Analysis for
Financial Management

The McGraw-Hill/Irwin Series in Finance, Insurance, and Real Estate

Analysis for Financial Management

Tenth Edition

ROBERT C. HIGGINS
Marguerite Reimers
Professor of Finance
The University of Washington

The McGraw·Hill Companies

**Mc
Graw
Hill** **McGraw-Hill
Irwin**

ANALYSIS FOR FINANCIAL MANAGEMENT, TENTH EDITION

Published by McGraw-Hill, a business unit of The McGraw-Hill Companies, Inc., 1221
Avenue of the Americas, New York, NY 10020. Copyright ©2012 by The McGraw-Hill
Companies, Inc. All rights reserved. Previous editions © 2009, 2007, and 2004. No part of this
publication may be reproduced or distributed in any form or by any means, or stored in a
database or retrieval system, without the prior written consent of The McGraw-Hill
Companies, Inc., including, but not limited to, in any network or other electronic storage or
transmission, or broadcast for distance learning.

Some ancillaries, including electronic and print components, may not be available to customers
outside the United States.

This book is printed on acid-free paper.

3 4 5 6 7 8 9 0 DOC/DOC 1 0 9 8 7 6 5 4

ISBN 978-0-07-803468-8
MHID 0-07-803468-X

Vice president and editor-in-chief: *Brent Gordon*
Publisher: *Douglas Reiner*
Executive editor: *Michele Janicek*
Editorial coordinator: *Kaylee Putbrese*
Marketing manager: *Melissa Caughlin*
Marketing specialist: *Jennifer M. Jelinski*
Project manager: *Pat Frederickson*
Buyer: *Debra Sylvester*
Full service project manager: *Vasundhara Sawhney*
Designer: *Joanne Mennemeier*
Media project manager: *Suresh Babu, Hurix Private Ltd.*
Media project manager: *Balaji Sundararaman, Hurix Private Ltd.*
Cover image: *Brand X Pictures/PunchStock*
Typeface: *10.5/13 Janson*
Compositor: *Cenveo Publisher Services*
Printer: *RRD Crawfordsville*

Library of Congress Cataloging-in-Publication Data

Higgins, Robert C.
    Analysis for financial management / Robert C. Higgins.—10th ed.
       p. cm.—(The McGraw-Hill/Irwin series in finance, insurance and real estate)
    Includes index.
    ISBN-13: 978-0-07-803468-8 (alk. paper)
    ISBN-10: 0-07-803468-X (alk. paper)
    1. Corporations—Finance.   I. Title.

HG4026.H496   2012
658.15'1—dc23   2011036536

www.mhhe.com

In memory of my son

STEVEN HIGGINS

1970–2007

Brief Contents

Contents

Preface

Like its predecessors, the tenth edition of *Analysis for Financial Management* is for nonfinancial executives and business students interested in the practice of financial management. It introduces standard techniques and recent advances in a practical, intuitive way. The book assumes no prior background beyond a rudimentary, and perhaps rusty, familiarity with financial statements—although a healthy curiosity about what makes business tick is also useful. Emphasis throughout is on the managerial implications of financial analysis.

Analysis for Financial Management should prove valuable to individuals interested in sharpening their managerial skills and to executive program participants. The book has also found a home in university classrooms as the sole text in Executive MBA and applied finance courses, as a companion text in case-oriented courses, and as a supplementary reading in more theoretical finance courses.

Analysis for Financial Management is my attempt to translate into another medium the enjoyment and stimulation I have received over the past three decades working with executives and college students. This experience has convinced me that financial techniques and concepts need not be abstract or obtuse; that recent advances in the field such as agency theory, market signaling, market efficiency, capital asset pricing, and real options analysis are important to practitioners; and that finance has much to say about the broader aspects of company management. I also believe that any activity in which so much money changes hands so quickly cannot fail to be interesting.

Part One looks at the management of existing resources, including the use of financial statements and ratio analysis to assess a company's financial health, its strengths, weaknesses, recent performance, and future prospects. Emphasis throughout is on the ties between a company's operating activities and its financial performance. A recurring theme is that a business must be viewed as an integrated whole and that effective financial management is possible only within the context of a company's broader operating characteristics and strategies.

The rest of the book deals with the acquisition and management of new resources. Part Two examines financial forecasting and planning with particular emphasis on managing growth and decline. Part Three considers the financing of company operations, including a review of the principal security types, the markets in which they trade, and the proper choice of security type by the issuing company. The latter requires a close look at financial leverage and its effects on the firm and its shareholders.

Part Four addresses the use of discounted cash flow techniques, such as the net present value and the internal rate of return, to evaluate investment opportunities. It also deals with the difficult task of incorporating risk into investment appraisal. The book concludes with an examination of business valuation and company restructuring within the context of the ongoing debate over the proper roles of shareholders, boards of directors, and incumbent managers in governing America's public corporations.

An extensive glossary of financial terms and suggested answers to odd-numbered, end-of-chapter problems follow the last chapter.

Changes in the Tenth Edition

Readers familiar with earlier editions of *Analysis for Financial Management* will note several changes and refinements in this edition, including:

- Use of Sensient Technologies Corporation (SXT), world's largest food and beverage color company, as the extended example throughout the book.

- Examination of Kraft Foods Corporation's hostile $23 billion takeover of British confectioner Cadbury Plc, including the role played by activist investor Nelson Peltz.

- Discussion of relevant aspects of the recent financial crisis, with emphasis on the possible roles played by the efficient market hypothesis, fair value accounting, and the financial rating agencies in precipitating the crisis.

- Expanded coverage of real options analysis, including decision trees.

- An update of the empirical evidence on corporate restructuring and shareholder value creation.

A welcome addition to the supplementary materials and teaching aids accompanying this edition is the test bank prepared by Professor Eric Wehrly, a veteran of past editions. Additionally, Hersh Shefrin has updated the PowerPoint images to reflect changes in the tenth edition.

As in earlier editions, you will continue to find annotated website references and recommended further readings at the end of each chapter. Also available is an *Analysis for Financial Management* website containing the following:

- A password-protected instructor's page containing suggested answers to all even-numbered problems appearing in the text.

- A test bank consisting of 20-30 questions per chapter, including multiple-choice, short-answer, and essay questions. Each question provides students with feedback and is tagged for level of difficulty.

- A student's page with spreadsheet-based problems and additional supplementary end-of-chapter problems and suggested answers.

- A list of the URLs of all websites mentioned in the book.

- An annotated list of suggested cases to accompany the book.

- PowerPoint versions of selected tables and figures.

- Complimentary software.

The complimentary software consists of three easy-to-use Excel programs, which I have found helpful when analyzing financial statements, projecting financing needs, and evaluating investment opportunities. The URL for this cornucopia of treats is **www.mhhe.com/higgins10e.**

A word of caution: *Analysis for Financial Management* emphasizes the application and interpretation of analytic techniques in decision making. These techniques have proved useful for putting financial problems into perspective and for helping managers anticipate the consequences of their actions. But techniques can never substitute for thought. Even with the best technique, it is still necessary to define and prioritize issues, to modify analysis to fit specific circumstances, to strike the proper balance between quantitative analysis and more qualitative considerations, and to evaluate alternatives insightfully and creatively. Mastery of technique is only the necessary first step toward effective management.

I want to thank Jared Stanfield for help on this edition's end-of-chapter problems. I am certain he will be a fine finance teacher as he begins his career at the University of New South Wales. I am indebted to Andy Halula and Scott Hossfeld of Standard & Poor's for providing timely updates to Research Insight. The ability to access current Compustat data continues to be a great help in providing timely examples of current practice. I also owe a large thank you to the following people for their insightful reviews of the ninth edition and their constructive advice. They did an excellent job; any remaining short-comings are mine not theirs.

Dr. Alexander Amati
Rutgers University

Richard T. Bliss
Babson College

Cheryl A. Brolyer
Preston University

Tom Burrell
Western Oregon University

Lawrence Byerly
Thomas More College

Neil G. Cohen
The George Washington University

Sanjiv Das
Santa Clara University

Yee-Tien Fu
Stanford University

Alexander Hittle
Washington University in St. Louis

George M. Jabbour
The George Washington University

Dee Ledford Malone
Park University

Dr. James N. Marshall
Muhlenberg College

Todd Mitton
Brigham Young University

Scott E. Pardee
Middlebury College

Peyton Foster Roden
University of North Texas

Salil K. Sarkar
The University of Texas at Arlington

Nikhil P. Varaiya
San Diego State University

I appreciate the exceptional direction provided by Michele Janicek, Kaylee Putbrese, Melissa Caughlin, Pat Frederickson, Debra Sylvester, and Joanne Mennemeier of McGraw-Hill on the development, design, and editing of the book. Bill Alberts, David Beim, Dave Dubofsky, Bob Keeley, Jack McDonald, George Parker, Megan Partch, Larry Schall, and Alan Shapiro have my continuing gratitude for their insightful help and support throughout the book's evolution. Thanks go as well to my daughter, Sara Higgins, for writing and editing the accompanying software. Finally, I want to express my appreciation to students and colleagues at the University of Washington, Stanford University, IMD, The Pacific Coast Banking School, The Koblenz Graduate School of Management, The Gordon Institute of Business Science, The Swiss International Business School ZfU AG, Boeing, and Microsoft, among others, for stimulating my continuing interest in the practice and teaching of financial management.

I envy you learning this material for the first time. It's a stimulating intellectual adventure.

Robert C. (Rocky) Higgins

Marguerite Reimers Professor of Finance

Foster School of Business

University of Washington

rhiggins@uw.edu

PART ONE

Assessing the Financial
Health of the Firm

CHAPTER ONE

Interpreting Financial Statements

Financial statements are like fine perfume; to be sniffed but not swallowed.

Abraham Brilloff

Accounting is the scorecard of business. It translates a company's diverse activities into a set of objective numbers that provide information about the firm's performance, problems, and prospects. Finance involves the interpretation of these accounting numbers for assessing performance and planning future actions.

The skills of financial analysis are important to a wide range of people, including investors, creditors, and regulators. But nowhere are they more important than within the company. Regardless of functional specialty or company size, managers who possess these skills are able to diagnose their firm's ills, prescribe useful remedies, and anticipate the financial consequences of their actions. Like a ballplayer who cannot keep score, an operating manager who does not fully understand accounting and finance works under an unnecessary handicap.

This and the following chapter look at the use of accounting information to assess financial health. We begin with an overview of the accounting principles governing financial statements and a discussion of one of the most abused and confusing notions in finance: cash flow. Two recurring themes will be that defining and measuring profits is more challenging than one might expect, and that profitability alone does not guarantee success, or even survival. In Chapter 2, we look at measures of financial performance and ratio analysis.

The Cash Flow Cycle

Finance can seem arcane and complex to the uninitiated. However, a comparatively few basic principles should guide your thinking. One is that *a company's finances and operations are integrally connected.* A company's

FIGURE 1.1 The Cash Flow–Production Cycle

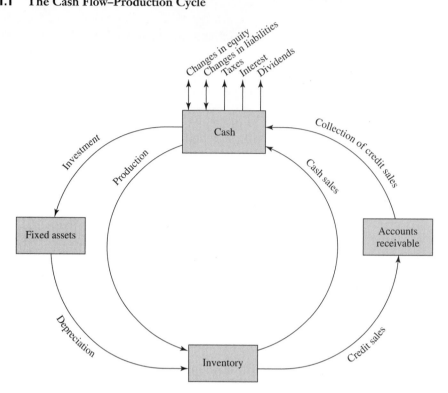

activities, method of operation, and competitive strategy all fundamentally shape the firm's financial structure. The reverse is also true: Decisions that appear to be primarily financial in nature can significantly affect company operations. For example, the way a company finances its assets can affect the nature of the investments it is able to undertake in future years.

The cash flow–production cycle in Figure 1.1 illustrates the close interplay between company operations and finances. For simplicity, suppose the company shown is a new one that has raised money from owners and creditors, has purchased productive assets, and is now ready to begin operations. To do so, the company uses cash to purchase raw materials and hire workers; with these inputs, it makes the product and stores it temporarily in inventory. Thus, what began as cash is now physical inventory. When the company sells an item, the physical inventory changes back into cash. If the sale is for cash, this occurs immediately; otherwise, cash is not realized until some later time when the account receivable is collected. This simple movement of cash to inventory, to accounts receivable, and back to cash is the firm's *operating*, or *working capital, cycle.*

Another ongoing activity represented in Figure 1.1 is investment. Over a period of time, the company's fixed assets are consumed, or worn out, in the creation of products. It is as though every item passing through the business takes with it a small portion of the value of fixed assets. The accountant recognizes this process by continually reducing the accounting value of fixed assets and increasing the value of merchandise flowing into inventory by an amount known as *depreciation*. To maintain productive capacity and to finance additional growth, the company must invest part of its newly received cash in new fixed assets. The object of this whole exercise, of course, is to ensure that the cash returning from the working capital cycle and the investment cycle exceeds the amount that started the journey.

We could complicate Figure 1.1 further by including accounts payable and expanding on the use of debt and equity to generate cash, but the figure already demonstrates two basic principles. First, *financial statements are an important window on reality*. A company's operating policies, production techniques, and inventory and credit-control systems fundamentally determine the firm's financial profile. If, for example, a company requires payment on credit sales to be more prompt, its financial statements will reveal a reduced investment in accounts receivable and possibly a change in its revenues and profits. This linkage between a company's operations and its finances is our rationale for studying financial statements. We seek to understand company operations and predict the financial consequences of changing them.

The second principle illustrated in Figure 1.1 is that *profits do not equal cash flow*. Cash—and the timely conversion of cash into inventories, accounts receivable, and back into cash—is the lifeblood of any company. If this cash flow is severed or significantly interrupted, insolvency can occur. Yet the fact that a company is profitable is no assurance that its cash flow will be sufficient to maintain solvency. To illustrate, suppose a company loses control of its accounts receivable by allowing customers more and more time to pay, or suppose the company consistently makes more merchandise than it sells. Then, even though the company is selling merchandise at a profit in the eyes of an accountant, its sales may not be generating sufficient cash soon enough to replenish the cash outflows required for production and investment. When a company has insufficient cash to pay its maturing obligations, it is insolvent. As another example, suppose the company is managing its inventory and receivables carefully, but rapid sales growth is necessitating an ever-larger investment in these assets. Then, even though the company is profitable, it may have too little cash to meet its obligations. The company will literally be "growing broke." These brief examples illustrate why a manager must be concerned at least as much with cash flows as with profits.

To explore these themes in more detail and to sharpen your skills in using accounting information to assess performance, we need to review the basics of financial statements. If this is your first look at financial accounting, buckle up because we will be moving quickly. If the pace is too quick, take a look at one of the accounting texts recommended at the end of the chapter.

The Balance Sheet

The most important source of information for evaluating the financial health of a company is its financial statements, consisting principally of a balance sheet, an income statement, and a cash flow statement. Although these statements can appear complex at times, they all rest on a very simple foundation. To understand this foundation and to see the ties among the three statements, let us look briefly at each.

A *balance sheet* is a financial snapshot, taken at a point in time, of all the assets the company owns and all the claims against those assets. The basic relationship, and indeed the foundation for all of accounting, is

$$\text{Assets} = \text{Liabilities} + \text{Shareholders' equity}$$

It is as if a herd (flock? column?) of accountants runs through the business on the appointed day, making a list of everything the company owns, and assigning each item a value. After tabulating the firm's assets, the accountants list all outstanding company liabilities, where a liability is simply an obligation to deliver something of value in the future—or more colloquially, some form of an "IOU." Having thus totaled up what the company *owns* and what it *owes*, the accountants call the difference between the two *shareholders' equity*. Shareholders' equity is the accountant's estimate of the value of the shareholders' investment in the firm just as the value of a homeowner's equity is the value of the home (the asset), less the mortgage outstanding against it (the liability). Shareholders' equity is also known variously as *owners' equity, stockholders' equity, net worth,* or simply *equity*.

It is important to realize that the basic accounting equation holds for individual transactions as well as for the firm as a whole. Thus, when a retailer pays $1 million in wages, cash declines $1 million and shareholders' equity falls by the same amount. Similarly, when a company borrows $100,000, cash rises by this amount, as does a liability entitled something like *loans outstanding*. And when a company receives a $10,000 payment from a customer, one asset, cash, rises while another asset, accounts receivable, falls by this amount. In each instance the double-entry nature of accounting guarantees that the basic accounting equation holds for each transaction, and when summed across all transactions, for the company as a whole.

To see how the repeated application of this single formula underlies the creation of company financial statements, consider Worldwide Sports (WWS), a newly founded retailer of value-priced sporting goods. In January 2011, the founder invested $150,000 of his personal savings and borrowed an additional $100,000 from relatives to start the business. After buying furniture and display materials for $60,000 and merchandise for $80,000, WWS was ready to open its doors.

The following six transactions summarize WWS's activities over the course of its first year.

- Sell $900,000 worth of sports equipment, receiving $875,000 in cash with $25,000 still to be paid.

- Pay $190,000 in wages.

- Purchase $380,000 of merchandise at wholesale, with $20,000 still owed to suppliers, and $30,000 worth still in inventory at year-end.

- Spend $210,000 on other expenses, including utilities, rent, and taxes.

- Depreciate furniture and fixtures by $15,000.

- Pay $10,000 interest on loan from relatives.

Table 1.1 shows how an accountant would record these transactions. WWS's beginning balance, the first line in the table, shows cash of $250,000, a loan of $100,000, and equity of $150,000. But these numbers change quickly as the company buys fixtures and an initial inventory of merchandise. And they change further as each of the listed transactions occurs.

TABLE 1.1 Worldwide Sports Financial Transactions 2011 ($ thousands)

	Assets				=	Liabilities	+	Equity
	Cash	Accounts Receivable	Inventory	Fixed Assets		Accounts Payable	Loan from Relatives	Owners' Equity
Beginning balance 1/1/11	$ 250						$100	$ 150
Initial purchases	(140)		80	60				
Sales	875	25						900
Wages	(190)							(190)
Merchandise purchases	(360)		30			20		(350)
Other expenses	(210)							(210)
Depreciation				(15)				(15)
Interest payment	(10)							(10)
Ending balance 12/31/11	$ 215	$25	$110	$ 45		$20	$100	$ 275

Abstracting from the accounting details, there are two important things to note here. First, the basic accounting equation holds for each transaction. For every line in the table, assets equal liabilities plus owners' equity. Second, WWS's year-end balance sheet at the bottom of the table is just its beginning balance sheet plus the cumulative effect of the individual transactions. For example, ending cash on December 31, 2008, is beginning cash of $250,000 plus, or minus, the cash involved in each transaction. Incidentally, WWS's first year appears to have been an excellent one; owners' equity is up $125,000 over the course of the year.

If the balance sheet is a snapshot in time, the income statement and the cash flow statement are videos, highlighting changes in two especially important balance sheet accounts over time. Business owners are naturally interested in how company operations have affected the value of their investment. The income statement addresses this question by partitioning observed changes in owners' equity into revenues and expenses, where revenues are increases in owners' equity generated by sales, and expenses are reductions in owner's equity incurred to earn the revenue. The difference between revenues and expenses is earnings, or net income.

The focus of the cash flow statement is solvency, having enough cash in the bank to pay bills as they come due. The cash flow statement provides a detailed look at changes in the company's cash balance over time. As an organizing principle, the statement segregates changes in cash into three broad categories: cash provided, or consumed, by operating activities, by investing activities, and by financing activities. Figure 1.2 is a simple schematic diagram showing the close conceptual ties among the three principal financial statements.

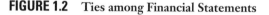

SENSIENT®

See **www.sensient.com.** Select button under "Investor Information" for financial statements.

To illustrate the techniques and concepts presented throughout the book, I will refer whenever possible to Sensient Technologies Corporation. If you have ever marveled at the florescent-orange cheese, bright-red tomatoes, or

FIGURE 1.2 Ties among Financial Statements

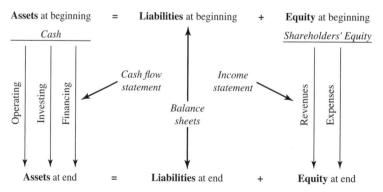

vibrant-green pickles lining grocery shelves, you probably have Sensient Technologies to thank. The company is a leading producer of flavors, colors, and aromas found in thousands of products ranging from food and beverages to a variety of pharmaceutical and household products. It produces some 25,000 flavors and 3,000 colors, and is said to be the largest food and beverage color company in the world with a leading position in flavor as well. In the words of chief executive Kenneth Manning, "We can match almost any color the customer would want." Yum!

Headquartered in Milwaukee, Wisconsin, with sales in excess of $1.3 billion, Sensient trades on the New York Stock Exchange and is a member of the Standard & Poor's 400 Midcap Stock Index. The company was originally founded in 1882 as a gin mill, Meadow Springs Distillery, but morphed into Red Star Yeast in the early 1920s when Prohibition put an abrupt end to the liquor business. In the early 1960s, the company went public, acquired Universal Foods, and took on its name. This lasted until 2000 when Universal Foods became Sensient Technologies Corporation, a pleasant-sounding but meaningless collection of letters perhaps suggesting a scientific approach to the human senses. Tables 1.2 and 1.3 present Sensient's balance sheets and income statements for fiscal years 2009 and 2010. If the precise meaning of every asset and liability category in Table 1.2 is not immediately apparent, be patient. We will discuss many of them in the following pages. In addition, all of the accounting terms used appear in the glossary at the end of the book.

See **www.nysscpa.org/ glossary** for an exhaustive glossary of accounting terms.

Sensient Technologies's balance sheet equation for 2010 is

$$\text{Assets} \qquad = \text{Liabilities} \qquad + \text{Shareholders' equity}$$
$$\$1{,}599.3 \text{ million} = \$615.5 \text{ million} \quad + \$983.8 \text{ million}$$

Current Assets and Liabilities

By convention, accountants list assets and liabilities on the balance sheet in order of decreasing liquidity, where liquidity refers to the speed with which an item can be converted to cash. Thus among assets cash, marketable securities, and accounts receivable appear at the top, while land, plant, and equipment are toward the bottom. Similarly on the liabilities side, short-term loans and accounts payable are toward the top, while shareholders' equity is at the bottom.

Accountants also arbitrarily define any asset or liability that is expected to turn into cash within one year as *current* and all others assets and liabilities as *long-term*. Inventory is a current asset because there is reason to believe it will be sold and will generate cash within one year. Accounts payable are short-term liabilities because they must be paid within one year. Note that almost half of Sensient's assets are current, a fact we will say more about in the next chapter.

TABLE 1.2 Sensient Technologies Corporation, Balance Sheets ($ millions)*

	December 31		Change in Account
	2009	2010	
Assets			
Cash and marketable securities	$ 12.2	$ 14.3	$ 2.1
Accounts receivable, less reserve for possible losses	200.2	218.6	18.4
Inventories	390.0	392.2	2.2
Other current assets	55.7	47.3	(8.4)
Total current assets	658.1	672.4	
Gross property, plant, and equipment	993.3	1,025.1	31.8
Less accumulated depreciation and amortization	567.6	592.6	25.0
Net property, plant, and equipment	425.7	432.5	6.8
Goodwill and intangible assets, net	469.6	458.3	(11.3)
Other assets	38.3	36.1	(2.2)
Total assets	$1,591.7	$1,599.3	
Liabilities and Shareholders' Equity			
Long-term debt due in one year	$ —	$ —	$ —
Short-term borrowings	39.2	25.5	(13.7)
Trade accounts payable	88.9	95.9	7.0
Taxes payable	0.7	7.1	6.4
Accrued expenses	87.4	76.6	(10.8)
Total current liabilities	216.2	205.1	
Long-term debt	388.9	324.4	(64.5)
Accrued employee and retiree benefits	50.8	52.7	1.9
Deferred taxes	12.8	21.0	8.2
Other long-term liabilities	14.4	12.3	(2.1)
Total liabilities	683.1	615.5	
Common stock	5.4	5.4	
Additional paid-in capital	85.5	89.0	
Retained earnings	921.7	976.5	
Treasury stock	(103.9)	(87.1)	
Total shareholders' equity	908.7	983.8	75.1
Total liabilities and shareholders' equity	$1,591.8	$1,599.3	

*Totals may not add due to rounding.

A Word to the Unwary

Nothing puts a damper on a good financial discussion (if such exists) faster than the suggestion that if a company is short of cash, it can always spend some of its shareholders' equity. Equity is on the liabilities side of the balance sheet, not the asset side. It represents owners' claims against existing assets. In other words, that money has already been spent.

TABLE 1.3 Sensient Technologies Corporation, Income Statements ($ millions)

	December 31	
	2009	**2010**
Net sales	$1,201.4	$1,328.2
Cost of goods sold	790.2	876.4
Gross profit	411.2	451.8
Selling, general and administrative expenses	210.8	235.2
Depreciation and amortization	42.2	43.4
Total operating expenses	253.0	278.6
Operating income	158.2	173.2
Interest expense	23.8	20.4
Other nonoperating expenses (income)	11.3	(1.5)
Total nonoperating expenses	35.1	18.9
Income before income taxes	123.1	154.3
Provision for income taxes	36.6	47.1
Net income	$ 86.5	$ 107.2

Shareholders' Equity

A common source of confusion is the large number of accounts appearing in the shareholders' equity portion of the balance sheet. Sensient has four, beginning with common stock and ending with treasury stock (see Table 1.2). Unless forced to do otherwise, my advice is to forget these distinctions. They keep accountants and attorneys employed, but seldom make much practical difference. As a first cut, just add up everything that is not an IOU and call it shareholders' equity.

The Income Statement

Looking at Sensient's operating performance in 2010, the basic income statement relation appearing in Table 1.3 is

Revenues − Expenses = Net income

$$\text{Net sales} - \text{Cost of goods sold} - \text{Operating expenses} - \text{Nonoperating expenses} - \text{Taxes} = \text{Net income}$$

$$\$1,328.2 - \$876.4 - \$278.6 - \$18.9 - \$47.1 = \$107.2$$

Net income records the extent to which net sales generated during the accounting period exceeded expenses incurred in producing the sales. For variety, net income is also commonly referred to as *earnings* or *profits*, frequently with the word *net* stuck in front of them; net sales are often called *revenues* or *net revenues*; and cost of goods sold is labeled *cost of sales*. I have never found a meaningful distinction between these terms. Why so many words to say the same thing? My personal belief is that accountants are so rule-bound in their calculations of the various amounts that their creativity runs a bit amok when it comes to naming them.

Income statements are commonly divided into operating and nonoperating segments. As the names imply, the operating segment reports the results of the company's major, ongoing activities, while the nonoperating segment summarizes all ancillary activities. In 2010, Sensient reported operating income of $173.2 million and nonoperating expenses of $18.9 million, consisting largely of interest expense.

Measuring Earnings

This is not the place for a detailed discussion of accounting. But because earnings, or lack of same, are a critical indicator of financial health, several technical details of earnings measurement deserve mention.

Accrual Accounting

The measurement of accounting earnings involves two steps: (1) identifying revenues for the period and (2) matching the corresponding costs to revenues. Looking at the first step, it is important to recognize that revenue is not the same as cash received. According to the *accrual principle* (a cruel principle?) of accounting, revenue is recognized as soon as "the effort required to generate the sale is substantially complete and there is a reasonable certainty that payment will be received." The accountant sees the timing of the actual cash receipts as a mere technicality. For credit sales, the accrual principle means that revenue is recognized at the time of sale, not when the customer pays. This can result in a significant time lag between the generation of revenue and the receipt of cash. Looking at Sensient, we see that revenue in 2010 was $1,328.2 million, but accounts receivable increased $18.4 million. We conclude that cash received from sales during 2010 was only $1,309.8 million ($1,328.2 million − $18.4 million). The other $18.4 million still awaits collection.

Depreciation

Fixed assets and their associated depreciation present the accountant with a particularly challenging problem in matching. Suppose that in 2012, a company constructs for $50 million a new facility that has an expected productive life of 10 years. If the accountant assigns the entire cost of the facility to expenses in 2012, some weird results follow. Income in 2012 will appear depressed due to the $50 million expense, while income in the following nine years will look that much better as the new facility contributes to revenue but not to expenses. Thus, charging the full cost of a long-term asset to one year clearly distorts reported income.

The preferred approach is to spread the cost of the facility over its expected useful life in the form of depreciation. Because the only cash outlay associated with the facility occurs in 2012, the annual depreciation listed as a cost on the company's income statement is not a cash outflow. It is a *noncash charge* used to match the 2012 expenditure with resulting revenue. Said differently, depreciation is the allocation of past expenditures to future time periods to match revenues and expenses. A glance at Sensient's income statement reveals that in 2010, the company included a $43.4 million noncash charge for depreciation and amortization among their operating expenses. In a few pages, we will see that during the same year, the company spent $55.8 million acquiring new property, plant, and equipment.

To determine the amount of depreciation to take on a particular asset, three estimates are required: the asset's useful life, its salvage value, and the method of allocation to be employed. These estimates should be based on economic and engineering information, experience, and any other objective data about the asset's likely performance. Broadly speaking, there are two methods of allocating an asset's cost over its useful life. Under the *straight-line* method, the accountant depreciates the asset by a uniform amount each year. If an asset costs $50 million, has an expected useful life of 10 years, and has an estimated salvage value of $10 million, straight-line depreciation will be $4 million per year ([$50 million − $10 million]/10).

The second method of cost allocation is really a family of methods known as *accelerated depreciation*. Each technique charges more depreciation in the early years of the asset's life and correspondingly less in later years. Accelerated depreciation does not enable a company to take more depreciation in total; rather, it alters the timing of the recognition. While the specifics of the various accelerated techniques need not detain us here, you should recognize that the life expectancy, the salvage value, and the allocation method a company uses can fundamentally affect reported earnings. In general, if a company is conservative and depreciates its assets rapidly, it will tend to understate current earnings, and vice versa.

Taxes

A second noteworthy feature of depreciation accounting involves taxes. Most U.S. companies, except very small ones, keep at least two sets of financial records: one for managing the company and reporting to shareholders and another for determining the firm's tax bill. The objective of the first set is, or should be, to accurately portray the company's financial performance. The objective of the second set is much simpler: to minimize taxes. Forget objectivity and minimize taxes. These differing objectives mean the accounting principles used to construct the two sets of books differ substantially. Depreciation accounting is a case in point. Regardless of the method used to report to shareholders, company tax books will minimize current taxes by employing the most rapid method of depreciation over the shortest useful life the tax authorities allow.

This dual reporting means that actual cash payments to tax authorities usually differ from the provision for income taxes appearing on a company's income statement, sometimes trailing the provision and other times exceeding it. To illustrate, Sensient's $47.1 million provision for income taxes appearing on its 2010 income statement is the tax payable according to the accounting techniques used to construct the company's published statements. But because Sensient used different accounting techniques when reporting to the tax authorities, taxes actually paid in 2010 were lower than this amount. To confirm this fact, note that Sensient has two tax accounts on the liabilities side of its balance sheet labeled "taxes payable," a short-term liability, and "deferred taxes," a long-term liability. The liability accounts reflect tax obligations incurred in past periods but not yet paid. The net change in these balance sheet accounts during 2010 indicates that Sensient's tax liability rose $14.6 million over the year, so that taxes paid must have been $14.6 million less than the provision for taxes appearing on the income statement. Sensient's aggressive deferral of tax obligations incurred during the year resulted in a 2010 tax payment less than the tax obligation appearing on its income statement. Here is the detailed accounting with figures in millions:

Provision for income taxes	$47.1
— Increase in taxes payable	6.4
— Increase in deferred taxes	8.2
Taxes paid	$32.5

At the end of 2010, Sensient's net tax liability appearing on its balance sheet was $28.1 million ($7.1 million taxes payable + $21.0 million deferred taxes). This sum represents money Sensient must pay tax authorities in future years, but in the meantime can be used to finance the business. Tax deferral techniques create the equivalent of interest-free loans from the government. In Japan and other countries that do not allow the use of separate accounting techniques for tax and reporting purposes, these complications never arise.

Research and Marketing

Now that you understand how accountants use depreciation to spread the cost of long-lived assets over their useful lives to better match revenues and

and are all sources of cash to the company. On the liabilities side of the balance sheet, an increase in a bank loan and the sale of common stock are increases in liabilities, which again generate cash.

- *A company also uses cash in two ways: to increase an asset account or to reduce a liability account.* Adding to inventories or accounts receivable and building a new plant all increase assets and all use cash. Conversely, the repayment of a bank loan, the reduction of accounts payable, and an operating loss all reduce liabilities and all use cash.

Because it is difficult to spend money you don't have, total uses of cash over an accounting period must equal total sources.

Table 1.4 presents a 2010 sources and uses statement for Sensient Technologies. It reveals that the company got over 60 percent of its cash from an increase in total shareholders' equity—due largely to retained profits—and, in turn, used almost 70 percent of the cash to reduce long-term debt and increase accounts receivable.

TABLE 1.4   **Sensient Technologies Corporation, Sources and Uses Statement, 2010 ($ millions)***

Sources	
Reduction in other current assets	$ 8.4
Reduction in net goodwill and intangible assets	11.3
Reduction in other assets	2.2
Increase in trade accounts payable	7.0
Increase in taxes payable	6.4
Increase in accrued employee and retiree benefits	1.9
Increase in deferred taxes	8.2
Increase in total shareholders' equity	75.1
Total sources	$120.5
Uses	
Increase in cash and marketable securities	$ 2.1
Increase in accounts receivable	18.4
Increase in inventories	2.2
Increase in net property, plant, and equipment	6.8
Reduction in short-term borrowings	13.7
Reduction in accrued expenses	10.8
Reduction in long-term debt	64.5
Reduction in other long-term liabilities	2.1
Total uses	$120.6

*Totals may not add due to rounding.

How Can a Reduction in Cash Be a Source of Cash?

One potential source of confusion in Table 1.4 is that the reduction in cash and marketable securities in 2010 appears as a source of cash. How can a reduction in cash be a source of cash? Simple. It is the same as when you withdraw money from your checking accounts. You reduce your bank balance but have more cash on hand to spend. Conversely, a deposit into your bank account increases your balance but reduces spendable cash in your pocket.

The Two-Finger Approach

I personally do not spend a lot of time constructing sources and uses statements. It might be instructive to go through the exercise once or twice just to convince yourself that sources really do equal uses. But once beyond this point, I recommend using a "two-finger approach." Put the two balance sheets side by side, and quickly run any two fingers down the columns in search of big changes. This should enable you to quickly observe that the majority of Sensient's cash came from retained profits and that much of it went to creditors. In 30 seconds or less, you have the essence of a sources and uses analysis and are free to move on to more stimulating activities. The other changes are largely window dressing of more interest to accountants than to managers.

The Cash Flow Statement

Identifying a company's principal sources and uses of cash is a useful skill in its own right. It is also an excellent starting point for considering the cash flow statement, the third major component of financial statements along with the income statement and the balance sheet.

In essence, a cash flow statement just expands and rearranges the sources and uses statement, placing each source or use into one of three broad categories. The categories and their values for Sensient in 2010 are as follows:

Category	Source (or Use) of Cash ($ millions)
1. Cash flows from operating activities	$155.8
2. Cash flows from investing activities	($55.1)
3. Cash flows from financing activities	($98.5)

Double-entry bookkeeping guarantees that the sum of the cash flows in these three categories equals the change in cash balances over the accounting period.

TABLE 1.5   Sensient Technologies Corporation, Cash Flow Statement, 2010 ($ millions)*

Cash Flows from Operating Activities	
Net income	$ 107.2
Adjustments to reconcile net income to net cash provided by operating activities:	
Depreciation and amortization	43.4
Deferred income taxes	8.7
Stock-based compensation expense	5.7
Loss on sale of assets	1.4
Changes in assets and liabilities:	
Increase in trade accounts receivable	(20.2)
Increase in inventories	(4.2)
Decrease in accounts payable and accrued liabilities	(2.7)
Increase in accrued income taxes	2.7
Other assets and liabilities, net change	13.8
Net cash provided by operating activities	155.8
Cash Flows from Investing Activities	
Capital expenditures	(55.8)
Other investing activities	0.7
Net cash used by investing activities	(55.1)
Cash flows from financing activities	
Net increase in borrowings	(72.6)
Dividends paid	(39.0)
Cash received from exercise of stock options	14.1
Effect of exchange rate changes on cash and cash equivalents	(1.0)
Net cash provided by financing activities	(98.5)
Net increase (decrease) in cash	2.2
Cash and marketable securities at beginning of year	12.2
Cash and marketable securities at end of year	$ 14.3

*Totals may not add due to rounding.

Table 1.5 presents a complete cash flow statement for Sensient Technologies in 2010. The first category, "cash flows from operating activities," can be thought of as a rearrangement of Sensient's financial statements to eliminate the effects of accrual accounting on net income. First, we add all noncash charges, such as depreciation and amortization, back to net income, recognizing that these charges did not entail any cash outflow. Then we add the changes in current assets and liabilities to net income, acknowledging, for instance, that some sales did not increase cash because customers had not yet paid, while some expenses did not reduce cash because the company had not yet paid. Changes in other current assets and liabilities, such as inventories, appear here because the accountant, following the matching principle, ignored these cash flows when calculating net income. Interestingly, the cash generated by Sensient's operations was almost 50 percent more than the firm's income. A principal reason for the difference is that the income statement includes a $43.4 million non-cash charge for depreciation.

If cash flow statements were just a reshuffling of sources and uses statements, as many textbook examples suggest, they would be redundant, for a reader could make his own in a matter of minutes. A chief attraction of the cash flow statements is that companies reorganize their cash flows into new and sometimes revealing categories. To illustrate, a glance at Sensient's sources and uses statement in Table 1.4 shows that accounts receivable increased $18.4 million during 2010. Yet the entry for "increase in accounts receivable" in the upper portion of its cash flow statement reads $20.2 million. Why the difference? The explanation is that the $18.4 million figure includes the effects of exchange rate changes, while the $20.2 million figure omits them. Sensient Technologies has operations in 35 countries, most with their own local currency–denominated receivables. At the end of each accounting period, Sensient's auditors use a prevailing exchange rate to translate these various balances into U.S. dollars in order to calculate an aggregate figure. This is the source of the $18.4 million. However, when the exchange rates used in this exercise change over the period, a portion of the measured change in accounts receivable will be due to exchange rate changes, not company activities. And because these exchange rate–induced changes are not cash flows, Sensient omits them from the number appearing on its cash flow statement, resulting in the $20.2 million figure. Taken together, we can say that Sensient's accounts receivable balance increased $20.2 million in 2010, but the dollar value of these receivables declined $1.8 million ($20.2 – $18.4) due to a strengthening dollar over the period. (Another source of such discrepancies arises when companies divide changes in current assets and liabilities into two parts: those attributable to existing activities, and those due to newly acquired businesses, with the first appearing in "cash flows from operations," and the second in "investing activities.")

As another example, note that Sensient's cash flow statement lists two sources of cash involving employee stock options that do not appear on its sources and uses statement. They are "cash received from exercise of stock options," and "stock-based compensation expense." When an employee exercises a stock option, she purchases her employer's stock at a price originally specified in the option agreement, and known as the option's strike price. This is the origin of the $14.1 million in "cash received from exercise of stock options," appearing as part of Sensient's financing activities. When the employee purchases the stock, she incurs a tax liability on the difference between the price of the stock on the exercise date and its strike price. The tax consequences for the company, however, are just the reverse. It is entitled to claim a tax-deductible expense for precisely the same amount—even though it never makes a cash outlay at any time over the entire life of the option. This is the $5.7 million source appearing as part of "cash flow from operations." It is a source of cash because, like depreciation, it is a noncash expense that must be added back to net income when calculating cash flow. These same two quantities, of course, lie buried somewhere among the various accounts on the company's sources and statement, but management has chosen to highlight them on its cash flow statement. (To enhance perceived performance, many companies record the tax benefit of employee stock options as an addition to cash flows from operating activities, as Sensient has done. Others take a more conservative route and record it as part of financing activities.)

A $5.7 million tax reduction is a tidy benefit for Sensient, but to appreciate what is really possible with employee stock options, we need to look at Cisco Systems. In 2000, this leading manufacturer of Internet networking gear reported record net income of $2.7 billion and a tax benefit from the exercise of employee stock options equal to $2.5 billion. Stock options are complex, and this is certainly not the place for a detailed discussion of the topic. At the same time, I can't resist noting that the enthusiasm for stock options evinced by many high-tech executives is easier to understand after learning that options can help companies report record profits and greatly reduced taxes in the same year.

Some analysts maintain that net cash provided by operating activities, appearing on the cash flow statement, is a more reliable indicator of firm performance than net income. They argue that because net income depends on myriad estimates, allocations, and approximations, devious managers can easily manipulate it. Numbers appearing on a company's cash flow statement, on the other hand, record the actual movement of cash, and are thus more objective measures of performance.

There is certainly some merit to this view, but also two problems. First, low or even negative net cash provided by operating activities does not necessarily indicate poor performance. Rapidly growing businesses in particular must customarily invest in current assets, such as accounts receivable and inventories, to support increasing sales. And although such investments reduce net cash provided by operating activities, they do not in any way suggest poor performance. Second, cash flow statements turn out to be less objective, and thus less immune to manipulation than might be supposed. Here's a simple example. Suppose two companies are identical except that one sells its product on a simple open account, while the other loans its customers money enabling them to pay cash for the product. In both cases, the customer has the product and owes the seller money.

What Is Cash Flow?

So many conflicting definitions of *cash flow* exist today that the term has almost lost its meaning. At one level, cash flow is very simple. It is the movement of money into or out of a cash account over a period of time. The problem arises when we try to be more specific. Here are four common types of cash flow you are apt to encounter.

$$\text{Net cash flow} = \text{Net income} + \text{Noncash items}$$

Often known in investment circles as cash earnings, net cash flow is intended to measure the cash a business generates, as distinct from the earnings—a laudable objective. Applying the formula to Sensient's 2010 figures (Table 1.5), net cash flow was $166.4 million, equal to net income plus depreciation, and other noncash charges.

A problem with net cash flow as a measure of cash generation is that it implicitly assumes a business's current assets and liabilities are either unrelated to operations or do not change over time. In Sensient's case, the cash flow statement reveals that changes in a number of current assets and liabilities consumed $10.6 million in cash. A more inclusive measure of cash generation is therefore cash flow from operating activities as it appears on the cash flow statement.

$$\text{Cash flow from operating activities} = \text{Net cash flow} \pm \text{Changes in current assets and liabilities}$$

A third, even more inclusive measure of cash flow, popular among finance specialists is

$$\text{Free cash flow} = \frac{\text{Total cash available for distribution to owners and creditors}}{\text{after funding all worthwhile investment activities}}$$

Free cash flow extends cash flow from operating activities by recognizing that some of the cash a business generates must be plowed back into the business, in the form of capital expenditures, to support growth. Abstracting from a few technical details, free cash flow is essentially cash flow from operating activities less capital expenditures. As we will see in Chapter 9, free cash flow is a fundamental determinant of the value of a business. Indeed, one can argue that the principal means by which a company creates value for its owners is to increase free cash flow.

Yet another widely used cash flow is

$$\text{Discounted cash flow} = \frac{\text{A sum of money today having the same value}}{\text{as a future stream of cash receipts and disbursements}}$$

Discounted cash flow refers to a family of techniques for analyzing investment opportunities that take into account the time value of money. A standard approach to valuing investments and businesses uses discounted cash flow techniques to calculate the present value of projected free cash flows. This is the focus of the last three chapters of this book.

My advice when tossing cash flow terms about is to either use the phrase broadly to refer to a general movement of cash or to define your terms carefully.

But the increase in accounts receivable recorded by the first company on each sale will lower its cash flows from operating activities relative to the second, which can report the customer loan as part of investing activities. Because the criteria for apportioning cash flows among operating, investing, and financing activities are ambiguous, subjective judgment must be used in the preparation of cash flow statements.

Much of the information contained in a cash flow statement can be gleaned from careful study of a company's income statement and balance sheet. Nonetheless, the statement has three principal virtues. First, accounting neophytes and those who do not trust accrual accounting have at least some hope of understanding it. Second, the statement provides more accurate information about certain activities, such as the tax effects of employee stock options than one can infer from income statements and balance sheets alone. Third, it casts a welcome light on the issue of firm solvency by highlighting the extent to which operations are generating or consuming cash.

Financial Statements and the Value Problem

To this point, we have reviewed the basics of financial statements and grappled with the distinction between earnings and cash flow. This is a valuable start, but if we are to use financial statements to make informed business decisions, we must go further. We must understand the extent to which accounting numbers reflect economic reality. When the accountant tells us that Sensient Technologies's total assets were worth $1,599.3 million on December 31, 2010, is this literally true, or is the number just an artificial accounting construct? To gain perspective on this issue, and in anticipation of later discussions, I want to conclude by examining a recurring problem in the use of accounting information for financial decision making.

Market Value vs. Book Value

Part of what I will call the *value problem* involves the distinction between the market value and the book value of shareholders' equity. Sensient's 2010 balance sheet states that the value of shareholders' equity is $983.8 million. This is known as the *book value* of Sensient's equity. However, Sensient is not worth $983.8 million to its shareholders or to anyone else, for that matter. There are two reasons. One is that financial statements are largely *transactions-based*. If a company purchased an asset for $1 million in 1950, this transaction provides an objective measure of the asset's value, which the accountant uses to value the asset on the company's balance sheet. Unfortunately, it is a 1950 value that may or may not have much relevance today. To further confound things, the accountant attempts to reflect the gradual deterioration of an asset over time by periodically subtracting depreciation from its balance sheet value. This practice makes sense as far as it goes, but depreciation is the only change in value an American accountant customarily recognizes. The $1 million asset purchased in 1950 may be technologically obsolete and therefore virtually worthless today; or, due to inflation, it may be worth much more than its original purchase price. This is especially true of land, which can be worth several times its original cost.

For more of fair value accounting and many other accounting topics, see **www.cfo.com**.

It is tempting to argue that accountants should forget the original costs of long-term assets and provide more meaningful current values. The problem is that objectively determinable current values of many assets do not exist, and it is probably not wise to rely on incumbent mangers to make the necessary adjustments. Faced with a choice between relevant but subjective current values and irrelevant but objective historical costs, accountants opt for irrelevant historical costs. Accountants prefer to be precisely wrong than approximately right. This means it is the user's responsibility to make any adjustments to historical-cost asset values she deems appropriate.

Prodded by regulators and investors, the Financial Accounting Standards Board, accounting's principal rule-making fraternity, increasingly stresses what is known as *fair value* accounting, according to which certain assets and liabilities must appear on company financial statements at their market values instead of their historical costs. Such "marking to market" applies to selected assets and liabilities that trade actively on financial markets, including many common stocks and bonds. Proponents of fair value accounting acknowledge it will never be possible to eliminate historical-cost accounting entirely, but maintain that market values should be used whenever possible. Skeptics respond that mixing historical costs and market values in the same financial statement only heightens confusion, and that periodically revaluing company accounts to reflect changing market values introduces unwanted subjectivity, distorts reported earnings, and greatly increases earnings volatility. They point out that under fair value accounting, changes in owners' equity no longer mirror the results of company operations but also include potentially large and volatile gains and losses from changes in the market values of certain assets and liabilities. The gradual movement toward fair value accounting was initially greeted with howls of protest, especially from financial institutions concerned that the move would increase apparent earnings volatility and, more menacingly, might reveal that some enterprises are worth less than historical-cost financial statements suggest. To these firms the appearance of benign stability is apparently more appealing than the hint of an ugly reality.

To understand the second, more fundamental reason Sensient is not worth $983.8 million, recall that equity investors buy shares for the future income they hope to receive, not for the value of the firm's assets. Indeed, if all goes according to plan, most of the firm's existing assets will be consumed in generating future income. The problem with the accountant's measure of shareholders' equity is that it bears little relation to future income. There are two reasons for this. First, because the accountant's numbers are backward-looking and cost-based, they often provide few clues about the future income a company's assets might generate. Second, companies typically have a great many assets and liabilities that do not appear

Fair Value Accounting and the Financial Crisis of 2008

The financial crisis of 2008 revealed several quirks and problems with fair value accounting. Among the quirks is fair value's treatment of company liabilities. Many financial institutions saw the market value of their publicly traded debt plummet during the crisis as investors lost faith in the institutions' ability to honor their obligations—clearly bad news. Yet fair value accounting forced the organizations to report this drop in value as a gain on the theory that it would now cost them that much less to repurchase and retire the debt. Similarly, when the crisis eased and debt values rose, the same institutions found themselves recording losses as the cost of repurchase went up. As one example, investment bank Morgan Stanley reported a $5.5 billion gain in 2008 on declining debt values, followed in 2009 by a $5.4 billion loss as the price of their debt recovered.

More worrisome, some observers maintain that fair value accounting may actually have contributed to the crisis. They argue that panic selling during the collapse made observed market prices more an indicator of investor fears than of asset values. Moreover, they claim that reliance on these distressed prices to value assets set in motion a vicious cycle whereby falling prices prompted creditors to demand payment of the debt, increased collateral, or increased equity relative to debt, all of which forced the debtors into more panic selling. While not abandoning fair value accounting, this criticism has forced accountants and regulators to allow managers some discretion in estimating fair values in distressed markets.[c]

[c]For more on this topic, see Christian Laux, and Christian Leuz, "The Crisis of Fair Value Accounting: Making Sense of the Recent Debate," *Accounting, Organizations and Society*, April, 2009. Available at ssrn.com/abstract=1392645.

on their balance sheets but affect future income nonetheless. Examples include patents and trademarks, loyal customers, proven mailing lists, superior technology, and, of course, better management. It is said that in many companies, the most valuable assets go home to their spouses in the evening. Examples of unrecorded liabilities include pending lawsuits, inferior management, and obsolete production processes. The accountant's inability to measure assets and liabilities such as these means that book value is customarily a highly inaccurate measure of the value perceived by shareholders.

It is a simple matter to calculate the market value of shareholders' equity when a company's shares are publicly traded: Simply multiply the number of common shares outstanding by the market price per share. On December 31, 2010, the last trading day of the month, Sensient's common shares closed on the New York Stock Exchange at $36.73 per share. With 49.6 million shares outstanding, this yields a value of $1,821.8 million, or 1.9 times the book value ($1,821.8/$983.8 million). This $1,821.8 million is the market value of Sensient's equity, often referred to as the firm's market capitalization or market cap.

Table 1.6 presents the market and book values of equity for 15 representative companies. It demonstrates clearly that book value is a poor proxy for market value.

TABLE 1.6 The Book Value of Equity Is a Poor Surrogate for the Market Value of Equity, December 31, 2010

Company	Value of Equity ($ millions)		Ratio, Market Value to Book Value
	Book	Market	
Aetna Inc.	9,891	12,207	1.2
Amazon.com Inc.	6,864	80,791	11.8
Coca-Cola Co.	31,003	152,720	4.9
Dynegy Inc.	22,522	23,590	1.0
Duke Energy	2,746	679	0.2
Google, Inc.	46,241	147,546	3.2
Harley-Davidson Inc.	2,207	8,166	3.7
Hewlett-Packard Co.	40,449	92,217	2.3
IBM	49,430	117,305	2.4
Intel Corp.	23,046	182,329	7.9
Kraft Foods	35,834	55,041	1.5
Sensient Technologies	984	1,822	1.9
Susquehanna Bancshares	1,985	1,256	0.6
Tesla Motors Corp	207	2,484	12.0
U.S. Cellular Corp.	3,481	2,634	0.8

Goodwill

There is one instance in which intangible assets, such as brand names and patents, find their way onto company balance sheets. It occurs when one company buys another at a price above book value. Suppose an acquiring firm pays $100 million for a target firm and the target's assets have a book value of only $40 million and an estimated replacement value of only $60 million. To record the transaction, the accountant will allocate $60 million of the acquisition price to the value of the assets acquired and assign the remaining $40 million to a new asset commonly known as "goodwill." The acquiring company paid a handsome premium over the fair value of the target's recorded assets because it places a high value on its unrecorded, or intangible, assets. But not until the acquisition creates a piece of paper with $100 million written on it is the accountant willing to acknowledge this value.

Looking at Sensient Technologies's balance sheet in Table 1.2 under the heading "Goodwill and intangible assets, net," we see that the company has over $450 million of goodwill, its largest single asset and 29 percent of total assets. To put this number in perspective, the median ratio of goodwill to total assets among Standard & Poor's 500 companies—a diversified group of large firms—was 15 percent in 2010. Stericycle, Inc., a provider of specialized waste management services to medical organizations, topped the list with a goodwill-to-total assets ratio of 61 percent.[1]

Economic Income vs. Accounting Income

A second dimension of the value problem is rooted in the accountant's distinction between *realized* and *unrealized* income. To anyone who has not studied too much accounting, income is what you could spend during the period and be as well off at the end as you were at the start. If Mary Siegler's assets, net of liabilities, are worth $100,000 at the start of the year and rise to $120,000 by the end, and if she receives and spends $70,000 in wages during the year, most of us would say her income was $90,000 ($70,000 in wages + $20,000 increase in net assets).

But not the accountant. Unless Mary's investments were in marketable securities with readily observable prices, he would say Mary's income was only $70,000. The $20,000 increase in the value of assets would not qualify as income because the gain was not *realized* by the sale of the assets. Because the value of the assets could fluctuate in either direction before the assets are sold, the gain is only *on paper*, and accountants generally do not recognize paper gains or losses. They consider *realization* the objective evidence necessary to record the gain, despite the fact that Mary is probably just as pleased with the unrealized gain in assets as with another $20,000 in wages.

It is easy to criticize accountants' conservatism when measuring income. Certainly the amount Mary could spend, ignoring inflation, and be as well off as at the start of the year is the commonsense $90,000, not the accountant's $70,000. Moreover, if Mary sold her assets for $120,000 and immediately repurchased them for the same price, the $20,000 gain would become realized and, in the accountant's eyes, become part of income. That income could depend on a sham transaction such as this is enough to raise suspicions about the accountant's definition.

However, we should note three points in the accountant's defense. First, if Mary holds her assets for several years before selling them, the gain or loss the accountant recognized on the sale date will equal the sum of the annual gains and losses we nonaccountants would recognize. So it's really not total income that is at issue here but simply the timing of its

---

[1]For many years, accounting authorities required companies to write goodwill off as a noncash expense against income over a number of years. Now they acknowledge that most goodwill is not necessarily a wasting asset and only require a write down when there is evidence the value of goodwill has declined. There is no offsetting provision requiring the write-up of goodwill when values appear to have risen. If this sounds vague and capricious, I agree.

recognition. Second, accountants' increasing use of fair value accounting, where at least some long-term assets and liabilities are revalued periodically to reflect changes in market value, reduces the difference between accounting and economic income. Third, even when accountants want to use fair value accounting, it is extremely difficult to measure the periodic change in the value of many assets and liabilities unless they are actively traded. Thus, even if an accountant wanted to include "paper" gains and losses in income, she would often have great difficulty doing so. In the corporate setting, this means the accountants frequently must be content to record realized rather than economic income.

Imputed Costs

A similar but subtler problem exists on the cost side of the income statement. It involves the cost of equity capital. Sensient's accountants acknowledge that in 2010 the company had use of $983.8 million of shareholders' money, measured at book value. They would further acknowledge that Sensient could not have operated without this money and that this money is not free. Just as creditors earn interest on loans, equity investors expect a return on their investments. Yet if you look again at Sensient's income statement (Table 1.3), you will find no mention of the cost of this equity; interest expense appears, but a comparable cost for equity does not.

While acknowledging that equity capital has a cost, the accountant does not record it on the income statement because the cost must be imputed, that is, estimated. Because there is no piece of paper stating the amount of money Sensient is obligated to pay owners, the accountant refuses to recognize any cost of equity capital. Once again, the accountant would rather be reliably wrong than make a potentially inaccurate estimate. The result has been serious confusion in the minds of less knowledgeable observers and continuing "image" problems for corporations.

Following is the bottom portion of Sensient's 2010 income statement as prepared by its accountant and as an economist might prepare it. Observe that while the accountant shows earnings of $107.2 million, the economist records a profit of only $8.8 million. These numbers differ because the economist includes a $98.4 million charge as a cost of equity capital, while the accountant pretends equity is free. (We will consider ways to estimate a company's cost of equity capital in Chapter 8. Here, for illustrative purposes only, I have assumed a 10 percent annual equity cost and applied it to the book value of Sensient's equity [$98.4 million = 10% × $983.8 million].)

($ in millions)	Accountant	Economist
Operating income	$173.2	$173.2
Interest expense	20.4	20.4
Other nonoperating expenses	(1.5)	(1.5)
Cost of equity		98.4
Income before taxes	154.3	55.9
Provision for taxes	47.1	47.1
Accounting earnings	$107.2	
Economic earnings		$ 8.8

The distinction between accounting earnings and economic earnings might be only a curiosity if everyone understood that positive accounting earnings are not necessarily a sign of superior or even commendable performance. But when many labor unions and politicians view accounting profits as evidence that a company can afford higher wages, higher taxes, or more onerous regulation, and when most managements view such profits as justification for distributing handsome performance bonuses, the distinction can be an important one. Keep in mind, therefore, that the right of equity investors to expect a competitive return on their investments is every bit as legitimate as a creditor's right to interest and an employee's right to wages. All voluntarily contribute scarce resources, and all are justified in expecting compensation. Remember too that a company is not shooting par unless its economic profits are zero or greater. By this criterion, Sensient had a decent but not fantastic year in 2010. On closer inspection, you will find that many companies reporting apparently large earnings are really performing like weekend duffers when the cost of equity is included.

We will look at the difference between accounting and economic profits again in more detail in Chapter 8 under the rubric of economic value added, or EVA. In recent years, EVA has become a popular yardstick for assessing company and managerial performance.

In sum, those of us interested in financial analysis eventually develop a love-hate relationship with accountants. The value problem means that financial statements typically yield distorted information about company earnings and market value. This limits their applicability for many important managerial decisions. Yet financial statements frequently provide the best information available, and if we bear their limitations in mind, they can be a useful starting point for analysis. In the next chapter, we consider the use of accounting data for evaluating financial performance.

SUMMARY

1. The cash flow cycle
   - Describes the flow of cash through a company.
   - Illustrates that profits and cash flow are not the same.
   - Reminds a manager she must be at least as concerned with cash flows as with profits.

2. The balance sheet
   - Is a snapshot at a point in time of what a company owns and what it owes.
   - Rests on the fundamental accounting equation, assets = liabilities + owners' equity, which applies to individual transactions as well as entire balance sheets.
   - Lists assets and liabilities with maturities of less than a year as current.
   - Shows shareholders' equity on the liability side of the balance sheet as the accounting value of owners' claims against existing assets.

3. The income statement
   - Divides changes in owners' equity occurring over a period of time into revenues and expenses, where revenues are increases in equity and expenses are reductions.
   - Defines net income, or earnings, as the difference between revenues and expenses.
   - Identifies revenues generated during the period and matches the corresponding costs incurred in generating the revenue.
   - Embodies the accrual principle, which records revenues and expenses when there is reasonable certainty payment will be made, not when cash is received or disbursed.
   - Records depreciation as the allocation of past expenditures for long-lived assets to future time periods to match revenues and expenses.

4. The cash flow statement
   - Focuses on solvency, having enough cash to pay bills as they come due.
   - Is an elaboration of a simple sources and uses statement, according to which increases in asset accounts and reductions in liability accounts are uses of cash, while opposite changes in assets and liabilities are sources of cash.

5. The value problem
   - Emphasizes that accounting statements suffer from several limitations when used to assess economic performance or value businesses:
     - Many accounting values are transactions-based and hence backward-looking, while market values are forward-looking.

- – Accounting often creates a false dichotomy between realized and unrealized income.
- – Accountants refuse to assign a cost to equity capital, thereby suggesting to lay observers that positive accounting profit means financial health.
- • Is diminished by the use of fair value accounting, according to which the value of widely traded assets and liabilities appear at market price rather than historical cost but at the potential cost of distortions, volatility, complexity, and subjectivity.

ADDITIONAL RESOURCES

Anthony, Robert N.; and Leslie P. Breitner. *Essentials of Accounting*. 10th ed. Englewood Cliffs, NJ: Prentice Hall, 2009. 360 pages.

> The lead author is a distinguished emeritus Harvard professor. A great way to review or pick up the basics of accounting on your own. Available in paperback, about $56.

Downes, John; and Jordan Elliot Goodman. *Dictionary of Finance and Investment Terms*. 8th ed. New York: Barron's Educational Services, Inc., 2010. 880 pages.

> More than 5,000 terms clearly defined. Available in paperback, about $10.

Horngren, Charles T.; Gary L. Sundem; John A. Elliott and Donna Philbrick. *Introduction to Financial Accounting*. 10th ed. Englewood Cliffs, NJ: Prentice Hall, 2010. 656 pages.

> The high-octane stuff—best-selling college text. Everything you ever wanted to know about the topic and then some. Less than $170.

Tracy, John A. *How to Read a Financial Report: Wringing Vital Signs Out of the Numbers*. 7th ed. New York: John Wiley & Sons, 2009. 216 pages.

> A lively, accessible look at practical aspects of financial statement analysis. Available in paperback, about $12.

Welton, Ralph E.; and George T. Friedlob. *Keys to Reading an Annual Report*. 4th ed. New York: Barron's Educational Services, Inc., 2008. 208 pages.

> A no-nonsense, practical guide to understanding financial reports. About $9.

WEBSITES

www.Stanford.edu/class/msande271/onlinetools/HowToReadFinancial.pdf
From this site you can download a free copy of Merrill Lynch's classic "How to Read a Financial Report" as a PDF file.

Visit us at www.mhhe.com/higgins10e

www.duke.edu/~charvey/Classes/wpg/glossary.htm

Duke Professor Campbell Harvey's glossary of finance with more than 8,000 terms defined and more than 18,000 hyperlinks.

www.secfilings.com

Edgar, a Securities and Exchange Commission site, contains virtually all filings of public companies in the United States. It is a treasure trove of financial information, including annual and quarterly reports. The referenced site offers a slick way to access Edgar, including direct downloading of individual filings in PDF and RTF formats. It's free, and I use it often.

www.cfo.com

An informative, practitioner-oriented website provided by the publishers of CFO magazine. Articles on current issues in accounting and finance.

PROBLEMS

Answers to odd-numbered problems appear at the end of the book. For additional problems with answers, see **www.mhhe.com/higgins10e.**

1. a. What does it mean when cash flow from operations on a company's cash flow statement is negative? Is this bad news? Is it dangerous?

   b. What does it mean when cash flow from investing activities on a company's cash flow statement is negative? Is this bad news? Is it dangerous?

   c. What does it mean when cash flow from financing activities on a company's cash flow statement is negative? Is this bad news? Is it dangerous?

2. DuHurst Corporation has $4 billion in assets, $3 billion in equity, and earned a profit last year as the economy boomed of $100 million. Senior management proposes paying themselves a large cash bonus in recognition of their performance. As a member of DuHurst's board of directors, how would you respond to this proposal?

3. True or false?

   a. If a company gets into financial difficulty, it can use some of its shareholders' equity to pay its bills for a time.

   b. It is impossible for a firm to have a negative book value of equity without the firm going into bankruptcy.

   c. You can construct a sources and uses statement for 2013 if you have a company's balance sheets for 2012 and 2013.

   d. The "goodwill" account on the balance sheet is an attempt by accountants to measure the benefits that result from a company's public relations efforts in the community.

   e. A reduction in an asset account is a use of cash, while a reduction in a liability account is a source of cash.

4. Explain briefly how each of the following transactions would affect a company's balance sheet. (Remember, assets must equal liabilities plus owners' equity before and after the transaction.)

   a. Sale of used equipment with a book value of $300,000 for $500,000 cash.

   b. Purchase of a new $80 million building, financed 40 percent with cash and 60 percent with a bank loan.

   c. Purchase of a new building for $60 million cash.

   d. A $40,000 payment to trade creditors.

   e. A firm's repurchase of 10,000 shares of its own stock at a price of $24 per share.

   f. Sale of merchandise for $80,000 in cash.

   g. Sale of merchandise for $120,000 on credit.

   h. Dividend payment to shareholders of $50,000.

5. Why do you suppose financial statements are constructed on an accrual basis rather than a cash basis when cash accounting is so much easier to understand?

6. Table 3.1 in Chapter 3 presents financial statements over the period 2008–2011 for R&E Supplies, Inc.

   a. Construct a sources and uses statement for the company over this period (one statement for all three years).

   b. What insights, if any, does the sources and uses statement give you about the financial position of R&E Supplies?

7. You are responsible for labor relations in your company. During heated labor negotiations, the General Secretary of your largest union exclaims, "Look, this company has $15 billion in assets, $7.5 billion in equity, and made a profit last year of $300 million—due largely, I might add, to the effort of union employees. So don't tell me you can't afford our wage demands." How would you reply?

8. You manage a real estate investment company. One year ago, the company purchased 10 parcels of land distributed throughout the community for $10 million each. A recent appraisal of the properties indicates that five of the parcels are now worth $8 million each, while the other five are worth $16 million each.

   Ignoring any income received from the properties and any taxes paid over the year, calculate the investment company's accounting earnings and its economic earnings in each of the following cases:

   a. The company sells all of the properties at their appraised values today.

   b. The company sells none of the properties.

Visit us at www.mhhe.com/higgins10e

c. The company sells the properties that have fallen in value and keeps the others.

d. The company sells the properties that have risen in value and keeps the others.

e. After returning from a property management seminar, an employee recommends the company adopt an end-of-year policy of always selling properties that have risen in value since purchase, and always retaining properties that have fallen in value. The employee explains that with this policy the company will never show a loss on its real estate investment activities. Do you agree with the employee? Why, or why not?

9. Please ignore taxes for this problem. During 2010, Mead, Inc. earned a net income of $400,000. The firm increased its accounts receivable during the year by $250,000. The book value of its assets declined by an amount equal to the year's depreciation charge, or $180,000, and the market value of its assets increased by $20,000. Based only on this information, how much cash did Mead generate during the year?

10. Jonathan currently is a brew master for Acme Brewery. He really enjoys his job, but is intrigued by the prospect of quitting and starting his own brewery. He currently makes $62,000 at Acme Brewery. Jonathan anticipates that his new brewery will have annual revenues of $230,000, and total annual expenses for operating the brewery, outside of any payments to Jonathan, will be $190,000. Jonathan comes to you with his idea. He believes that he would be equally happy with either option, but that starting his own brewery is the right decision in light of its profitability. Ignoring what might happen beyond the first year, do you agree with him? Why or why not?

11. Selected information for Blake's Restaurant Supply follows.

	($ in millions)	
	2010	2011
Net sales	$694	$782
Cost of goods sold	450	502
Depreciation	51	61
Net income	130	142
Finished goods inventory	39	29
Accounts receivable	57	87
Accounts payable	39	44
Net fixed assets	404	482
Year-end cash balance	$ 86	$135

a. During 2011, how much cash did Blake's collect from sales?

b. During 2011, what was the cost of goods produced by the company?

c. Assuming the company neither sold nor salvaged any assets during the year, what were the company's capital expenditures during 2011?

d. Assuming that there were no financing cash flows during 2011 and basing your answer solely on the information provided, what was Blake's cash flow from operations in 2011?

12. The following are summary cash flow statements for three roughly equal-sized companies

	($ millions)		
	A	**B**	**C**
Net cash flows from operating activities	$(300)	$(300)	$ 300
Net cash used in investing activities	(900)	(30)	(90)
Net cash from financing activities	1,200	210	(240)
Cash balance at beginning of year	150	150	150

a. Calculate each company's cash balance at the end of the year.

b. Explain what might cause company C's net cash from financing activities to be negative.

c. Looking at companies A and B, which company would you prefer to own? Why?

d. Is company C's cash flow statement cause for any concern on the part of C's management or shareholders? Why or why not?

13. Epic Trucking's equity has a market value of $15 million with 700,000 shares outstanding. The book value of its equity is $9 million.

a. What is Epic's stock price per share? What is its book value per share?

b. If the company repurchases 25 percent of its shares in the stock market at their current price, how will this affect the book value of equity if all else remains the same?

c. If there are no taxes or transaction costs, and investors do not change their perceptions of the firm, what should the market value of the firm be after the repurchase?

d. Instead of a share repurchase, the company decides to raise money by selling an additional 20 percent of its shares on the market. If it can issue these additional shares at the current market price, how will this affect the book value of equity if all else remains the same?

e. If there are no taxes or transaction costs, and investors do not change their perception of the firm, what should the market value of the firm be after this stock issuance? Its price per share?

eXcel

14. An Excel spreadsheet containing the Whistler Corporation's financial statements is available for download at **www.mhhe.com/higgins10e.** (Select Student Edition > Choose a Chapter > Files.) Use the statements to create a sources and uses statement and a cash flow statement for the company in 2011. If you are new to Excel, see http://people.usd.edu/~bwjames/tut/excel/ or http://office.microsoft.com/en-us/excel/default.aspx for free tutorials.

CHAPTER TWO

Evaluating Financial Performance

You can't manage what you can't measure.

William Hewlett

The cockpit of a 747 jet looks like a three-dimensional video game. It is a sizable room crammed with meters, switches, lights, and dials requiring the full attention of three highly trained pilots. When compared to the cockpit of a single-engine Cessna, it is tempting to conclude that the two planes are different species rather than distant cousins. But at a more fundamental level, the similarities outnumber the differences. Despite the 747's complex technology, the 747 pilot controls the plane in the same way the Cessna pilot does: with a stick, a throttle, and flaps. And to change the altitude of the plane, each pilot makes simultaneous adjustments to the same few levers available for controlling the plane.

Much the same is true of companies. Once you strip away the facade of apparent complexity, the levers with which managers affect their companies' financial performance are comparatively few and are similar from one company to another. The executive's job is to control these levers to ensure a safe and efficient flight. And like the pilot, the executive must remember that the levers are interrelated; one cannot change the business equivalent of the flaps without also adjusting the stick and the throttle.

The Levers of Financial Performance

In this chapter, we analyze financial statements for the purpose of evaluating performance and understanding the levers of management control. We begin by studying the ties between a company's operating decisions, such as how many units to make this month and how to price them, and its financial performance. These operating decisions are the levers by which management controls financial performance. Then we broaden the discussion to consider the uses and limitations of ratio analysis as a tool for evaluating performance. To keep things practical, we will again use the financial statements for Sensient Technologies Corporation, presented in Tables 1.2, 1.3, and 1.5 of the last chapter, to illustrate the techniques. The chapter concludes with an evaluation of Sensient's financial performance relative to its competition. (See Additional Resources at the end of the chapter for information about HISTORY, complimentary software for calculating company ratios. Also at the end of the chapter, Table 2.5 presents summary definitions of the principal ratios appearing throughout the chapter.)

Return on Equity

By far the most popular yardstick of financial performance among investors and senior managers is the *return on equity (ROE)*, defined as

$$\text{Return on equity} = \frac{\text{Net income}}{\text{Shareholders' equity}}$$

Sensient's ROE for 2010 was

$$\text{ROE} = \frac{\$107.2}{\$983.8} = 10.9\%$$

It is not an exaggeration to say that the careers of many senior executives rise and fall with their firms' ROEs. ROE is accorded such importance because it is a measure of the *efficiency* with which a company employs owners' capital. It is a measure of earnings per dollar of invested equity capital or, equivalently, of the percentage return to owners on their investment. In short, it measures bang per buck.

Later in this chapter, we will consider some significant problems with ROE as a measure of financial performance. For now, let us accept it provisionally as at least widely used and see what we can learn.

The Three Determinants of ROE

To learn more about what management can do to increase ROE, suppose we rewrite ROE in terms of its three principal components:

$$\text{ROE} = \frac{\text{Net income}}{\text{Sales}} \times \frac{\text{Sales}}{\text{Assets}} \times \frac{\text{Assets}}{\text{Shareholders' equity}}$$

Denoting the last three ratios as the profit margin, asset turnover, and financial leverage, respectively, the expression can be written as

$$\frac{\text{Return on}}{\text{equity}} = \frac{\text{Profit}}{\text{margin}} \times \frac{\text{Asset}}{\text{turnover}} \times \frac{\text{Financial}}{\text{leverage}}$$

This says that management has only three levers for controlling ROE: (1) the earnings squeezed out of each dollar of sales, or the *profit margin*; (2) the sales generated from each dollar of assets employed, or the *asset turnover*; and (3) the amount of equity used to finance the assets, or the

TABLE 2.1 ROEs and Levers of Performance for 10 Diverse Companies, 2010*

	Return on Equity (ROE) (%)	=	Profit Margin (P) (%)	×	Asset Turnover (A) (times)	×	Financial Leverage (T) (times)
Adobe Systems	14.9	=	20.4	×	0.47	×	1.57
Chevron	18.1	=	10.0	×	1.03	×	1.76
Google	18.4	=	29.0	×	0.51	×	1.25
Hewlett-Packard	21.7	=	7.0	×	1.01	×	3.08
JPMorgan Chase	10.3	=	15.0	×	0.05	×	12.58
Norfolk Southern	14.0	=	15.7	×	0.34	×	2.64
Novartis	15.5	=	19.3	×	0.41	×	1.95
Safeway	11.8	=	1.4	×	2.71	×	3.03
Sensient Technoligies	10.9	=	8.1	×	0.83	×	1.63
Southern Company	12.6	=	11.7	×	0.32	×	3.40

*Totals do not add due to rounding.

financial leverage.[1] With few exceptions, whatever management does to increase these ratios increases ROE.

Note too the close correspondence between the levers of performance and company financial statements. Thus, the profit margin summarizes a company's income statement performance by showing profit per dollar of sales. The asset turnover ratio summarizes the company's management of the asset side of its balance sheet by showing the resources required to support sales. And the financial leverage ratio summarizes management of the liabilities side of the balance sheet by showing the amount of shareholders' equity used to finance the assets. This is reassuring evidence that despite their simplicity, the three levers do capture the major elements of a company's financial performance.

We find that Sensient's 2010 ROE was generated as follows:

$$\frac{\$107.2}{\$983.8} = \frac{\$107.2}{\$1,328.2} \times \frac{\$1,328.2}{\$1,599.3} \times \frac{\$1,599.3}{\$983.8}$$

$$10.9\% = 8.1\% \times 0.8 \times 1.6$$

Table 2.1 presents ROE and its three principal components for 10 highly diverse businesses. It shows quite clearly that there are many paths

---

[1] At first glance the ratio of assets to shareholders' equity may not look like a measure of financial leverage, but consider the following:

$$\frac{\text{Assets}}{\text{Equity}} = \frac{\text{Liabilities} + \text{Equity}}{\text{Equity}} = \frac{\text{Liabilities}}{\text{Equity}} + 1$$

And the liabilities-to-equity ratio clearly measures financial leverage.

to heaven: The companies' ROEs are quite similar, but the combinations of profit margin, asset turnover, and financial leverage producing this end result vary widely. Thus, ROE ranges from a high of 21.7 percent for Hewlett-Packard, a diversified technology company, to a low of 10.3 percent for banker JPMorgan Chase, while the range for the profit margin, to take one example, is from a low of 1.4 percent for grocery chain Safeway, Inc. to a high of 29.0 percent for Internet search firm Google. ROE differs by about 2 to 1 high to low, but the profit margin varies by a factor of over 20 to 1. Comparable ranges for asset turnover and financial leverage are 54 to 1 and 8 to 1, respectively.

Why are ROEs similar across firms while profit margins, asset turnovers, and financial leverages differ dramatically? The answer, in a word, is competition. Attainment of an unusually high ROE by one company acts as a magnet to attract rivals anxious to emulate the superior performance. As rivals enter the market, the heightened competition drives the successful company's ROE back toward the average. Conversely, unusually low ROEs repel potential new competitors and drive existing companies out of business so that over time, survivors' ROEs rise toward the average.

To understand how managerial decisions and a company's competitive environment combine to affect ROE, we will examine each lever of performance in more detail. In anticipation of the discussion of ratio analysis to follow, we will also consider related commonly used financial ratios. See Additional Resources at the end of the chapter for published sources of business ratios.

The Profit Margin

The profit margin measures the fraction of each dollar of sales that trickles down through the income statement to profits. This ratio is particularly important to operating managers because it reflects the company's pricing strategy and its ability to control operating costs. As Table 2.1 indicates, profit margins differ greatly among industries depending on the nature of the product sold and the company's competitive strategy.

Note too that profit margin and asset turnover tend to vary inversely. Companies with high profit margins tend to have low asset turns, and vice versa. This is no accident. Companies that add significant value to a product, such as Google and pharmaceutical company Novartis, can demand high profit margins. However, because adding value to a product usually requires lots of assets, these same firms tend to have lower asset turns. At the other extreme, grocery stores, such as Safeway, bring the product in the store on forklift trucks, sell for cash, and make the customer carry out his own purchases. Because they add little value to the product, they have very low profit margins and correspondingly high asset turns. It should be apparent, therefore, that a high profit margin is not necessarily better or worse than a low one—it all depends on the combined effect of the profit margin and the asset turnover.

Return on Assets

To look at the combined effect of margins and turns, we can calculate the *return on assets (ROA):*

$$\text{ROA} = \frac{\text{Profit}}{\text{margin}} \times \frac{\text{Asset}}{\text{turnover}} = \frac{\text{Net income}}{\text{Assets}}$$

Sensient's ROA in 2010 was

$$\text{Return on assets} = \frac{\$107.2}{\$1,599.3} = 6.7\%$$

This means Sensient earned an average of 6.7 cents on each dollar tied up in the business.

ROA is a basic measure of the efficiency with which a company allocates and manages its resources. It differs from ROE in that it measures profit as a percentage of the money provided by owners *and* creditors as opposed to only the money provided by owners.

Some companies, such as Google, Novartis, and Norfolk Southern, a railroad, produce their ROAs by combining a high profit margin with a low asset turn; others, such as Safeway, adopt the reverse strategy. A high profit margin *and* a high asset turn is ideal, but can be expected to attract considerable competition. Conversely, a low profit margin combined with a low asset turn will attract only bankruptcy lawyers.

Gross Margin

When analyzing profitability, it is often interesting to distinguish between variable costs and fixed costs. Variable costs change as sales vary, while fixed costs remain constant. Companies with a high proportion of fixed costs are more vulnerable to sales declines than other firms, because they cannot reduce fixed costs as sales fall.

Unfortunately, the accountant does not differentiate between fixed and variable costs when constructing an income statement. However, it is usually safe to assume that most expenses in cost of goods sold are variable, while most of the other operating costs are fixed. The gross margin enables us to distinguish, insofar as possible, between fixed and variable costs. It is defined as

$$\text{Gross margin} = \frac{\text{Gross profit}}{\text{Sales}} = \frac{\$451.8}{\$1,328.2} = 34.0\%$$

where gross profit equals net sales less cost of sales. Thirty-four percent of Sensient's sales dollar is a *contribution to fixed cost and profits:* 34 cents of every sales dollar is available to pay for fixed costs and to add to profits.

One common use of the gross margin is to estimate a company's breakeven sales volume. Sensient's income statement tells us that total operating expenses in 2010 were $278.6 million. If we assume these expenses are fixed and if 34 cents of each Sensient sales dollar is available to pay for fixed costs and add to profits, the company's zero-profit sales volume must be $278.6/0.340, or $819.4 million.[2] Assuming operating expenses and the gross margin are independent of sales, Sensient loses money when sales are below $819.4 million, and makes money when sales are above this figure.

Asset Turnover

Some newcomers to finance believe assets are a good thing: the more the better. The reality is just the opposite: Unless a company is about to go out of business, its value is in the income stream it generates, and its assets are simply a necessary means to this end. Indeed, the ideal company would be one that produced income without any assets; then no investment would be required, and returns would be infinite. Short of this fantasy, our ROE equation tells us that, other things constant, financial performance improves as asset turnover rises. This is the second lever of management performance.

The asset turnover ratio measures the sales generated per dollar of assets. Sensient Technologies's asset turnover of 0.8 means that Sensient generated 80 cents of sales for each dollar invested in assets. This ratio measures asset intensity, with a low asset turnover signifying an asset-intensive business and a high turnover the reverse.

The nature of a company's products and its competitive strategy strongly influence asset turnover. A steel mill will never have the asset turnover of a grocery store. But this is not the end of the story, because

[2]Income = Sales − Variable costs − Fixed costs = Sales × Gross margin − Fixed costs. Setting income to zero and solving for sales, Sales = Fixed costs/Gross margin.

management diligence and creativity in controlling assets are also vital determinants of a company's asset turnover. When product technology is similar among competitors, control of assets is often the margin between success and failure.

Control of current assets is especially critical. You might think the distinction between current and fixed assets based solely on whether the asset will revert to cash within one year is artificial. But more is involved than this. Current assets, especially accounts receivable and inventory, have several unique properties. One is that if something goes wrong—if sales decline unexpectedly, customers delay payment, or a critical part fails to arrive—a company's investment in current assets can balloon very rapidly. When even manufacturing companies routinely invest one-half or more of their money in current assets, it is easy to appreciate that even modest alterations in the management of these assets can significantly affect company finances.

A second distinction is that unlike fixed assets, current assets can become a source of cash during business downturns. As sales decline, a company's investment in accounts receivable and inventory should fall as well, thereby freeing cash for other uses. (Remember, a reduction in an asset account is a source of cash.) The fact that in a well-run company current assets move in an accordion-like fashion with sales is appealing to creditors. They know that during the upswing of a business cycle rising current assets will require loans, while during a downswing falling current assets will provide the cash to repay the loans. In bankers' jargon, such a loan is said to be *self-liquidating* in the sense that the use to which the money is put creates the source of repayment.

It is often useful to analyze the turnover of each type of asset on a company's balance sheet individually. This gives rise to what are known as *control ratios*. Although the form in which each ratio is expressed may vary, every control ratio is simply an asset turnover for a particular type of asset. In each instance, the firm's investment in the asset is compared to net sales or a closely related figure.

Why compare assets to sales? The fact that a company's investment in, say, accounts receivable has risen over time could be due to two forces: (1) Perhaps sales have risen and simply dragged receivables along, or (2) management may have slackened its collection efforts. Relating receivables to sales in a control ratio adjusts for changes in sales, enabling the analyst to concentrate on the more important effects of changing management control. Thus, the control ratio distinguishes between sales-induced changes in investment and other, perhaps more sinister causes. Following are some standard control ratios and their values for Sensient Technologies in 2010.

Inventory Turnover

Inventory turnover is expressed as

$$\text{Inventory turnover} = \frac{\text{Cost of goods sold}}{\text{Ending inventory}} = \frac{\$876.4}{\$392.2} = 2.2 \text{ times}$$

An inventory turn of 2.2 times means that items in Sensient's inventory turn over 2.2 times per year on average; said differently, the typical item sits in inventory about 166 days before being sold (365 days/2.2 times = 165.9 days).

Several alternative definitions of the inventory turnover ratio exist, including sales divided by ending inventory and cost of goods sold divided by average inventory. Cost of goods sold is a more appropriate numerator than sales because sales include a profit markup that is absent from inventory. But beyond this, I see little to choose from among the various definitions.

The Collection Period

The *collection period* highlights a company's management of accounts receivable. For Sensient

$$\text{Collection period} = \frac{\text{Accounts receivable}}{\text{Credit sales per day}} = \frac{\$218.6}{\$1,328.2/365} = 60.1 \text{ days}$$

Credit sales appear here rather than net sales because only credit sales generate accounts receivable. As a company outsider, however, I do not know what portion of Sensient's net sales, if any, are for cash, so I assume they are all on credit. Credit sales per day is defined as credit sales for the accounting period divided by the number of days in the accounting period, which for annual statements is obviously 365 days.

Two interpretations of Sensient's collection period are possible. We can say that Sensient has an average of 60.1 days' worth of credit sales tied up in accounts receivable, or we can say that the average time lag between sale and receipt of cash from the sale is 60.1 days.

Beware of Seasonal Companies

Interpreting ratios of companies with seasonal sales can be tricky. For example, suppose a company's sales peak sharply at Christmas, resulting in high year-end accounts receivable. A naïve collection period calculated by relating year-end accounts receivable to average daily sales for the whole year will produce an apparently very high collection period because the denominator is insensitive to the seasonal peak. To avoid being misled, a better way to calculate the collection period for a seasonal company is to use credit sales per day based only on the prior 60 to 90 days' sales. This matches the accounts receivable to the credit sales actually generating the receivables.

If we like, we can define a simpler asset turnover ratio for accounts receivable as just credit sales/accounts receivable. However, the collection period format is more informative, because it allows us to compare a company's collection period with its terms of sale. Thus, if a company sells on 90-day terms, a collection period of 65 days is excellent, but if the terms of sale were 30 days, our interpretation would be quite different.

Days' Sales in Cash

Sensient's days' sales in cash is

$$\frac{\text{Days' sales}}{\text{in cash}} = \frac{\text{Cash and securities}}{\text{Sales per day}} = \frac{\$14.3}{\$1,328.2/365} = 3.9 \text{ days}$$

Sensient has 3.9 days' worth of sales in cash and securities. It is difficult to generalize about whether or not this amount is appropriate for Sensient. Companies require modest amounts of cash to facilitate transactions and are sometimes required to carry substantially larger amounts as compensating balances for bank loans. In addition, cash and marketable securities can be an important source of liquidity for a firm in an emergency. So the question of how much cash and securities a company should carry is often closely related to the broader question of how important liquidity is to the company and how best to provide it. For comparison, the median figure for the 419 nonfinancial companies in the Standard & Poor's 500 Index in 2010 was 43.4 days, more than double the figure for 2000. In fact, the median days' sales in cash among the 75 information technology companies in the S&P 500 was 171.4 days, with Google clocking in at 435.4 and Microchip Technology at 467.7. In comparison, Sensient's 3.9 days is miniscule.

Payables Period

The *payables period* is a control ratio for a liability. It is simply the collection period applied to accounts payable. For Sensient

$$\frac{\text{Payables}}{\text{period}} = \frac{\text{Accounts payable}}{\text{Credit purchases per day}} = \frac{\$95.9}{\$876.4/365} = 39.9 \text{ days}$$

The proper definition of the payables period uses credit purchases, because they are what generate accounts payable. However, an outsider seldom knows credit purchases, so it is frequently necessary to settle for the closest approximation: cost of goods sold. This is what I have done above for Sensient; $876.4 million is Sensient's cost of goods sold, not its credit purchases. Cost of goods sold can differ from credit purchases for two reasons. First, the company may be adding to or depleting inventory, that is, purchasing at a different rate than it is selling. Second, all manufacturers add labor to material in the production process, thereby making cost

Google's Levers of Performance

Internet titan, Google's 2010 levers of performance make instructive reading. As shown in Table 2.1 and repeated in the following, the company combined an attractive profit margin and conservative financial leverage with an abysmally low asset turnover of only 0.51 times to generate a rather ordinary ROE of 18.4 percent. This is mediocre performance for a company selling at over 20 times earnings and perceived by most to be the dominant Internet player.

How can an Internet company generate an asset turnover more like that of a steel mill or a public utility? A look at Google's balance sheet explains the mystery. At year-end 2010, fully $35 billion, or over half of Google's assets, were in cash and marketable securities. It's as if the company had merged with a money market mutual fund. And Google is not alone. It is common practice among leading technology companies to build huge war chests, which they argue are necessary to finance continued growth and to facilitate possible acquisitions—like maybe if Panama or South Dakota ever came up for sale. Others, including Ralph Nader, see a more sinister purpose: to keep the money out of the hands of shareholders and to avoid taxes.

To focus on Google's operating performance apart from its ability to invest excess cash, we can strip cash and marketable securities out of the analysis. To do this, imagine the company returned 90 percent of its cash and securities to shareholders as a giant dividend. Alternatively, imagine Google split into two companies: an operating Internet company and a money market mutual fund charged with investing 90 percent of the firm's excess cash. This would cut the operating company's assets and shareholders' equity by $31.5 billion, while leaving the company with a still robust 43.6 days' sales in cash. Assuming a modest 2 percent after-tax return on cash and securities, this would knock $630 million from net income. The resulting revised levers of performance appear in the following summary. Asset turnover is now a more plausible, but still modest, 1.11 times, and ROE is up to a robust 53.4 percent. These numbers more accurately reflect the economics of Google's business.

	Return on Equity	=	Profit Margin	×	Asset Turnover	×	Financial Leverage
As reported	18.4%	=	29.0%	×	0.51	×	1.25
Revised	53.4%	=	26.9%	×	1.11	×	1.79

Totals do not add due to rounding.

of goods sold larger than purchases. Because of these differences, it is tricky to compare a manufacturing company's payables period, based on cost of goods sold, to its purchase terms. For Sensient, it is almost certain that cost of goods sold overstates credit purchases per day and that Sensient's suppliers are waiting a good bit longer than 39.9 days on average to receive payment.

Fixed-Asset Turnover

Companies or industries requiring large investments in long-lived assets to produce their goods are said to be capital intensive. Because a preponderance of their costs are fixed, capital-intensive businesses, such as auto manufacturers and airlines, are especially sensitive to the state of the economy, prospering in good times as sales rise relative to costs and suffering in bad as the reverse occurs. Capital intensity, also referred to as operating leverage, is of particular concern to creditors because it magnifies the basic business risks faced by a firm.

Fixed-asset turnover is a measure of capital intensity, with a low turnover implying high intensity. The ratio in 2010 for Sensient was

$$\frac{\text{Fixed-asset}}{\text{turnover}} = \frac{\text{Sales}}{\text{Net property, plant, and equipment}} = \frac{\$1,328.2}{\$432.5}$$

$$= 3.1 \text{ times}$$

where \$432.5 million is the book value of Sensient's net property, plant, and equipment.

Financial Leverage

The third lever by which management affects ROE is financial leverage. A company increases its financial leverage when it raises the proportion of debt relative to equity used to finance the business. Unlike the profit margin and the asset turnover ratio, where more is generally preferred to less, financial leverage is not something management necessarily wants to maximize, even when doing so increases ROE. Instead, the challenge of financial leverage is to strike a prudent balance between the benefits and costs of debt financing. Later we will devote all of Chapter 6 to this important financial decision. For now, it is sufficient to recognize that more leverage is not necessarily preferred to less and that while companies have considerable latitude in their choice of how much financial leverage to employ, there are economic and institutional constraints on their discretion.

As Table 2.1 suggests, the nature of a company's business and its assets influence the financial leverage it can employ. In general, businesses with highly predictable and stable operating cash flows, such as Southern Company, an electric utility, can safely undertake more financial leverage than firms facing a high degree of market uncertainty, such as Adobe System and Google. In addition, businesses such as banks, which before the recession we used to think of as having diversified portfolios of readily salable, liquid assets, can also safely use more financial leverage than the typical business.

Another pattern evident in Table 2.1 is that ROA and financial leverage tend to be inversely related. Companies with low ROAs generally employ more debt financing, and vice versa. This is consistent with the previous paragraph. Safe, stable, liquid investments tend to generate low returns but substantial borrowing capacity. Banks are extreme examples of this pattern.

JPMorgan Chase combines what by manufacturing standards would be a horrible 0.5 percent ROA with an astronomical leverage ratio of 12.58 to generate a modest ROE of 10.3 percent. The key to this pairing is the safe, liquid nature of the bank's assets. (Past loans to Third World dictators, Texas energy companies, and subprime mortgage, borrowers are, of course, another story—one the bank would just as soon forget.)

The following ratios measure financial leverage, or debt capacity, and the related concept of liquidity.

Balance Sheet Ratios

The most common measures of financial leverage compare the book value of a company's liabilities to the book value of its assets or equity. This gives rise to the *debt-to-assets ratio* and the *debt-to-equity ratio*, defined as

$$\text{Debt-to-assets ratio} = \frac{\text{Total liabilities}}{\text{Total assets}} = \frac{\$615.5}{\$1{,}599.3} = 38.5\%$$

$$\text{Debt-to-equity ratio} = \frac{\text{Total liabilities}}{\text{Shareholders' equity}} = \frac{\$615.5}{\$983.8} = 62.6\%$$

The first ratio says that money to pay for 38.5 percent of Sensient's assets, in book value terms, comes from creditors of one type or another. The second ratio says the same thing in a slightly different way: Creditors supply Sensient with 62.6 cents for every dollar supplied by shareholders. As footnote 1 demonstrated earlier, the lever of performance introduced earlier, the assets-to-equity ratio, is just the debt-to-equity ratio plus 1.

As many companies have built up large excess balances of cash and marketable securities, analysts have increasingly replaced debt in these equations with "net" debt, defined as total liabilities less cash and marketable securities. The idea is that as safe, interest-bearing assets, excess cash and marketable securities are essentially negative debt and, should thus be subtracted from liabilities when measuring aggregate indebtedness. I have no objection to this adjustment but do not believe it is an issue for Sensient Technologies given its modest cash and marketable securities balance.

Coverage Ratios

A number of variations on these balance sheet measures of financial leverage exist. Conceptually, however, there is no reason to prefer one over another, for they all focus on balance sheet values, and hence all suffer from the same weakness. The financial burden a company faces by using debt financing ultimately depends not on the size of its liabilities relative to assets or to equity but on its ability to meet the annual cash payments the debt requires. A simple example will illustrate the distinction. Suppose two companies, A and B, have the same debt-to-assets ratio, but A is very profitable and B is losing money. Chances are that B will have difficulty meeting its annual interest and principal obligations, while A will not. The obvious conclusion is that balance sheet ratios are of primary interest only in liquidation, when the proceeds of asset sales are to be distributed among creditors and owners. In all other instances, we should be more interested in comparing the annual burden the debt imposes to the cash flow available for debt service.

This gives rise to what are known as *coverage ratios*, the most common of which are *times interest earned* and *times burden covered*. Letting EBIT represent earnings before interest and taxes, the ratios are defined as:

$$\text{Times interest earned} = \frac{\text{EBIT}}{\text{Interest expense}} = \frac{\$173.2}{\$20.4} = 8.5 \text{ times}$$

$$\text{Times burden covered} = \frac{\text{EBIT}}{\text{Interest} + \dfrac{\text{Principal repayment}}{1 - \text{tax rate}}}$$

No numbers illustrating the calculation of Sensient's times burden covered ratio appear because the company had no principal repayment obligations in 2010.

Both ratios compare income available for debt service in the numerator to some measure of annual financial obligation. For both ratios, the income available is EBIT.[3] This is the earnings the company generates that can be used to make interest payments. EBIT is before taxes because interest payments are before-tax expenditures, and we want to compare like quantities. Sensient's times-interest-earned ratio of 8.5 means the company earned its interest obligation 8.5 times over in 2010; EBIT was 8.5 times as large as interest.

Though dentists may correctly claim that if you ignore your teeth they'll eventually go away, the same cannot be said for principal repayments. If a company fails to make a principal repayment when due, the outcome is the same as if it had failed to make an interest payment. In both cases, the company is in default and creditors can force it into bankruptcy. The times-burden-covered ratio reflects this reality by expanding the definition of annual financial obligations to include debt principal

[3]EBIT equals operating income from Table 1.3. An alternative definition is income before income taxes + interest expense. I believe the former is superior because it ignores nonoperating expenses and various special items that tend to be nonrecurring, noncash charges.

repayments as well as interest. When including principal repayment as part of a company's financial burden, we must remember to express the figure on a before-tax basis comparable to interest and EBIT. Unlike interest payments, principal repayments are not a tax-deductible expense. This means that if a company is in, say, the 50 percent tax bracket, it must earn $2 before taxes to have $1 after taxes to pay creditors. The other dollar goes to the tax collector. For other tax brackets, the before-tax burden of a principal repayment is found by dividing the repayment by 1 minus the company's tax rate. Adjusting the principal repayment in this manner to its before-tax equivalent is known in the trade as *grossing up* the principal—about as gross as finance ever gets.

An often-asked question is: Which of these coverage ratios is more meaningful? The answer is that both are important. If a company could always roll over its maturing obligations by taking out new loans as it repaid old ones, the *net* burden of the debt would be merely the interest expense, and times interest earned would be the more important ratio. The problem, as we were all vividly reminded during the recent financial panic, is that the replacement of maturing debt with new debt is not an automatic feature of capital markets. In some instances, when capital markets are unsettled or a company's fortunes decline, creditors may refuse to renew maturing obligations. Then the burden of the debt suddenly becomes interest plus principal payments, and the times-burden-covered ratio assumes paramount importance.

This is what happened beginning in the summer of 2007 when growing defaults on subprime mortgages prompted some short-term lenders to demand immediate payment from a variety of mortgage investment companies. These special purpose companies were issuing short-term debt to finance ownership of complex, long-term mortgage-backed securities. This was a nice business as long as lenders willingly rolled over maturing debts. But the minute they balked, a vicious circle ensued as borrowers sold their securities at cut-rate prices to repay short-term lenders, and short-term lenders, reacting to the falling prices, increasingly refused to rollover maturing obligations.

In sum, it is fair to conclude that the times-burden-covered ratio is too conservative because it assumes the company will pay its existing loans down to zero, but that the time-interest-earned ratio is too liberal because it assumes the company will always roll over all of its obligations as they mature.

Market Value Leverage Ratios

A third family of leverage ratios relates a company's liabilities to the *market value of its equity* or the *market value of its assets*. For Sensient

Technologies in 2010,

$$\frac{\text{Market value of debt}}{\text{Market value of equity}} = \frac{\text{Market value of debt}}{\text{Number of shares of stock} \times \text{Price per share}}$$

$$= \frac{\$615.5}{\$1,821.8} = 38.5\%$$

$$\frac{\text{Market value of debt}}{\text{Market value of assets}} = \frac{\text{Market value of debt}}{\text{Market value of debt} + \text{equity}}$$

$$= \frac{\$615.5}{\$615.5 + \$1,821.8} = 25.3\%$$

Note that I have assumed the market value of debt equals the book value of debt in both of these ratios. Strictly speaking, this is seldom true, but in most instances, the difference between the two quantities is small. Also, accurately estimating the market value of debt often turns out to be a tedious, time-consuming chore that is best avoided—unless, of course, you are being paid by the hour.

Market value ratios are clearly superior to book value ratios simply because book values are historical, often irrelevant numbers, while market values indicate the true worth of creditors' and owners' stakes in the business. Recalling that market values are based on investors' expectations about future cash flows, market value leverage ratios can be thought of as coverage ratios extended over many future periods. Instead of comparing income to financial burden in a single year as coverage ratios do, market value ratios compare today's value of expected future income to today's value of future financial burdens.

Market value ratios are especially helpful when assessing the financial leverage of rapidly growing, start-up businesses. Even when such companies have terrible or nonexistent coverage ratios, lenders may still extend them liberal credit if they believe future cash flows will be sufficient to service the debt. McCaw Communications offers an extreme example of this. At year-end 1990, McCaw had over $5 billion in debt; a debt-to-equity ratio, in book terms, of 330 percent; and annualized interest expenses of *more than 60 percent of net revenues*. Moreover, despite explosive growth, McCaw had never made a meaningful operating profit in its principal cellular telephone business. Why then did otherwise intelligent creditors loan McCaw $5 billion? Because creditors and equity investors believed it was only a matter of time before the company would begin to generate huge cash flows. This optimism was handsomely rewarded in late 1993 when AT&T paid $12.6 billion to acquire McCaw. Including the $5 billion in debt assumed by AT&T, the acquisition ranked as the second largest in corporate history at the time.

Another example is Amazon.com. In 1998 the company recorded its largest-ever loss of $124 million, had never earned a profit, and had only $139 million left in shareholders' equity. But not to worry: Lenders were still pleased to extend the company $350 million in long-term debt. Apparently, creditors are willing to overlook a number of messy details when a borrower's sales are growing 300 percent a year and the market value of its equity tops $17 billion—especially when the debt is convertible into equity. After all, in market value terms, Amazon's debt-to-equity ratio was only 3 percent. Today Amazon's equity is worth almost $83 billion, and it is debt-free.

Economists like market value leverage ratios because they are accurate indicators of company indebtedness at a point in time. But you should be aware that market value ratios are not without problems. One is that they ignore rollover risks. When creditors take the attitude that debt must be repaid with cash, not promises of future cash, modest market value leverage ratios can be of hollow comfort. Also, despite these ratios' conceptual appeal, few companies use them to set financing policy or to monitor debt levels. This may be due in part to the fact that volatile stock prices can make market value ratios appear somewhat arbitrary and beyond management's control.

Liquidity Ratios

One determinant of a company's debt capacity is the liquidity of its assets. An asset is liquid if it can be readily converted to cash, while a liability is liquid if it must be repaid in the near future. As the subprime mortgage debacle illustrates, it is risky to finance illiquid assets such as fixed plant and equipment with liquid, short-term liabilities, because the liabilities will come due before the assets generate enough cash to pay them. Such "maturity mismatching" forces borrowers to roll over, or refinance, maturing liabilities to avoid insolvency.

Two common ratios intended to measure the liquidity of a company's assets relative to its liabilities are the *current ratio* and the *acid test*. For Sensient,

$$\text{Current ratio} = \frac{\text{Current assets}}{\text{Current liabilities}}$$

$$= \frac{\$672.4}{\$205.1} = 3.3 \text{ times}$$

$$\text{Acid test} = \frac{\text{Current assets} - \text{Inventory}}{\text{Current liabilities}}$$

$$= \frac{\$672.4 - \$392.2}{\$205.1} = 1.4 \text{ times}$$

The current ratio compares the assets that will turn into cash within the year to the liabilities that must be paid within the year. A company with a low current ratio lacks liquidity in the sense that it cannot reduce its current assets for cash to meet maturing obligations. It must rely instead on operating income and outside financing.

The acid-test ratio, sometimes called the *quick ratio*, is a more conservative liquidity measure. It is identical to the current ratio except that the numerator is reduced by the value of inventory. Inventory is subtracted because it is frequently illiquid. Under distress conditions, a company or its creditors may realize little cash from the sale of inventory. In liquidation sales, sellers typically receive 40 percent or less of the book value of inventory.

You should recognize that these ratios are rather crude measures of liquidity, for at least two reasons. First, rolling over some obligations, such as accounts payable, involves virtually no insolvency risk provided the company is at least marginally profitable. Second, unless a company intends to go out of business, most of the cash generated by liquidating current assets cannot be used to reduce liabilities because it must be plowed back into the business to support continued operations.

Is ROE a Reliable Financial Yardstick?

To this point, we have assumed management wants to increase the company's ROE, and we have studied three important levers of performance by which they can accomplish this: the profit margin, asset turnover, and financial leverage. We concluded that whether a company is IBM or the corner drugstore, careful management of these levers can positively affect ROE. We also saw that determining and maintaining appropriate values of the levers is a challenging managerial task that requires an understanding of the company's business, the way the company competes, and the interdependencies among the levers themselves. Now it is time to ask how reliable ROE is as a measure of financial performance. If company A has a higher ROE than company B, is it necessarily a better company? If company C increases its ROE, is this unequivocal evidence of improved performance?

ROE suffers from three critical deficiencies as a measure of financial performance, which I will refer to as the *timing* problem, the *risk* problem, and the *value* problem. Seen in proper perspective, these problems mean ROE is seldom an unambiguous measure of performance. ROE remains a useful and important indicator, but it must be interpreted in light of its limitations, and no one should automatically assume a higher ROE is always better than a lower one.

The Timing Problem

It is a cliché to say that successful managers must be forward-looking and have a long-term perspective. Yet ROE is precisely the opposite:

backward-looking and focused on a single year. So it is little wonder that ROE can at times be a skewed measure of performance. When, for example, a company incurs heavy startup costs to introduce a hot new product, ROE will initially fall. However, rather than indicating worsening financial performance, the fall simply reflects the myopic, one-period nature of the yardstick. Because ROE necessarily includes only one year's earnings, it fails to capture the full impact of multiperiod decisions.

The Risk Problem

Business decisions commonly involve the classic "eat well–sleep well" dilemma. If you want to eat well, you had best be prepared to take risks in search of higher returns. If you want to sleep well, you will likely have to forgo high returns in search of safety. Seldom will you realize both high returns and safety. (And when you do, please give me a call.)

The problem with ROE is that it says nothing about what risks a company has taken to generate it. Here is a simple example. Take-a-Risk, Inc., earns an ROA of 6 percent from wildcat oil exploration in Sudan, which it combines with an assets-to-equity ratio of 5.0 to produce an ROE of 30 percent (6% × 5.0). Never-Dare, Ltd., meanwhile, has an ROA of 10 percent on its investment in government securities, which it finances with equal portions of debt and equity, yielding an ROE of 20 percent (10% × 2.0). Which company is the better performer? My answer is Never-Dare. Take-a-Risk's ROE is high, but its high business risk and extreme financial leverage make it a very uncertain enterprise. I would prefer the more modest but eminently safer ROE of Never-Dare.[4] Security analysts would make the same point by saying that Take-a-Risk's ROE might be higher but that the number is much lower quality than Never-Dare's ROE, meaning that it is much riskier. In sum, because ROE looks only at return while ignoring risk, it can be an inaccurate yardstick of financial performance.

Return on Invested Capital

To circumvent the distorting effects of leverage on ROE and ROA, I recommend calculating *return on invested capital (ROIC)*, also known as *return on net assets (RONA)*:

$$\text{ROIC} = \frac{\text{EBIT}(1 - \text{Tax rate})}{\text{Interest-bearing debt} + \text{Equity}}$$

[4] Even if I preferred eating well to sleeping well, I would still choose Never-Dare and finance my purchase with a little personal borrowing to lever my return on investment. See the appendix to Chapter 6 for more on the substitution of personal borrowing for company borrowing.

Sensient's 2010 ROIC was

$$\frac{\$173.2(1 - \$47.1/\$154.3)}{\$25.5 + \$324.4 + \$983.8} = 9.0\%$$

The numerator of this ratio is the earnings after tax the company would report if it were all equity financed, and the denominator is the sum of all sources of cash to the company on which a return must be earned. Thus, while accounts payable are a source of cash to the company, they are excluded because they carry no explicit cost. In essence, ROIC is the rate of return earned on the total capital invested in the business without regard for whether it is called debt or equity.

To see the virtue of ROIC, consider the following example. Companies A and B are identical in all respects except that A is highly levered and B is all equity financed. Because the two companies are identical except for capital structure, we would like a return measure that reflects this fundamental similarity. The following table shows that ROE and ROA fail this test. Reflecting the company's extensive use of financial leverage, A's ROE is 18 percent, while B's zero-leverage position generates a lower but better-quality ROE of 7.2 percent. ROA is biased in the other direction, punishing company A for its extensive use of debt and leaving B unaffected. Only ROIC is independent of the different financing schemes the two companies employ, showing a 7.2 percent return for both firms. ROIC thus reflects the company's fundamental earning power before it is confounded by differences in financing strategies.

	Company	
	A	**B**
Debt @ 10% interest	$ 900	$ 0
Equity	100	1,000
Total assets	$1,000	$1,000
EBIT	$ 120	$ 120
– Interest expense	90	0
Earnings before tax	30	120
– Tax @ 40%	12	48
Earnings after tax	$ 18	$ 72
ROE	18.0%	7.2%
ROA	1.8%	7.2%
ROIC	7.2%	7.2%

The Value Problem

ROE measures the return on shareholders' investment; however, the investment figure used is the *book value* of shareholders' equity, not the *market value*. This distinction is important. Sensient's ROE in 2010 was 10.9 percent, and indeed this is the return you could have earned had you been able to buy the company's equity for its book value of $983.8 million. But that would have been impossible, for, as noted in the previous chapter, the market value of Sensient's equity was $1,821.8 million. At this price, your annual return would have been only 5.9 percent, not 10.9 percent ($107.2/$1,821.8 = 5.9%). The market value of equity is more significant to shareholders because it measures the current, realizable worth of the shares, while book value is only history. So even when ROE measures management's financial performance, it may not be synonymous with a high return on investment to shareholders. Thus, it is not enough for investors to find companies capable of generating high ROEs; these companies must be unknown to others, because once they are known, the possibility of high returns to investors will melt away in higher stock prices.

The Earnings Yield and the P/E Ratio

It might appear that we can circumvent the value problem by simply replacing the book value of equity with its market value in the ROE. But the resulting *earnings yield* has problems of its own. For Sensient,

$$\text{Earnings yield} = \frac{\text{Net income}}{\text{Market value of shareholders' equity}}$$

$$= \frac{\text{Earnings per share}}{\text{Price per share}} = \frac{\$2.16}{\$36.73} = 5.9\%$$

Is earnings yield a useful measure of financial performance? No! The problem is that a company's stock price is very sensitive to investor expectations about the future. A share of stock entitles its owner to a portion of *future* earnings as well as present earnings. Naturally, the higher an investor's expectations of future earnings, the more she will pay for the stock. This means that a bright future, a high stock price, and a *low* earnings yield go together. Clearly, a high earnings yield is not an indicator of superior performance; in fact, it is more the reverse. Said another way, the earnings yield suffers from a severe timing problem of its own that invalidates it as a performance measure.

Turning the earnings yield on its head produces the *price-to-earnings ratio*, or *P/E ratio*. Sensient's 2010 P/E ratio is

$$\frac{\text{Price per share}}{\text{Earnings per share}} = \frac{\$36.73}{\$2.16} = 17.0 \text{ times}$$

The P/E ratio adds little to our discussion of performance measures, but its wide use among investors deserves comment. The P/E ratio is the price of one dollar of current earnings and is a means of normalizing stock prices for different earnings levels across companies. At year end 2010, investors were paying $17.0 per dollar of Sensient's earnings. A company's P/E ratio depends principally on two things: its future earnings prospects and the risk associated with those earnings. Stock price, and hence the P/E ratio, rises with improved earnings prospects and falls with increasing risk. A sometimes confusing pattern occurs when a company's earnings are weak but investors believe the weakness is temporary. Then prices remain buoyant in the face of depressed earnings, and the P/E ratio *rises*. In general, the P/E ratio says little about a company's current financial performance, but it does indicate what investors believe about future prospects.

ROE or Market Price?

For years, academicians and practitioners have been at odds over the proper measure of financial performance. Academicians criticize ROE for the reasons just cited and argue that the correct measure of financial performance is the firm's stock price. Moreover, they contend that management's goal should be to maximize stock price. Their logic is persuasive: Stock price represents the value of the owners' investment in the firm, and if managers want to further the interests of owners, they should take actions that increase value to owners. Indeed, the notion of "value creation" has become a central theme in the writings of many academicians and consultants.

Practitioners acknowledge the logic of this reasoning but question its applicability. One problem is the difficulty of specifying precisely how operating decisions affect stock price. If we are not certain what impact a change in, say, the business strategy of a division will have on the company's stock price, the goal of increasing price cannot guide decision making. A second problem is that managers typically know more about their company than do outside investors, or at least think they do. Why, then, should managers consider the assessments of less informed investors when making business decisions? A third practical problem with stock price as a performance measure is that it depends on a whole array of factors outside the company's control. One can never be certain whether an increase in stock price reflects improving company performance or an improving external economic environment. For these reasons, many practitioners remain skeptical of stock market–based indicators of performance, even while academicians and consultants continue to work on translating value creation into a practical financial objective. One popular effort along these lines is *economic value added (EVA)*, popularized by the consulting firm Stern Stewart Management Services. We will look more closely at EVA in Chapter 8.

Can ROE Substitute for Share Price?

Figures 2.1 and 2.2 suggest that the gulf between academicians and practitioners over the proper measure of financial performance may be narrower than supposed. The graphs plot the market value of equity divided by the book value of equity against ROE for two representative groups of companies. The ROE figure is a weighted-average ROE over the most recent three years. The solid line in each figure is a regression line indicating the general relation between the two variables. The noticeable positive relationship visible in both graphs suggests that high-ROE companies tend to have high stock prices relative to book value, and vice versa. Hence, working to increase ROE appears to be generally consistent with working to increase stock price.

The proximity of the company dots to the fitted regression line is also interesting. It shows the importance of factors other than ROE in determining a company's market-to-book ratio. As we should expect, these other factors play an important role in determining the market value of a company's shares.

For interest, I have indicated the positions of several companies on the graphs. Note in Figure 2.1 that Sensient Technologies is a bit below the regression line, indicating that based purely on historical ROE, Sensient's stock is modestly under-priced compared to those of other firms in the specialty chemical and related industries. Two other highlighted companies, with market-to-book ratios way above the regression line, are Green Mountain Coffee Roasters and Balchem Corporation. Green Mountain is a small coffee company with a patent-protected position in gourmet, single-brew coffees. Investors are excited about the prospects for single-brew systems and apparently think Green Mountain can give Starbucks a run for its money, although the results are not fully apparent. Balchem is most likely well above the regression line because it is growing rapidly. Earnings rose 38 percent two years ago and were up another 21 percent last year. Cal-Maine Foods, the country's largest egg producer, appears to be the Rodney Dangerfield of the market. Despite a very attractive ROE, it is well below the regression line, due possibly to salmonella-related recalls in recent months. Interestingly, the company is located neither in California nor Maine, but in Jackson, Mississippi.

Figure 2.2 shows the same information for 80 nonfinancial firms in Standard & Poor's 100 Index of the largest U.S. firms. Microsoft takes the prize here for the highest ROE with a figure of over 40 percent, although Amazon.com wins market-to-book honors at almost 12 times. Perhaps this has something to do with the fact that Amazon's sales have grown at an average rate of 27 percent a year over the past decade and 67 percent a year over the past 15 years. At the other end of the spectrum, AT&T, Dell, and Microsoft all lie well below the regression line.

To summarize, these graphs offer tantalizing evidence that despite its weaknesses, ROE may serve as at least a crude proxy for share price in measuring financial performance.

FIGURE 2.1   **Market to Book Value of Equity vs. Return on Equity for 50 Companies in the Specialty Chemicals and Packaged Foods and Meats Industries**

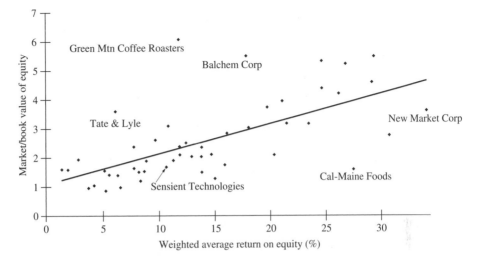

The regression equation is MV/BV = 1.1 + 10.5 ROE, where MV/BV is the market value of equity relative to the book value of equity in March 2011, and ROE is a weighted-average of return on equity in 2010 and the prior two years. Smaller companies with market values below $500 million and outliers with negative values or ROEs above 45 percent were eliminated. Adjusted R^2 = 0.41, the t-statistic for the slope coefficient is 5.9.

FIGURE 2.2   **Market to Book Value of Equity vs. Return on Equity for 80 Large Corporations**

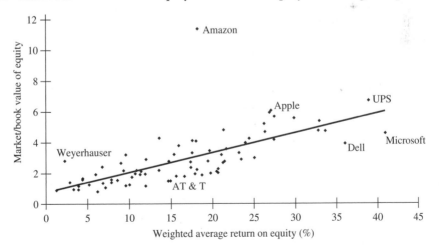

Companies are members of Standard & Poor's 100 Index of the largest U.S. corporations. Those with negative values and outliers with ROEs above 45 percent were eliminated. The regression equation is MV/BV = 0.78 + 12.8 ROE, where MV/BV is the market value of equity relative to the book value of equity in March 2011 and ROE is a weighted average return on equity for 2010 and the prior two years. Adjusted R^2 = 0.45. The t-statistic for the slope coefficient = 8.2.

Ratio Analysis

In our discussion of the levers of financial performance, we defined a number of financial ratios. It is now time to consider the systematic use of these ratios to analyze financial performance. Ratio analysis is widely used by managers, creditors, regulators, and investors. At root it is an elementary process involving little more than comparing a number of company ratios to one or more performance benchmarks. Used with care and imagination, the technique can reveal much about a company. But there are a few things to bear in mind about ratios. First, a ratio is simply one number divided by another, so it is unreasonable to expect the mechanical calculation of one or even several ratios to automatically yield important insights into anything as complex as a modern corporation. It is best to think of ratios as clues in a detective story. One or even several ratios might be misleading, but when combined with other knowledge of a company's management and economic circumstances, ratio analysis can tell a revealing story.

A second point to bear in mind is that a ratio has no single correct value. Like Goldilocks and the three bears, the observation that the value of a particular ratio is too high, too low, or just right depends on the perspective of the analyst and on the company's competitive strategy. The current ratio, previously defined as the ratio of current assets to current liabilities, is a case in point. From the perspective of a short-term creditor, a high current ratio is a positive sign suggesting ample liquidity and a high likelihood of repayment. Yet an owner of the company might look on the same current ratio as a negative sign suggesting that the company's assets are being deployed too conservatively. Moreover, from an operating perspective, a high current ratio could be a sign of conservative management or the natural result of a competitive strategy that emphasizes liberal credit terms and sizable inventories. In this case, the important question is not whether the current ratio is too high but whether the chosen strategy is best for the company.

Using Ratios Effectively

If ratios have no universally correct values, how do you interpret them? How do you decide whether a company is healthy or sick? There are three approaches, each involving a different performance benchmark: Compare the ratios to rules of thumb, compare them to industry averages, or look for changes in the ratios over time. Comparing a company's ratios to rules of thumb has the virtue of simplicity but has little else to recommend it. The appropriate ratio values for a company depend too much on the analyst's perspective and on the company's specific circumstances for rules of thumb to be very helpful. The most positive thing one can say about them is that over the years, companies conforming to these rules of thumb apparently go bankrupt somewhat less frequently than those that do not.

Comparing a company's ratios to industry ratios provides a useful feel for how the company measures up to its competitors, provided you bear in mind that company-specific differences can result in entirely justifiable deviations from industry norms. Also, there is no guarantee that the industry as a whole knows what it is doing. The knowledge that one railroad was much like its competitors was cold comfort in the depression of the 1930s, when virtually all railroads got into financial difficulties.

The most useful way to evaluate ratios involves trend analysis: Calculate ratios for a company over several years, and note how they change over time. Trend analysis avoids the need for cross-company and cross-industry comparisons, enabling the analyst to draw firmer conclusions about the company's financial health and its variation over time.

Moreover, the levers of performance suggest one logical approach to trend analysis: Instead of calculating ratios at random, hoping to stumble across one that might be meaningful, take advantage of the structure implicit in the levers. As Figure 2.3 illustrates, the levers of performance organize ratios into three tiers. At the top, ROE looks at the performance of the

FIGURE 2.3   **The Levers of Performance Suggest One Road Map for Ratio Analysis**

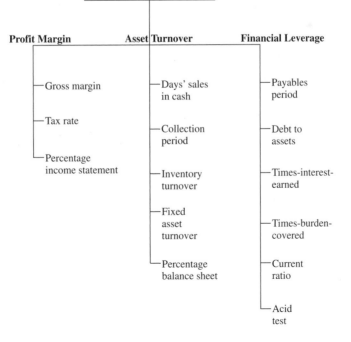

enterprise as a whole; in the middle, the levers of performance indicate how three important segments of the business contributed to ROE; and on the bottom, many of the other ratios discussed reveal how the management of individual income statement and balance sheet accounts contributed to the observed levers. To take advantage of this structure, begin at the top by noting the trend in ROE over time. Then narrow your focus and ask what changes in the three levers account for the observed ROE pattern. Finally, get out your microscope and study individual accounts for explanations of the observed changes in the levers. To illustrate, if ROE has plunged while the profit margin and financial leverage have remained constant, examine the control of individual asset accounts in search of the culprit or culprits.

Ratio Analysis of Sensient Technologies Corporation

As a practical demonstration of ratio analysis, let us see what the technique can tell us about Sensient Technologies. Table 2.2 presents previously discussed ratios for Sensient over the years 2006–2010 and average industry figures for 2010. (For summary definitions of the ratios, see Table 2.5 at the end of chapter.) The comparison industry consists of six representative competitors noted at the bottom of the table. As an example of similar, readily available industry data, Table 2.4 at the end of the chapter presents selected ratios from Dun & Bradstreet Information Services for representative industries, including median, upper-quartile, and lower-quartile values for the represented ratios.[5]

Beginning with Sensient's profitability ratios, we see a company making steady improvement, but to a distinctly mediocre level. The company's return on equity in 2010 is only 10.9 percent, barely more than one-half the industry average of 18.1 percent. It is tempting to attribute this disparity to Sensient's modest use of debt financing, but a glance at the company's return on invested capital reveals that this is not the whole story. At 9.0 percent, Sensient's ROIC is little more than two-thirds the industry average of 12.5 percent. Recall that ROIC abstracts from company financing to reveal the basic earning power of the firm's assets. To put these figures in broader perspective, the average ROE chalked up by a broad cross-section of large American companies in 2010 was 17.6 percent, while the corresponding ROIC was 13.1 percent.[6]

---

[5]For any ratio, if we array all of the values for the companies in the industry from the highest to the lowest, the figure falling in the middle of the series is the *median,* the ratio halfway between the highest value and the median is the *upper quartile,* and the ratio halfway between the lowest value and the median is the *lower quartile.* Data are from *Industry Norms and Key Business Ratios: Library Edition 2009–10,* Dun & Bradstreet Credit Services, 2010.

[6]These numbers are the mean return on equity and return on invested capital in 2010 for the 419 nonfinancial firms in Standard & Poor's 500 Index, generally the largest 500 companies in the United States. Comparable median percentages were 14.8 and 11.8, respectively.

TABLE 2.2 Ratio Analysis of Sensient Technologies Corporation, 2006–2010, and Industry Medians, 2010

	2006	2007	2008	2009	2010	Industry Average*
Profitability ratios:						
Return on equity (%)	**9.4**	**9.6**	**11.1**	**9.5**	**10.9**	**18.1**
Return on assets (%)	4.6	5.0	6.0	5.4	6.7	7.5
Return on invested capital (%)	7.4	7.8	8.7	7.7	9.0	12.5
Profit margin (%)	**6.0**	**6.6**	**7.3**	**7.2**	**8.1**	**8.4**
Gross margin (%)	34.2	34.3	34.0	34.2	34.0	33.5
Price-to-earnings ratio (X)	17.2	17.2	12.7	14.8	17.0	17.7
Turnover-control ratios:						
Asset turnover (X)	**0.8**	**0.8**	**0.8**	**0.8**	**0.8**	**0.9**
Fixed-asset turnover (X)	2.8	2.8	3.1	2.8	3.1	4.0
Inventory turnover (X)	2.2	2.2	2.2	2.0	2.2	4.1
Collection period (days)	59.2	60.5	58.0	60.8	60.1	58.9
Days' sales in cash (days)	1.7	3.2	2.5	3.7	3.9	32.9
Payables period (days)	40.8	41.7	36.6	41.1	39.9	51.3
Leverage and liquidity ratios:						
Assets to equity (X)	**2.1**	**1.9**	**1.9**	**1.8**	**1.6**	**2.4**
Debt to assets (%)	51.6	47.9	46.3	42.9	38.5	57.3
Debt to equity (%)	106.5	92.1	86.3	75.2	62.6	139.7
Times interest earned (X)	3.6	4.1	5.0	6.7	8.5	10.1
Times burden covered (X)	3.6	4.1	5.0	6.7	8.5	5.4
Debt to assets (market value, %)	39.6	35.9	38.1	34.7	25.3	32.5
Debt to equity (market value, %)	65.5	56.0	61.5	53.2	33.8	50.5
Current ratio (X)	2.1	2.7	3.2	3.0	3.3	2.2
Acid test (X)	0.8	1.1	1.3	1.2	1.4	1.5

*Sample consists of six representative firms in the specialty chemicals and related industries: Agrium, Albemarle, Cabot, Corn Products, Int'l Flavors & Fragrances, and McCormick.

Looking next at the company's levers of performance, Sensient's profit margin is improving but still modestly below the industry average. The company's asset turnover is highly stable but again modestly below the industry figure. Lastly, Sensient's assets-to-equity has declined steadily to where it is now just two-thirds the peer group average. To put this decline in perspective, the company's ROE in 2010 would have been almost 25 percent higher had its financial leverage not declined (8.1% × 0.8 × 2.1 = 13.6%).

Digging a little deeper into these broad trends, Sensient's improving profit margin is not reflected in its gross margin, which has been stable and is a bit above the industry average in 2010. This suggests the improvement is due to tightening control of the company's selling, general, and administrative expenses, although more work remains before Sensient can get its profit margin up to that of its peers.

Sensient's mediocre asset utilization masks two sharp differences from its peers. Although rising over time, Sensient's cash balances are much less than the industry average. This is evidenced by a days' sales-in-cash ratio of only 3.9, compared to an industry ratio of 32.9 days, a difference of over eight times. More than offsetting Sensient's efficient use of cash are its distressingly low fixed-asset and inventory turnover ratios. Fixed-asset turnover has improved a bit since 2006 but is still only about three-quarters the industry figure, while the inventory turnover has not improved and registers little more than one-half of the industry norm. It is possible that these differences, especially the lower fixed-asset turnover, reflect the more capital-intensive nature of Sensient's products, but it is just as likely that they reflect management inefficiencies. Moreover, if these low asset turns were due to more capital-intensive products, I would expect Sensient to command higher operating margins than its peers, but this is not the case. I am left to suspect that Sensient is not very good at managing its assets.

Looking at Sensient's indebtedness ratios, it is apparent that the company has been aggressively reducing its reliance on other peoples' money. According to the balance sheet ratios—both book and market value versions—it appears the company is now quite conservatively financed relative to its peers. However, the times interest earned ratio is less comforting. Sensient's lower profit margin and less efficient asset utilization mean that its interest coverage is still about 15 percent below the industry figure. (The times burden covered ratio is not particularly meaningful here simply because Sensient had no sinking fund obligations during the period.)

Table 2.3 presents what are known as **common-size financial statements** for Sensient Technologies over the same period, as well as peer averages for 2010. A common-size balance sheet presents each asset and liability as a percentage of total assets. A common-size income statement is analogous except that all items are scaled in proportion to net sales rather than total assets. The purpose of scaling financial statements in this fashion is to concentrate on the underlying trends by abstracting from changes in the dollar figures caused by growth or decline. In addition, common-size statements are useful for removing simple scale effects when comparing companies of different sizes.

Looking at Sensient's balance sheet, the numbers look quite stable. The largest changes on the asset side are increases in every single current asset, led by increased inventories. This is partially offset by a decline in goodwill and intangible assets. Note that 42.0 percent of Sensient's assets are now short-term, a figure that again highlights the importance of working-capital management to most businesses. When a large portion of a company's investment is in assets as volatile as inventory and accounts receivable, that investment bears close watching.

TABLE 2.3 Sensient Technologies Corporation, Common-Size Financial Statements, 2006–2010, and Industry Averages, 2010

	2006	2007	2008	2009	2010	Industry Average*
Assets						
Cash & marketable securities	0.4%	0.7%	0.6%	0.8%	0.9%	7.8%
Accounts receivable, less reserve for possible losses	12.3	12.6	13.0	12.6	13.7	14.5
Inventories	22.9	23.1	25.0	24.5	24.5	15.2
Other current assets	2.4	2.7	2.6	3.5	3.0	5.6
Total current assets	37.9	39.0	41.1	41.4	42.0	43.2
Gross plant, property & equipment	59.9	60.6	61.0	62.4	64.1	64.5
Less accumulated depreciation and amortization	33.0	33.9	34.6	35.7	37.1	38.1
Net property, plant, and equipment	26.9	26.7	26.4	26.7	27.1	26.3
Goodwill and intangible assets, net	31.9	31.4	29.8	29.5	28.7	25.3
Other assets	3.3	2.8	2.7	2.4	2.3	5.2
Total assets	100.0%	100.0%	100.0%	100.0%	100.0%	100.0%
Liabilities and Shareholders' Equity						
Long-term debt due in one year	0.0%	0.0%	0.0%	0.0%	0.0%	1.5%
Short-term borrowings	6.3	3.7	2.2	2.5	1.6	0.9
Trade accounts payable	5.6	5.7	5.4	5.6	6.0	8.4
Taxes payable	1.0	0.2	0.1	0.0	0.5	0.6
Accrued expenses & other current liabilities	5.1	5.2	5.1	5.5	4.8	10.1
Total current liabilities	17.9	14.7	12.9	13.6	12.8	21.5
Long-term debt	30.4	28.7	29.2	24.4	20.3	24.8
Deferred taxes	-	0.8	1.0	0.8	1.3	2.9
Other long-term liabilities	3.3	3.7	3.3	4.1	4.1	8.6
Total liabilities	51.6	47.9	46.3	42.9	38.5	57.3
Total shareholders' equity	48.4	52.1	53.7	57.1	61.5	41.6
Total liabilities and shareholders' equity	100.0%	100.0%	100.0%	100.0%	100.0%	100.0%
Income Statements						
Net sales	100.0%	100.0%	100.0%	100.0%	100.0%	100.0%
Cost of goods sold	65.8	65.7	66.1	65.8	66.0	66.5
Gross profit	34.2	34.3	34.0	34.2	34.0	33.5
Selling, general and administrative expenses	18.5	18.1	17.5	17.5	17.7	17.1
Depreciation and amortization	3.9	3.7	3.6	3.5	3.3	3.2
Total operating expenses	22.4	21.9	21.1	21.1	21.0	20.3
Operating income	11.8	12.4	12.9	13.2	13.0	13.2
Interest expense	3.3	3.1	2.6	2.0	1.5	1.3
Other nonoperating expense (income)	-	-	-	0.9	(0.1)	0.4
Total nonoperating expense	3.3	3.1	2.6	2.9	1.4	1.8
Income before income taxes	8.5	9.4	10.3	10.3	11.6	11.4
Provision for income taxes	2.5	2.8	3.1	3.1	3.5	2.9
Net income	6.1%	6.6%	7.3%	7.2%	8.1%	8.4%

*See footnote to Table 2.2 for companies comprising industry sample.

The decline in goodwill is largely due to management write downs of past acquisitions caused by the recent recession. Accounting rules require managements to periodically assess the value of past acquisitions and to reduce their accounting values when it appears their market values have declined. In case you are wondering, no, managements may not increase the book values when they think values have risen—it is a one-way street. On the liabilities side of the balance sheet, we again see the sharp decline in both short- and long-term debt.

Comparing Sensient's 2010 numbers to industry averages, we see the earlier noted low cash balance and high inventories. In fact, Sensient's inventories now equal almost one-quarter of total assets, compared to an industry figure of just over 15 percent. This is a large difference. The company's investment in net property, plant, and equipment is roughly similar to the industry figure, an observation that seems at odds with our earlier comment that the firm's fixed-asset turnover was well below the industry average. The explanation is that the turnover ratio compares fixed assets to sales, while the percentage balance sheet compares them to total assets, and, as already noted, Sensient has more assets per dollar of sales than its peers. Finally, note that Sensient makes much less use of "accrued expenses and other current liabilities" than its peers. In fact, it relies on all four of the "catch-all" assets and liabilities appearing on the balance sheet much less than its peers do. What does this imply? I have no idea because I have no notion of what these "catch-all" quantities are.

Sensient's common size income statement shows declining selling, general, and administrative expenses, although they still exceed industry averages. Other differences between Sensient's numbers and those of its peers include lower "other nonoperating expense"—although this number is quite volatile year to year—and a higher provision for taxes. Together, Sensient's higher cost of goods sold and selling, general, and administrative expenses add 1.1 percent to its costs relative to peers. This might not seem like much at first glance, but it is important to remember that although small percentage differences on an income statement may appear inconsequential, they seldom are when compared to net income. Because Sensient's income before tax in 2010 was only 11.6 percent of sales, the 1.1 percent cost differential measured relative to sales translates into a meaningful 9.5 percent shortfall in net income. Small percentage differences compared to sales can be large differences compared to income, and income matters much more than sales.

Some beginners are inclined to think all operating expenses are fixed and to fault management for allowing them to rise with sales. Why aren't Sensient's selling, general, and administrative expenses constant over time they ask? Where are the economies of scale? The answer is that scale economies are not so simple. If they were, very large companies, like Sears and General Motors, would quickly dominate smaller competitors and eventually monopolize markets. In fact, it appears that while some activities exhibit economies of scale, others are subject to diseconomies of scale, meaning the company becomes less efficient with size. (Imagine how many more meetings are required to coordinate the activities of a 100-person team than a 10-person team.) Moreover, many activities exhibit scale economies over only a limited range of activity and then require a large investment to increase capacity. So on balance, I see no reason to criticize Sensient management for the fact that percentage selling, general, and administrative expenses have not fallen more steeply over the past five years. At the same time, I remain concerned that the number is still above the industry average.

To summarize, our ratio analysis of Sensient Technologies reveals a highly stable, conservatively financed company capable of sailing through the recent major recession with barely a pause. Recent performance is improving nicely relative to peers but remains mediocre in terms of operating margins, inventory turns, and returns on both capital and equity. Despite these weak spots, the company's improving performance and modest capital expenditure needs have enabled it to generate more cash than necessary to run the business. The size of the challenge is clear from Sensient's cash flow statements. Over the five years ending in 2010, the company's cash flow from operations totaled close to $600 million, while its capital expenditures and dividend payments came to just two-thirds of this amount. The problem: What to do with the other $200 million? To date, management's answer has been to pay down debt, which has fallen by just over $200 million since 2006. There are, however, two problems with this as a long-run answer to Sensient's cash flow problem. At the current rate of retirement, Sensient's debt will disappear entirely in five years, and more importantly, a low debt level may not be in the company's or shareholders' best interest (Chapter 6 considers this issue in detail).

Finding ways to spend excess cash might sound like fun, but Kenneth Manning, Sensient's boss, knows better. He realizes that unless he finds productive uses for this cash by increasing capital expenditures, acquiring other businesses, or returning the money to shareholders, he risks depressing the company's stock price, antagonizing his board and shareholders, and possibly inviting attack or takeover by activist investors. We will have more to say about Sensient's financial challenges and the wisdom of its aggressive deleveraging in coming chapters.

TABLE 2.4 Selected Ratios for Representative Industries, 2009 (upper-quartile, median, and lower-quartile values)

Lines of Business and Number of Firms Reporting	Current Ratio (times)	Total Liabilities to Net Worth (%)	Collection Period (days)	Net Sales to Inventory (times)	Total Assets to Net Sales (%)	Profit Margin (%)	Return on Assets (%)	Return on Equity (%)
Agriculture, forestry, and fishing:								
Ornamental nursery products (35)	5.2	17.5	10.2	13.8	46.6	5.5	8.1	17.5
	2.4	**76.6**	**23.9**	**7.1**	**75.5**	**1.7**	**2.7**	**3.8**
	1.2	164.6	46.0	4.2	94.6	(1.3)	(3.7)	(1.6)
Lawn and garden services (144)	4.1	33.2	19.4	135.9	25.4	6.2	16.3	27.7
	2.2	**71.1**	**35.8**	**42.2**	**37.0**	**2.0**	**5.1**	**11.7**
	1.4	164.1	57.3	16.8	50.3	0.1	0.2	1.0
Manufacturing:								
Chemicals and allied products (609)	4.2	28.7	26.7	14.3	58.1	7.3	8.3	19.1
	2.4	**70.4**	**42.9**	**8.5**	**105.0**	**1.0**	**0.8**	**5.2**
	1.4	175.1	59.3	5.1	194.0	(30.8)	(24.0)	(21.5)
Motors and generators (25)	3.0	31.4	26.3	9.4	49.3	7.8	7.7	12.5
	2.3	**98.7**	**42.0**	**5.7**	**77.9**	**0.5**	**0.7**	**(6.6)**
	0.9	244.9	51.5	2.8	255.1	(194.0)	(35.6)	(87.0)
Semiconductors and related devices (152)	6.4	16.4	34.2	11.1	92.4	8.3	6.4	9.5
	3.7	**32.0**	**47.5**	**7.6**	**136.5**	**(2.6)**	**(1.4)**	**(1.4)**
	2.0	82.7	66.1	5.2	184.0	(24.8)	(17.6)	(22.4)
Process control instruments (53)	7.7	13.3	38.0	10.9	35.8	8.4	16.0	28.2
	3.7	**38.5**	**48.6**	**7.4**	**54.3**	**3.9**	**7.3**	**10.1**
	2.3	84.0	64.6	4.4	78.6	0.1	0.2	0.6
Wholesale trade:								
Sporting and recreational goods (72)	4.2	27.6	15.5	14.1	20.6	4.4	14.1	23.2
	2.3	**59.7**	**29.9**	**6.8**	**32.7**	**1.8**	**5.8**	**11.9**
	1.4	186.1	46.4	4.5	51.2	0.2	0.6	1.6
Women's and children's clothing (56)	3.4	55.6	25.9	15.1	22.7	5.2	17.2	50.7
	1.9	**139.9**	**37.2**	**9.0**	**34.3**	**2.0**	**6.7**	**21.1**
	1.4	304.2	53.7	5.5	44.5	0.4	1.5	4.4

Lines of Business and Number of Firms Reporting	Current Ratio (times)	Total Liabilities to Net Worth (%)	Collection Period (days)	Net Sales to Inventory (times)	Total Assets to Net Sales (%)	Profit Margin (%)	Return on Assets (%)	Return on Equity (%)
Retail trade:								
Department stores (66)	5.8	20.3	1.5	6.8	36.0	3.8	7.8	13.8
	3.3	**47.5**	**6.4**	**4.8**	**54.7**	**2.0**	**3.6**	**4.2**
	2.1	110.8	16.8	2.8	74.1	(0.1)	–	(0.1)
Grocery stores (185)	3.0	33.1	1.1	34.3	15.9	2.6	11.9	25.9
	1.9	**95.1**	**3.3**	**19.8**	**22.1**	**1.3**	**4.6**	**11.5**
	1.3	213.5	6.9	13.7	35.2	0.4	1.9	4.1
Jewelry stores (114)	6.0	22.1	1.5	3.2	47.2	4.7	8.0	15.0
	3.1	**55.4**	**13.9**	**2.2**	**74.4**	**1.0**	**1.5**	**3.0**
	1.8	142.3	30.7	1.6	100.8	(1.3)	(1.7)	(1.6)
Services:								
Hotels and motels (84)	3.1	26.0	3.3	169.3	72.0	7.7	6.6	17.8
	1.1	**151.4**	**6.6**	**108.9**	**176.2**	**1.5**	**1.2**	**5.8**
	0.6	339.1	17.9	34.9	275.5	(9.3)	(3.2)	(2.3)
Prepackaged software (195)	2.6	35.7	37.6	212.3	54.4	9.4	10.0	21.8
	1.5	**62.7**	**55.9**	**48.2**	**98.3**	**1.4**	**1.2**	**3.8**
	0.8	126.7	78.7	15.9	177.3	(15.3)	(18.7)	(7.7)
College and universities (108)	2.9	29.1	17.0	208.1	191.1	10.0	2.9	5.5
	1.9	**54.1**	**28.5**	**98.9**	**310.1**	**1.8**	**0.6**	**1.1**
	1.3	89.5	50.6	44.1	437.9	(8.3)	(2.0)	(3.4)

Source: Industry Norms & Key Business Ratios, 2009–2010, Desktop Edition, Dun & Bradstreet, a company of The Dun & Bradstreet Corporation. Reprinted with permission.

When interpreting these figures and the earlier table, it is important to bear in mind that publicly traded firms are not necessarily representative of the economy as a whole. This is especially true in developing economies where publicly traded firms represent a small and often elite portion of the total economy. Note too that the similarity of debt levels among companies trading in U.S. markets evident in Table 2A.1 may well reflect the expectations of U.S. investors rather than any inherent similarities among home country practices. It is entirely possible that the elite firms trading in U.S. markets will have similar capital structures, while other, purely domestic firms carry much different debt loads.

Why these observed patterns? It is always dangerous to generalize about diverse countries scattered across the globe, but here is my take on the situation. Begin by noting two common characteristics among developing economies, whether in East Asia or Latin America. First, wealthy families and the state control a high percentage of public firms. For example, Stijn Claessens and colleagues report that in 1996 the top 10 families in Korea, Thailand, and Indonesia controlled between 37 and 58 percent of the *total* value of listed equities in these countries.[2] Second, public financial markets in emerging economies are generally small, unstable, and potentially corrupt. As a result, most company financing comes from one of three sources: controlling family members, state-owned or (often) influenced banks, or the state itself.

A principal reason Korean, Thai, and Indonesian companies are heavily indebted is that the state in these countries has historically used the banking system to implement economic development strategies. This involves directing or encouraging banks to lend generously to targeted companies and, when necessary, cajoling banks to bail out troubled targets without excessive regard to creditworthiness. In return, the governments have not been above pumping public money into the banking system to keep favored companies and the banking system itself afloat—not unlike what the U.S. government has done of late.

Conversely, companies in other developing regions evidence more modest debt financing because governments there are less committed to top-down economic development and have been less inclined to view their banking systems as vehicles for allocating resources among companies. As a result, bank lending more accurately reflects the creditworthiness of borrowers and the absence of implicit government guarantees.

Furthermore, the tendency toward short-term debt in developing regions is the product of occasionally high and volatile inflation, characteristic

---

[2]Stijn Claessens, Simeon Djankov, and Larry H. P. Lang, "The Separation of Ownership and Control in East Asian Corporations," *Journal of Financial Economics,* October–November 2000, pp. 81–112.

of those economies. Because economic instability and erratic inflation greatly increase the risks borne by creditors, few lenders are willing to make long-term commitments in such an environment.

The Move Toward International Accounting Standards

A problem inherent in any cross-country comparison of accounting numbers is that accountants in different countries do not always keep score by the same rules. Companies in German-speaking countries, for example, have a long tradition of secrecy. Indeed, it was not many years ago that *Fortune* magazine remarked of Roche, the giant Swiss pharmaceutical company, "The only number in Hoffman-LaRoche's annual report you can believe is the year on the front."

See **www.fasb.org/intl/** for information on convergence of U.S. and international accounting standards.

Happily, times have changed, and what optimists might call international accounting standards are rapidly emerging. The European Union (EU) has taken the lead in this initiative as part of its much broader effort to hammer out a common, integrated marketplace among member countries. After some 30 years of study, debate, and political wrangling, the accounting initiative became a reality on January 1, 2005, when all 7,000 publicly traded companies in Europe dumped their national accounting rules in favor of the newly designated International Financial Accounting Standards (IFAS). Today over 100 countries spread over six continents have also adopted IFAS, either directly or by aligning national rules to the new international standards.

Even Japan and the United States look set to join the club. Japan began bringing its accounting rules in line with Western practices in 1996 and now expects to complete the task in 2012 when it formally adopts International Financial Reporting Standards (IFRS).

United States accounting authorities have traditionally viewed American accounting rules as the gold standard to which other countries could only hope to aspire. And their approach to international accounting standards has been to invite the rest of the world to adopt ours. But accounting scandals at Enron and WorldCom, and the ensuing demise of the accounting firm Arthur Andersen, have made Americans a bit more humble about their accounting rules and a bit more willing to compromise.

Historically, a major barrier to greater transatlantic cooperation on accounting standards has been differing philosophical perspectives on the role such standards should play. The European philosophy has been to articulate broad accounting principles and to charge accountants and executives to prepare company accounts consistent with the spirit of those principles. Concerned that principles alone leave too much room for manipulation, the American approach has been to lay down voluminous, detailed rules defining how each transaction is to be recorded and to demand strict conformance to the letter of those rules.

Ironically, this rules-based philosophy seems to have backfired in recent years. Rather than limiting accounting manipulation, the American "bright-line" approach appears on occasion to have encouraged it by shifting executives' focus from preparing fair and accurate statements to figuring out how best to beat the rules. The ability to argue "we didn't break any rules, so we must be innocent" appears to have given some executives a rationale for shirking their professional responsibilities in pursuit of better looking numbers. One response to this breakdown in U.S. accounting standards was passage of the Sarbanes-Oxley Act of 2002. Among numerous changes to corporate governance and reporting practices, Sarbanes-Oxley requires chief executive officers and chief financial officers to personally attest to the appropriateness, fairness, and accuracy of their company's financial reports.

A second response has been to express growing enthusiasm for the European, broad-brush approach, and to promote the possibility of increased international cooperation. Indeed, in late 2007 the Securities and Exchange Commission (SEC) dropped a requirement that foreign companies with U.S. stock market listings reconcile their results to U.S. accounting rules. Henceforth, foreign companies may use international financial accounting standards when filing with the U.S. regulator. This change set the stage for broader consideration of whether the U.S. should abandon domestic accounting rules entirely and move to the international standards. The SEC has endorsed the move in principle, and U.S. accounting authorities have been working for several years with their international counterparts on technical aspects of the conversion, but an irrevocable, date-certain commitment to IFRS has not yet been made.

In sum, our cursory review of accounting practices internationally indicates that differences in national standards are rapidly diminishing and that further integration is likely. This trend is driven by several forces, including the growing globalization of business and finance, EU attempts to create a single marketplace among member countries, Japan's efforts to revive their stagnating economy, and U.S. reactions to accounting scandals. The era of a single, world standard may well be at hand. A distinct benefit of this trend is that the challenge inherent in making cross-border comparisons of accounting numbers is falling rapidly and may all but vanish in future years.

SUMMARY

1. The levers of performance
   - Are the same for all companies from corner stores to multinational corporations.
   - Highlight the means by which managers can influence return on equity.
   - Consist of three ratios:
     - The profit margin.
     - Asset turnover.
     - Financial leverage.
   - Can vary widely across industries depending on the technology and business strategies employed.

2. Return on equity (ROE)
   - Is a widely used measure of company financial performance.
   - Equals the product of the profit margin, asset turnover, and financial leverage.
   - Is broadly similar across industries due to competition.
   - Suffers from three problems as a performance measure:
     - A timing problem because business decisions are forward-looking, while ROE is a backward-looking, one-period measure.
     - A risk problem because financial decisions involve balancing risk against return, while ROE only measures return.
     - A value problem because owners are interested in return on the market value of their investment, while ROE measures return on the accounting book value, a problem that is not solved by measuring the return on the market value of equity.
   - Despite its problems can serve as a rough proxy for share price in measuring financial performance.

3. The profit margin
   - Summarizes income statement performance.
   - Measures the fraction of each sales dollar that makes its way to profits.

4. Asset turnover
   - Summarizes asset management performance.
   - Measures the value of sales generated per dollar invested in assets.
   - Is a control ratio in that it relates sales, or cost of sales, to a specific asset or liability; other control ratios are
     - inventory turnover.
     - collection period.
     - days' sales in cash.
     - payables period.
     - fixed-asset turnover.

Visit us at www.mhhe.com/higgins10e

5. Financial leverage
   - Summarizes the company's use of debt relative to equity financing.
   - Adds to owners' risk and is thus not something to be maximized.
   - Is best measured in the form of coverage ratios that relate operating earnings to the annual financial burden imposed by the debt.
   - Is also measured using balance sheet ratios that relate debt to assets, measured using book or market values.

6. Ratio analysis
   - Is the systematic use of a number of ratios to analyze financial performance.
   - Involves trend analysis and comparison of company ratios to peer group numbers.
   - Requires considerable judgment, as there is no single correct value for any ratio.

ADDITIONAL RESOURCES

Fridson, Martin S.; and Fernando Alvarez. *Financial Statement Analysis: A Practitioner's Guide*. 4th ed. John Wiley and Sons, 2011. 400 pages.

An executive and an academic combine to write a thorough practical overview of the topic. $48.

Palepu, Krishna G.; Paul M. Healy; and Victor L. Bernard. *Business Analysis and Valuation: Using Financial Statements: IFRS Edition*, 2nd ed. Cengage Learning, 2010. 784 pages.

Part finance, part accounting. An innovative look at the use of accounting information to address selected financial questions, especially business valuation. Available in paperback. $68.

Jiambalvo, James. *Managerial Accounting*. 4th ed. New York: John Wiley & Sons, Inc., 2009. 600 pages.

A straightforward and concise introduction to the use of managerial accounting in planning, budgeting, management control, and decision making. (Full disclosure: Jim is my dean, but we are still friends and it is a good book.) $158.

SOFTWARE

Designed to accompany this text, HISTORY produces a financial analysis of up to five years of user-supplied, historical financial data about a company. Results appear in four convenient tables of one page each. Balance sheet and income statement entries can be customized to a limited degree to reflect the reporting practices of individual companies. For a complimentary copy, visit **www.mhhe.com/higgins10e**.

WEBSITES

www.reuters.com
www.businessweek.com
finance.yahoo.com
online.wsj.com

All of these sites provide vast amounts of information on publicly traded companies, including overviews, stock quotes, financial statements, ratios, charts, and much more.

SSRN.com/abstract=982481

For a recent look at the uneven convergence of U.S. and international accounting standards, check out this working paper by Elaine Henry, Steve W. J. Lin, and Ya-wen Yong entitled "The European-U.S. GAAP Gap: Amount, Type, Homogeneity, and Value Relevance of IFRST U.S. GAAP Form 20-F Reconciliations," September 2008.

SOURCES FOR BUSINESS RATIOS

Check your library for the following:

Troy, Leo. *Almanac of Business and Industrial Ratios 2011 Edition*. Toolkit Media Group, 2010. 824 pages.

Based on IRS tax filings. Especially good on ratios for small companies.

Dun & Bradstreet Business Credit Services. *Industry Norms and Key Business Ratios*. New York: published annually.

Percentage balance sheets and 14 ratios for more than 1 million U.S. corporations, partnerships, and proprietorships, both public and private, representing 800 lines of business as defined by SIC codes. Median-, upper-, and lower-quartile values.

Annual Statement Studies 2010–2011: Financial Ratio Benchmarks. Risk Management Association. Philadelphia: published annually.

Common-size financial statements and widely used ratios in many business lines. Ratios broken out into six size ranges by sales and by assets. Also contains comparative historical data. One limitation is that only companies with assets of $250 million or less are included. Excellent bibliography entitled "Sources of Composite Financial Data."

Standard & Poor's. *Analysts Handbook*. New York: published annually, with monthly supplements.

Visit us at www.mhhe.com/higgins10e

7. Answer the questions below based on the following information. The tax rate is 35 percent and all dollars are in millions.

	Locktite Inc.	Stork Systems
Earnings before interest and taxes	$380	$ 394
Debt (at 10% interest)	$240	$1,240
Equity	$760	$ 310

   a. Calculate each company's ROE, ROA, and ROIC.
   b. Why is Stork's ROE so much higher than Locktite's? Does this mean Stork is a better company? Why or why not?
   c. Why is Locktite's ROA higher than Stork's? What does this tell you about the two companies?
   d. How do the two companies' ROICs compare? What does this suggest about the two companies?

8. Table 3.1 in Chapter 3 presents financial statements over the period 2008 through 2011 for R&E Supplies, Inc.

   a. Use these statements to calculate as many of the ratios in Table 2.2 as you can.
   b. What insights do these ratios provide about R&E's financial performance? What problems, if any, does the company appear to have?

9. You are trying to prepare financial statements for Bartlett Pickle Company, but seem to be missing its balance sheet. You have Bartlett's income statement, which shows sales last year were $420 million with a gross profit margin of 40 percent. You also know that credit sales equaled three-quarters of Bartlett's total revenues last year. In addition, Bartlett had a collection period of 55 days, a payables period of 40 days, and an inventory turnover of eight times based on the cost of goods sold. Calculate Bartlett's year-ending balance for accounts receivable, inventory, and accounts payable.

10. In 2010, Natural Selection, a nationwide computer dating service, had $500 million of assets and $200 million of liabilities. Earnings before interest and taxes were $120 million, interest expense was $28 million, the tax rate was 40 percent, principal repayment requirements were $24 million, and annual dividends were 30 cents per share on 20 million shares outstanding.

   a. Calculate:
      i. Natural Selection's liabilities-to-equity ratio
      ii. Times interest earned ratio
      iii. Times burden covered

b. What percentage decline in earnings before interest and taxes could Natural Selection have sustained before failing to cover:

    i. Interest payment requirements?

    ii. Principal and interest requirements?

    iii. Principal, interest, and common dividend payments?

11. Given the following information, complete the balance sheet shown next.

Collection period	71 days
Days' sales in cash	34 days
Current ratio	2.6
Inventory turnover	5 times
Liabilities to assets	75%
Payables period	36 days

(All sales are on credit. All calculations assume a 365-day year. Payables period is based on cost of goods sold.)

Assets	
Current:	
Cash	$1,100,000
Accounts receivable	
Inventory	1,900,000
Total current assets	
Net fixed assets	————
Total assets	8,000,000
Liabilities and shareholders' equity	
Current liabilities:	
Accounts payable	
Short-term debt	————
Total current liabilities	
Long-term debt	
Shareholders' equity	————
Total liabilities and equity	

12. An Excel spreadsheet containing Men's Wearhouse, Inc., financial statements for fiscal years 2006–2010 is available for download at **www.mhhe.com/higgins10e.** (Select Student Edition > Choose a Chapter > Files.)

a. Use the spreadsheet to calculate as many of the company's profitability, turnover-control, and leverage and liquidity ratios as you can for these years (see Table 2.5).

b. What do these ratios suggest about the company's performance over this period?

repay you," the lending officer for Suburban National Bank is apt to be of two minds about this result. On the one hand, R&E has a projected 2012 accounts receivable balance equal to $3.6 million, which would probably provide excellent security for a $1.4 million loan. On the other hand, R&E's cavalier attitude toward financial planning and the president's obvious lack of knowledge about where his company is headed are definite negatives. But before getting too involved in the implications of the forecast, we need to recall that our projection does not yet include the higher interest expense on the new, larger loan.

Interest Expense

One thing that bothers attentive novices about pro forma forecasting is the circularity involving interest expense and indebtedness. As noted earlier, interest expense cannot be estimated accurately until the amount of external funding required has been determined. Yet because the external funding depends in part on the amount of interest expense, it would appear one cannot be accurately estimated without the other.

There are two common ways around this dilemma. The more responsible approach is to use a computer spreadsheet to solve for the interest expense and external funding simultaneously. We will look at this approach in more detail in the section titled Computer-Based Forecasting. The other, more cavalier approach is to ignore the problem with the expectation that the first-pass estimate will be close enough. Given the likely errors in predicting sales and other variables, the additional error caused by a failure to determine interest expense accurately is usually not all that critical.

To illustrate, R&E Supplies' first-pass pro formas assumed a net interest expense of $90,000, whereas the balance sheet indicates total interest-bearing debt of almost $2.2 million. At a 10 percent interest rate, this implies an interest expense of about $220,000, or $130,000 more than our first-pass estimate. But think what happens as we trace the impact of a $130,000 addition to interest expense through the income statement. First, the $130,000 expense is before taxes. At a 45 percent tax rate, the decline in earnings after tax will be only $71,500. Second, because R&E Supplies distributes half of its earnings as dividends, a $71,500 decline in earnings after tax will result in only a $35,750 decline in the addition to retained earnings. So after all the dust settles, our estimate of the addition to retained earnings and, by implication, the external funding required will be about $35,750 low. But when the need for new external financing is already over $1.4 million, what's another $35,750 among friends? Granted, increased interest expense has a noticeable percentage effect on earnings, but by the time the increase filters through taxes and dividend payments, the effect on the external funding needed is modest. The moral to the story is that quick-and-dirty financial forecasts really can be quite useful. Unless you are naturally inclined toward green eyeshades or have the luxury of charging by the hour, you will find that handmade forecasts are just fine for many purposes.

Seasonality

A more serious potential problem with pro forma statements—and, indeed, with all of the forecasting techniques mentioned in this chapter—is that the results are applicable only on the forecast date. The pro formas in Table 3.3 present an estimate of R&E Supplies' external financing requirements on December 31, 2012. They say nothing about the company's need for financing on any other date before or after December 31. If a company has seasonal financing requirements, knowledge of year-end loan needs may be of little use in financial planning, since the year end may bear no relation whatever to the date of the company's peak financing need. To avoid this problem, you should make monthly or quarterly forecasts rather than annual ones. Or, if you know the date of peak financing need, you can simply make this date the forecast horizon.

Pro Forma Statements and Financial Planning

To this point, R&E's pro forma statements simply display the financial implications of the company's operating plans. This is the forecasting half of the exercise. It is time now for R&E to do some serious financial planning. Using the techniques described in earlier chapters, management must analyze the forecast carefully to decide if it is acceptable or whether it must be changed to avoid identified problems. In particular, R&E management must decide whether the estimated external funding requirement is too large. If the answer is yes, either because R&E does not want to borrow $1.4 million or because the bank is unwilling to grant such a large loan, management must change its plans to conform to the financial realities. This is where operating plans and financial plans merge (or, too often, collide) to create a coherent strategy. Fortunately, the pro forma forecast provides an excellent template for such iterative planning.

To illustrate the process, suppose that Suburban National Bank, concerned about R&E management's obvious lack of financial acumen, will not lend the company more than $1 million. Ignoring the possibility of trying another bank, or selling new equity, R&E's challenge is to modify its operating plans to shave $400,000 off the projected external funding requirement. There are many ways to meet this challenge, each involving subtle trade-offs among growth, profitability, and funding needs. And while we are not in a position to evaluate these trade-offs, as R&E management would be, we can illustrate the mechanics. Suppose that after much debate management decides to test the following revised operating plan:

- Tighten up collection of accounts receivable so that the collection period falls from 51 days to 47.

- Settle for a more modest improvement in trade payables so that the payables period rises from 59 days to 60.

Finally, because a tougher collection policy will drive away some customers and higher trade payables will sacrifice some prompt payment discounts, let us presume that management believes the revised plan will reduce sales growth from 25 percent to 20 percent and increase general, selling, and administrative expenses from 12 percent to 12.5 percent.

To test this revised operating plan we need only make the indicated changes in assumptions and roll out a revised pro forma forecast. Table 3.4 presents the results of this exercise. The good news is that external funding required is now below the $1 million target; the bad news is that this improvement is not free. Earnings after tax in the revised forecast trail the original projection in Table 3.3 by 34 percent [($234 − $155)/$234].

Is R&E Supplies' revised operating plan optimal? Is it superior to all other possible plans? We cannot say; these are fundamental questions of business strategy that can never be answered with complete assurance. We can say, however, that pro forma forecasts contribute mightily to the planning process by providing a vehicle for evaluating alternative plans, by quantifying the anticipated costs and benefits of each, and by indicating which plans are financially feasible.

Computer-Based Forecasting

Readily available spreadsheets have made it possible for anyone with a modicum of computer skill to spin out elegant (and occasionally useful) pro forma forecasts and sophisticated risk analysis. To demonstrate how easy computer-based forecasting is, Table 3.5 (page 100) presents an abbreviated one-year forecast for R&E Supplies as it might appear on a computer screen. (If you are a computer novice, I suggest skipping this section or developing a basic understanding of spreadsheet programs before continuing.) The first area on the simulated screen is an *assumptions box*, containing all of the information and assumptions required to construct the forecast. (It is a good idea to leave some room here initially so that if you are unable to think of all the necessary information immediately, you can add it later.) Gathering all of the necessary input information in an assumptions box can be a real timesaver later if you want to

TABLE 3.4 Revised Pro Forma Financial Statements for R&E Supplies, Inc., December 31, 2012 ($ thousands, changes in bold)

Income Statement		
	2012	**Comments**
Net sales	$24,736	**20% increase**
Cost of goods sold	21,273	86% of sales
Gross profit	3,463	
Expenses:		
General, selling, and administrative expenses	**3,092**	**12.5% sales**
Net interest expense	90	Initially constant
Earnings before tax	281	
Tax	126	45% tax rate
Earnings after tax	$ 155	
Balance Sheet		
Assets		
Current assets:		
Cash and securities	$ 1,220	18 days sales
Accounts receivable	**3,185**	**47-day collection period**
Inventories	2,364	9 times turnover
Prepaid expenses	20	Rough estimate
Total current assets	6,789	
Net fixed assets	280	See text discussion
Total assets	$ 7,069	
Liabilities and Owners' Equity		
Current liabilities:		
Bank loan	$ 0	
Accounts payable	**3,497**	**60-day payables period**
Current portion of long-term debt	100	See text discussion
Accrued wages	22	Rough estimate
Total current liabilities	3,619	
Long-term debt	660	
Common stock	150	
Retained earnings	1,657	See text discussion
Total liabilities and owners' equity	$ 6,086	
External funding required	$ 982	

change assumptions. The 2012 data in the assumptions box correspond closely to the data used earlier in our original handmade forecast for R&E Supplies.

The forecast begins immediately below the assumptions box. The first column, labeled "Equations 2012," is included for explanatory purposes

TABLE 3.5 Forecasting with a Computer Spreadsheet: Pro Forma Financial Forecast for R&E Supplies, Inc., December 31, 2012 ($ thousands)

	A	B	C	D
1				
2	Year	2011 Actual	2012	2013
3	Net sales	$20,613		
4	Growth rate in net sales		25.0%	
5	Cost of goods sold/net sales		86.0%	
6	Gen., sell., and admin. expenses/net sales		12.0%	
7	Long-term debt	$ 760	$660	
8	Current portion long-term debt	$ 100	$100	
9	Interest rate		10.0%	
10	Tax rate		45.0%	
11	Dividend/earnings after tax		50.0%	
12	Current assets/net sales		29.0%	
13	Net fixed assets		$280	
14	Current liabilities/net sales		14.5%	
15	Owners' equity	$1,730		
16	**INCOME STATEMENT**			
17		Equations	Forecast	Forecast
18	Year	2012	2012	2013
19	Net sales	=B3 + B3*C4	$25,766	
20	Cost of goods sold	=C5*C19	22,159	
21	Gross profit	=C19 − C20	3,607	
22	Gen., sell., and admin. exp.	=C6*C19	3,092	
23	Interest expense	=C9*(C7 + C8 + C40)	231	
24	Earnings before tax	=C21 − C22 − C23	285	
25	Tax	=C10*C24	128	
26	Earnings after tax	=C24 − C25	156	
27	Dividends paid	=C11*C26	78	
28	Additions to retained earnings	=C26 − C27	78	
29				
30	**BALANCE SHEET**			
31	Current assets	=C12*C19	7,472	
32	Net fixed assets	=C13	280	
33	Total assets	=C31 + C32	7,752	
34				
35	Current liabilities	=C14*C19	3,736	
36	Long-term debt	=C7	660	
37	Equity	=B15 + C28	1,808	
38	Total liabilities and shareholders'	=C35 + C36 + C37	6,204	
39	equity			
40	**EXTERNAL FUNDING REQUIRED**	=C33 − C38	$ 1,548	

Why Are Lenders So Conservative?

Some would answer, "Too much Republican in-breeding," but there is another possibility: low returns. Simply put, if expected loan returns are low, lenders cannot accept high risks.

Let us look at the income statement of a representative bank lending operation with, say, 100, $1 million loans, each paying 10 percent interest:

($ thousands)	
Interest income (10% × 100 × $1 million)	$10,000
Interest expense	7,000
Gross income	3,000
Operating expenses	1,000
Income before tax	2,000
Tax at 40% rate	800
Income after tax	$ 1,200

The $7 million interest expense represents a 7 percent return the bank must promise depositors and investors to raise the $100 million lent. (In bank jargon, these loans offer a 3 percent lending margin, or spread.) Operating expenses include costs of the downtown office towers, the art collection, wages, and so on.

These numbers imply a minuscule return on assets of 1.2 percent ($1.2 million/100 × $1 million). We know from the levers of performance that to generate any kind of reasonable return on equity, banks must pile on the financial leverage. Indeed, to generate a 12 percent ROE, our bank needs a 10-to-1 assets-to-equity ratio or, equivalently, $9 in liabilities for every $1 in equity.

Worse yet, our profit figures are too optimistic because they ignore the reality that not all loans are repaid. Banks typically are able to recover only about 40 percent of the principal value of defaulted loans, implying a loss of $600,000 on a $1 million default. Ignoring tax losses on defaulted loans, this means that if only two of the bank's 100 loans go bad annually, the bank's $1.2 million in expected profits will evaporate. Stated differently, a loan officer must be almost certain that each loan will be repaid just to break even. (Alternatively, the officer must be almost certain of being promoted out of lending before the loans start to go bad.) So why are lenders conservative? Because the aggressive ones have long since gone bankrupt.

and would not appear on a conventional forecast. Entering the equations shown causes the computer to calculate the quantities appearing in the second column, labeled "Forecast 2012." The third column, labeled "Forecast 2013," is presently blank.

Two steps are required to get from the assumptions to the completed forecast. First, it is necessary to enter a series of equations tying the inputs to the forecasted outputs. These are the equations appearing in the first column. Here is how to read them. The first equation for net sales is = B3 + B3 * C4. This instructs the computer to get the number in cell B3 and add to it that number times the number in cell C4, in other words, $20,613 + $20,613 × 25%. The second equation instructs the computer to multiply forecasted net sales by the forecasted cost of goods sold percentage. The third says to calculate gross profit by subtracting cost of goods sold from net sales.

There are only three tricky equations. Interest expense, row 23, is the interest rate times end-of-period long-term debt, including the current portion, plus the forecasted external funding required. As discussed earlier, the tricky part here is the interdependency between interest expense and external funding required. (I will talk more about this in step 2.) The other two equations are simple by comparison. The equity equation, row 37, is end-of-period equity plus additions to retained earnings; the external funding required equation, row 40, is total assets minus total liabilities and shareholders' equity.

The second required step is to incorporate the interdependence between interest expense and external funding required. Without some adjustment on your part, the computer will likely stall and signal "Circular Reference Warning" when you enter the equation for interest expense. To avoid this, you need to modify the way the computer calculates formulas in this file. For Excel 2007 or newer, click the "Microsoft Office Button" in the upper left corner of the spreadsheet; click "Excel Options," and the "Formulas" category. In the "Calculation Options" section, select the "Enable iterative calculation" box and then click "OK". Your forecast should now be complete.

Now the fun begins. To modify a forecast assumption, just change the appropriate entry in the assumptions box, and *voilà:* The computer instantly makes all the necessary changes and shows the revised forecast. To extend the forecast one more year, just complete the entries in the assumptions box, highlight the 2012 forecast, and copy or fill one column to the right. Then make some obvious changes in the equations for net sales and equity, and the computer does the rest. (See Additional Resources at the end of the chapter for information about PROFORMA, complimentary software for constructing pro forma forecasts.)

Coping with Uncertainty

Sensitivity Analysis

Several techniques exist to help executives grapple with the uncertainty inherent in all realistic financial projections. The simplest is *sensitivity analysis,* known colloquially as "what if" questions: What if R&E's sales grow by 15 percent instead of 25 percent? What if cost of goods sold is

84 percent of sales instead of 86 percent? It involves systematically changing one of the assumptions on which the pro forma statements are based and observing how the forecast responds. The exercise is useful in at least two ways. First, it provides information about the range of possible outcomes. For example, sensitivity analysis on R&E Supplies' original forecast might reveal that depending on the future sales volume attained, the company's need for external financing could vary between $1.4 million and $2 million. This would tell management that it had better have enough flexibility in its financing plans to add an extra $600,000 in external funding as the future unfolds. Second, sensitivity analysis encourages management by exception. It enables managers to determine which assumptions most strongly affect the forecast and which are secondary. This allows them to concentrate their data-gathering and forecasting efforts on the most critical assumptions. Subsequently, during implementation of the financial plan, the same information enables management to focus on those factors most critical to the plan's success.

Scenario Analysis

Sensitivity analysis has its uses, but it is important to realize that forecasts seldom err on one assumption at a time. That is, whatever events throw one assumption in a financial forecast off the mark will likely affect other assumptions as well. For example, suppose we want to estimate R&E Supplies' external financing needs assuming sales fall 15 percent below expectations. Sensitivity analysis would have us simply cut forecasted sales growth by 15 percent and recalculate the external financing required. However, this approach implicitly assumes the shortfall in sales will not affect any of the other estimates underlying the forecast. If the proper assumptions are that inventories will initially rise when sales drop below expectations and the profit margin will decline as the company slashes prices to maintain volume, failure to include these complementary effects will cause an underestimate of the need for outside financing.

Instead of manipulating one assumption at a time, *scenario analysis* broadens the perspective to look at how a number of assumptions might change in response to a particular economic event. The first step in a scenario analysis is to identify a few carefully chosen events, or scenarios, that might plausibly befall the company. Common scenarios include loss of a major customer, successful introduction of a major new product, or entry of an important new competitor. Then, for each scenario identified, the second step is to carefully rethink the variables in the original forecast to either reaffirm the original assumption or substitute a new, more accurate one. The last step in the analysis is to generate a separate forecast for each scenario. The result is a limited number of detailed projections describing the range of contingencies the business faces.

Simulation

Simulation is a computer-assisted extension of sensitivity analysis. To perform a simulation, begin by assigning a probability distribution to each uncertain element in the forecast. The distribution describes the possible values the variable could conceivably take on and states the probability of each value occurring. Next, ask a computer to pick at random a value for each uncertain variable consistent with the assigned probability distribution and generate a set of pro forma statements based on the selected values. This creates one trial. Performing the last step many times produces a large number of trials. The output from a simulation is a table or, more often, a graph summarizing the results of many trials.

As an example, Figure 3.1 displays the results of a simulation of R&E's external funding needs using Crystal Ball, a popular simulation program. Our original forecast assumed a 25 percent sales growth in 2012, but this, of course, is only a guess. The figure shows a frequency chart of R&E's external funds required as the estimated sales growth varies in a range of about 10 to 40 percent. To generate the chart, I selected a bell-shaped, normal distribution for the sales growth estimate from the gallery of distributions provided by Crystal Ball and shown at the bottom of the figure. Then, using the spreadsheet model in Table 3.5, I asked Crystal Ball to display the results of 500 trials as a frequency chart. In less than a minute, I had the result shown. I could have allowed virtually all of the assumptions in the spreadsheet to vary, and to vary in correlation with one another, but this is enough to provide a taste of how easy simulations have become.

The principal advantage of simulation relative to sensitivity analysis and scenario analysis is that it allows all of the uncertain input variables to change at once. The principal disadvantage, in my experience, is that the results are often hard to interpret. One reason is that few executives are used to thinking about future events in terms of probabilities. The frequency chart in Figure 3.1 indicates there is a 2.00 percent chance that R&E's external funding needs will exceed $1.844 million. Is a 2.00 percent chance so remote that R&E can safely raise less than $1.844 million, or might the prudent course be to raise even more just in case? How big a chance should the company be willing to take that it will be unable to meet its external funding requirement: 10 percent, 2 percent, or is

FIGURE 3.1 Simulating R&E Supplies' Need for External Funding: Frequency Chart and Distribution Gallery for Sales Growth

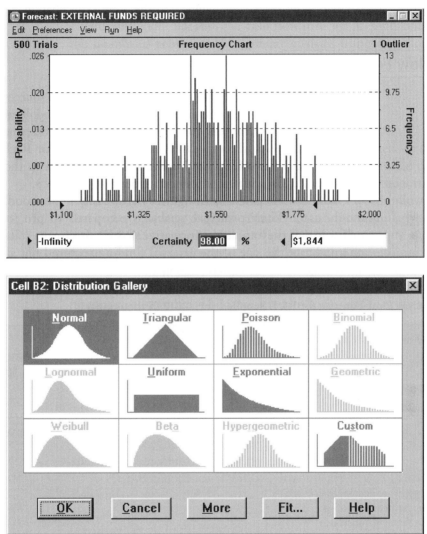

.02 percent the right number? The answer isn't obvious. A second difficulty with simulation in practice recalls President Eisenhower's dictum "It's not the plans but the planning that matters." With simulation much of the "planning" goes on inside the computer, and managers too often see only the results. Consequently, they may not gain the depth of insight into the company and its future prospects that they would if they used simpler techniques.

A Problem with Depreciation

XYZ Corporation is forecasting its financing needs for next year. The original forecast shows an external financing need of $10 million. On reviewing the forecast, the production manager, having just returned from an accounting seminar, recommends increasing depreciation next year—for reporting purposes only, not for tax purposes—by $1 million. She explains, rather condescendingly, that this will reduce net fixed assets by $1 million and, because a reduction of an asset is a source of cash, this will reduce the external funding required by a like amount. Explain why the production manager is incorrect.

Answer: Increasing depreciation will reduce net fixed assets. However, it will also reduce provision for taxes and earnings after tax by the same amount. Since both are liability accounts and reduction of a liability is a use of cash, the whole exercise is a wash with respect to determination of external financing requirements. This is consistent with cash budgeting, which ignores depreciation entirely. Here is a numerical example:

	Original Depreciation	Increase in Depreciation	Change in Liability Account
Operating income	$10,000	$10,000	
Depreciation	4,000	5,000	
Earnings before tax	6,000	5,000	
Provision for tax @ 40%	2,400	2,000	−400
Earnings after tax	3,600	3,000	
Dividends	1,000	1,000	
Additions to retained earnings	$ 2,600	$ 2,000	−$ 600
Total change in liabilities			−$1,000

The integration of these detailed divisional budgets at headquarters produces the corporation's financial forecast. If management has been realistic about available resources throughout the planning process, the forecast will contain few surprises. If not, headquarters executives may discover that in the aggregate, the spending plans of the divisions exceed available resources and some revisions in division budgets will be necessary.

As company plans evolve from broad strategies to concrete marching orders, the forecasting techniques described in this chapter take on increasing importance, first as a means of articulating the financial implications of a chosen strategy, and then as a vehicle for testing alternative strategies. In proper perspective, then, financial forecasting is a family of techniques for translating creative ideas and strategies into concrete action plans, and while proper technique cannot guarantee success, the lack of same certainly heightens the odds of failure.

SUMMARY

1. Pro Forma Statements
   - Are the principal means by which operating managers can predict the financial implications of their decisions.
   - Are predictions of what a company's financial statements will look like at the end of the forecast period.
   - Are commonly used to estimate a company's future need for external funding and a great way to test the feasibility of current operating plans.
   - Are often based on percent-of-sales forecasts that assume many balance sheet and income statement entries vary in constant proportion to sales.
   - Involve four steps:
     - Review of past financial statements to identify quantities that have varied in proportion to sales historically.
     - Careful projection of future sales.
     - Preparation of independent projections of quantities, such as fixed plant and equipment, that have not varied in proportion to sales historically.
     - Testing the sensitivity of forecast results to variations in projected sales.
   - Generate forecasts that are strictly applicable only on the forecast date and thus require care when dealing with seasonal businesses.
   - Contain a circularity involving interest expense and total debt outstanding, which can be easily handled with a computer spreadsheet set to enable iterative calculation.
   - Are a great platform for effective financial planning where management carefully analyzes their forecast to decide if it is acceptable or whether it must be changed to avoid identified problems.
2. Cash flow forecasts
   - Project external funding required as the difference between anticipated sources and uses of cash over the forecast period.
   - Yield the same need for external funding as a pro forma projection, given the same assumptions.
   - Are less informative than pro forma forecasts because they do not provide information useful for evaluating how best to meet the indicated need for financing.

PROBLEMS

Answers to odd-numbered problems appear at the end of the book. For additional problems with answers, see **www.mhhe.com/higgins10e.**

1. Suppose you constructed a pro forma balance sheet for a company and the estimate for external financing required was negative. How would you interpret this result?

2. Pro forma financial statements, by definition, are predictions of a company's financial statements at a future point in time. So why is it important to analyze the historical performance of the company before constructing pro forma financial statements?

3. Suppose you constructed a pro forma balance sheet and a cash budget for a company for the same time period and the external financing required from the pro forma forecast exceeded the cash deficit estimated on the cash budget. How would you interpret this result?

4. Diamond Window Corporation's sales, half of which are for cash, over the past three months were:

March	April	May
$140,000	$240,000	$160,000

   a. Estimate Diamond's cash receipts in May if the company's collection period is 60 days.

   b. Estimate Diamond's cash receipts in May if the company's collection period is 45 days.

   c. What would be the May balance of Accounts Receivable for Diamond Window if the company's collection period is 60 days? 45 days?

5. Table 3.3 shows the December 31, 2012, pro forma balance sheet and income statements for R&E Supplies, Inc. The pro forma balance sheet shows that R&E Supplies will need external funding from the bank of $1.4 million. However, they show almost $1.3 million in cash and short-term securities. Why are they talking to the bank for such a large amount when they have most of this sum in their cash account?

6. Table 3.5 presents a computer spreadsheet for estimating R&E Supplies' external financing required for 2012. The text mentions that, with modifications to the equations for equity and net sales, the forecast can easily be extended through 2013. Write the modified equations for equity and net sales.

7. An Excel spreadsheet containing R&E Supplies' 2012 pro forma financial forecast as shown in Table 3.5 is available for download at **www.mhhe.com/higgins10e.** (Select Student Edition > Choose a Chapter > Files.) Using this spreadsheet, the information presented in the following list of figures, and the modified equations determined earlier in question 6, extend the forecast for R&E Supplies contained in Table 3.5 through 2013.

R&E Supplies Assumptions for 2013 ($ thousands)			
Growth rate in net sales	30.0%	Tax rate	45.0%
Cost of goods sold/net sales	86.0%	Dividend/earnings after tax	50.0%
Gen., sell., & admin.		Current assets/net sales	29.0%
expenses/net sales	11.0%	Net fixed assets	$270
Long-term debt	$560	Current liabilities/net sales	14.4%
Current portion long-term debt	$100		
Interest rate	10.0%		

a. What is R&E's projected external financing required in 2013? How does this number compare to the 2012 projection?

b. Perform a sensitivity analysis on this projection. How does R&E's projected external financing required change if the ratio of cost of goods sold to net sales declines from 86.0 percent to 84.0 percent?

c. Perform a scenario analysis on this projection. How does R&E's projected external financing required change if a severe recession occurs in 2013? Assume net sales decline 5 percent, cost of goods sold rises to 88 percent of net sales due to price cutting, and current assets increase to 35 percent of net sales as management fails to cut purchases promptly in response to declining sales.

8. This and the following two problems demonstrate that pro forma forecasts, cash budgets, and cash flow forecasts all yield the same estimated need for external financing—provided you don't make any mistakes. For problems 8, 9, and 10, you may ignore the effect of added borrowing on interest expense.

The treasurer of Pepperton, Inc., a wholesale distributor of household appliances, wants to estimate his company's cash balances for the first three months of 2012. Using the information in the following chart, construct a monthly cash budget for Pepperton for January 2012 through March 2012. Does it appear from your results that the treasurer should be concerned about investing excess cash or looking for a bank loan?

Sustainable Growth

We can think of successful companies as passing through a predictable life cycle. The cycle begins with a startup phase in which the company loses money while developing products and establishing a foothold in the market. This is followed by a rapid growth phase in which the company is profitable but is growing so rapidly that it needs regular infusions of outside financing. The third phase is maturity, characterized by a decline in growth and a switch from absorbing outside financing to generating more cash than the firm can profitably reinvest. The last phase is decline, during which the company is perhaps marginally profitable, generates more cash than it can reinvest internally, and suffers declining sales. Mature and declining companies frequently devote considerable time and money to seeking investment opportunities in new products or firms that are still in their growth phase.

We begin our discussion by looking at the growth phase, when financing needs are most pressing. Later we will consider the growth problems of mature and declining firms. Central to our discussion is the notion of sustainable growth. Intuitively, sustainable growth is merely a formalization of the old adage "It takes money to make money." Increased sales require more assets of all types, which must be paid for. Retained profits and the accompanying new borrowing generate some cash, but only limited amounts. Unless the company is prepared to sell common stock or borrow excessive amounts, this limit puts a ceiling on the growth it can achieve without straining its resources. This is the firm's sustainable growth rate.

The Sustainable Growth Equation

Let's begin by writing a simple equation to express the dependence of growth on financial resources. For this purpose, assume

- The company has a target capital structure and a target dividend policy it wishes to maintain.

- Management is unable or unwilling to sell new equity.

We will say more about these assumptions soon. For now, it is enough to realize that although they may not be appropriate for all firms, the assumptions describe a great many.

Figure 4.1 shows the rapidly growing company's plight. It represents the firm's balance sheet as two rectangles, one for assets and the other for liabilities and owners' equity. The two long, unshaded rectangles

FIGURE 4.1   **New Sales Require New Assets, Which Must Be Financed**

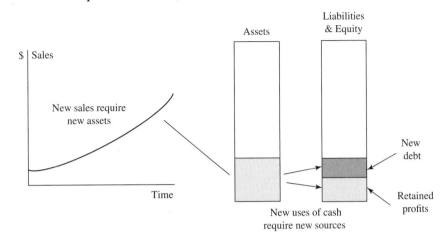

represent the balance sheet at the beginning of the year. The rectangles are, of course, the same height because assets must equal liabilities plus owners' equity. Now, if the company wants to increase sales during the coming year, it must also increase assets such as inventory, accounts receivable, and productive capacity. The shaded area on the assets side of the figure represents the value of new assets necessary to support the increased sales. Because the company will not be selling equity by assumption, the cash required to pay for this increase in assets must come from retained profits and increased liabilities.

We want to know what limits the rate at which the company in Figure 4.1 can increase sales. Assuming, in effect, that all parts of a business expand in strict proportion like a balloon, what limits the rate of this expansion? To find out, start in the lower-right corner of the figure with owners' equity. As equity grows, the firm can borrow more money without altering the capital structure; together, the growth of liabilities and the growth of equity determine the rate at which assets expand. This, in turn, limits the growth rate in sales. So after all the dust settles, what limits the growth rate in sales is the rate at which owners' equity expands. A company's sustainable growth rate therefore is nothing more than its growth rate in equity.

Letting g^* represent the sustainable growth rate,

$$g^* = \frac{\text{Change in equity}}{\text{Equity}_{\text{bop}}}$$

where bop denotes beginning-of-period equity. Because the firm will not be selling any new shares by assumption, the only source of new equity will be from retained profits, so we can rewrite this expression as

$$g^* = \frac{R \times \text{Earnings}}{\text{Equity}_{\text{bop}}}$$

where R is the firm's "retention rate." R is the fraction of earnings retained in the business, or 1 minus the dividend payout ratio. If a company's target dividend policy is to distribute 10 percent of earnings as dividends, its retention ratio is 90 percent.

The ratio "Earnings/Equity" in this expression should look familiar; it is the firm's return on equity, or ROE. Thus,

$$g^* = R \times \text{ROE}_{\text{bop}}$$

Finally, recalling the levers of performance discussed in Chapter 2, we can rewrite this expression yet again as

$$g^* = PRA\hat{T}$$

where P, A, and $\hat{T}$ are our old friends from Chapter 2, the levers of performance. Recall that P is the profit margin, A is the asset turnover ratio, and $\hat{T}$ is the assets-to-equity ratio. The assets-to-equity ratio wears a hat here as a reminder that it is assets divided by *beginning-of-period* equity instead of end-of-period equity as defined in Chapter 2.

This is the sustainable growth equation.[1] Let's see what it tells us. Given the assumptions just noted, the equation says that a company's sustainable growth rate in sales, g^*, equals the product of four ratios, P, R, A, and $\hat{T}$. Two of these ratios, P and A, summarize the operating performance of the business, while the other two describe the firm's principal financial policies. Thus, the retention rate, R, captures management's attitudes toward the distribution of dividends, and the assets-to-equity ratio, $\hat{T}$, reflects its policies regarding financial leverage.

An important implication of the sustainable growth equation is that g^* *is the only growth rate in sales that is consistent with stable values of the four ratios.* If a company increases sales at any rate other than g^*, one or more of the ratios *must* change. This means that when a company grows at a rate in excess of its sustainable growth rate, it had better improve operations (represented by an increase in the profit margin or the asset turnover ratio) or prepare to alter its financial policies (represented by increasing its retention rate or its financial leverage).

---

[1] I shall refrain from admonishing you to avoid "pra$\hat{t}$" falls.

Too Much Growth

This is the crux of the sustainable growth problem for rapidly expanding firms: Because increasing operating efficiency is not always possible and altering financial policies is not always wise, we see that it is entirely possible for a company to grow too fast for its own good. This is particularly true for smaller companies, which may do inadequate financial planning. Such companies see sales growth as something to be maximized and think too little of the financial consequences. They do not realize that rapid growth has them on a treadmill; the faster they grow, the more cash they need, even when they are profitable. They can meet this need for a time by increasing leverage, but eventually they will reach their debt capacity, lenders will refuse additional credit requests, and the companies will find themselves without the cash to pay their bills. All of this can be prevented if managers understand that growth above the company's sustainable rate creates financial challenges that must be anticipated and managed.

Please understand; I am not suggesting that a company's actual growth rate should always equal its sustainable growth rate, or even closely approximate it. Rather, I am saying that management must anticipate any disparity between actual and sustainable growth and have a plan in place for managing that disparity. The challenge is, first, to recognize the disparity and, second, to create a viable strategy to manage it.

Balanced Growth

Here is another way to think about sustainable growth. Recalling that a company's return on assets, ROA, can be expressed as the product of its profit margin times its asset turnover, we can rewrite the sustainable growth equation as[2]

$$g^* = R\hat{T} \times \text{ROA}$$

Here R and $\hat{T}$ reflect the company's financial policies, while ROA summarizes its operating performance. So if a company's retention ratio is 25 percent and its assets-to-equity ratio is 1.6, its sustainable growth equation becomes simply

$$g^* = 0.4 \times \text{ROA}$$

This equation says that given stable financial policies, sustainable growth varies linearly with return on assets. Figure 4.2 graphs this relationship with sales growth on the vertical axis, ROA on the horizontal axis, and the

---

[2]Strictly speaking, this equation should be expressed in terms of return on invested capital, not return on assets, but the gain in precision is too modest to justify the added mathematical complexity. See Gordon Donaldson, *Managing Corporate Wealth* (New York: Praeger, 1984), Chapter 4, for a more rigorous exposition.

FIGURE 4.2 **A Graphical Representation of Sustainable Growth**

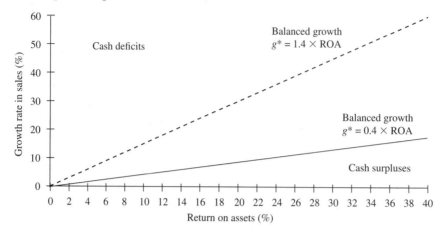

sustainable growth equation as the upward-sloping, solid, diagonal line. The line bears the label "Balanced growth" because the company can self-finance only the sales growth–ROA combinations lying on this line. All growth-return combinations lying off this line generate either cash deficits or cash surpluses. Thus, rapidly growing, marginally profitable companies will plot in the upper-left portion of the graph, implying cash deficits, while slowly expanding, highly profitable companies will plot in the lower-right portion, implying cash surpluses. I should emphasize that the phrase "self-finance" does not imply constant debt but rather a constant debt-to-equity ratio. Debt can increase but only in proportion to equity.

When a company experiences unbalanced growth of either the surplus or the deficit variety, it can move toward the balanced growth line in any of three ways: It can change its growth rate, alter its return on assets, or modify its financial policies. To illustrate the last option, suppose the company with the balanced growth line depicted in Figure 4.2 is in the deficit region of the graph and wants to reduce the deficit. One strategy would be to increase its retention ratio to, say, 50 percent and its assets-to-equity ratio to, say, 2.8 to 1, thereby changing its sustainable growth equation to

$$g^* = 1.4 \times \text{ROA}$$

In Figure 4.2, this is equivalent to rotating the balanced growth line upward to the left, as shown by the dotted line. Now any level of profitability will support a higher growth rate than before.

In this perspective, the sustainable growth rate is the nexus of all growth-return combinations yielding balanced growth, and the sustainable growth challenge is that of managing the surpluses or deficits caused by unbalanced growth. We will return to strategies for managing growth after looking at a numerical example.

Medifast's Sustainable Growth Rate

To illustrate the growth management challenges a rapidly growing business faces, let's look at Medifast Inc., the producer and marketer of Medifast 5&1 weight-loss meals and other health and weight-loss products. Table 4.1 presents the company's actual and sustainable growth rates from 2006 through 2010. For each year, I calculated Medifast's sustainable growth rate by plugging the four required ratios for the relevant year into the sustainable growth equation. I calculated the ratios from the company's financial statements, which are not shown. Observe that Medifast's sales grew over 45 percent a year on average over the period, more than double the firm's average sustainable growth rate.

How did Medifast cope with actual growth above sustainable levels? A look at the four required ratios reveals that the company almost doubled its asset turnover. Profit margin and financial leverage increased marginally over the period, but these improvements pale in comparison to the improvement in asset utilization. Illustrating the importance of Medifast's increased asset turnover, it is easy to show that, absent this change, the company's financial leverage would have had to rise to a precariously high 3.93 times to produce the same 2010 sustainable growth rate.[3] (To appreciate why this might be a perilous debt level for a rapidly growing company, take a look at Chapter 6.)

TABLE 4.1 A Sustainable Growth Analysis of Medifast Inc., 2006–2010

	2006	2007	2008	2009	2010
Required ratios:					
Profit margin, P (%)	6.0	7.0	4.6	5.2	7.2
Retention ratio, R (%)	99.5	100.0	100.0	100.0	100.0
Asset turnover, A (times)	1.33	2.02	1.92	2.07	2.64
Financial leverage, T (times)	1.61	1.69	1.57	1.57	1.64
Medifast's sustainable growth rate, g^* (%)	12.8	23.9	13.9	16.9	31.2
Medifast's actual growth rate in sales, g (%)	46.8	84.6	13.1	25.9	57.1

	What If?		
	Profit Margin 8.2%	Financial Leverage 1.8 Times	Both Occur
Medifast's sustainable growth rate in 2010 (%)	35.5	34.3	39.1

*Totals may not add due to rounding.

[3]Assume Medifast's profit margin, retention rate, and asset turnover had remained at 2006 levels of 6.0%, 0.995, and 1.33 times, respectively, and let Y equal the financial leverage ratio required to generate the company's 2010 sustainable growth rate. $31.3\% = 6.0\% \times 99.5\% \times 1.33 \times Y$. Solving for Y, $Y = 3.93$ times.

FIGURE 4.3 Medifast's Sustainable Growth Challenges, 2006–2010

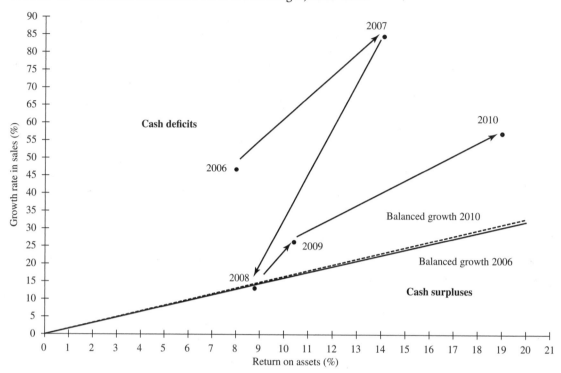

Figure 4.3 says the same thing graphically. It shows Medifast's balanced growth lines in 2006 and 2010, and the growth-return combinations the company achieved each year. Despite a very modest increase in the slope of the company's balanced growth line produced by a small increase in financial leverage, Medifast remained in the cash deficit portion of the graph every year except 2008 when the recession knocked sales growth down to "only" 13.1 percent. The growing gap between the yearly growth-return combinations and the balanced growth lines since 2008 confirms that Medifast's rapid growth challenges remain.

"What If" Questions

When management faces sustainable growth problems, the sustainable growth equation can be useful in searching for solutions. This is done by asking a series of "what if" questions as shown in the bottom portion of Table 4.1. We see, for example, that in coming years Medifast can raise its sustainable growth rate to 35.5 percent by increasing its profit margin to 8.2 percent. Alternatively, it can boost its sustainable growth rate to 34.3 percent by raising financial leverage to 1.8 times. Doing both simultaneously will raise sustainable growth to 39.1 percent.

What to Do When Actual Growth Exceeds Sustainable Growth

We have now developed the sustainable growth equation and illustrated its use for rapidly growing companies. The next question is: What should management do when actual growth exceeds sustainable growth? The first step is to determine how long the situation will continue. If the company's growth rate is likely to decline in the near future as the firm reaches maturity, the problem is only a transitory one that can probably be solved by further borrowing. In the future, when the actual growth rate falls below the sustainable rate, the company will switch from being an absorber of cash to being a generator of cash and can repay the loans. For longer-term sustainable growth problems, some combination of the following strategies will be necessary.

- Sell new equity
- Increase financial leverage
- Reduce the dividend payout
- Prune away marginal activities
- Outsource some or all of production
- Increase prices
- Merge with a "cash cow"

Let's consider each of these strategies in more detail.

Sell New Equity

If a company is willing and able to raise new equity capital by selling shares, its sustainable growth problems vanish. The increased equity, plus whatever added borrowing it makes possible, become sources of cash with which to finance further growth.

The problem with this strategy is that it is unavailable to many companies and unattractive to others. In many countries throughout the world, equity markets are poorly developed or nonexistent. To sell equity in these countries, companies must go through the laborious and expensive task of seeking out investors one by one to buy the new shares. This is a difficult undertaking because without active stock market trading of the shares, new investors will be minority owners of illiquid securities. In effect, they will be along for the ride, unable to steer the corporate ship and without a graceful way to bail out. Consequently, those investors interested in buying the new shares will be limited largely to family and friends of existing owners.

Dell Grows Up

Even well-known, successful companies such as $30 billion Dell, Inc., have experienced life-threatening growing pains. The company's young founder, Michael Dell, now admits that in 1993 Dell's growth spurt had come at the expense of a sound financial position. He says the company's cash reserves were down to $20 million at one point. "We could have used that up in a day or two. For a company our size, that was ridiculous. I realized we had to change the priorities."

Had Dell's priorities remained "growth, growth, growth," it might not be around today. Michael Dell founded Dell Computer before he was 20 years old. After several years of prodigious growth and with his company at the financial precipice, he lacked the expertise to manage the growth. Fortunately, he had the sense to hire more seasoned managers who could calm security analysts and steer Dell in a more conservative direction. Those managers urged Dell to focus on earnings and liquidity rather than sales growth. Slowing growth in 1994 cost the company market share, but it also helped convert a loss a year earlier into a $106.6 million profit. The company also instituted formal planning and budgeting processes. Today Dell is one of the world's largest computer manufacturers, with a healthy balance sheet, solid growth, and cash balances approximating 40 percent of assets.

Even in countries with well-developed stock markets, such as the United States and Britain, many companies find it very difficult to raise new equity. This is particularly true of smaller concerns that, unless they have a glamorous product, find it difficult to attract venture capital money or to secure the services of an investment banker to help them sell the shares to other investors. Without such help, the firms might just as well be in a country without developed markets, for a lack of trading in the stock will again restrict potential buyers largely to family and friends.

Finally, even many companies that are able to raise new equity prefer not to do so. This is evidenced in Table 4.2, which shows the sources of capital to U.S. nonfinancial corporations over the past decade. Observe that internal sources, depreciation and retained profits, were by far the most important sources of corporate capital, accounting for over 65 percent of the total. At the other extreme, *new equity has been not a source of capital at all but a use*, meaning American corporations on average retired more stock than they issued over this period.

We will return to the puzzling question of why companies do not issue more new equity at the end of the chapter. For now, let us provisionally accept that many companies cannot or will not sell new stock, and consider other strategies for managing unsustainably rapid growth.

TABLE 4.2 Sources of Capital to U.S. Nonfinancial Corporations, 2001–2010

Source: Federal Reserve System, *Flow of Funds Accounts of the United States.* **www.federalreserve.gov/releases/z1/current/data.htm.**

Internal		
Retained profits	17.9%	
Depreciation	48.0%	
Subtotal	65.9%	
External		
Increased liabilities	51.4%	
New equity issues	−17.3%	
Subtotal	34.1%	
Total		100.0%

Increase Leverage

If selling new equity is not a solution to a company's sustainable growth problems, two other financial remedies are possible. One is to cut the dividend payout ratio, and the other is to increase financial leverage. A cut in the payout ratio raises sustainable growth by increasing the proportion of earnings retained in the business, while increasing the leverage ratio raises the amount of debt the company can add for each dollar of retained profits.

I like to think of increasing leverage as the "default" option, in two senses of the word. From a computer programming perspective, an increase in leverage will be what occurs by default when management does not plan ahead. Over time, the company will find there is too little cash to pay creditors in a timely fashion, and accounts payable will rise by default. Increasing leverage is also the default option in the financial sense that creditors will eventually balk at rising debt levels and force the company into default—step one on the path to bankruptcy.

We will have considerably more to say about financial leverage in the next two chapters. It should be apparent already, however, that there is an upper limit to a company's use of debt financing. And part of the growth management challenge is to identify an appropriate degree of financial leverage for a company and to ensure this ceiling is not broached.

Reduce the Payout Ratio

Just as there is an upper limit to leverage, there is a lower limit of zero to a company's dividend payments, and most companies are already at this limit. Over half of the almost 10,000 public companies for which data are available on Standard & Poor's Compustat data service paid no dividends at all in 2010.[4] In general, owners' interest in dividend payments varies inversely with their perceptions of the company's investment opportunities. If owners believe the retained profits can be put to productive use earning attractive rates of return, they will happily forgo current dividends in favor of higher future ones. (There have been few complaints among Google's shareholders about the lack of dividends.) On the other hand, if company investment opportunities do not promise attractive returns, a dividend cut will anger shareholders, prompting a decline in stock price. An additional concern for closely held companies is the effect of dividend changes on owners' income and on their tax obligations.

Profitable Pruning

Beyond modifications in financial policy, a company can make several operating adjustments to manage rapid growth. One is called "profitable pruning." During much of the 1960s and early 1970s, some financial experts emphasized the merits of product diversification. The idea was that companies could reduce risk by combining the income streams of businesses in different product markets. The thought was that as long as these income streams were not affected in exactly the same way by economic events, the variability inherent in each stream would "average out" when combined with others. We now recognize two problems with this conglomerate diversification strategy. First, although it may reduce the risks seen by management, it does nothing for the shareholders. If shareholders want diversification, they can get it on their own by just purchasing shares of different independent companies. Second, because companies have limited resources, and a limited ability to manage disparate activities, they cannot be important competitors in a large number of product markets at the same time. Instead, they are apt to be followers in many markets, unable to compete effectively with the dominant firms.

Profitable pruning is the opposite of conglomerate merger. This strategy recognizes that when a company spreads its resources across too many products, it may be unable to compete effectively in any. Better to sell off marginal operations and plow the money back into remaining businesses.

---

[4] This does not imply that dividends are in any way insignificant or unimportant in the U.S. economy. For in the same year that less than half of companies were paying dividends, 77 percent of the nation's largest firms, represented by members of the S&P 500 Index, were distributing over $221 billion to shareholders, a sum equal to more than one-third of earnings. The proper inference is that small, young firms tend not to pay dividends, while large, mature ones do, and that there are many more small, young firms in our economy than large, mature ones.

Profitable pruning reduces sustainable growth problems in two ways: It generates cash directly through the sale of marginal businesses, and it reduces actual sales growth by eliminating some of the sources of the growth. Many businesses have successfully employed this strategy in recent years, including Cooper Industries, a large Texas company. Beginning in the 1970s, Cooper sold several of its operations, not because they were unprofitable but because Cooper believed it lacked the resources to become a dominant factor in the markets involved.

Profitable pruning is also possible for a single-product company. Here the idea is to prune out slow-paying customers or slow-turning inventory. This lessens sustainable growth problems in three ways: It frees up cash, which can be used to support new growth; it increases asset turnover; and it reduces sales. Sales decline because tightening credit terms and reducing inventory selection drive away some customers.

Outsourcing

Outsourcing involves the decision of whether to perform an activity in-house or purchase it from an outside vendor. A company can increase its sustainable growth rate by outsourcing more and doing less in-house. When a company outsources, it releases assets that would otherwise be tied up in performing the activity, and it increases its asset turnover. Both results diminish growth problems. An extreme example of this strategy is a franchisor that sources out virtually all of the company's capital-intensive activities to franchisees and, as a result, has very little investment.

The key to effective outsourcing is to determine where the company's unique abilities—or, as consultants would put it, "core competencies"—lie. If certain activities can be performed by others without jeopardizing the firm's core competencies, these activities are candidates for outsourcing.

Pricing

An obvious inverse relationship exists between price and volume. When sales growth is too high relative to a company's financing capabilities, it may be necessary to raise prices to reduce growth. If higher prices increase the profit margin, the price increase will also raise the sustainable growth rate.

In effect, the recommendation here is to make growth itself a decision variable. If rapid growth is a problem, attack the problem directly by cutting growth. And while closing early on alternate Wednesdays or turning away every 10th customer might get the job done, the most effective way to cut growth is usually to raise prices.

Is Merger the Answer?

When all else fails, it may be necessary to look for a partner with deep pockets. Two types of companies are capable of supplying the needed cash. One is a mature company, known in the trade as a "cash cow," looking for profitable investments for its excess cash flow. The other is a conservatively financed company that would bring liquidity and borrowing capacity to the marriage. Acquiring another company or being acquired is a drastic solution to growth problems, but it is better to make the move when a company is still financially strong than to wait until excessive growth forces the issue.

Too Little Growth

Slow-growth companies—those whose sustainable growth rate exceeds actual growth—have growth management problems too, but of a different kind. Rather than struggling continually for fresh cash to stoke the fires of growth, slow-growth companies face the dilemma of what to do with profits in excess of company needs. This might appear to be a trivial or even enviable problem, but to an increasing number of enterprises it is a very real and occasionally frightening one.

To get a closer look at the difficulties insufficient growth creates, let's look at Jos. A. Bank Clothiers, Inc., a direct marketer of men's clothing with 473 retail stores in 42 states. Table 4.3 presents a five-year, sustainable growth analysis of J.A. Bank. Despite healthy profit margins and an annual sales growth exceeding 10 percent, the company's sustainable growth rate exceeded its actual growth rate by a sizeable margin in every year. What did management do with the excess cash? Much like Sensient Technologies discussed in earlier chapters, the company's chief use of the cash has been to reduce financial leverage, accompanied by a more modest

TABLE 4.3   **A Sustainable Growth Analysis of Jos. A. Bank Clothiers, Inc., 2006–2010***

	2006	2007	2008	2009	2010
Required ratios:					
Profit margin, P (%)	7.9	8.3	8.4	9.2	10.0
Retention ratio, R (%)	100.0	100.0	100.0	100.0	100.0
Asset turnover, A (times)	1.48	1.37	1.42	1.39	1.30
Financial leverage, T (times)	2.40	2.11	1.88	1.73	1.68
J.A. Bank's sustainable growth rate, g^* (%)	28.1	24.0	22.4	22.1	21.8
J.A. Bank's actual growth rate, g (%)	17.6	10.5	15.2	10.7	11.4

*Totals may not add due to rounding.

FIGURE 4.4   Jos. A. Bank Clothiers, Inc. Sustainable Growth Challenges, 2006–2010

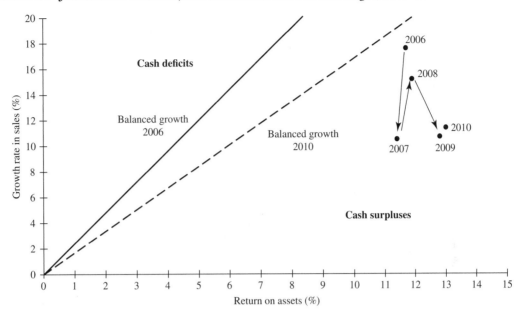

decline in asset turnover. From 2006 through 2010, financial leverage fell by 30 percent. In fact, a look at the company's balance sheets reveals that interest-bearing debt was eliminated in 2006 and that cash and marketable securities have since risen dramatically to 41 percent of total assets. No wonder asset turnover has been declining. What has J.A. Bank done with the money? They have largely sat on it.

Figure 4.4 says the same thing graphically. J.A. Bank's returns and growth rates are clustered in the upper-right corner of the figure, a great place to be were it not for the fact they continue to generate more cash than necessary to run the business. The company's reduction in financial leverage has lowered its balanced growth line noticeably, but excess cash continues to roll in. Time for management to decide how best to redeploy this money.

What to Do When Sustainable Growth Exceeds Actual Growth

The first step in addressing problems of inadequate growth is to decide whether the situation is temporary or longer term. If temporary, management can simply continue accumulating resources in anticipation of future growth.

When the difficulty is longer term, the issue becomes whether the lack of growth is industrywide—the natural result of a maturing market—or unique to the company. If the latter, the reasons for inadequate growth and possible sources of new growth are to be found within the firm. In this event, management must look carefully at its own performance to identify and remove the internal constraints on company growth, a potentially painful process involving organizational changes as well as increased developmental expenses. The nerve-wracking aspect of such soul searching is that the strategies initiated to enhance growth must bear fruit within a few years or management will be forced to seek other, often more drastic solutions.

When a company is unable to generate sufficient growth from within, it has three options: ignore the problem, return the money to shareholders, or buy growth. Let us briefly consider each alternative.

Ignore the Problem

This response takes one of two forms: Management can continue investing in its core businesses despite the lack of attractive returns, or it can simply sit on an ever-larger pile of idle resources. The difficulty with either response is that, like dogs to a fire hydrant, underutilized resources attract unwelcome attention. Poorly utilized resources depress a company's stock price and make the firm a feasible and attractive target for a raider. If a raider has done her sums correctly, she can redeploy the target firm's resources more productively and earn a substantial profit in the process. And among the first resources to be redeployed in such a raid are usually incumbent managers, who find themselves suddenly reading help-wanted ads. Even if a hostile raid does not occur, boards of directors and activist shareholders are increasingly likely to give the boot to underperforming managements.

Another way to characterize the relationship between investment and growth is to distinguish between good growth and its evil twin, bad growth. Good growth occurs when the company invests in activities offering returns in excess of cost, including the cost of capital employed. Good growth benefits owners and is rewarded by a higher stock price and reduced threat of takeover. Bad growth involves investing in activities with returns at or below cost. Because ill-advised activities are always readily available, a bad growth strategy is easy to execute. If all else fails, the company can always overpay to purchase the sales and assets of another business. Such a strategy disposes of excess cash and makes the firm larger, but these cosmetic results only mask the fact that a bad growth strategy wastes valuable resources—and stock markets are increasingly adept at distinguishing between good and bad growth, and punishing the latter. The moral to the story, then, is that it is not enough for slow-growth companies to grow more rapidly; they must do so in a way that benefits shareholders. All other forms of growth are a snare and a delusion. (We will say more about value-creating investment activities in Chapters 7 and 8.)

Return the Money to Shareholders

The most direct solution to the problem of idle resources is to simply return the money to owners by increasing dividends or repurchasing shares. However, while this solution is becoming more common, it is still not the strategy of choice among many executives. The chief reason is that many executives appear to have a bias in favor of growth, even when the growth creates little or no value for shareholders. At the personal level, these executives resist paying large dividends because the practice hints of failure. Shareholders entrust managers with the task of profitably investing their capital, and for the company to return the money suggests an inability to perform a basic managerial function. A cruder way to say the same thing is that dividends reduce the size of management's empire, an act counter to basic human nature.

Gordon Donaldson and others also document a bias toward growth at the organizational level.[5] In a carefully researched review and synthesis of the decision-making behavior of senior executives in a dozen large companies, Donaldson noted that executives commonly opt for growth, even uneconomic growth, out of concern for the long-run viability of their organizations. As senior managers see it, size offers some protection against the vagaries of the marketplace. Moreover, growth contributes significantly to company morale by creating stimulating career opportunities for employees throughout the organization, and when growth slackens, the enterprise risks losing its best people.

Buy Growth

The third way to eliminate slow-growth problems is to buy growth. Motivated by pride in their ability as managers, concern for retaining key employees, and fear of raiders, managers often respond to excess cash flow by attempting to diversify into other businesses. Management systematically searches for worthwhile growth opportunities in other, more vibrant industries. And because time is a factor, this usually involves acquiring existing businesses rather than starting new ones from scratch.

The proper design and implementation of a corporate acquisition program is a challenging task that need not detain us here. Two points, however, are worth noting. First, in many important respects, the growth management problems of mature or declining companies are just the mirror image of those faced by rapidly growing firms. Slow-growth businesses are generally seeking productive uses for their excess cash, while rapidly growing ones are in search of additional cash to finance their

[5] Donaldson, *Managing Corporate Wealth*.

unsustainably rapid growth. It is natural, therefore, that high- and low-growth companies frequently solve their respective growth management problems by merging so that the excess cash generated by one organization can finance the rapid growth of the other. Second, after a flurry of optimism in the 1960s and early 1970s, accumulating evidence increasingly suggests that, from the shareholders' perspective, buying growth is distinctly inferior to returning the money to owners. More often than not, the superior growth prospects of potential acquisitions are fully reflected in the target's stock price, so that after paying a substantial premium to acquire another firm, the buyer is left with a mediocre investment or worse. The conflict between managers and owners in this regard is a topic of Chapter 9.

Sustainable Growth and Inflation

Growth comes from two sources: increasing volume and rising prices. Unfortunately, the amount of money a company must invest to support a dollar of inflationary growth is about the same as the investment required to support a dollar of real growth. Imagine a company that has no real growth—it makes and sells the same number of items every year—but is experiencing 10 percent inflationary growth. Then, even though it has the same number of units in inventory, each unit will cost more dollars to build, so the total investment in inventory will be higher. The same is true of accounts receivable: The same volume of customers will purchase the same number of units, but because each unit has a higher selling price, the total investment in accounts receivable will rise.

A company's investment in fixed assets behaves similarly under inflation, but with a delay. When the inflation rate increases, there is no immediate need for more fixed assets. The existing fixed assets can produce the same number of units. But as existing assets wear out and are replaced at higher prices, the company's investment in fixed assets rises.

This inflationary increase in assets must be financed just as if it were real growth. It is fair to say, then, that inflation worsens a rapidly expanding company's growth management problems. How much worse depends primarily on the extent to which management and creditors understand the impact of inflation on company financial statements.

Inflation does at least two things to company financial statements. First, as just noted, it increases the amount of external financing required. Second, in the absence of new equity financing, it increases the company's debt-to-equity ratio *when measured on its historical-cost financial statements.* This combination can spell trouble. If management or creditors require that the company's historical-cost debt-to-equity ratio stay constant over time, inflation will lower the company's real sustainable growth rate. If the sustainable growth rate is 15 percent without inflation, the real sustainable growth rate will fall to about 5 percent when the inflation rate is 10 percent. Intuitively, under inflation, cash that would otherwise support real growth must be used to finance inflationary growth.

If managers and creditors understand the effects of inflation, this inverse relation between inflation and the sustainable growth rate need not exist. True, the amount of external financing required does rise with the inflation rate, but because the real value of liabilities declines as companies become able to repay their loans with depreciated dollars, the *net* increase in external financing may be little affected by inflation.

In sum, with historical-cost financial statements, inflationary growth appears to substitute for real growth on almost a one-for-one basis; each percentage point increase in inflation appears to reduce the real sustainable growth rate by the same amount. More accurate, inflation-adjusted financial statements show, however, that inflation turns out to have relatively little effect on sustainable growth. Let us hope that executives can convince their bankers of this fact. I have not been able to do so.

Sustainable Growth and Pro Forma Forecasts

It is important to keep the material presented here in perspective. I find that comparison of a company's actual and sustainable growth rates reveals a great deal about the principal financial concerns confronting senior management. When actual growth exceeds sustainable growth, management's focus will be on getting the cash to fund expansion; conversely, when actual growth falls below sustainable growth, the financial agenda will swing 180 degrees to one of productively spending the excess cash flow. The sustainable growth equation also describes the way many top executives view their jobs: Avoid external equity financing and work to balance operating strategies, growth targets, and financial policies so that the disparity between actual and sustainable growth is manageable. Finally, for nonfinancial types, the sustainable growth equation is a useful way to highlight the tie between a company's growth rate and its financial resources.

The sustainable growth equation, however, is essentially just a simplification of pro forma statements. If you really want to study a company's growth management problems in detail, therefore, I recommend that you take the time to construct pro forma financial statements. The sustainable growth equation may be great for looking at the forest but is considerably less helpful when studying individual trees.

New Equity Financing

Earlier in the chapter I noted that a fundamental assumption of sustainable growth analysis is that the company cannot or will not issue new equity. Consistent with this assumption I also noted in Table 4.2 that over the past decade new equity has been a use of cash to American companies, not a source, meaning that businesses have retired more stock than they have issued. It is time now to explore this phenomenon in more detail with particular emphasis on explaining why companies are so reticent to sell new stock.

Figure 4.5 shows the value of new equity issues, net of repurchases, on a year-by-year basis for the United States from 1975 through 2010. Net new equity issues grew erratically to about $28 billion in 1983, then plunged sharply, and have been essentially negative ever since. The figure reached an all-time low of minus $787 billion in 2007 when companies took advantage of healthy internal cash flows and low borrowing rates to repurchase shares aggressively. The repurchase binge ended abruptly the following year, however, when the sharp recession cut internal cash flows and increased the perceived importance of corporate liquidity.

Companies reduce common stock outstanding in two ways: by repurchasing their own stock or by acquiring the stock of another firm for cash or debt. The best available evidence suggests that the sharp reduction in

FIGURE 4.5   **Net New Equity Issues, 1975–2010**

Sources: Federal Reserve System, *Flow of Funds Accounts of the United States,* **www.federalreserve.gov/releases/z1/current/data.htm.**

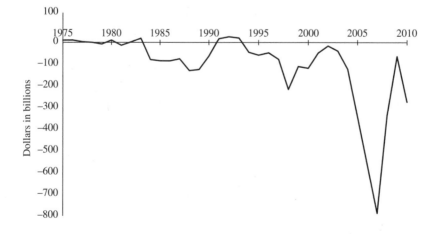

equity outstanding in recent decades was initially triggered by the hostile takeover battles that swept through the economy in the last half of the 1980s.

In more recent years, the reduction in U.S. equity appears attributable to the growing popularity of share repurchase as a way to distribute cash to shareholders and to manage reported earnings per share. If stock analysts are projecting a 15 percent growth in earnings-per-share but management believes they can only increase earnings 10 percent, one way to meet the analysts' target is to repurchase five percent of the shares outstanding.

These data suggesting that new equity capital is not a source of financing to American business are consistent with evidence showing that in an average year, only about 5 percent of publicly traded companies in the United States sell additional common stock. This means that a typical publicly traded company raises new equity capital in public markets only once every 20 years.[6]

Recalling the tale of the statistician who drowned crossing the stream because he had heard it was only 5 feet deep on average, we need to remember that the equity figures presented are the net result of new issues and retirements. Figure 4.6 shows the gross proceeds from new common stock sales in the U.S. from 1980 to 2010. The 30-year average was $98.3 billion, and the high in 2009 was $234.0 billion. The spike in equity issues during the years of the recent recession is due to the frantic fund raising efforts by the nation's banks, who accounted for almost three-quarters of total equity raised as they fought to avoid collapse.

To put these numbers in perspective, gross proceeds from new stock sales by nonfinancial corporations over the past decade equaled 4.0 percent of total sources of capital over the period. The comparable figure as a percent of external sources was 11.6 percent.

Figure 4.6 also shows the money raised from initial public offerings of common stock (IPOs) from 1980 through 2010. Observe that the aggregate amount of money raised is comparatively modest, amounting to about one-quarter of gross new equity proceeds over the period. In 2000, the peak year for IPOs, total money raised equaled only 5 percent of total corporate external sources of capital. The fact that IPO proceeds have trended downward over the past decade is a source of growing concern to many.

---

[6] U.S. Securities and Exchange Commission, *Report of the Advisory Committee on the Capital Formation and Regulatory Process,* July 24, 1996, Figure 4.

FIGURE 4.6 Gross New Stock Issues by Corporations and Initial Public Offerings, 1980–2010

Source: *Federal Reserve Bulletin*, Table 1.46, "New Security Issues U.S. Corporations," various issues, new stock issues by corporations; Jay Ritter, "Initial Public Offerings: Tables Updated Through 2010," Table 8. **bear.warrington.ufl.edu/ritter/IPOs2010statistics111.pdf.**

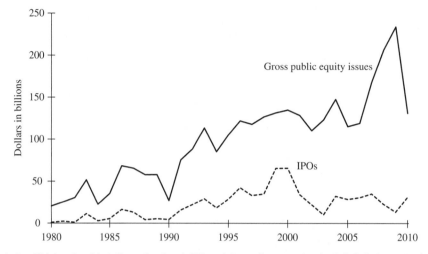

Note: New equity is publicly issued stock including preferred stock. IPOs exclude overallotment options but include the international tranche, if any.

I see these graphs as a testament to the dynamism of the American economy in which many firms are retiring equity at the same time others are selling new shares. On balance, the appropriate conclusion is that while the stock market is not an important source of capital to corporate America in the aggregate, it is critical to some companies. Companies making extensive use of the new equity market tend to be what brokers call "story paper," potentially high-growth enterprises with a particular product or concept that brokers can hype to receptive investors (the words high-tech and biotech come most readily to mind).

Why Don't U.S. Corporations Issue More Equity?

Here are several reasons. We will consider others in Chapter 6 when we review financing decisions in more detail.

- In recent years, companies in the aggregate simply did not need new equity. Retained profits and new borrowing were sufficient.

- Equity is expensive to issue. Issues costs commonly run in the neighborhood of 5 to 10 percent of the amount raised, and the percentage on small issues is even higher. These figures are at least twice as high as the issue costs for a comparable-size debt issue. (On the other hand, the equity can be outstanding forever, so its effective annualized cost is less onerous.)

- Many managers, especially U.S. managers, have a fixation with earnings per share (EPS). They translate a complicated world into the simple notion that whatever increases EPS must be good and whatever reduces EPS must be bad. In this view, a new equity issue is bad because, at least initially, the number of shares outstanding rises but earnings do not. EPS is said to be *diluted*. Later, as the company makes productive use of the money raised, earnings should increase but in the meantime, EPS suffers. Moreover, as we will see in Chapter 6, EPS is almost always higher when debt financing is used in favor of equity.

- Then there is the "market doesn't appreciate us" syndrome. When a company's stock is selling for $10 a share, management tends to think the price will be a little higher in the future as soon as the current strategy begins to bear fruit. When the price rises to $15, management begins to believe this is just the beginning and the price will be even higher in the near future. Managers' inherent enthusiasm for their company's prospects produces a feeling that the firm's shares are undervalued at whatever price they currently command, and this view creates a bias toward forever postponing new equity issues. A 2001 survey of 371 chief financial officers of U.S. corporations by John Graham and Campbell Harvey at Duke University illustrates this syndrome. Despite the fact that the Dow Jones Industrial Averages were approaching a new record high at the time of the survey, fewer than one-third of respondents thought the stock market correctly valued their stock; only 3 percent believed their stock was overvalued, and fully 69 percent felt it was undervalued.[7]

- Finally, many managers perceive the stock market to be an unreliable funding source. In addition to uncertainty about the price a company can get for new shares, managers also face the possibility that during some future periods the stock market will not be receptive to new equity issues on any reasonable terms. In finance jargon, the "window" is said to be shut at these times. Naturally, executives are reluctant to develop a growth strategy that depends on such an unreliable source of capital. Rather, the philosophy is to formulate growth plans that can be financed from retained profits and accompanying borrowing and relegate new equity finance to a minor backup role. More on this topic in later chapters.

---

[7] John R. Graham and Campbell R. Harvey, "The Theory and Practice of Corporate Finance: Evidence from the Field," *Journal of Financial Economics,* May–June 2001, pp. 187–243.

  c. Share repurchases usually increase earnings per share.

  d. Companies often buy back their stock because managers believe the shares are undervalued.

  e. Only rapidly growing firms have growth management problems.

  f. Increasing growth increases stock price.

4. Table 3.1 in the last chapter presents R&E Supplies's financial statements for the period 2008 through 2011, and Table 3.5 presents a pro forma financial forecast for 2012. Use the information in these tables to answer the following questions.

  a. Calculate R&E Supplies's sustainable growth rate in each year from 2009 through 2012.

  b. Comparing the company's sustainable growth rate with its actual and projected growth rates in sales over these years, what growth management problems does R&E Supplies appear to face in this period?

  c. How did the company cope with these problems? Do you see any difficulties with the way it addressed its growth problems over this period? If so, what are they?

  d. What advice would you offer management regarding managing future growth?

5. Looking at Figure 4.5, describe the trend in net equity financing in the U.S. during the last 30 years. What does this say about the use of equity financing in U.S. corporations?

6. Looking at Figure 4.6, describe the trend in gross public equity issues and IPOs in the U.S. during the last 30 years. How do you explain this trend given what we observe in Figure 4.5?

7. Biosite, Inc. is a developer, manufacturer, and marketer of medical diagnostic products in San Diego, California. If you wanted to test for parasites, drug abuse, or congestive heart failure, you would be wise to contact Biosite. Following are selected financial data for the company for the period 2000–2004.

	2000	2001	2002	2003	2004
Profit margin (%)	11.2	10.3	12.7	14.3	16.9
Retention ratio (%)	100.0	100.0	100.0	100.0	100.0
Asset turnover (X)	0.66	0.64	0.80	0.89	0.86
Assets (end of year, millions)	$83.0	$102.7	$131.3	$194.6	$283.5
Equity (end of year, millions)	$72.9	$ 90.9	$107.9	$152.9	$220.3
Growth rate in sales (%)	25.8	19.4	60.3	64.8	41.3

  a. Calculate Biosite's sustainable growth rate in each year from 2001 through 2004.

b. Comparing the company's sustainable growth rate with its actual growth rate in sales, what growth management problems did Biosite face over this period?

c. How did the company cope with these problems?

8. Genentech Inc. is a California-based biotech pioneer recently acquired by Swiss pharmaceutical giant Roche Holding AG. Roche paid $46.8 billion in cash for the 44 percent of Genentech it did not already own, implying a market value of over $100 billion for the entire company. For a look at Genentech's recent sustainable growth challenges, consider the following selected financial data.

	2003	2004	2005	2006	2007
Profit margin (%)	17.0	17.0	19.3	22.8	23.6
Retention ratio (%)	100.0	100.0	100.0	100.0	100.0
Asset turnover (X)	0.38	0.49	0.55	0.63	0.62
Financial leverage (X)	1.64	1.44	1.79	1.99	2.00
Growth rate in sales (%)	26.1	40.0	43.5	40.0	26.3

a. Calculate Genentech's annual sustainable growth rate for the years 2003–2007.

b. Did Genentech face a growth management challenge during this period? Please explain briefly.

c. How did Genentech cope with this challenge?

d. Calculate Genentech's sustainable growth rate in 2007 assuming an asset turnover of 0.72 times. Calculate the sustainable growth rate in 2007 assuming a financial leverage of 2.20 times. Calculate the sustainable growth rate in 2007 assuming both of these changes occur.

9. Harley Davidson, Inc., the iconic motorcycle company, has the following ratios for the years 2000 through 2004:

	2000	2001	2002	2003	2004
Profit margin (%)	11.4	12.3	13.5	15.5	16.7
Retention ratio (%)	91.3	91.9	92.8	92.2	86.6
Asset turnover (X)	1.25	1.14	1.11	1.00	0.97
Assets (end of year, millions)	$2,436	$3,118	$3,861	$4,923	$5,483
Equity (end of year, millions)	$1,406	$1,756	$2,233	$2,958	$3,219
Growth rate in sales (%)	17.8	16.4	21.4	14.0	8.5

a. Calculate Harley Davidson's annual sustainable growth rate from 2001 through 2004.

CHAPTER FIVE

Financial Instruments and Markets

Don't tell mom I'm an investment banker. She still thinks I play piano in a brothel.

Anonymous

A major part of a financial executive's job is to raise money to finance current operations and future growth. In this capacity, the financial manager acts much as a marketing executive. He or she has a product—claims on the company's future cash flow—that must be packaged and sold to yield the highest price to the company. The financial manager's customers are creditors and investors who put money into the business in anticipation of future cash flows. In return, these customers receive a piece of paper such as a stock certificate, a bond, or a loan agreement, that describes the nature of their claim on the firm's future cash flow. When the paper can be bought and sold in financial markets, it is customarily called a *financial security*.

In packaging the product, the financial executive must select or design a financial security that meets the needs of the company and is attractive to potential creditors and investors. To do this effectively requires knowledge of financial instruments, the markets in which they trade, and the merits of each instrument to the issuing company. In this chapter, we consider the first two topics, financial instruments and markets. In the next chapter, we look at a company's choice of the proper financing instrument.

Although corporate financing decisions are usually the responsibility of top executives and their finance staffs, there are several reasons managers at all levels need to understand the logic on which these decisions rest. First, we all make similar financing decisions in our personal lives whenever we borrow money to buy a home, a car, or return to school. Second, as investors, we are often consumers of the financial securities that companies issue, and it is always wise to be an informed consumer. Third, and most important for present purposes, sound financing decisions are central to effective financial management. This is witnessed by the fact that financial leverage is one of the levers of performance by which managers seek to generate competitive returns, and it is a principal determinant of a company's sustainable growth rate. So failure to appreciate the logic driving an enterprise's financing decisions robs managers of a complete understanding of their company and its challenges.

Before beginning, a few words about what this chapter is not. "Financial markets" is the name given to a dynamic, heterogeneous distribution system through which cash-surplus entities provide money to cash-deficit entities. Businesses are by no means the only, or even the most prominent players in these markets. Other active participants include national, state, and local governments and agencies, pension funds, endowments, individuals, commercial banks, insurance companies, and the list goes on and on. This chapter is not a balanced overview of financial markets; rather it is a targeted look at the financing instruments most used by nonfinancial corporations and the means by which they are sold. A further restriction is that we will not consider short-term instruments. When speaking of financial markets it is common to distinguish between *money markets*, in which securities having a maturity of less than one-year trade, and *capital markets*, in which longer-term instruments are bought and sold. Because nonfinancial businesses rely much more on capital markets for financing, we will say little about money markets, even though they are the larger and more liquid of the two. (For a more comprehensive look at financial markets and instruments, see one of the books recommended at the end of this chapter.)

Financial Instruments

Fortunately, lawyers and regulators have not yet taken all of the fun and creativity out of raising money. When selecting a financial instrument for sale in securities markets, a company is *not* significantly constrained by law or regulation. The company is largely free to select or design any instrument, provided only that the instrument appeals to investors and meets the needs of the company. Securities markets in the United States are regulated by the Securities and Exchange Commission (SEC) and, to a lesser extent, by state authorities. SEC regulation can create red tape and delay, but the SEC does not pass judgment on the investment merits of a security. It requires only that investors have access to all information relevant to valuing the security and have adequate opportunity to evaluate it before purchase. This freedom has given rise to such unusual securities as Foote Minerals' $2.20 cumulative, if earned, convertible preferred stock and Sunshine Mining's silver-indexed bonds. My favorite is a 6 percent bond issued by Hungary in 1983 that, in addition to paying interest, included a firm promise of telephone service within three years. The usual wait for a phone at the time was said to run up to 20 years. A close second is a bond proposed by a group of Russian vodka distillers. Known as *Lial*, or "Liter" bonds, they were to pay annual interest of 20 percent in hard currency or 25 percent in vodka. According to one of the promoters, "Vodka has been currency for 1,000 years. We have just made the relationship formal."

But, do not let the variety of securities obscure the underlying logic. When designing a financial instrument, the financial executive works with three variables: investors' claims on future cash flow, their right to participate in company decisions, and their claims on company assets in liquidation. We will now describe the more popular security types in terms of these three variables. In reading the descriptions, bear in mind that the characteristics of a specific financial instrument are determined by the terms of the contract between issuer and buyer, not by law or regulation. So the descriptions that follow should be thought of as indicating general security types rather than exact definitions of specific instruments.

Bonds

Economists like to distinguish between physical assets and financial assets. A physical asset, such as a home, a business, or a painting, is one whose value depends on its physical properties. A financial asset is a piece of paper or, more formally, a security representing a legal claim to future cash payouts. The entity agreeing to make the payouts is the issuer, and the recipient is the investor. It is often useful to draw a further distinction among financial assets depending on whether the claim to future payments is fixed as to dollar amount and timing or residual, meaning the investor receives any cash remaining after all prior fixed claims have been paid. Debt instruments offer fixed claims, while equity, or common stock, offers residual claims. Human ingenuity being what it is, you should not be surprised to learn that some securities, such as convertible preferred stock, are neither fish nor fowl, offering neither purely fixed nor purely residual claims.

Derivatives, also known as contingent claims, constitute a third fundamental security type. A derivative security is distinguished by the fact that its claim to future payments depends upon the value of some other underlying asset. For example, an option to purchase IBM stock is a derivative because its value depends on the price of IBM shares. The popularity and importance of derivatives have grown enormously since Fisher Black and Myron Scholes first proposed a rigorous way to value options in 1973. The appendix to this chapter considers derivatives briefly as part of a broader discussion of financial risk management, and Chapter 8 revisits the topic in the context of evaluating investment opportunities.

A bond, like any other form of indebtedness, is a *fixed-income* security. The holder receives a specified annual interest income and a specified amount at maturity—no more and no less (unless the company goes bankrupt). The difference between a bond and other forms of indebtedness such as trade credit, bank loans, and private placements is that bonds are sold to the public in small increments, usually $1,000 per bond. After issue, the bonds can be traded by investors on organized security exchanges.

I noted in the last chapter that internal financing, in the form of retained profits and depreciation, has provided about 65 percent of the money used by American business over the past decade. Looking at external financing, aggregate data indicate that over the past two decades corporate bonds have been the largest source, accounting for about 37 percent of the total. Loans and advances of various kinds from banks and others have contributed another 11 percent. Before dismissing bank loans as of only secondary importance, it is important to bear in mind that although they are not a major source of financing in the aggregate, they are important to smaller firms. For example, in 2010 the ratio of bank loans to total liabilities among billion dollar–plus manufacturing firms was only 8 percent, while the comparable number for small manufacturers having assets of $25 million or less was 34 percent.[1]

Three variables characterize a bond: its *par value*, its *coupon rate*, and its *maturity date*. For example, a bond might have a $1,000 par value, a 7 percent coupon rate, and a maturity date of December 31, 2018. The par value is the amount of money the holder will receive on the bond's maturity date. By custom, the par value of bonds issued in the United States is usually $1,000. The coupon rate is the percentage of par value the issuer promises to pay the investor annually as interest income. Our bond will pay $70 per year in interest (7% × $1,000), usually in two semiannual payments of $35 each. On the maturity date, the company will pay the bondholder $1,000 per bond and will cease further interest payments.

On the issue date, companies usually try to set the coupon rate on the new bond equal to the prevailing interest rate on other bonds of similar maturity and quality. This ensures that the bond's initial market price will about equal its par value. After issue, the market price of a bond can differ substantially from its par value as market interest rates and credit risk perceptions change. As we will see in Chapter 7, when interest rates rise, bond prices fall, and vice versa.

---

[1] U.S. Federal Reserve, "Flow of Funds Accounts of the United States," **www.federalreserve.gov/releases/z1/**. U.S. Census Bureau, "Quarterly Financial Report for Manufacturing, Mining, Trade, and Selected Service Industries: 2010" Tables 1.1 and 80.1. **www.census.gov/csd/qfr/qfr10q4.pdf**.

When Investing Internationally, What You See Isn't Always What You Get

A 10 percent interest rate on a dollar-denominated bond is not comparable to a 6 percent rate on a yen bond or a 14 percent rate on a British sterling bond. To see why, let's calculate the rate of return on $1,000 invested today in a one-year, British sterling bond yielding 14 percent interest. Suppose today's exchange rate is 1£ = $1.50 and the rate in one year is 1£ = $1.35.

$1,000 will buy £666.67 today ($1,000/1.50 = £666.67), and in one year interest and principal on the sterling bond will total £760 (£666.67 [1 + 0.14] = £760). Converting this amount back into dollars yields $1,026 in one year (£760 × 1.35 = $1,026). So the investment's rate of return, measured in dollars, is only 2.6 percent ([$1,026 − $1,000]/$1,000 = 2.6%).

Why is the dollar return so low? Because investing in a foreign asset is really two investments: purchase of a foreign-currency asset and speculation on future changes in the dollar value of the foreign currency. Here the foreign asset yields a healthy 14 percent, but sterling depreciates 10 percent against the dollar ([$1.50 − $1.35]/$1.50); so the combined return is roughly the difference between the two. The exact relationship is

$$(1 + \text{Return}) = (1 + \text{Interest rate})(1 + \text{Change in exchange rate})$$
$$(1 + \text{Return}) = (1 + 14\%)(1 - 10\%)$$
$$\text{Return} = 2.6\%$$

Incidentally, we know that sterling depreciated relative to the dollar over the year because a pound costs less at the end of the year than at the start.

Most forms of long-term indebtedness require periodic repayment of principal. This principal repayment is known as a *sinking fund*. Readers who have studied too much accounting will know that technically a sinking fund is a sum of money the company sets aside to meet a future obligation, and this is the way bonds used to work, but no more. Today a bond sinking fund is a direct payment to creditors that reduces principal. Depending on the indenture agreement, there are several ways a firm can meet its sinking-fund obligation. It can repurchase a certain number of bonds in securities markets, or it can retire a certain number of bonds by paying the holders par value. When a company has a choice, it will naturally repurchase bonds if the market price of the bonds is below par value.

I have just described a fixed-interest-rate bond. An alternative more common to loans than bonds is floating-rate debt in which the interest rate is tied to a short-term interest rate such as the 90-day U.S. Treasury bill rate. If a floating-rate instrument promises to pay, say, one percentage point over the 90-day bill rate, the interest to be paid on each payment date will be calculated anew by adding one percentage point to the then prevailing 90-day bill rate. Because the interest paid on a floating-rate instrument varies in harmony with changing interest rates over time, the instrument's market value always approximates its principal value.

Call Provisions

Some corporate bonds contain a clause giving the issuing company the option to retire the bonds prior to maturity. Frequently the call price for early retirement will be at a modest premium above par; or the bond may have a *delayed call*, meaning the issuer may not call the bond until it has been outstanding for a specified period, usually 5 or 10 years.

Companies want call options on bonds for two obvious reasons. One is that if interest rates fall, the company can pay off its existing bonds and issue new ones at a lower interest cost. The other is that the call option gives a company flexibility. If changing market conditions or changing company strategy requires it, the call option enables management to re-arrange its capital structure.

At first glance, it may appear that a call option works entirely to the company's advantage. If interest rates fall, the company calls the bonds and refinances at a lower rate. But if rates rise, investors have no similar option. They must either accept the low interest income or sell their bonds at a loss. From the company's perspective, it looks like "heads I win, tails you lose," but investors are not so naive. As a general rule, the more attractive the call provisions to the issuer, the higher the coupon rate on the bond.

Covenants

Under normal circumstances, no creditors, including bondholders, have a direct voice in company decisions. Bondholders and other long-term cred-itors exercise control through *protective covenants* specified in the indenture agreement. Typical covenants include a lower limit on the company's cur-rent ratio, an upper limit on its debt-to-equity ratio, and perhaps a re-quirement that the company not acquire or sell major assets without prior creditor approval. Creditors have no say in company operations as long as the firm is current in its interest and sinking-fund payments and no covenants have been violated. If the company falls behind in its payments or violates a covenant, it is in *default*, and creditors gain considerable power. At the extreme, creditors can force the company into bankruptcy and possible liquidation. In liquidation, the courts supervise the sale of company assets and distribution of the proceeds to the various claimants.

Rights in Liquidation

The distribution of liquidation proceeds in bankruptcy is determined by what is known as the *rights of absolute priority*. First in line are, naturally, the government for past-due taxes. Among investors, the first to be repaid are *senior* creditors, then *general* creditors, and finally *subordinated* credi-tors. Preferred stockholders and common shareholders bring up the rear. Because each class of claimant is paid off in full before the next class re-ceives anything, equity shareholders frequently get nothing in liquidation.

Secured Creditors

A *secured credit* is a form of senior credit in which the loan is collateralized by a specific company asset or group of assets. In liquidation, proceeds from the sale of this asset go only to the secured creditor. If the cash generated from the sale exceeds the debt to the secured creditor, the excess cash goes into the pot for distribution to general creditors. If the cash is insufficient, the lender becomes a general creditor for the remaining liability. Mortgages are a common example of a secured credit in which the asset securing the loan is land or buildings.

Bonds as an Investment

For many years, investors thought bonds to be very safe investments. After all, interest income is specified and the chances of bankruptcy are remote. However, this reasoning ignored the pernicious effects of inflation on fixed-income securities. For although the *nominal* return on fixed-interest-rate bonds is specified, the value of the resulting interest and principal payments to the investor is much less when inflation is high. This implies that investors need to concern themselves with the *real*, or inflation-adjusted, return on an asset, not the nominal return. And according to this yardstick, even default-free bonds can be quite risky in periods of high and volatile inflation.

Table 5.1 presents the nominal rate of return U.S. investors earned on selected securities over the period 1900 to 2010. Looking at long-term corporate bonds, you can see that had an investor purchased a representative portfolio of corporate bonds in 1899 and held them through 2010 (while reinvesting all interest income and principal payments in similar bonds), the annual return would have been 5.7 percent over the entire 111-year period. By comparison, the annual return on an investment in long-term U.S. government bonds would have been 5.2 percent over the same period. We can attribute the 0.5 percent difference to a "risk premium." This is the added return investors in corporate bonds earn over

TABLE 5.1   **Rate of Return on Selected Securities, 1900–2010**

Source: Elroy Dimson, Paul Marsh, and Mike Staunton. *Credit Suisse Global Investment Returns Sourcebook* opyright © 2011 Elroy Dimson, Paul Marsh and Mike Staunton. Used with permission Return on long-term corporate bonds estimated by author.

Security	Return*
Common stocks	11.4%
Long-term corporate bonds	5.7
Long-term government bonds	5.2
Short-term government bills	4.0
Consumer price index	3.1

*Arithmetic mean annual returns ignoring taxes and assuming reinvestment of all interest and dividend income.

government bonds as compensation for the risk that the corporations will default on their liabilities or call their bonds prior to maturity.

The bottom entry in Table 5.1 contains the annual percentage change in the consumer price index over the period. Subtracting the annual inflation rate from 1900 through 2010 of 3.1 percent from these nominal returns yields real, or inflation-adjusted, returns of 2.6 percent for corporates and 2.1 percent for governments.[2] Long-term bonds did little more than keep pace with inflation over this period.

Bond Ratings

Several companies analyze the investment qualities of many publicly traded bonds and publish their findings in the form of bond ratings. A bond rating is a letter grade, such as AA, assigned to an issue that reflects the analyst's appraisal of the bond's default risk. Analysts determine these ratings using many of the techniques discussed in earlier chapters, including analysis of the company's balance sheet debt ratios and its coverage ratios relative to competitors. Table 5.2 contains selected debt-rating definitions of Standard & Poor's, a major rating firm. Table 6.5 in the next chapter shows the differences in key performance ratios by rating category.

Junk Bonds

A company's bond rating is important because it affects the interest rate the company must offer. Moreover, many institutional investors are prohibited from investing in bonds that are rated less than "investment" grade, usually defined as BBB− and above. As a result, there have been periods in the past when companies with lower-rated bonds had great difficulty raising debt in public markets. Below-investment-grade bonds are known variously as *speculative*, *high-yield*, or simply *junk* bonds.

Until the emergence of a vibrant market for speculative-grade bonds in the 1980s, public debt markets were largely the preserve of huge, blue-chip corporations. Excluded from public bond markets, smaller, less prominent companies in need of debt financing were forced to rely on bank and insurance company loans. Although bond markets are still closed to most smaller businesses, the junk bond market has been a boon to many mid-size and emerging companies, which now find public debt an attractive alternative to traditional bank financing. The market has also been an important financing source to corporate raiders and private equity investors for use in highly levered transactions.

---

[2] These numbers are approximate. The exact equation is $i_r = (1 + i_n)/(1 + p) - 1$, where i_r = real return, i_n = nominal return, and p = inflation rate. Applying this equation, the real returns on corporate and government bonds are 2.5 percent and 2.0 percent, respectively.

TABLE 5.2   **Selected Standard & Poor's Debt-Rating Definitions**

Source: Standard and Poor's Long-Term Issue Credit Ratings, **www.standardpoors.com.**

A Standard & Poor's issue credit rating is a current opinion of the creditworthiness of an obligor with respect to a specific financial obligation, a specific class of financial obligations, or a specific financial program . . . It takes into consideration the creditworthiness of guarantors, insurers, or other forms of credit enhancement on the obligation and takes into account the currency in which the obligation is denominated. The issue credit rating is not a recommendation to purchase, sell, or hold a financial obligation, inasmuch as it does not comment as to market price or suitability for a particular investor. . .

Issue credit ratings are based, in varying degrees, on the following considerations:

(1) Likelihood of payment, capacity, and willingness of the obligor to meet its financial commitment on an obligation in accordance with the terms of the obligation.
(2) Nature of and provisions of the obligation.
(3) Protection afforded by, and relative position of, the obligation in the event of bankruptcy, reorganization, or other arrangement under the laws of bankruptcy and other laws affecting creditors' rights. . .

AAA An obligation rated 'AAA' has the highest rating assigned by Standard & Poor's. The obligor's capacity to meet its financial commitment on the obligation is extremely strong.

•
•

BBB An obligation rated 'BBB' exhibits adequate protection parameters. However, adverse economic conditions or changing circumstances are more likely to lead to a weakened capacity of the obligor to meet its financial commitment on the obligation.

•
•

CCC An obligation rated 'CCC' is currently vulnerable to nonpayment, and is dependent upon favorable business, financial, and economic conditions for the obligor to meet its financial commitment on the obligation. In the event of adverse business, financial, or economic conditions, the obligor is not likely to have the capacity to meet its financial commitment on the obligation.

•
•

D An obligation rated 'D' is in payment default. The 'D' rating category is used when payments on an obligation are not made on the date due even if the applicable grace period has not expired, unless Standard & Poor's believes that such payments will be made during such a grace period. The 'D' rating also will be used upon the filing of a bankruptcy petition or the taking of a similar action if payments on an obligation are jeopardized.

Plus (+) or minus (−): The ratings from 'AA' to 'CCC' may be modified by the addition of a plus (+) or minus (−) sign to show relative standing within the major rating categories.

Rating agencies have been justly criticized for their role in fostering the recent financial crisis when their ratings of complex mortgage-based securities proved to be wildly optimistic. They appear to have made two egregious errors. First, based on the review of limited historical evidence in a rapidly changing market, the agencies discounted the possibility that housing prices could fall nationwide. Their models convinced them that any decline in housing prices would be only regional, not national. As Mark Adelson, former senior director at Moody's rating agency put it later, their method was "like observing 100 years of weather in Antarctica

What Do Bond Ratings Tell Investors About the Chance of Default?

Take a look at the following figures showing bond default rates by rating category and investment horizon. The numbers span the years 1970–2006 and are from Moody's Investors Service. Note, for instance, that on average only 0.52 percent of Aaa rated bonds defaulted over a 10-year holding period, while the same figure for C rated bonds of all types was 69.25 percent. Default is clearly a distinct possibility among lower rated bonds; no wonder they carry higher interest rates.

The fact that default rates consistently rise as bond ratings fall offers convincing evidence that ratings are indeed useful predictors of default. Notice, too, the sharp break between investment grade and speculative grade bonds. At, say, a five-year investment horizon the default rate on Baa bonds—the lowest investment rating—is just under 2 percent, while the same figure for Ba bonds—the highest speculative rating—is over 10 percent.

Historical Average Cumulative Bond Default Rates 1970–2006

Bond Rating	Time Horizon (Years)		
	1	5	10
Aaa	0.00%	0.10%	0.52%
Aa	0.01%	0.18%	0.52%
A	0.02%	0.47%	1.29%
Baa	0.18%	1.94%	4.63%
Ba	1.20%	10.21%	19.10%
B	5.24%	26.79%	43.32%
Caa-C	19.47%	52.66%	69.25%

Source: Richard Cantor, David T. Hamilton, and Jennifer Tennant, Exhibit 2, "Confidence Intervals for Corporate Default Rates," 2007. Available on the Web at **ssrn.com/abstract=995545**.

to forecast the weather in Hawaii."[3] Second, the agencies all but ignored the possibility that loan origination standards might deteriorate, assuming instead that the credit quality of the mortgages underpinning the securities to be rated was constant over time. In their minds, it was not appropriate to study individual loan files because their job was to rate the quality of the securities, not the underlying mortgages. In the words of Claire Robinson, a 20-year veteran at Moody's, "We aren't loan officers. Our expertise is as statisticians on an aggregate basis."[4]

Common Stock

Common stock is a *residual income* security. The stockholder has a claim on any income remaining after the payment of all obligations, including interest on debt. If the company prospers, stockholders are the chief

---

[3] Roger Lowenstein, "Triple-A-Failure," *New York Times Magazine*, April 27, 2008.
[4] *Ibid.*

beneficiaries; if it falters, they are the chief losers. The amount of money a stockholder receives annually depends on the dividends the company chooses to pay, and the board of directors, which makes this decision quarterly, is under no obligation to pay any dividend at all.

Shareholder Control

At least in theory, stockholders exercise control over company affairs through their ability to elect the board of directors. In the United States, the wide distribution of share ownership and the laws governing election of the board have frequently combined to greatly reduce this authority, although the winds of change are blowing. In some companies, ownership of as little as 10 percent of the stock has been sufficient to control the entire board. In many others, there is no dominant shareholder group, and management has been able to control the board even if it owns little or none of the company's shares.

This does not imply that managers in such companies are free to ignore shareholder interests entirely, for they face at least two potential constraints on their actions. One is created by their need to compete in product markets. If management does not make a product or provide a service efficiently and sell it at a competitive price, the company will lose market share to more aggressive rivals and will eventually be driven from the industry. The actions managers take to compete effectively in product markets are most often consistent with shareholder interests.

Securities markets provide a second check on management discretion. If a company wants to raise debt or equity capital in future years, it must maintain its profitability to attract money from investors. Moreover, if managers ignore shareholder interests, stock price will suffer, and the firm may become the target of a hostile takeover. Even when not facing a takeover, a growing number of company boards, often prodded by large institutional shareholders, have become more diligent in monitoring management performance and replacing poor performers. In recent years, more than 20 percent of chief executive departures were forced by their boards.[5] We will have more to say about corporate takeovers and the evolving role of the board of directors in Chapter 9.

German and Japanese owners exercise much more direct control over company managements than do their U.S. or English counterparts. In Germany, the legal ability of banks to hold unlimited equity stakes in industrial companies, combined with the historical insignificance of public financial markets, has led to high concentrations of ownership in many companies. Banks are controlling shareholders of many German businesses,

---

[5] "CEO Turnover Rate" *The Economist,* May 20, 2010.

with representation on the board of directors and effective control over the business's access to debt and equity capital. German managers are thus inclined to think twice before ignoring shareholder interests.

Like their American counterparts, Japanese banks are prohibited from owning more than 5 percent of an industrial company's shares, and Japanese capital markets are more highly developed than German markets. Nonetheless, Japan's *keiretsu* form of organization produces results similar to those in Germany. As noted in the appendix to Chapter 2, a *keiretsu* is a group of companies, usually including a lead bank, that purchase sizable ownership interests in one another as a means of cementing important business relations. When the majority of a company's stock is in the hands of business partners and associates through cross-share holdings, managers ignore shareholder interests only at their peril.

Whether the more direct control exercised by German and Japanese shareholders is any better economically than the more indirect American variety is open to question. For while the German and Japanese models may facilitate a direct shareholder voice in company affairs, they also tend to encourage a clubby, "old-boy" approach to corporate governance that can be inimical to necessary change and innovation. Moreover, evidence is accumulating that both the German and Japanese approaches to corporate governance are in decline. In Germany, a growing interest on the part of companies in raising capital on public markets rather than from banks has undermined banks' authority, while in Japan an increasing emphasis on stock price performance as opposed to business relationships as the principal criterion for holding shares has recently led to sharp declines in cross-share holdings.

Common Stock as an Investment

Common stockholders receive two types of investment return: dividends and possible share price appreciation. If d_1 is the dividends per share during the year and p_0 and p_1 are the beginning-of-the-year and end-of-the-year stock price, respectively, the *annual income* a stockholder earns is

$$d_1 + p_1 - p_0$$

Dividing by the beginning-of-the-year stock price, the *annual return* is

$$\frac{\text{Annual}}{\text{return}} = \frac{\text{Dividend}}{\text{yield}} + \frac{\text{Percentage change in}}{\text{share price}}$$

$$= \frac{d_1}{p_0} + \frac{p_1 - p_0}{p_0}$$

Over the 1928–2010 period, equity investors in large-company common stocks received an average dividend yield of 3.9 percent and average capital appreciation of 7.2 percent. Over the past decade, these figures have been 1.9 percent and 1.7 percent, respectively.

Common stocks are an ownership claim against primarily real, or productive, assets. If companies can maintain profit margins during inflation, real, inflation-adjusted profits should be relatively unaffected by inflation. For years this reasoning led to the belief that common stocks are a hedge against inflation, but this did not prove to be the case during the bout of high inflation during the 1970s. Looking at Table 5.1 again, we see that had an investor purchased a representative portfolio of common stocks in 1899 and reinvested all dividends received in the same portfolio, his average annual return in 2010, over the entire 111 years, would have been 11.4 percent. However, from 1973 through 1981, a period when prices rose an average of 9.2 percent a year, the average annual nominal return on common stocks was only 5.2 percent. This implies a negative *real* return of about 4 percent. The comparable figures for corporate bonds over this period were a nominal return of 2.5 percent and a negative real return of about 6.7 percent.

The common stock return of 11.4 percent from 1900 through 2010 compares with a return of 5.2 percent on government bonds over the same period. The difference between the two numbers of 6.2 percent can be thought of as a *risk premium*, the extra return common stockholders earned as compensation for the added risks they bore. Comparing the return on common stocks to the annual percentage change in consumer prices, we see that the *real* return to common stock investors over the period was about 8.3 percent (11.4% − 3.1%).

Figure 5.1 presents much of the same information more dramatically. It shows an investor's wealth at year-end 2010 had she invested $1 in various assets at year-end 1899. Common stocks are the clear winners here. By 2010, the original $1 investment in common stock would have grown to a whopping $21,766. In contrast, $1 invested in long-term government bonds would have been worth only $191 in 2010. Reflecting the pernicious effect of inflation, the corresponding real numbers are $850.70 for common stock

---

Do Dividends Increase Annual Return?

It may appear from the preceding equation that annual return rises when dividends rise. But the world is not so simple. An increase in current dividends means one of two things: The company will have less money to invest, or it will have to raise more money from external sources to make the same investments. Either way, an increase in current dividends reduces the stockholders' claim on future cash flow, which reduces share price appreciation. Depending on which effect dominates, annual returns may or may not increase as dividends rise.

FIGURE 5.1 **If Your Great-Grandmother Had Invested Only a Dollar in 1900; Nominal Returns on U.S. Assets, 1900–2010**

(Assumed initial investment of $1 at year-end 1899; includes reinvestment income.)

Source: Elroy Dimson, Paul Marsh, and Mike Staunton, *Credit Suisse Global Investment Returns Sourcebook. 172.* Copyright © 2011 E. Dimson, P. Marsh, and M. Staunton. Used with permission.

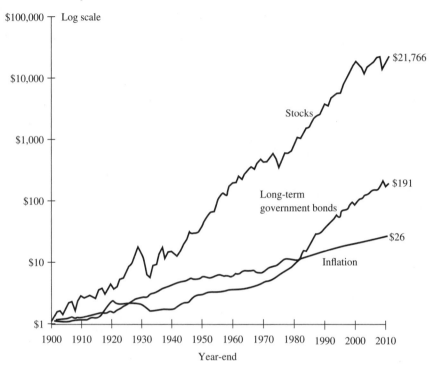

and $7.50 for government bonds. Common stocks, however, have proven to be a much more volatile investment than bonds, as Figure 5.2 attests.

Preferred Stock

Preferred stock is a hybrid security: like debt in some ways, like equity in others. Like debt, preferred stock is a fixed-income security. It promises the investor an annual fixed dividend equal to the security's coupon rate times its par value. Like equity, the board of directors need not distribute this dividend unless it chooses. Also like equity, preferred dividend payments are *not* a deductible expense for corporate tax purposes. For the same coupon rate, this makes the *after-tax* cost of bonds about two-thirds that of preferred shares. Another similarity with equity is that although preferred stock may have a call option, it frequently has no maturity. The preferred shares are outstanding indefinitely unless the company chooses to call them.

FIGURE 5.2 **Distribution of Annual Return on Stocks and Bonds, 1928–2010**

Source: Professor Aswath Damodaran's Website: **pages.stern.nyu.edu/~adamodar/.**

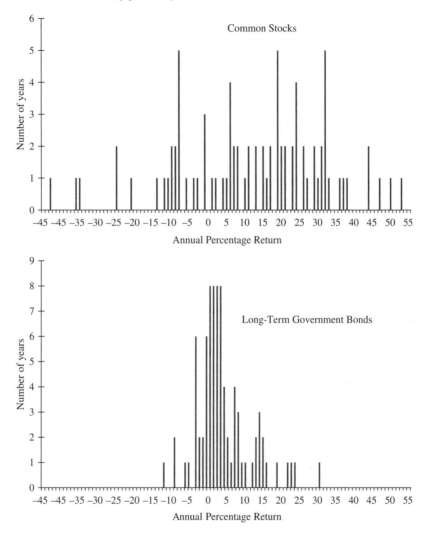

Cumulative Preferred

Company boards of directors have two strong incentives to pay preferred dividends. One is that preferred shareholders have priority over common shareholders with respect to dividend payments. Common shareholders receive no dividends unless preferred holders are paid in full. Second, virtually all preferred stocks are *cumulative*. If a firm passes a preferred dividend, the arrearage accumulates and must be paid in full before the company can resume common dividend payments.

The control preferred shareholders have over management decisions varies. In some instances, preferred shareholders' approval is routinely required for major decisions; in others, preferred shareholders have no voice in management unless dividend payments are in arrears.

Preferred stock is not a widely used form of financing. Some managers see preferred stock as *cheap equity*. They observe that preferred stock gives management much of the flexibility regarding dividend payments and maturity dates that common equity provides. Yet because preferred shareholders have no right to participate in future growth, they see preferred stock as less expensive than equity. The majority, however, see preferred stock as *debt with a tax disadvantage*. Because few companies would ever omit a preferred dividend payment unless absolutely forced to, most managers place little value on the flexibility of preferred stock. To them the important fact is that interest payments on bonds are tax deductible, whereas dividend payments on preferred stock are not.

Financial Markets

Having reviewed the basic security types, let us now turn to the markets in which these securities are issued and traded. Of particular interest will be the provocative notion of market efficiency.

Broadly speaking, financial markets are the channels through which investors provide money to companies. Because these channels differ greatly depending on the nature of the company and securities involved, they can best be described by considering the financing needs of three representative firms: a startup, a candidate for an initial public offering, and a multinational. Although these brief vignettes certainly do not exhaust the topic, I hope they offer a useful overview of financial markets and their more important participants.

Private Equity Financing

Janet Holmes has developed a promising new medical device and now wants to start a company to capitalize on her research. Her problem is determining where to find the financing. After a brief inquiry, she learns that conventional financing sources such as bank loans and public stock or bond offerings are out of the question. Her venture is far too risky to qualify for a bank loan and too small to attract public funding. A banker has expressed interest in a small loan collateralized by accounts receivable, machinery, and any personal assets she owns, but this will not be nearly enough. Instead, it looks as if Janet will have to rely primarily on the traditional four-Fs of new venture financing: founders, family, friends, and fools. Other possible financing sources are strategic investors and venture capitalists, from whom Ms. Holmes might legitimately aspire to raise as much as $15 million in return for a large fraction, possibly controlling interest, of her new company.

Strategic investors are operating companies—frequently potential competitors—that make significant equity investments in startups as a way to gain access to promising new products and technology. Some strategic investors, including Microsoft, Intel, and Cisco Systems, have come to view new venture investing as a means of outsourcing research and development. Rather than develop all new products in-house, they sprinkle money across a number of promising startups, expecting to acquire any that prove successful.

Venture capitalists come in two flavors: wealthy individuals, often referred to as "angel investors," and professional venture capital companies. Venture capital companies are financial investors who make high-risk equity investments in entrepreneurial businesses deemed capable of rapid growth and high investment returns. They purchase a significant fraction of a company and take an active policy role in management. Their goal is to liquidate the investment in five or six years when the company goes public or sells out to another firm. Venture capital firms routinely consider dozens of candidates for every investment made and expect to suffer a number of failures for each investment success. In return, they expect winners to return 5 to 10 times their initial investment. Most of their investments are in technology firms of one kind or another.

Venture capital companies are prominent examples of what are known as "private equity" firms. Although private equity firms invest in a wide variety of opportunities, including new ventures, leveraged buyouts, and distressed businesses, they all share two important traits: their investments are high-risk, and they employ an unusual organizational form known as a private equity partnership. Instead of the conventional public-company form, private equity investments are structured as limited partnerships with a specified duration, usually of 10 years. Acting as the general partner, the private equity firm raises a pool of money from limited partners, consisting primarily of institutional investors, such as pension funds, college endowments, and insurance companies. As limited partners, these investors enjoy the same limited liability protections afforded conventional shareholders. The private equity sponsor then invests the money raised, actively manages the investments for a period of years, liquidates the portfolio, and returns the proceeds to the limited partners. In return, the private equity firm charges the limited partners handsome fees consisting of an annual management charge equaling about 2 percent of the original investment, plus what is known as *carried interest*, typically 20 percent or more of any capital appreciation earned on the portfolio. For example, the carried interest on a $1 billion portfolio subsequently liquidated for $3 billion would be $400 million ($400 million = 20% × [$3 billion − $1 billion]). At any one time, private equity firms may be managing a number of limited partnerships of differing size and years to maturity.

Private equity partnerships are becoming increasingly popular investment vehicles because they appear to address several incentive problems inherent in more conventional investment forms.

- The partnership form minimizes any differences between owners and managers. As knowledgeable, active owners, private equity investors make it clear that management works for them and that their goal is not to meet artificial short-run earnings targets, but to create value for owners.

- The fixed life of the partnership imposes an aggressive, buy-fix-sell attitude on managers, prompting them to take decisive actions.

- As Dave Barry might put it, the limited time horizon also assures investors that they will eventually get their money back, rather than having to stand by idly watching management feed it to chipmunks.

How big is the private equity business? Big. Malcolm Gladwell, in his *New Yorker* story on the rescue of General Motors, notes "In the past twenty-five years, private equity has risen from obscurity to become one of the most powerful forces in the American economy."[6] According to *The Economist*, "When the Service Employees International Union (SEIU) added up the numbers of workers at the companies in [private equity] firms' portfolios, it found that five of the ten biggest American employers were private-equity firms. KKR with 826,710 workers in its domain (from HCA, a health-care giant, to Toys "R" Us, a retailer) is second only to Walmart, the world's largest retailer, which has 1.9m employees worldwide."[7]

Initial Public Offerings

Genomic Devices got its start six years ago when it raised $15 million from three venture capital firms. After two more rounds of venture financing totaling $40 million, Genomic is now a national company with sales of $125 million and an annual growth rate of more than 40 percent. To finance this rapid growth, management estimates the company needs another $25 million

---

[6]Malcolm Gladwell, "Overdrive: Who Really Rescued General Motors?" *The New Yorker,* November 1, 2010.
[7]"Face value: Bashing the Barbarians," *The Economist,* August 2, 2008.

equity infusion. At the same time, company founders and venture capital investors are anxious to see some cash from their years of toil. This has led to active consideration of an initial public offering (IPO) of common stock. By creating a public market for the company's shares, an IPO will provide desired liquidity to existing owners as well as supplying necessary funding.

Investment Banking

Genomic Devices' first step toward an IPO will be to conduct what is known in the trade as a "bake-off." This involves reviewing proposals from several investment bankers detailing the mechanics of how they would sell the new shares and what a great job each could do for the company. Investment bankers can be thought of as the grease that keeps financial markets running smoothly. They are finance specialists who assist companies in raising money. Other activities include stock and bond brokerage, investment counseling, merger and acquisition analysis, corporate consulting and proprietary trading with their own money. Some banking companies, such as Bank of America, employ thousands of brokers and have offices all over the world. Others, such as Lazard Ltd., specialize in working with companies or trading securities, and consequently are less in the public eye. As to the range of services provided, H. F. Saint said it best in his Wall Street thriller *Memoirs of an Invisible Man:* "[Investment bankers] perform all sorts of interesting services and acts—in fact any service or act that can be performed in a suit, this being the limitation imposed by their professional ethics."[8]

When a company is about to raise new capital on public markets, an investment banker's responsibilities are not unlike his fees: many and varied. (Capital raising techniques differ from one country to another depending on custom and law. In the interest of space, and with apologies to non-American readers, I will confine my comments here to the American scene.) The winner of the bake-off receives the mantle "managing underwriter" and immediately begins advising the company on detailed design of the security to be issued. Then the banker helps the company register the issue with the SEC. This usually takes 30 to 90 days and includes detailed public disclosure of information about the company's finances, its officer compensation, plans, and so on—information some managements would prefer to keep confidential.

While the registration wends its way toward approval, the managing underwriter orchestrates the "road show," during which top company executives market the issue to institutional investors in New York and other financial centers. The managing underwriter also puts together a

---

[8]H. F. Saint, *Memoirs of an Invisible Man* (New York: Dell, 1987), p. 290.

selling and an *underwriting syndicate*. A syndicate is a team of as many as 100 or more investment banking firms that join forces for a brief time to sell new securities. Each member of the selling syndicate accepts responsibility for selling a specified portion of the new securities to investors. Members of the underwriting syndicate in effect act as wholesalers, purchasing all of the securities from the company at a guaranteed price and attempting to sell them to the public at a higher price. The "Rules of Fair Practice" of the National Association of Securities Dealers prohibit underwriters from selling new securities to the public at a price above the original offer price quoted to the company. If necessary, however, the syndicate may sell them at a lower price.

Given the volatility of stock markets and the length of time required to go through registration, it may appear that underwriters bear significant risks when they guarantee the issuer a fixed price for the shares. This is not the way the world works, however. Underwriters do not commit themselves to a firm price on a new security until just hours before the sale, and if all goes as planned, the entire issue will be sold to the public on the first day of offer. It is the company, not the underwriters, that bears the risk that the terms on which the securities can be sold will change during registration.

The life of a syndicate is brief. Syndicates form several months prior to an issue for the purpose of "building the book," or preselling the issue, and disband as soon as the securities are sold. Even on unsuccessful issues, the syndicate breaks up several weeks after the issue date, leaving the underwriters to dispose of their unsold shares on their own. I will have more to say about the issue costs and pricing of IPOs in a few paragraphs.

Seasoned Issues

Our third representative firm in need of financing is Trilateral Enterprises, a multinational consumer products company with annual sales of almost $90 billion. Trilateral wants to raise $200 million in new debt and has narrowed the choices down to a "shelf registration," a "private placement," or an international issue executed through the company's Netherlands Antilles subsidiary.

Shelf Registration

First authorized in 1982, a shelf registration allows frequent security issuers to avoid the cumbersome traditional registration process by filing a general-purpose registration, good for up to two years, indicating in broad terms the securities the company may decide to issue. Once the registration is approved by the SEC, and provided it is updated periodically, the company can put the registration on the "shelf," ready for use as desired. A shelf registration cuts the time lag between the decision to issue a security and receipt of the proceeds from several months to as little as 48 hours. Because 48 hours is far too little time for investment bankers to throw a syndicate together, shelf registrations tend to be "bought deals" in which a single investment house buys the entire issue in the hope of reselling it piecemeal at a profit. Also, because it is just as easy for the issuer to get price quotes from two banks as from one, shelf registrations increase the likelihood of competitive bidding among banks. As a result, issue costs for shelf-registered issues are as much as 10 percent to 50 percent lower than for traditionally registered issues, depending on the type of security and other factors.[9]

Shelf-registered equity issues are also possible. When first authorized in 1990, such issues were quite rare, but recent figures indicate they are growing rapidly in popularity and now account for something like half of all money raised in seasoned equity issues.[10] (A seasoned equity issue, or SEO, refers to an equity issue by a company that is already publicly traded. It contrasts with an initial public offering, undertaken by a private firm.) Companies appear attracted to shelf-registered equity because it enables them to time issues in response to temporary stock price movements. Moreover, the advent of "universal" shelf registrations, covering both debt and equity issues, allows the issuer to defer the choice of whether to issue debt or equity to a later date, and enables management to avoid signaling investors that it is even considering an equity issue. I will have more to say about market signaling in the next chapter.

Private Placement

If it wishes, Trilateral Enterprises can avoid SEC registration entirely by placing its debt privately with one or more large institutional investors. The SEC does not regulate such private placements on the expectation that large investors, such as insurance companies and pension funds, can fend for themselves without government protection. Because private placements are unregulated, there are no accurate figures on the size of the market. Best guesses are that, excluding bank loans, private placements are about half the size of public markets in terms of total funds provided.[11]

---

[9]Robert J. Rogowski and Eric H. Sorensen, "Deregulation in Investment Banking, Shelf Registrations, Structure, and Performance," *Financial Management,* Spring 1985, pp. 5–15. See also Sanjai Bhagat, M. Wayne Marr, and G. Rodney Thompson, "The Rule 415 Experiment: Equity Markets," *Journal of Finance,* December 1985, pp. 1385–1402.

[10]Bernardo Bortolotti, William L. Megginson, and Scott B. Smart, "The Rise of Accelerated Seasoned Equity Underwritings," FEEM Working Paper, January 11, 2007. **ssrn.com/abstract=957389**. See also Don Autore, Raman Kumar, and Dilip Shome, "The Revival of Shelf-Registered Corporate Equity Offerings," *Journal of Corporate Finance,* Vol.14 No.1, 2008.

[11]Stephen D. Prowse, "The Economics of Private Placements: Middle-Market Corporate Finance, Life Insurance Companies, and a Credit Crunch," *Economic Review,* Federal Reserve Bank of Dallas, Third Quarter 1997, pp. 12–24. **www.dallasfed.org/research/er/1997/er9703b.pdf**.

Private placements are especially attractive to smaller, less well-known firms and to so-called "information-problematic" companies whose complex organization structures or financing needs make them difficult for individual investors to evaluate. Private placements can also be custom-tailored to specific company needs, arranged quickly, and renegotiated as needed with comparative ease.

A major disadvantage of private placements has traditionally been that as unregistered securities the SEC prohibits their purchase or sale on public financial markets. As a result, issuers have historically found it necessary to offer more favorable terms on private placements than on public issues to compensate for their lack of liquidity. This began to change, at least for less information-problematic issuers, in 1990 when the SEC released Rule 144A permitting the trading of private placements among large institutional investors. Rule 144A is part of a determined effort by the SEC to encourage what are essentially two parallel markets for corporate securities: a closely regulated public market for individual investors and a more loosely monitored private market for institutional investors.

International Markets

Large corporations can raise money on any of three types of markets: *domestic*, *foreign*, or *international*. A domestic financial market is the market in the company's home country, while foreign markets are the domestic markets of other countries. U.S. financial markets are thus domestic to IBM and General Motors but foreign to Sony Corporation and British Petroleum; Japanese markets are domestic to Sony but foreign to IBM, General Motors, and British Petroleum.

Companies find it attractive to raise money in foreign markets for a variety of reasons. When the domestic market is small or poorly developed, a company may find that only foreign markets are large enough to absorb the contemplated issue. Companies may also want liabilities denominated in the foreign currency instead of their own. For example, when Walt Disney expanded into Japan, it sought yen-denominated liabilities to reduce the foreign exchange risk created by its yen-denominated revenues. Finally, issuers may believe foreign-denominated liabilities will prove cheaper than domestic ones in view of anticipated exchange rate changes.

Access to foreign financial markets has historically been a sometime thing. The Swiss and Japanese governments have frequently restricted access to their markets by limiting the aggregate amount of money foreigners may raise in a given time period or imposing firm size and credit quality constraints on foreign issuers. Even U.S. markets, the largest and time. In contrast, the issuer of a registered security maintains records of the owner and the payments made. Because bearer securities facilitate tax avoidance, they are illegal in the United States. This is why Trilateral Enterprises anticipates issuing their bonds to non-U.S. residents through its Netherlands Antilles subsidiary. The use of bearer bonds in international markets means international bonds can carry lower coupon rates than comparable domestic bonds and still yield the same after-tax returns.

The ability of international financial markets to draw business away from domestic markets has sharply accelerated the deregulation of domestic financial markets. As long as companies and investors can avoid onerous domestic regulations by simply migrating to international markets, regulators face a Hobson's choice: They can either remove the offending regulations or keep the regulations and watch international markets grow at the expense of domestic ones. The interest equalization tax is an apt example. When first imposed, the tax had the desired effect of restricting foreign companies' access to dollar financing. Over time, however, borrowers found they could avoid the tax by simply going to the international markets. The longer-run effect of the IET, therefore, was to shift business away from the United States without greatly affecting the total volume of dollar financing. Indeed, an avowed goal in repealing the IET was to make U.S. markets more competitive with international markets.

Some wonder if we are starting down a similar path with recent legislation intended to strengthen U.S. public markets. The concern is that the long-term effect of regulatory initiatives, including the Sarbanes-Oxley Act of 2002 and the Dodd-Frank Wall Street Reform and Consumer Protection Act of 2010, will be simply to drive business offshore and on to private markets. Although largely circumstantial, evidence consistent with this concern is accumulating. It includes diminished IPO activity over the past decade,[12] apparent increased popularity of going-private transactions among smaller public companies,[13] growth of unregulated private markets, called "shadow markets," on which investors can buy and trade shares of private companies, and decisions by Facebook, Twitter, and other hot IPO prospects to defer public issues.

Not all regulations are bad, of course. Regulatory oversight of financial markets and the willingness of governments to combat financial panics have greatly stabilized markets and economies for over 70 years. The ongoing question is whether the recent wave of new regulations improves public markets or drives business to less fettered, murkier locales. Stay tuned.

[12]Craig Doidge, George Karolyi, and Rene Stulz, "The U.S. Left Behind: The Rise of IPO Activity Around the World," Charles A. Dice Center working paper, March 25, 2011. **ssrn.com/abstract=1795423**.
[13]Ellen Engel, Rachel Hayes, and Xue Wang "The Sarbanes-Oxley Act and Firms' Going-Private Decisions," *Journal of Accounting and Economics,* September 2007.

traditionally most open markets in the world, have not alv
restricted access to foreigners. Beginning in the late 1960s
for almost a decade, foreign borrowers in the United Sta
to a surcharge known as the interest equalization tax (IE
purportedly to compensate for low U.S. interest rates, bu
saw it as an attempt to bolster a weak dollar in foreign e:
by constraining foreign borrowing.

The third type of market on which companies can rai
national financial markets, is best viewed as a free marke
regulatory constraints endemic in domestic and foreign i
action is said to occur in the international financial marl
currency employed is outside the control of the issuing r
ity. A dollar-denominated loan to an American compa
euro-denominated loan to a Japanese company in Singap
pound bond issue by a Dutch company underwritten in
examples of international financial market transactions.
the transaction occurs in a locale that is beyond the direc
of the issuing monetary authority. Thus, the U.S. Fe⟨
trouble regulating banking activities in London even w
involve American companies and are denominated in
the European Central Bank has difficulty regulating
Singapore.

International financial markets got their start in Lo
World War II and were originally limited to dollar trans
From this beginning, the markets have grown enormo
most major currencies and trading centers around
international financial markets give companies acces:
capital, at very competitive prices, with minimal regul
requirements.

Two important reasons international markets have
offer lower-cost financing than domestic markets are
serve requirements on international bank deposits
issue bonds in what is known as *bearer form*. In the
many other domestic markets, banks must abide k
ments stipulating that they place a portion of each ⟨
account at the central bank. Because these reserv⟨
without yielding a competitive return, domestic l
higher interest rate than international loans to yield

The chief appeal of bearer bonds is that they make i
to avoid paying taxes on interest income. The comp
bond never knows the bond's owners and simply make
pal payments to anyone who presents the proper coup⟨

Issue Costs

Financial securities impose two kinds of costs on the issuer: annual costs, such as interest expense, and issue costs. We will consider the more important annual costs later. Issue costs are the costs the issuer and its shareholders incur on initial sale. For privately negotiated transactions, the only substantive cost is the fee charged by the investment banker in his or her capacity as agent. On a public issue, there are legal, accounting, and printing fees, plus those paid to the managing underwriter. The managing underwriter states his fee in the form of a *spread*. To illustrate, suppose ABC Corporation is a publicly traded company that wants to sell 10 million new shares of common stock using traditional registration procedures, and its shares presently trade at $20 on the New York Stock Exchange. A few hours prior to public sale, the managing underwriter might inform ABC management, "Given the present tone of the markets, we can sell the new shares at an issue price of $19.00 and a spread of $1.50, for a net to the company of $17.50 per share." This means the investment banker intends to *underprice* the issue $1.00 per share ($20 market price less $19 issue price) and is charging a fee of $1.50 per share, or $15 million, for his services. This fee will be split among the managing underwriter and the syndicate members by prior arrangement according to each bank's importance in the syndicates.

To underprice an issue means to offer the new shares at a price below that of existing shares, or in the case of an IPO, below the market price of the shares shortly after the issue is completed. One obvious motivation investment bankers have for underpricing is to make their own job easier. Selling something worth $20 for $19 is a lot easier than selling for $20. But there appears to be more to the practice than this. In any public sale of securities, well-informed insiders are selling paper of uncertain value to less informed outsiders. One way to quell outsiders' natural concern with being victimized by insiders is to consistently underprice new issues. This gives uninformed buyers the expectation the shares will more likely rise than fall after issue. Underpricing is not an out-of-pocket cost to the company, but it is a cost to shareholders. The greater the underpricing, the more securities a company must issue to raise a given amount of money. If the securities are bonds, this translates into higher interest expense, and if they are shares, it translates into a reduced percentage ownership for existing owners.

Empirical studies of issue costs confirm two prominent patterns. First, equity is much more costly than debt. Representative costs of raising capital in public markets, ignoring underpricing, average about 2.2 percent of proceeds for straight debt, 3.8 percent for convertible bonds, and 7.1 percent for offerings of equity by publicly traded companies. This figure rises to

Despite its occasional complexity, operating executives need to understand the basics of financial risk management for at least three reasons:

- Statistics put the total value of derivative contracts of all types outstanding in mid-2010 at $583 *trillion*.[1] While the amount of money actually at risk is closer to "only" $10 *trillion*, the markets are huge by any measure, and size alone warrants a basic familiarity.

- The fact that a number of otherwise sophisticated companies, including Procter & Gamble and Volkswagen, have reported multimillion-dollar losses on what were originally intended as risk-reducing activities highlights the damage derivative securities can wreak in the wrong hands. All executives need to appreciate the risks of misusing derivatives and how best to avoid them.

- Financial risk management is an indisputably valuable activity, but not a panacea. Executives throughout the firm need a clear understanding of what the techniques can and cannot do if they are to use them effectively.

This appendix looks briefly at two important weapons in the manager's risk management arsenal: forward contracts and options. We begin by examining the use of these weapons to implement a simple risk management technique known as hedging. The appendix concludes with a brief overview of the determinants of an option's value and how to price it. In the interest of brevity, I will confine the hedging discussion to the task of managing foreign exchange risks, although I might just as well have focused on interest rate, commodity price, or credit risks. The story in each instance would be much the same. (For a more in-depth look at financial risk management, I recommend one of the following books.[2])

Forward Markets

Most markets are *spot* markets, in which a price is set today for immediate exchange. In a *forward* market, the price is set today but exchange occurs at some stipulated future date. Buying bread at the grocery store is a spot market transaction, while reserving a hotel room to be paid for later is a forward market transaction. Most assets trading in forward

---

[1]Bank for International Settlements, Table 19: Amounts outstanding of over-the-counter (OTC) derivatives, **www.bis.org/statistics/derstats.htm**.

[2]Michael Crouhy, Dan Galei, and Robert Mark, *Essentials of Risk Management* (New York: McGraw-Hill, 2005). Steven Allen, *Financial Risk Management: A Practitioner's Guide to Managing Market and Credit Risk* (New York: John Wiley & Sons, 2003).

markets also trade spot. To illustrate these markets, the spot price of one euro today in currency markets is $1.4892, meaning payment of this amount will buy one euro for immediate delivery. In contrast, the 180-day forward rate is $1.4805, meaning payment of this slightly smaller amount in 180 days will buy one euro for delivery at that time. A forward transaction involves an irrevocable contract, most likely with a bank, in which the parties set the price today at which they will trade euros for dollars at a future date.

Speculating in Forward Markets

Although our focus in this appendix is on risk avoidance, we will begin at the opposite end of the spectrum by looking at forward market speculation. As you will see, speculation—especially the creative use of one speculation to counteract another—is the essence of the risk management techniques to be described. To demonstrate this important fact, imagine that an irresistible impulse has prompted you to remortgage your home and bet $100,000 on the New York Knicks to beat the Boston Celtics in an upcoming basketball game. Your spouse, however, is not amused to learn of your wager and threatens serious consequences unless you immediately cancel the bet. But, of course, bets are seldom canceled without a broken kneecap or two.

So what do you do? You hedge your bet. Acknowledging your mother was wrong all those years ago—that two wrongs may indeed make one right—you place a second wager, but this time on the Celtics to beat the Knicks. Now, no matter who wins, the proceeds from your winning wager will cover the cost of your losing one, and except for the bookie's take, it's just as though you had never made the first bet. You have covered your bet. Companies use financial market "wagers" analogously to manage unavoidable commercial risks.

For a closer look at forward market speculation, suppose the treasurer of American Merchandising, Inc. (AMI) believes the euro will weaken dramatically over the next six months. Forward currency markets offer a simple way for the treasurer to bet on his belief by executing a modest variation on the old "buy-low, sell-high" strategy. Here he will sell high first and buy low later: sell euros forward today at $1.4805, wait 180 days as the euro plummets, and then purchase euros in the spot market for delivery on the forward contract. If the treasurer is correct, the forward price at which he sells the euros today will exceed the spot price at which he buys them in six months, and he will profit from the difference. Of course, the reverse is also possible: If the euro strengthens relative to the dollar, the forward selling price could be below the spot buying price, and the treasurer will lose money.

Putting this into equation form, the treasurer's gain or loss on, say, a €1 million forward sale is

$$\text{Gain or loss} = (F - \tilde{S})\,€1 \text{ million}$$

where F is the 180-day forward price and $\tilde{S}$ is the spot price 180 days hence. The spot price has a tilde over it as a reminder that it is unknown today.

A convenient way to represent such transactions is with a *position diagram* showing the transaction's gain or loss on the vertical axis as a function of the uncertain future spot rate. As Figure 5A.1(a) shows, the treasurer's gamble is a winner when the future spot price is below today's forward rate and a loser when it is above that rate. We will refer to this and similar position diagrams throughout the appendix.

Hedging in Forward Markets

We are now ready to see how currency speculation can reduce the risk of loss on cross-border transactions. Set aside the treasurer's bet on the euro for a moment and suppose AMI has just booked a €1 million sale to a German buyer, with payment to be received in 180 days. The dollar value of this account receivable, of course, depends on the future exchange rate. In symbols,

$$\$ \text{ Value of AMI's receivable} = \tilde{S}(€1 \text{ million})$$

where $\tilde{S}$ is again the spot exchange rate. AMI faces foreign exchange risk, or exposure, because the dollar value of its German receivable in six months depends on the uncertain, future spot rate.

Figure 5A.1(b) is a position diagram for AMI's account receivable. It shows the change in the dollar value of AMI's receivable as the exchange rate changes. If the spot rate remains at $1.4892, the receivable will show neither a gain nor a loss in value, but as the price of the euro changes, so does the value of the receivable. In particular, an unlucky fall in the euro in coming months could turn an expected profit on the German sale into a loss—not exactly a morale booster for the operating folks who worked so hard to make the sale.

By generating the German account receivable, AMI has inadvertently bet that the euro will strengthen. If it wants to shed this risk, it can easily do so by instructing the treasurer to place an offsetting bet in the forward market. In this instance, the treasurer needs to sell €1 million 180 days forward, just as before. Upon adding the gain or loss on the forward sale

FIGURE 5A.1   **Forward Market Hedge**

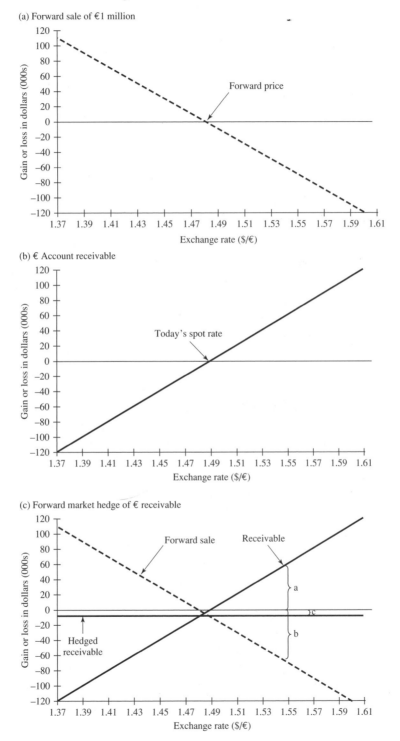

(a) Forward sale of €1 million

(b) € Account receivable

(c) Forward market hedge of € receivable

to the dollar value of the account receivable, we find that AMI has "locked in" a value for the German receivable of $1,480,500:

$$\text{Gain or loss on forward sale} + \text{\$ Value of receivable}$$

$$(F - \tilde{S}) \text{€} 1 \text{ million} + (\tilde{S}) \text{€} 1 \text{ million}$$

$$= (F) \text{€} 1 \text{ million}$$

$$= (\$1.4805) \text{€} 1 \text{ million}$$

$$= \$1,480,500$$

The elimination of $\tilde{S}$ from the equation indicates that the treasurer's judicious combination of two opposing bets eliminates AMI's currency exposure. Now, regardless of what happens to the spot rate, AMI will receive $1,480,500 in 180 days. The treasurer has executed a *forward market hedge,* the effect of which is to replace the unknown future spot rate with the known forward rate in determining the dollar value of the receivable. AMI has locked in the forward rate.

How does the forward market hedge differ from the forward market speculation described earlier? It doesn't; the transactions are identical. The only difference is one of intent. In the speculation, the treasurer intends to benefit from his belief that the euro will fall. In the hedge, the treasurer presumably has no opinion about the euro's future price and intends only to avoid the risk of losing money on the account receivable. When the same transaction can be either a risky speculation or a risk-reducing hedge depending only on the intent of the person rolling the dice, it should come as no surprise to learn that companies frequently have trouble controlling their risk management activities.

Figure 5A.1(c) shows the forward market hedge graphically. The solid, upward-sloping line is the gain or loss on the unhedged receivable from (b), while the dotted, downward-sloping line is the position diagram for the forward sale from (a). The bold horizontal line represents the combined effect of the receivable and the forward sale. When both are undertaken, the *net* outcome is independent of the future spot rate. The forward hedge eliminates risk just as opposing bets on the Celtics–Knicks game did.

Instead of manipulating equations to determine the net effect of hedging, it is usually simpler to do the same thing graphically by adding the position diagram from one bet to that of the other at each exchange rate. For instance, adding the gain on the receivable, denoted by *a* in Figure 5A.1(c), to the loss on the forward sale, *b*, yields the net result, *c*. The fact that the net result at each exchange rate lies on a horizontal line confirms that the value of the hedged receivable does not depend on the future spot rate. In other words, the hedge eliminates exchange risk.[3]

Hedging in Money and Capital Markets

The treasurer eliminated exchange risk on AMI's euro asset by creating a euro liability of precisely the same size and maturity. In the jargon of the trader, he *covered* the company's *long position* by creating an offsetting *short position*, where a long position refers to a foreign-currency asset and a short position corresponds to a foreign-currency liability. By offsetting one against the other, he *squared* the position.

A second way to create a short position in euros is to borrow euros today, promising to repay 1 million euros in 180 days, and sell the euros immediately in the spot market for dollars. Then, in 180 days, the 1 million euros received in payment of the account receivable can be used to repay the loan. After the dust settles, such a *money market* hedge enables AMI to receive a known sum of dollars today in return for 1 million euros in 180 days. As you might expect in efficient markets, the costs of hedging in forward markets and in money and capital markets are almost identical.

Hedging with Options

Options are for those who tire of Russian roulette—unless, of course, the options are one leg of a hedge. An *option* is a security entitling the holder to either buy or sell an underlying asset at a specified price and for a specified time. Options come in two flavors: A *put* option conveys the right to sell the underlying asset, while a *call* is the right to buy it. To illustrate, for a payment of $48,800 today, you can purchase *put* options on the euro giving you the right to sell €1 million for $1.49 each at any time over the next 180 days. As a matter of semantics, $1.49 is known as the option's *exercise*, or *strike*, price, and 180 days is its *maturity*. The $48,800 purchase price, payable today, is referred to as the *premium*.

Figure 5A.2(a) shows the position diagram for these put options at maturity for different exchange rates. The lower, dotted line includes the premium, while the solid line omits it. Concentrating first on the solid

---

[3]The hedged position in Figure 5A.1(c) appears to result in a loss. But this is not correct. Instead, the apparent loss is a mechanical result of the fact that the euro is at a forward discount to the dollar, which, in turn, is due to the fact that euro area interest rates are above U.S. rates. If the euro were not at a forward discount, U.S. investors could earn riskless arbitrage profits by borrowing dollars, buying euros spot, investing the euros at attractive rates, and selling the proceeds forward for dollars. Hence, the euro must sell at a forward discount. A hedge involves an expected loss only when the forward rate is below the treasurer's *expected future* spot rate, not the current rate. The figure implicitly assumes the treasurer's expected future spot rate equals the current spot, which clearly need not be true.

FIGURE 5A.2 **Option Market Hedge**

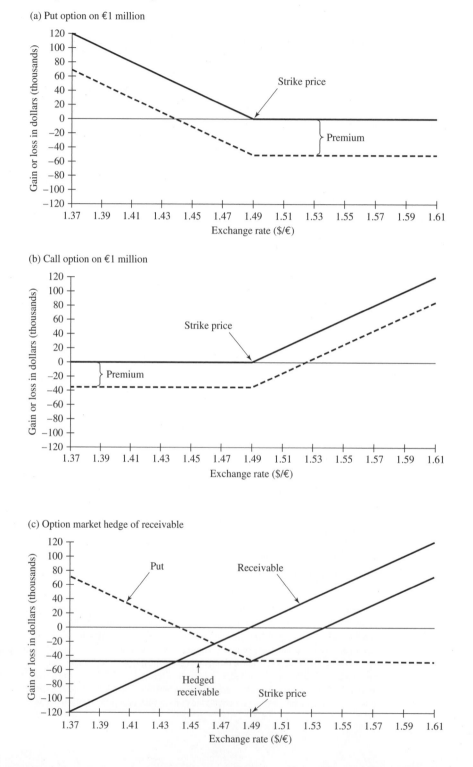

(a) Put option on €1 million

(b) Call option on €1 million

(c) Option market hedge of receivable

line, we see that the puts are worthless at maturity when the spot exchange rate exceeds the option's strike price. The right to sell euros for $1.49 each obviously isn't very enticing when they command a higher price in the spot market. In this event, the options will expire worthless, and you will have spent the $48,800 premium for nothing. The outcome is very different, however, when the spot rate is below the strike price at maturity. If the spot exchange rate falls to $1.45, for instance, the option to sell € 1 million at $1.49 is worth $40,000, and this number rises rapidly as the euro sinks further toward zero. In the best of all worlds (provided you're not European), the euro will be worthless, and your puts will garner $1.49 million—not a bad return on a $48,800 investment.

The position diagram for call options is just the reverse of that for puts. Based on today's closing prices, 180-day call options on € 1 million with a strike price of $1.49 are available for a premium of approximately $37,100. As shown in Figure 5A.2(b), these calls will expire worthless unless the spot price rises above the strike price; the right to buy something for more than its spot price has no value. But once above the strike price, the value of the calls rises penny for penny with the spot.

To understand why options appeal to serious speculators, suppose you believe the euro will rise to $1.55 in six months. Using the forward market to speculate on your belief, you can purchase € 1 million forward today for $1.4805 each and sell them in six months for $1.55, thereby generating a return of 4.4 percent [(1.55 − 1.4805)/1.4805 = 4.4]. Alternatively, you can purchase the call options for $37,100, followed in six months by exercise of the call and immediate sale of the euros for $1.55 each, thereby producing a heart-skipping return of 62 percent ([(1.55 − 1.49) × $1 million − $37,100]/$37,000 = 62%)—more than 10 times higher than the forward market speculation. Of course, the downside risks are equally stimulating; a fall in the euro to $1.43 would generate a loss of only 3.2 percent in the forward market compared to a 262 percent loss with options.

How might AMI use options to reduce exchange risk on the company's German receivable? Because the receivable makes the company long in euros, the treasurer will want to create an offsetting short position; that is, he will want to purchase put options. Calls would only add to AMI's currency risk.

Analyzing the hedge graphically, Figure 5A.2(c) shows the combined effect of AMI's German receivable and purchase of the described put options. As before, the upward-sloping, solid line represents the gain or loss in the dollar value of the receivable, and the bent, dotted line shows the payoff on the puts, including the premium. Adding the two together at each exchange rate yields the kinked solid line, portraying AMI's exchange risk after hedging with options.

Comparing the forward market hedge in Figure 5A.1 with the option hedge, we see that the option works much like an insurance policy, limiting

AMI's loss when the euro weakens while still enabling the company to benefit when it strengthens. The cost of this policy is the option's premium.

Options are especially attractive hedging vehicles in two circumstances. One is when the hedger has a view about which way currencies will move but is too cowardly to speculate openly. Options enable the hedger to benefit when her views prove correct but limits losses when they are incorrect. Options are also attractive when the exposure is contingent. When a company bids on a foreign contract, its currency exposure obviously depends on whether the bid is accepted. Hedging this contingent exposure in forward markets results in unintended, and possibly costly, reverse exposure whenever the bid is rejected. The worst possible outcome with an option hedge, however, is loss of the premium.

Limitations of Financial Market Hedging

Because new initiates to the world of hedging frequently overestimate the technique's power, a few cautionary reflections on the severe limitations of financial market hedges are in order.

Two basic conditions must hold before commercial risks can be hedged effectively in financial markets. One is that the asset creating the risk, or one closely correlated with it, must trade in financial markets. In our example, this means euros must be a traded currency. For this reason, an exposure in Indian rupees is much harder to manage than one in euros.

The second necessary condition for effective foreign-currency hedging in financial markets is that the amount and the timing of the foreign cash flow be known with reasonable certainty. This is usually not a problem when the cash flow is a foreign receivable or payable, but when it is an operating cash flow, such as expected sales, cost of sales, or earnings, the story is quite different. For example, suppose the treasurer of an American exporter to Germany anticipates earnings next year of 1 million euros, and she wants to lock in the dollar value of these profits today. What should she do? At first glance, the answer is obvious: Sell 1 million euros forward for dollars. But further consideration will reveal severe problems with this strategy. First, the exporter's long position in euros equals not next year's profits but next year's sales, a much larger number. Second, instead of hedging a known future cash flow as in our account receivable example, the exporter must hedge an unknown, expected amount. Moreover, because changes in the dollar-euro exchange rate will affect the competitiveness of the American exporter's products in Germany, we know that expected sales are themselves dependent on the future exchange rate. In terms of a position diagram, this means the foreign cash flow we seek to hedge cannot be represented by a straight line, which greatly complicates any hedging strategy. Third, if the American company expects to continue exporting to Germany into the foreseeable future,

Currency and Interest Rate Swaps

Another derivative security, known as a *swap,* has altered the way many financial executives think about issuing and managing company debt. A swap is a piece of paper documenting the trade of future cash flows between two parties in which each commits to pay or receive the other's cash flows. The market value of a swap at any time equals the difference in the value of the underlying cash flows exchanged. A *currency* swap involves the trade of liabilities denominated in different currencies, while an *interest rate* swap entails the trade of fixed-rate payments for floating-rate ones. Swaps do not appear on the participating companies' financial statements, and lenders typically are unaware a swap has occurred. Swaps have become so commonplace that an active market now exists in which standard swaps are bought and sold over the phone much like stocks and bonds. If your company has a 10-year, Swiss franc liability and would prefer one denominated in U.S. dollars, phone a swap dealer for a quote.

Swaps inevitably seem exotic and a bit pathological on first acquaintance, but the underlying concept is really an elementary one. Whenever each of two parties has something the other wants, a trade can benefit both. A swap is such a trade in which the items exchanged are future interest and principal payments. Some swaps, denoted as asset swaps, involve rights to *receive* future payments, while more common liability swaps involve the obligation to *make* future payments.

Swaps have proven to be valuable financing tools for at least two reasons. First, swaps help solve a fundamental problem facing many companies when raising capital. Prior to the advent of swaps, a company's decision about what type of debt to issue often involved a compromise between what the company really wanted and what investors were willing to buy. An issuer might have wanted fixed-rate, French franc debt but settled for floating-rate, Canadian dollar debt because the terms were better. But with swaps, the issuer can have his cake and eat it too. Just issue floating-rate, Canadian dollar debt and immediately swap into fixed-rate, French franc debt. In effect, swaps enable the issuer to separate concerns about what type of debt the company needs from those regarding what type investors want to buy, thereby greatly simplifying the issuance decision and reducing borrowing costs.

A second virtue of swaps is that they are a slick tool for interest rate and currency risk management. Worried the Swiss franc will soon strengthen, increasing the dollar burden of your company's Swiss franc debt? No problem: Swap out of francs into dollars. Worried that interest rates are about to fall, saddling your company with a pile of high-cost, fixed-rate debt? Piece of cake: Swap into floating-rate debt and watch borrowing costs float down with the rates.

its exposure extends far beyond next year's sales. So even if it successfully hedges next year's sales, this represents only a small fraction of the company's total euro exposure. We conclude that hedging the risks of individual transactions such as those generating accounts receivable is a straightforward task, but hedging the much larger risks inherent in operating cash flows in financial markets is a complex, nearly impossible undertaking.

Our final caveat about financial market hedging is more philosophical. Empirical studies suggest that foreign exchange, commodity, and debt markets are all "fair games," meaning the chance of benefiting from unexpected price changes in these markets about equals the chance of losing. If this is so, companies facing repeated exchange exposures, or those with a number of exposures in different currencies, might justifiably dispense with hedging altogether on the grounds that over the long run, losses will about equal gains anyway. According to this philosophy, financial market hedging is warranted only when the company seldom faces currency exposures, when the potential loss is too big for the company to absorb gracefully, or when the elimination of exchange exposure yields administrative benefits such as more accurate performance evaluation or improved employee morale.

Valuing Options

Because options are finding increasing applications in corporate finance ranging from incentive compensation to analysis of investment opportunities, a brief primer on option valuation is appropriate.

Suppose you hold a five-year option to purchase 100 shares of Cisco Systems stock for $27 a share when the stock is selling for $25, and you want to know what the option is worth today. It is apparent that your option would be worthless if you had to exercise it immediately, for the privilege of buying something for $27 when it is freely available elsewhere for $25 is not highly prized. Your option is said to be "out of the money." But fortunately, you do not have to exercise the option immediately. You can wait for up to five years before acting. Looking to the future, chances are good that sometime before the option matures, Cisco stock will sell for more than $27. The option will then be "in the money," in which case you can exercise it and sell the stock for a profit. We conclude that the value of the option today depends fundamentally on two things: the chance that Cisco's stock will rise above the option's strike price prior to maturity and the potential amount by which it might exceed the strike price. The challenge in valuing an option is to decide what these two things are worth.

Options have been around for many years, but it was not until 1973 that Fisher Black and Myron Scholes offered the first practical solution to this valuation challenge. Their solution is remarkable both for what it contains and for what it omits. Black and Scholes demonstrated that the value of an option depends on five variables, four of which are readily available in the newspaper. They are

- The current price of the underlying asset (which in our example is Cisco stock).

- The option's time to maturity.

- The option's strike price.

- The interest rate.

As you might expect, the value of a call option rises with the price of the underlying asset and the option's time to maturity, but falls with the strike price. The Cisco call option is more valuable when Cisco is selling at $50 than at $25 and when the option is good for 10 years as opposed to 5.

Conversely, it is worth less when its strike price is $40 as opposed to $27. The value of a call rises as interest rates rise because a call option can be viewed as a delayed purchase of the underlying asset, and the higher the interest rate, the more valuable this deferral privilege becomes.

The one unobservable determinant of an option's value is the expected volatility of return on the underlying asset. In English, the value of the Cisco option depends on how uncertain investors are about the return on Cisco stock over the life of the option. The standard approach to estimating expected volatility is to look at the stock's past volatility, as measured by the standard deviation of past returns. (Standard deviation is a widely used statistical measure of dispersion, which we will consider in more detail in Chapter 8.) If the standard deviation of return on Cisco stock in the recent past has been 25 percent, this is a plausible estimate of its future volatility.

The intriguing thing about volatility is that option value **rises** with volatility. In other words, a call option on a speculative stock is actually worth more than an identical option on a blue chip. That's right. Options are contrary to intuition and to most of finance, where volatility means risk and risk is bad. With options, volatility is good. To see why, recall that an option allows its owner to walk away unscathed when things go poorly. In our example, if Cisco stock never rises above $27, the worst that can happen is you will have some new wallpaper. This means that an option owner is only concerned with upside potential, and the greater the volatility, the greater this potential. If you received a dollar every time a batter hit a home run, wouldn't you rather back an erratic slugger than a steady singles hitter? The same is true of options. Uncertainty is good for options.

The input variable that is surprisingly missing from the Black-Scholes formula is the predicted future value of the underlying asset. In our example, there is no need to forecast the value of Cisco stock over the next five years to value the option because the market's forecast is already embedded in the current price.

With the Black-Scholes option-pricing formula in hand, valuing an option is now a straightforward, three-step process. First, find the current values of the four observable variables. Second, estimate the future volatility of the underlying asset's return, usually by extrapolating its past volatility. And third, throw these numbers into the Black-Scholes option pricing formula, or one of its latter-day extensions, and wait for the computer to disgorge an answer. As an example, let's value the Cisco option under the following conditions:

Option strike price	$27
Option maturity	5 years
Current Cisco stock price	$25
5-yr government interest rate	2.50%
Volatility of Cisco stock price	22.02%

My volatility estimate is from Robert's Online Option Pricer, a handy Website that, among other things, provides historical volatilities for many stocks. The number used is Cisco's annualized historical volatility over the prior month as measured on May 9, 2011. Rather than manipulating the Black-Scholes formula myself—a tedious task—I will use Robert's Option Pricer, available on the same Website. Plugging the requisite five numbers into the option pricer, we learn that the estimated value of the option on 100 Cisco shares is $539. At a volatility of 35 percent, the value jumps to $806.[4]

Growth of the options industry since introduction of the Black-Scholes pricing model recalls Mark Twain's quip, "If your only tool is a hammer, pretty soon all the world appears to be a nail." The ability to price options with reasonable accuracy has led to a remarkable growth in the volume and variety of options traded, including those on interest rates, stocks, stock indices, foreign exchange, weather, and a wide variety of physical commodities. In addition to traded options, we have discovered the presence of embedded options lurking in many conventional financial instruments such as home mortgages and commercial bank loans. In the past, these options were either ignored or only crudely reflected in the pricing of the instrument. Now it is possible to value each option separately and price it accordingly. From the discovery of embedded options in conventional instruments, it has been a small step to the creation of innovative new instruments that include heretofore unavailable options. Finally, we have recently begun to realize that many corporate investment decisions, such as whether or not to introduce a new product, contain embedded options that, at least in theory, can be priced using the techniques described. Examples of what are known as *real options* include the choice to expand production, to terminate production, or to change the product mix. The ability to price these options promises to greatly improve corporate investment decisions. (We will say more on this topic in Chapter 8.) Once you know how to price them, all the world indeed appears to be an option.

---

[4] Robert's Online Applications are available at **www.intrepid.com/robertl/index.html**. I have taken several liberties with the material in this section in the interest of simplicity. First, the pricing formula used in Robert's Option Pricer is an extension of Black-Scholes. In addition to the five variables discussed, the formula requires the dividend yield, which for Cisco is zero. It is also necessary to specify that the Cisco option is an "American" option because it can be exercised at any time prior to maturity.

SUMMARY

1. Financial instruments
   - Are claims to a company's cash flows and assets designed to meet the financing needs of the business and to appeal to investors.
   - Are not greatly constrained by law or regulation but are subject to full disclosure requirements.
   - Are often grouped into four categories:
     - Fixed-income securities known as bonds.
     - Residual-income securities known as common stock.
     - Hybrid securities having characteristics of both bonds and of stocks.
     - Derivative securities whose value depends on that of some underlying asset.
2. Realized returns on U.S. common stocks over the years since 1900 have
   - Averaged 11.4 percent a year.
   - Outpaced inflation by an average of 8.1 percent a year.
   - Been more volatile, and thus riskier, than returns on bonds.
   - Exceeded the return on government bonds by an average of 6.2 percent a year.
3. Financial markets
   - Are the channels through which companies sell financial instruments to investors
   - Include such diverse segments as
     - Private equity financing: where buyout and venture capital firms, organized as limited partnerships, make high risk, intermediate-term investments.
     - Initial public offerings: where private companies, with the help of investment bankers, sell ownership interests to public investors.
     - Seasoned issues: where larger public companies use often-specialized techniques such as private placements, shelf registrations, and Rule 144A offerings to raise money.
     - Cross-border financing: where large companies raise money in other countries' financial markets, or in international markets, which are best thought of as a free market response to regulatory constraints imposed in domestic markets.

Visit us at www.mhhe.com/higgins10e

4. Efficient markets
- Are markets in which prices respond rapidly to new information such that current prices fully reflect available information about the assets traded.
- Typically impound new information into prices in a matter of seconds.
- Are often divided into three categories:
  - Weak-form efficient: when current prices fully reflect all information about past prices.
  - Semistrong-form efficient: when current prices fully reflect all publicly available information.
  - Strong-form efficient: when current prices fully reflect all information public or private.
- Is a relative term in that the same market can be simultaneously efficient to retail investors and inefficient to market specialists

5. In semistrong-form efficient markets, in the absence of private information
- Publicly available information is not helpful in forecasting future prices.
- The best forecast of future price is current price, perhaps adjusted for a long-run trend.
- A company cannot improve the terms on which it sells securities by attempting to time the issue.
- Investors should not expect to consistently earn above-average returns without accepting above average risks.

ADDITIONAL RESOURCES

Dimson, Elroy, Paul Marsh, and Mike Staunton. *Triumph of the Optimists: 101 Years of Global Investment Returns.* Princeton, NJ: Princeton University Press, 2002. 302 pages.

An elegant book by three British academics providing detailed information about returns earned on financial instruments in 16 countries over the twentieth century. An authoritative source of important information. About $120. Updated annually in *Credit Suisse Global Investment Returns Yearbook.*

Fox, Justin. *The Myth of the Rational Market: A History of Risk, Reward, and Delusion on Wall Street.* New York: Harper Paperbacks, 2011. 416 pages.

Tells the story of the rise and fall of the rational markets hypothesis. An excellent intellectual history of modern finance. *A New York Times* Notable Book of 2009. In paperback. $12.

Gladstone, David, and Laura Gladstone. *Venture Capital Handbook: An Entrepreneur's Guide to Raising Venture Capital*, revised edition. London: Financial Times Prentice Hall, 2002. 448 pages.

> If you intend to raise venture capital money or to become a venture capitalist, read this book. About $30.

Malkiel, Burton G. *A Random Walk Down Wall Street*. Completely revised edition. New York: W.W. Norton & Company, 2007. 445 pages.

> The classic best-selling introduction to market efficiency and personal investing by someone who knows both the academic and professional sides of the story. About $15.

Mishkin, Frederic S., and Stanley G. Eakins. *Financial Markets and Institutions*. 6th ed. Reading, MA: Addison Wesley, 2008. 752 pages.

> An introduction to financial markets including money, bond, stock, mortgage, and foreign exchange markets. Also covers the management of financial institutions and the conduct of monetary policy. About $160.

Reinhart, Carmen M., and Kenneth Rogoff. *This Time is Different: Eight Centuries of Financial Folly*. Princeton N.J.: Princeton University Press, 2009. 512 pages.

> A valuable historical perspective by two distinguished economists on the recurring self-delusion and economic crashes plaguing society over many years. The panic of 2008 appears quite ordinary by comparison. $21.

WEBSITES

www.cboe.com

Home of the Chicago Board Options Exchange. Site includes option prices, a dictionary, and online complimentary courses.

www.intrepid.com/robertl/index.html

Robert's Online Applications. Lots of information on stock options and related topics. You give the option pricer the five bits of information necessary to price an option, and it returns the estimated price. Also contains information on the volatility of stock prices. Check out "About options" at the bottom of the option pricer page for a witty introduction to options. Anyone who answers the question "How are options priced?" with "Usually with a lot of difficulty" deserves a look.

www.sandhillecon.com

Creators of the Dow Jones index of venture capital designed to reveal the return and volatility of venture investing. The site of a number of interesting, rigorous studies of venture investing.

www.vnpartners.com

Includes an informative primer on venture capital.

PROBLEMS

Answers to odd-numbered problems appear at the end of the book. For additional problems with answers, see **www.mhhe.com/higgins10e.**

1. Table 5.1 indicates that the average annual rate of return on common stocks over many years has exceeded the return on government bonds in the United States. Why do we observe this pattern?

2. Suppose the realized rate of return on government bonds exceeded the return on common stocks one year. How would you interpret this result?

3. What is more important to investors: the number of a company's shares they own, the price of the company's stock, or the percentage of the company's equity they own? Why?

4. Two 20-year bonds are identical in all respects except that one allows the issuer to call the bond in return for $1,000 cash at any time after five years while the other contains no call provisions. Will the yield to maturity on the two bonds differ? If so, which will be higher? Why?

5. The return an investor earns on a bond over a period of time is known as the *holding period return*, defined as interest income plus or minus the change in the bond's price, all divided by the beginning bond price.

   a. What is the holding period return on a bond with a par value of $1,000, and a coupon rate of 6 percent if its price at the beginning of the year was $1,050, and its price at the end was $940? Assume interest is paid annually.

   b. Can you give two reasons the price of the bond might have fallen over the year?

6. Information about three securities appears below.

	Beginning-of-year Price	End-of-year Price	Interest/dividend paid
Stock 1	$ 42.50	$ 46.75	$ 1.50
Stock 2	$ 1.25	$ 1.36	$ 0.00
Bond 1	$1,020	$1,048	$41.00

   a. Assuming interest and dividends are paid annually, calculate the annual holding period return on each security.

   b. During the year, management of Stock 2 spent $10 million, or $0.50 a share, repurchasing 7.7 million of the company's shares. How, if at all, does this information affect calculation of the holding period return on Stock 2?

7. A company wants to raise $500 million in a new stock issue. Its investment banker indicates that the sale of new stock will require 8 percent underpricing and a 7 percent spread. (Hint: the underpricing is 8 percent of the current stock price, and the spread is 7 percent of the issue price.)

    a. Assuming the company's stock price does not change from its current price of $75 per share, how many shares must the company sell and at what price to the public?

    b. How much money will the investment banking syndicates earn on the sale?

    c. Is the 8 percent underpricing a cash flow? Is it a cost? If so, to whom?

8. Why do you suppose that smaller firms tend to rely on bank financing while larger companies are more apt to sell bonds in financial markets?

9. You see an article in the newspaper that details the performance of mutual funds over the last five years. Out of 5,600 actively managed mutual funds in the study, 104 outperformed the market in each of the last five years. The author of the article argues that these mutual funds are examples of market inefficiency. "If markets are efficient, you would expect to see mutual funds outperforming the market for short periods of time. But when more than 100 mutual funds are able to outperform the market in each of the last five years, you can no longer suppose that markets are truly efficient. Obviously, these 100 fund managers have figured out a way to beat the market every year." Do you think that this is evidence that markets are not efficient?

10. Suppose in Figure 5.3 that the stock prices of target firms in acquisitions responded to acquisition announcements over a three-day period rather than almost instantly.

    a. Would you describe such an acquisition market as efficient? Why, or why not?

    b. Can you think of any trading strategy to take advantage of the delayed price response?

    c. If you and many others pursued this trading strategy, what would happen to the price response to acquisition announcements?

    d. Some argue that market inefficiencies contain the seeds of their own destruction. In what ways does your answer to this problem illustrate the logic of this statement, if at all?

    e. Immediately after some merger announcements, the stock price of the target firm jumps to a level higher than the bid price. Is this proof of market inefficiency? What might explain this price pattern?

11. a. Suppose that Liquid Force's stock price consistently falls by an amount equal to one-half the dividend it pays on the payment date. Ignoring taxes, can you think of an investment strategy to take advantage of this information?

    b. If you and many others pursued this strategy, predict what would happen to Liquid Force's stock price on the dividend payment date.

c. Suppose that Liquid Force's stock price consistently falls by an amount equal to twice the dividend payment on the payment date. Ignoring taxes, can you think of an investment strategy to take advantage of this information?

d If you and many others pursued this strategy, predict what would happen to Liquid Force's stock price on the dividend payment date.

e. In an efficient market, ignoring taxes and transaction costs, how do you think stock prices will change on dividend payment dates?

f. Given that investors receive returns from common stock in the form of dividends and capital appreciation, do you think that increasing dividends will benefit investors in the absence of taxes and transactions costs?

12. If the stock market in the United States is efficient, how do you explain the fact that some people make very high returns? Would it be more difficult to reconcile very high returns with efficient markets if the same people made extraordinary returns year after year?

Problems 13 and 14 test your understanding of the chapter appendix.

13. Some refer to common stock in a company with debt outstanding as an option on a company's assets. Do you see any logic to this statement? What is the logic, if any?

14. The common shares of Fortune Brands, Inc. (FO), owner of many brands including Knob Creek bourbons, Wild Horse wines, Titleist golf products, and Swingline staplers, are trading today on the New York Stock Exchange for $54.04 a share. You have employee stock options to purchase 1,000 FO shares for $54 per share. The options mature in three years. The annualized volatility of FO stock according to the Chicago Board Option Exchange (CBOE, **www.cboe.com/data/ historicalvolatility.aspx**) in a recent month was 19.846 percent. The company's dividend yield is 1.41%, and the interest rate is 2.5 percent. (Assume the options are European options that may only be exercised at the maturity date.)

a. Is this option a call or a put?

b. Using Robert's Option Pricer at **www.intrepid.com/robertl/ option-pricer1.html** or any other calculator you prefer, estimate the value of your FO options.

c. What is the estimated value of the options if their maturity is five months instead of three years? Why does the value of the options decline as the maturity declines?

d. What is the estimated value of the options if their maturity is three years, but FO's volatility is 45 percent? Why does the value of the options increase as volatility increases?

CHAPTER SIX

The Financing Decision

Equity Capital: The least amount of money owners can invest in a business and still obtain credit.

Michael Sperry

In the last chapter, we began our inquiry into financing a business by looking at financial instruments and the markets in which they trade. In this chapter, we examine the company's choice of the proper financing instruments.

Selecting the proper financing instruments is a two-step process. The first step is to decide how much external capital is required. Frequently this is the straightforward outcome of the forecasting and budgeting process described in Chapter 3. Management estimates sales growth, the need for new assets, and the money available internally. Any remaining monetary needs must be met from outside sources. Often, however, this is only the start of the exercise. Next comes a careful consideration of financial markets and the terms on which the company can raise capital. If management does not believe it can raise the required sums on agreeable terms, a modification of operating plans to bring them within budgetary constraints is initiated.

Once the amount of external capital to be raised has been determined, the second step is to select—or, more accurately, design—the instrument to be sold. This is the heart of the financing decision. As indicated in the last chapter, an issuer can choose from a tremendous variety of financial securities. The proper choice will provide the company with needed cash on attractive terms. An improper choice will result in excessive costs, undue risk, or an inability to sell the securities. In this context, it is important to keep in mind that most operating companies make money by creatively acquiring and deploying assets, not by dreaming up clever ways to finance these assets. This means that the focus of the financing decision should generally be on supporting the company's business strategy, and that care should be taken to avoid financing choices that carry even a modest chance of derailing this strategy. Better to make company financing the passive handmaiden of operating strategy than to jeopardize that strategy in pursuit of marginally lower financing costs. This is especially true for rapidly growing companies where aggressive financing choices can be especially costly.

For simplicity, we will concentrate on a single financing choice: XYZ Company needs to raise $200 million this year; should it sell bonds or stock? But do not let this narrow focus obscure the complexity of the topic. First, bonds and stocks are just extreme examples of a whole spectrum of possible security types. Fortunately, the conclusions drawn regarding these extremes will apply to a modified degree to other instruments along the spectrum. Second, many businesses, especially smaller ones, are often unable or unwilling to sell stock. For these firms, the relevant financing question is not whether to sell debt or equity but how much debt to sell. As will become apparent later in the chapter, the inability to raise equity forces companies to approach financing decisions as part of the broader challenge of managing growth. Third and most important, financing decisions are seldom one-time events. Instead, the raising of money at any point in time is just one event in an evolving financial strategy. Yes, XYZ Company needs $200 million today, but it will likely need $150 million in two years and an undetermined amount in future years. Consequently, a major element of XYZ's present financing decision is the effect today's choice will have on the company's future ability to raise capital. Ultimately, then, a company's financing strategy is closely intertwined with its long-run competitive goals and the way it intends to manage growth.

A word of warning before we begin: Questions of how best to finance a business recall the professor's admonition to students in a case discussion class: "You will find that there are no right answers to these cases, but many wrong ones." In the course of this chapter, you will learn there is no single right answer to the question of how best to finance a business, but you will also discover some important guidelines to help you avoid the many wrong answers.

This chapter addresses a central topic in finance known as OPM: other people's money. We look first at how OPM fundamentally affects the risk and return faced by the owners of any risky asset. We then examine several practical tools for measuring these risk-return effects in a corporate setting, and we conclude by reviewing current thinking on the determinants of the optimal use of debt by a business. In the course of our review, we will consider the tax implications of various financing instruments, the distress costs a company faces when it relies too heavily on OPM, the incentive effects of high leverage, the challenges faced by companies unable to sell new equity, and what are known as signaling effects. These refer to the way a company's stock price reacts to news that the company intends to sell a particular financing instrument. The chapter appendix takes up a major conceptual building block in finance known variously as the irrelevance proposition or the M&M theorem.

Financial Leverage

In physics, a lever is a device to increase force at the cost of greater movement. In business, OPM, or what is commonly called *financial leverage*, is a device to increase owners' expected return at the cost of greater risk. Mechanically, financial leverage involves the substitution of fixed-cost debt financing for owners' equity, and because this substitution increases fixed interest expenses, it follows that financial leverage increases the variability of returns to owners— a common surrogate for risk. Financial leverage is, thus, the proverbial two-edged sword, increasing owners' expected return, but also, their risk.

Table 6.1 illustrates this fundamental point in the form of a very simple risky investment. Ignoring taxes, the investment requires a $1,000 outlay today in return for a 50-50 chance at either $900 or $1,400 in one year. We are interested in how the owners' expected return and risk vary as we alter the type of financing. Panel A at the top of the table assumes all-equity financing. Observe that the investment promises an equal chance at a return of minus 10 percent or plus 40 percent (a $400 profit on a $1,000 investment implies a 40 percent return). Looking at the bold figures in Panel A,

TABLE 6.1 **Debt Financing Increases Expected Return and Risk to Owners**

The Investment: Pay $1,000 today for a 50-50 change at $900 or $1,400 in one year.

Panel A: 100% Equity Financing. Owners Invest $1,000.

Investment Outcome	Probability	To Owners	Return to Owners	Probability Weighted Return
$ 900	0.50	$ 900	−10%	−5%
1,400	0.50	1,400	40	20
			Expected return =	**15%**

Panel B: 80% Debt Financing; 1-Year Loan at 10% Interest. Owners Invest $200.

Investment Outcome	Probability	Due Lender	Residual to Owners	Return to Owners	Probability Weighted Return
$ 900	0.50	$880	$ 20	−90%	−45%
1,400	0.50	880	520	160	80
				Expected return =	**35%**

we see that these numbers imply an expected return on the investment of 15 percent with a range of possible outcomes between -10 percent and $+40$ percent.

Now let's pile on the debt and see what happens. Assume we finance 80 percent of the cost of the same investment with an $800, one-year loan at an interest rate of 10 percent. This reduces the owners' investment to $200. Panel B of Table 6.1 shows that while the investment cash flows are unchanged, the residual cash flows to owners change dramatically. Because owners must pay $880 in principal and interest to creditors before receiving anything, they now stand an equal chance of getting back $20 or $520 on their $200 investment. Looking again at the bold numbers in Panel B, this translates into an attractive expected return of 35 percent and a daunting range of possible outcomes between -90 percent and $+160$ percent.

This example clearly demonstrates that debt financing does two things to owners: It increases their expected return and it increases their risk. The example also illustrates that a single risky investment can be converted into a wide variety of risk-return combinations by simply varying the means of financing. Want to minimize risk and return on an investment? Finance with equity. Willing to take a gamble? Make the same investment, but finance it with some debt. Want to really roll the dice? Crank up the leverage. These same observations apply to companies as well as individual investments: Financial leverage increases expected return and risk to shareholders, and companies are able to generate a wide array of shareholder, risk-return combinations by varying the way they finance the business. (Incidentally, if you are worried about what happens to the $800 owners have left over in Panel B, don't. The same conclusions follow if we assume owners combine their $1,000 of equity with $4,000 of borrowed money to invest $5,000 in the risky asset. All of the dollar figures in Panel B go up, but the returns remain the same.)

A second way to look at financial leverage is to note that it is a close cousin to *operating leverage*, defined as the substitution of fixed-cost methods of production for variable-cost methods. Replacing hourly workers with a robot increases operating leverage because the robot's initial cost pushes up fixed costs, while the robot's willingness to work longer hours without additional pay reduces variable costs. This produces two effects: Sales required to cover fixed costs rise, but once break-even is reached, profits grow more quickly with additional sales. Analogously, the substitution of debt for equity financing increases fixed costs in the form of higher interest and principal payments, but because creditors do not share in company profits, it also reduces variable costs. Increased financial leverage thus has two effects as well: More operating income is required to cover fixed financial costs, but once breakeven is achieved, profits grow more quickly with additional operating income.

To see these effects more clearly, let's look at the influence of financial leverage on return on equity. Recall from Chapter 2 that despite some problems, ROE is a widely used measure of financial performance defined as profit after tax divided by owners' equity. As shown in the following footnote, ROE can be written for our purposes as

$$ROE = ROIC + (ROIC - i')\, D/E$$

where ROIC is the company's return on invested capital (defined in Chapter 2 as EBIT after tax divided by all sources of cash on which a return must be earned), i' is the after-tax interest rate, $(1-t)i$, D is interest-bearing debt, and E is the book value of equity.[1] You can think of ROIC as the return a company earns before the effects of financial leverage are considered. Looking at i', recall that because interest is a tax-deductible expense, a company's tax bill declines whenever its interest expense rises; i' captures this effect.

To illustrate this equation, we can write ROE for Sensient Technologies Corporation in 2010 as

$$ROE = 9.0\% + (9.0\% - 3.7\%)\, \$349.9/\$983.8$$
$$10.9\% = 9.0\% + 1.9\%$$

where 3.7 percent is Sensient's after-tax borrowing rate, $349.9 million is its interest-bearing debt, and $983.8 million is its book value of equity. Sensient earned a basic return of 9.0 percent on its assets, which it levered into a 10.9 percent return on equity by substituting $349.9 million of debt for equity in its capital structure.

This revised expression for ROE is revealing. It shows clearly that the impact of financial leverage on ROE depends on the size of ROIC relative to i'. If ROIC exceeds i', financial leverage, as measured by D/E, increases ROE. The reverse is also true: If ROIC is less than i', leverage reduces ROE. In English, the equation says that when a company earns more on borrowed money than it pays in interest, return on equity will rise, and vice versa. Leverage thus improves financial performance when things are going well but worsens performance when things are going poorly. It is the classic fair-weather friend.

---

[1] Write profit after tax as $(EBIT - iD)(1-t)$, where EBIT is earnings before interest and tax, iD is interest expense—written as the interest rate, i, times interest-bearing debt outstanding, D—and t is the firm's tax rate. This equation reflects the steps an accountant goes through to calculate profit after tax from EBIT. The rest is algebra, as shown in the following equation.

$$ROE = \frac{(EBIT - iD)(1 - t)}{E} = \frac{EBIT(1 - t)}{E} - \frac{iD(1 - t)}{E} = ROIC \times \frac{D + E}{E} - i'\frac{D}{E},$$

And lest you think that earning a return above borrowing cost is an easy target, be aware that in 2010 only 43 percent of the publicly traded, non-financial firms tracked by Standard & Poor's accomplished this feat. Even among larger firms with sales above $200 million, the comparable figure was just 60 percent. In business as in other walks of life, expectations are often unfulfilled.

Figure 6.1 is a graphical representation of the earlier ROE equation. The steeply pitched, solid curve represents a typical distribution of possible ROEs for an all-equity company. Note that the expected ROE is 10 percent and the range of possible outcomes is from a loss of about 12 percent to a gain of 35 percent. The flatter, dotted curve shows the possible ROEs for the same distribution of all-equity returns when the company's debt-to-equity ratio is 2.0 and the after-tax borrowing rate is 4 percent. Debt financing levers the expected ROE from 10 percent up to 22 percent but also greatly broadens the range of possible outcomes. Now a loss of as much as 40 percent or a gain of 80 percent can occur.

For at least two reasons, it is appropriate to think of the range of possible ROEs as a measure of risk. First, a larger range of possible outcomes means greater uncertainty about what ROE the company will earn. Second, a larger range of possible outcomes means a greater

FIGURE 6.1 **Leverage Increases Risk and Expected Return**

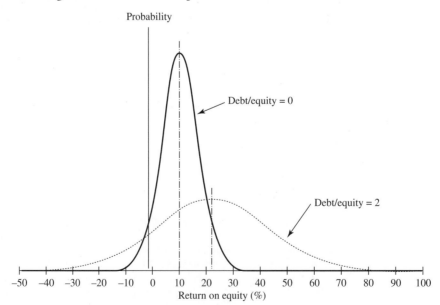

chance of bankruptcy. Look at the left-side tails of the two distributions, it is apparent that with zero leverage, the worst the company will do is lose about 12 percent on equity, but with a debt-to-equity ratio of 2 to 1, the same level of operating income generates a loss of about 40 percent, more than a threefold increase. In this situation, operating income is not sufficient to cover interest expense, and debt magnifies the loss. If the loss is large enough or persistent enough, bankruptcy can occur. We see again that financial leverage increases both expected return to owners and risk.

Measuring the Effects of Leverage on a Business

For a practical look at measuring the risks and rewards of debt financing in a corporate setting, let us return to the challenge faced by Sensient Technologies Corporation in 2010. Recall from Chapter 2 that Sensient is a stable, conservatively financed company with improving, but still mediocre, performance. Its chief financial challenge is what to do with the excess cash it is generating. Lately, the company has been paying down long-term debt, but at the current rate, debt will disappear entirely in about five years.

Here is my fictionalized account of an important financing decision faced by the company. Suppose that in late 2010 Sensient reaches a tentative agreement to purchase a division of General Electric Company that it has been coveting for several years. The agreed-upon price is $450 million, and Richard Hobbs, Sensient's chief financial officer, must decide how to best finance it. The firm's investment bankers indicate the company can easily raise the money in either of two ways:

- Sell 12 million new shares of common stock at a net price of $37.50 a share.
- Sell $450 million of bonds with an interest rate of 6 percent and 10 years to maturity. The bonds would carry an annual sinking fund of $25 million, with the remaining principal of $200 million due in a single balloon payment at maturity.

Historically, Sensient has sought to limit capital expenditures to an amount that could be financed out of internally generated cash and modest new borrowings. However, the board of directors deems this opportunity too important to pass up and has directed Mr. Hobbs to prepare a financing recommendation for consideration at their next board meeting. Complicating Mr. Hobbs's decision is the fact that several younger members of senior management have recently criticized what they perceive to be Sensient's overly timid financing policies. In their words, "We're leaving money on the table and short changing our share-holders by not levering up this business." One source of their enthusi-asm for debt financing appears to be the perception that higher leverage will increase return on equity and earnings per share, key determinants of the company's executive bonuses. These executives see the current situation as an ideal opportunity to right the balance by financing with debt. Mr. Hobbs is less certain.

Looking to the future, Mr. Hobbs believes the acquisition would in-crease Sensient's earnings before interest and taxes (EBIT) to about $250 million in 2011. As shown in the following figures, the company's EBIT has been quite stable in the recent past. Mr. Hobbs further anticipates that Sensient's need for outside financing in coming years will be quite mod-est, unless another acquisition opportunity arises. The company expects to pay annual dividends of 85 cents a share in 2011, and Hobbs believes the board would be quite reluctant to reduce this amount in future years.

	2003	2004	2005	2006	2007	2008	2009	2010	2011F
EBIT ($ millions)	131	129	112	129	147	162	158	173	250F

F = forecast.

Table 6.2 presents selected information about the two financing op-tions in 2011. It shows that in the absence of any new financing, Sensient will have $300 million in debt outstanding, interest expenses of $17 million, and a $20 million sinking fund repayment. All these numbers escalate sharply with $450 million in new debt financing. New stock, on the other hand, will leave these quantities unchanged but will increase common shares outstanding from 50 to 62 million and total dividend payments from $43 to $53 million.

TABLE 6.2 Selected Information about Sensient Technologies Corporation's Financing Options in 2011 ($ millions)

	2011 Projected		
	Before New Financing	**Stock Financing**	**Bond Financing**
Interest-bearing debt outstanding	$ 300	$ 300	$ 750
Interest expense	17	17	44
Principal payments	20	20	45
Shareholders' equity (book value)	1,100	1,550	1,100
Common shares outstanding	50	62	50
Dividends paid at $0.85 per share	43	53	43

Leverage and Risk

Mr. Hobbs's first task in analyzing the financing options should be to decide if Sensient can safely carry the financial burden imposed by the new debt. The best way to do this is to compare the company's forecasted operating cash flows to the annual financial burden imposed by the debt. There are two ways to do this: construct pro forma financial forecasts of the type discussed in Chapter 3, perhaps augmented by sensitivity analysis and simulations, or more simply, calculate several coverage ratios. To provide a flavor of the analysis without repeating much of Chapter 3, I will confine discussion here to coverage ratios on the understanding that if real money were involved, detailed financial forecasting would be the order of the day. Because coverage ratios were treated in Chapter 2, our discussion can be brief.

The before- and after-tax burdens of Sensient's financial obligations under the two financing options appear in the top portion of Table 6.3. Recall that because we want to compare these financial obligations to the company's EBIT, a before-tax number, we must gross up the after-tax amounts to their before-tax equivalents. This involves dividing the after-tax numbers by $(1 - t)$ where t is the company's tax rate. For this analysis $t = 40\%$.

TABLE 6.3   **Sensient Technologies's Projected Financial Obligations and Coverage Ratios in 2011 ($ millions)**

Expected EBIT = $250	Tax rate = 40%			
Financial Obligations				
	Stock		**Bonds**	
	After Tax	**Before Tax**	**After Tax**	**Before Tax**
Interest expense		$17		$44
Principal payment	$20	$33	$45	$75
Common dividends	$53	$88	$43	$72

Coverage Ratios				
	Stock		**Bonds**	
	Coverage	**Percentage EBIT Can Fall**	**Coverage**	**Percentage EBIT Can Fall**
Times interest earned	14.7	93%	5.7	82%
Times burden covered	5.0	80%	2.1	52%
Times common covered	1.8	45%	1.3	24%

Three coverage ratios, corresponding to the progressive addition of each financial obligation listed in Table 6.3, appear in the bottom portion of the table for a projected EBIT of $250 million. To illustrate the calculation of these ratios, "times common covered" equals $250 million EBIT divided by the sum of all three financial burdens stated in before-tax dollars. [For the bond financing option, $1.3 = 250/(44 + 75 + 72)$.] Note that our analysis here is not an incremental one. We are interested in the total burden imposed by new *and* existing debt, not just that of the new borrowings.

The column headed "Percentage EBIT Can Fall" offers a second way to interpret coverage ratios. It is the percentage amount that EBIT can decline from its expected level before coverage drops to 1.0. For example, interest expense with bond financing is $44 million; thus, EBIT can fall from $250 million to $44 million, or 82 percent, before times interest earned equals 1.0. A coverage of 1.0 is critical, because any lower coverage indicates that operating income will be insufficient to cover the financial burden under consideration, and another source of cash must be available.

As expected, these figures confirm the greater risk inherent in debt financing. In every instance, Sensient's coverage of its financial obligations will be worse with debt financing than without. In fact, with debt financing, a decline in EBIT of only 24 percent from the projected level will put the company's dividend in jeopardy. And although missing a dividend payment is admittedly less catastrophic than missing an interest or principal payment, it is still an eventuality most companies would just as soon avoid. At the same time, this risk may be an entirely manageable one for Sensient in light of its previously noted operating stability. In fact, earlier figures reveal that the company's steepest decline in EBIT since 2003 was only 13 percent, despite the harsh recession of recent years.

To put these numbers in further perspective, Mr. Hobbs will next want to compare them with various industry figures. As an example, the top part of Table 6.4 shows debt-to-asset and times-interest-earned ratios over the past decade for nonfinancial companies in the Standard & Poor's 500 stock index, while the bottom part shows the same information by selected industry in 2010. Note that both ratios show declining indebtedness until 2007 when a weakening economy and attractive interest rates lead to a reversal in the trend. In general, these figures demonstrate that corporate balance sheets never did show the extreme debt levels characteristic of consumers and governments and that by 2010 the figures were returning to pre-recession levels. Mr. Hobbs will be especially interested in numbers for the "materials" industry, of which Sensient is a member. Sensient's projected 5.7 times-interest-earned ratio with debt financing will be a bit below the industry figure of 5.9, while the corresponding number for stock financing of 14.7 times will be well above.

TABLE 6.4   Average Nonfinancial Corporate Debt Ratios 2001–2010 and Industry Debt Ratios 2010

Nonfinancial companies in Standard and Poor's 500 index and industry components, size-weighted averages. (Numbers in parentheses are the number of companies in sample.)

	2001	2002	2003	2004	2005	2006	2007	2008	2009	2010
Nonfinancial Companies in Standard & Poor's 500										
Debt to total assets* (%)	27	28	26	23	22	22	24	28	28	27
Times interest earned	5.5	5.7	6.5	7.8	8.1	8.8	8.1	6.7	5.2	7.0

Industry Debt Ratios 2010		
	Debt to total assets (%)	Times interest earned
Consumer discretionary (80)	32	5.4
Consumer staples (41)	29	9.4
Energy (41)	16	11.1
Health care (52)	21	14.1
Industrials (59)	41	4.7
Information technology (74)	13	26.0
Materials (30)	27	5.9
Telecommunications services (8)	28	4.0
Utilities (33)	35	3.2

*All interest-bearing debt; all quantities measured at book value.

Table 6.5 offers a second comparison. It shows the variation in key performance ratios across Standard & Poor's bond-rating categories in the 2007 through 2009 time period. Note that the median times-interest-earned ratio falls steadily across the rating categories, from a high of 30.5 times for AAA companies down to 1.4 times for B firms. By this yardstick, Sensient's prospective coverage ratio of 5.7 times with bonds would put it in the BBB range, right on the border between investment and speculative grade.

Leverage and Earnings

Our brief look at Sensient's coverage ratios under the two financing options suggests that a $450 million bond offering is at least feasible. Next, let's see how the two financing schemes are likely to affect reported income and return on equity. Mr. Hobbs can do this by looking at the company's projected income statement under the two options. Ignoring for the moment the possibility that the company's financing choice might affect its sales or operating income, Mr. Hobbs can begin his analysis with projected EBIT. Table 6.6 shows the bottom portion of a 2011 pro forma

TABLE 6.5 Median Values of Key Ratios by Standard & Poor's Rating Category

(Industrial long-term debt, three-year figures, 2007–2009)

	AAA	AA	A	BBB	BB	B
Times interest earned (X)	30.5	18.3	11.0	5.8	3.5	1.4
EBITDA interest coverage (X)	33.5	20.5	14.3	7.6	5.2	2.3
Funds from operations/total debt (%)	200.7	73.4	53.0	34.0	25.3	12.0
Pretax return on capital (%)	34.2	25.4	21.1	14.1	12.2	8.3
Total debt/capital (%)	15.1	34.7	35.7	44.7	50.4	73.1
Number of companies	4	16	92	213	245	325
Percent of sample companies (%)	0.4	1.8	10.3	23.8	27.4	36.3

Variable definitions:

EBITDA = Earnings before interest, taxes, depreciation, and amortization.

Funds from operations = Net income from continuing operations plus depreciation, amortization, deferred income taxes, and other noncash items.

Pretax return on capital = EBIT/Average of beginning and ending capital, including short-term debt, current maturities, long-term debt (including amount for operating lease debt equivalent), non-current deferred taxes, and equity.

Long-term debt/capital = Long-term debt (including amount for operating lease debt equivalent) / Long-term debt + shareholders' equity (including preferred stock) plus minority interest.

Note: These figures are not meant to be industry standards. Company data are adjusted to eliminate nonrecurring gains and losses and to include an amount for operating lease debt equivalent.
Source: David Lugg and Paulina Grabowiec, "CreditStats: 2009 Adjusted Key U.S.and European Industrial and Utility Financial Ratios," copyright 2009 by Standard & Poor's. Reproduced with permission of Standard & Poor's, a division of the McGraw-Hill Companies, Inc.

TABLE 6.6 Sensient Technologies Corporation's Partial Pro Forma Income Statements in 2010 under Bust and Boom Conditions ($ millions except EPS)

	Bust		Boom	
	Stock	Bonds	Stock	Bonds
EBIT	$ 100	$ 100	$ 400	$ 400
Interest expense	17	44	17	44
Earnings before tax	83	56	383	356
Tax at 40%	33	22	153	142
Earnings after tax	$ 50	$ 34	$ 230	$ 214
Number of shares (millions)	62	50	62	50
Earnings per share	$0.80	$ 0.67	$3.71	$ 4.27
Book value of equity (millions)	1,550	1,100	1,550	1,100
Return on equity	3.2%	3.1%	14.8%	19.4%

income statement for Sensient under boom and bust conditions. Bust corresponds to a recessionary EBIT of $100 million, while boom represents a healthy EBIT of $400 million.

Several noteworthy observations emerge from these figures. One involves the tax advantage of debt financing. Observe that Sensient's tax bill is always $11 million lower under bond financing than under the alternative, leaving more operating income to be divided among owners and creditors. It is as if the government pays companies a subsidy, in the form of reduced taxes, to encourage the use of debt financing. Letting t be the company's tax rate and I its interest expense, the subsidy equals tI annually. Many believe this subsidy, frequently referred to as the *interest tax shield* from debt financing, is a chief attraction of debt financing. It is available to any company using debt financing provided only that it has sufficient taxable income to shield.

A second observation is that debt financing reduces earnings after tax, an apparent disadvantage to debt. However, it is important to realize that this is only half the story, for although debt financing does reduce earnings after tax, it also reduces shareholders' investment in the firm. And personally, I would rather earn $90 on a $500 investment than $100 on a $1,000 investment. To capture both effects, it is useful to look at earnings per share and return on equity, two widely tracked indicators of equity performance. First, examining the boom conditions in Table 6.6 we see the expected effect of leverage on shareholder performance: EPS with debt financing is 15 percent higher than with equity, while ROE is a robust 31 percent higher. Under bust conditions, however, the reverse is true: Stock financing in difficult times produces a higher EPS and ROE than debt. This corresponds to our earlier example when the return on invested capital (ROIC) was less than the after-tax interest rate.

To display this information more informatively, Mr. Hobbs can construct a range of earnings chart relating either ROE or EPS, to EBIT. To do so using ROE, he need only plot the EBIT – ROE pairs calculated in Table 6.6 on a graph and connect the appropriate points with straight lines. Figure 6.2 shows the resulting range of earnings chart for Sensient Technologies. It presents the return on equity Sensient will report for any level of EBIT under the two financing options. Consistent with our boom-bust pro formas, note that the debt financing line passes through a ROE of 3.1 percent at $100 million EBIT and 19.4 percent at $400 million EBIT, while the corresponding figures for stock financing are 3.2 percent and 14.8 percent, respectively.

Mr. Hobbs will be particularly interested in two aspects of the range of earnings chart. One is the increase in ROE Sensient will report at the expected EBIT level if the company selects bonds over stock financing.

FIGURE 6.2 Range of Earnings Chart for Sensient Technologies Corporation

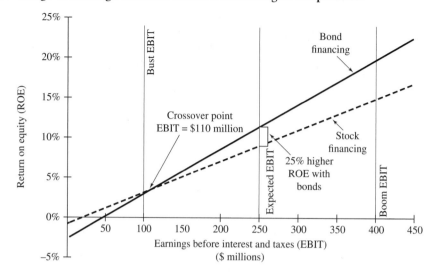

As the graph shows, this increase will be an attractive 25 percent at the expected EBIT of $250 million. Mr. Hobbs will also observe that in addition to generating an immediate increase in ROE, bond financing puts Sensient on a faster growth trajectory. This is represented by the steeper slope of the bond financing line. For each dollar Sensient adds to EBIT, ROE will rise more with bond financing than with equity. Unfortunately, the reverse is also true: For each dollar EBIT declines, ROE will fall more with bond financing than with equity financing.

The second aspect of the range of earnings chart that will catch Mr. Hobbs's eye is that debt financing does not always yield a higher ROE. If Sensient's EBIT falls below a critical crossover value of $110 million, ROE will actually be higher with stock financing than with bonds. Sensient's expected EBIT is comfortably above the crossover value today and past EBIT has been quite stable, but there are no guarantees going forward. Higher ROE with bond financing is clearly not a certainty.

How Much to Borrow

Coverage ratios, pro forma forecasts, and range of earnings charts yield important information about Sensient Technologies's ability to support various amounts of debt and about the effect of different debt levels on shareholder returns and earnings. With this foundation, it is now time to confront the chapter's central question: How do we determine what level of debt financing is best for a firm? How does Richard Hobbs decide whether Sensient should issue debt or equity? There is general agreement that the purpose of a firm's financing decision should be to increase firm value. But what does this imply for specific financing decisions? As noted earlier, the current state of the art will not enable us to answer this question definitively. We can, however, identify the key decision variables and suggest practical guides to Mr. Hobbs's deliberations.

Irrelevance

Speaking broadly, there are two possible channels by which financing decisions might affect firm value: by increasing the value investors attach to a given stream of operating cash flows, or by increasing the amount of the cash flows themselves. Some years ago, two economists eliminated the apparently more promising first channel. Franco Modigliani and Merton Miller, known universally today as M&M, demonstrated that when expected operating cash flows are unchanged, the amount of debt a company carries has no effect on its value and, hence, should be of no concern to value-maximizing managers or their shareholders. In their provocative words, when cash flows are constant, "the capital structure decision is irrelevant." In terms of risk and return, M&M demonstrated that what's important is the aggregate amount of each, not how they are divided up among shareholders and creditors.

See www.dfaus.com/2009/05/an-interview-with-merton-miller.html. for a candid interview with Merton Miller on the M&M theory and his philosophy of personal investing. See also interviews with Gene Fama and Rex Sinquefield.

Note the irony here. Questions of risk and return are centrally important to individuals. Strongly risk-averse people will prefer safe equity financing, while risk-indifferent folks will prefer debt. And, if financing choices are so important at the individual level, it seems only natural to conclude they must also be important to firms. However, this conclusion does not necessarily follow. Indeed, the genius of M&M's irrelevance proposition is to demonstrate that under certain conditions, firm financing choices need not affect value—despite the importance of financing decisions in our personal lives.

Intuitively, M&M's irrelevance argument comes down to this: Companies own physical assets, like trucks and buildings, and owe paper liabilities, like stocks and bonds. A company's physical assets are the true creators of value, and as long as the cash flows these assets stay constant, it is hard to imagine how simply renaming paper claims to the cash flows could create value. The company is worth no more with one set of paper claims than another.

Just for good measure, here is a second intuitive argument supporting the M&M irrelevance proposition, based on what is known as the "homemade" leverage. It rests on the observation that investors have two ways to lever an investment: They can rely on the company to borrow money, or they can borrow money themselves and buy the stock on margin. It is like a boat with two tillers, and whatever leverage tack the company takes with its corporate financing decision, the investor can override with her home-made decision. But if investors can readily substitute homemade leverage for corporate leverage, why would they care how much debt the company employs? How could firm leverage affect its value? (See the appendix to this chapter for more on the irrelevance proposition and homemade lever-age, including a numerical example.)

No rational executive believes M&M's irrelevance proposition is liter-ally true, but most acknowledge it to be the starting point for practical consideration of how financing decisions affect firm value. By demon-strating that renaming paper claims to a firm's cash flows alone does not affect value, M&M direct our attention to the second channel by which fi-nancing decisions might affect firm value. They thus confirm that firm fi-nancing decisions are important to the extent that they affect the *amount* of the cash flows themselves, and that the best capital structure is the one that maximizes these flows. To decide whether Sensient Technologies should issue debt or equity, Richard Hobbs needs to consider how the change in debt will affect company cash flows.

In the following pages, we examine five ways in which a company's fi-nancing decision can affect its cash flows. With a nod to Michael Porter, Figure 6.3 presents these forces as part of what I will modestly call the Higgins 5-Factor Model. The figure also shows each factor's direction of

FIGURE 6.3 **The Higgins 5-Factor Model for Financing Decisions**

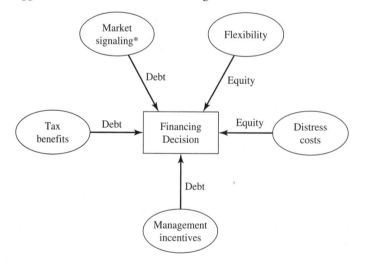

*Technically, market signaling affects investor perceptions of company cash flows, not the cash flows themselves. However, this distinction is not important for present purposes.

influence when considered in isolation. Thus, tax benefits considered alone suggest more debt financing, while distress costs caution more equity. Mr. Hobbs's job is to consider each of these five factors in light of Sensient's specific circumstances, and come to a reasoned judgment about their collective effect on company cash flows.

Tax Benefits

The tax advantages of debt financing are readily apparent. As noted in Table 6.6, Sensient's tax bill falls $11 million annually when it increases debt by $450 million—a clear benefit to the firm and its owners. As Warren Buffett so deftly put it, back in the days of a 48 percent corporate tax rate, "If you can eliminate the federal government as a 48 percent partner in your business, it's got to be worth more." As the tax bill goes down, the cash flow available for distribution to owners and creditors rises dollar for dollar.

Distress Costs

One popular perspective on selecting an appropriate debt level views the decision as a trade-off between the just-noted tax advantages of debt financing and various costs a company incurs when it uses too much debt. Collectively, these costs are known as the costs of *financial distress*. According to this view, the tax benefits of debt financing predominate at low debt levels, but as debt increases, the costs of financial distress grow to the point where they outweigh the tax advantages. The appropriate debt level, then, involves a judicious balancing of these offsetting costs and benefits.

The costs of financial distress are more difficult to quantify than the benefits of increased interest tax shields, but they are no less important to financing decisions. These costs come in at least three flavors, which we will review briefly under the headings of bankruptcy costs, indirect costs, and conflicts of interest.

Bankruptcy Costs

The expected cost of bankruptcy equals the probability bankruptcy will occur times the costs incurred when it does. As a glance at Sensient's coverage ratios attests, an obvious problem with aggressive debt financing is that rising debt levels increase the probability the business will be unable to meet its financial obligations. With high debt, what might otherwise be a modest downturn in profits can turn into a contentious bankruptcy as the company finds itself unable to make interest and principal payments in a timely manner.

Changing Attitudes Toward Bankruptcy

In recent decades, the public purpose of the bankruptcy process in the United States has shifted somewhat from protecting the rights of creditors toward protecting those of workers, communities, and society at large. Two things have changed in response. One is that creditors have factored the likelihood of greater losses in bankruptcy into their loan pricing by demanding higher rates. The other is that many managers have changed their attitude toward bankruptcy. Bankruptcy was once seen as a black hole in which companies were clumsily dismembered for the benefit of creditors and shareholders lost everything. Today some executives view it as a quiet refuge where the courts keep creditors at bay while management works on its problems. Manville Corporation was the first company to see the virtues of bankruptcy in August 1982, when, although solvent by any conventional definition, it declared bankruptcy in anticipation of massive product liability suits involving asbestos. Continental Airlines followed in September 1983, using bankruptcy protection to abrogate what it considered ruinous labor contracts. Subsequently, A. H. Robbins and Texaco, among others, have found bankruptcy an inviting haven while wrestling with product liability suits and a massive legal judgment, respectively. In all these instances, the companies expected to emerge from bankruptcy healthier and more valuable than when they entered.

While this is not the place for a complete review of bankruptcy laws and procedures, two points are worth making. First, bankruptcy does not necessarily imply liquidation. Many bankrupt companies are able to continue operations while they reorganize their business and are eventually able to leave bankruptcy and return to normal life. Second, bankruptcy in the United States is a highly uncertain process. For once in bankruptcy, a company's fate rests in the hands of a bankruptcy judge and a multitude of attorneys, each representing an aggrieved party and each determined to pursue the best interests of his or her client until justice is done or the money runs out. Bankruptcy today is thus akin to a high-stakes poker game in which the only certain winners are attorneys. And, depending on their luck, managers and owners can come away with a revitalized business or next to nothing.

Increased debt clearly heightens the probability of bankruptcy, but this is not the whole story. The other important consideration is the cost to the business if bankruptcy does occur. If bankruptcy involves only a few amicable meetings with creditors to reschedule debt, there is little need to limit borrowing to avoid bankruptcy. On the other hand, if bankruptcy spells immediate liquidation at fire-sale prices, aggressive borrowing is obviously foolhardy. A key factor in determining the cost of bankruptcy to an individual company is what can be called the "resale" value of its assets. Two simple examples will illustrate this notion.

First, suppose ACE Corporation's principal asset is an apartment complex and, due to local overbuilding and overly aggressive use of debt financing, ACE has been forced into bankruptcy. Because apartment complexes are readily salable, the likely outcome of the proceedings will be the sale of the complex to a new owner and distribution of the proceeds to creditors. The cost of bankruptcy in this instance will be correspondingly modest, consisting of the obvious legal, appraisal, and court costs, plus whatever price concessions are necessary to sell the apartments. In substance, because bankruptcy will have little effect on the operating income generated by the apartment complex, bankruptcy costs will be relatively low, and ACE can justify aggressive debt financing.

Note that the cost of bankruptcy here does *not* include the difference between what ACE and its creditors originally thought the apartments were worth and their value just prior to bankruptcy. This loss is due to overbuilding, not bankruptcy, and is incurred by the firm regardless of how it is financed or whether or not it declares bankruptcy. Even all-equity financing, while it may prevent bankruptcy, will not eliminate this loss.

At the other extreme, Moletek is a genetic engineering firm whose chief assets are a brilliant research team and attractive growth opportunities. If Moletek stumbles into bankruptcy, the cost is likely to be very high. Selling the company's assets individually in a liquidation will generate little cash, because most of the assets are intangible. It will also be difficult to realize value by keeping the company intact, either as an independent firm or in the hands of a new owner, for in such an unsettled environment it will be hard to retain key employees and to raise the funds needed to exploit growth opportunities. In essence, because bankruptcy will adversely affect Moletek's operating income, bankruptcy costs are likely to be high and Moletek would be wise to use debt sparingly.

In sum, our brief overview of bankruptcy costs suggests that they vary with the nature of a company's assets. If the resale value of the assets is high either in liquidation or when sold intact to new owners, bankruptcy costs are correspondingly modest. Such firms should be expected to make liberal use of debt financing. Conversely, when resale value is low because the assets are largely intangible and would be difficult to sell intact, bankruptcy costs are comparatively high. Companies matching this profile should use more conservative financing.

Another way to say the same thing is to suggest that the value of a company is composed of two types of assets: physical assets in place, and growth options. Growth options are the exciting investment opportunities a firm is positioned to undertake in coming years. While physical assets tend to retain value in times of financial distress, growth options clearly do not. Consequently, companies with valuable growth options are ill advised to use aggressive debt financing.

Indirect Costs

In addition to direct bankruptcy costs, companies frequently incur a number of more subtle indirect costs as the probability of bankruptcy grows. These costs are especially troublesome because they can be mutually reinforcing, causing a chain reaction in which one cost feeds on another. Internally, these costs include lost profit opportunities as management cuts back investment, R&D, and marketing to conserve cash. Externally, they include lost sales as customers become concerned about future parts and service availability, higher financing costs as investors worry about future payments, and increased operating costs as suppliers become reluctant to make long-run commitments or to provide trade credit. Lost sales and increased costs, in turn, pressure management to become even more conservative, risking further losses. And if this weren't enough, competitors, tasting blood in the water, are inclined to initiate price wars and to compete more aggressively for the company's customers.

Trade creditors in certain industries show an especially strong propensity to cut and run. With a portfolio of perhaps thousands of small-ticket receivables to manage, these suppliers are unwilling to work with ailing customers and instead rush for the exits at the first sign of trouble. With a conservative management, restless customers, aggressive competitors, and flighty suppliers, the slope between financial health and bankruptcy can be a slippery one.

Conflicts of Interest

Managers, owners, and creditors in healthy companies usually share the same fundamental objective: to see the business prosper. When a company falls into financial distress, however, this harmony can evaporate as the various parties begin to worry more about themselves than the firm. The resulting conflicts of interest are a third potential cost of aggressive debt financing. Here is an example of one such conflict. It is known as the over investment problem, but might more aptly be called the "go-for-broke" problem.

XYZ Company is in serious financial difficulty due to over-borrowing, and shareholders' equity is almost worthless. Realizing that shareholders are about to be wiped out, an opportunistic banker proposes a wildly risky investment scheme. Under normal conditions, the company would never consider the investment, but it presently offers one compelling attraction: a small chance at a very large payoff. Shareholders look at the scheme and reason, "This is a truly bad investment, but if we do nothing, our shares will likely end up worthless, while if we make this investment, there is at least a small chance of hitting the jackpot. Then we can settle our debts, and walk away with a little something for ourselves. So what have we got to lose? Let's go-for-broke." This reasoning accurately describes the U.S. savings and loan industry in the late 1980s when many owners, faced with the near certainty their equity would soon be wiped out, took wild risks with depositors' money in the hope of a big score.[2]

So what do these musings about the relative importance of taxes and financial distress costs imply about how to finance a business? Our analysis suggests that managers should consider the following three firm-specific factors when making financing choices:

1. The ability of the company to utilize additional interest tax shields over the life of the debt.

2. The increased probability of incurring financial distress costs created by any new leverage.

3. The magnitude of the distress costs should they occur.

Applying this checklist to Sensient Technologies, we can say that the first consideration should be no barrier to increased debt in as much as the company appears to have plenty of income to take advantage of the increased interest tax shields. Similarly, the company's past income stability suggests the increased chance of incurring financial distress due to the new, higher debt level is probably not excessive. Finally, the distress costs incurred by Sensient, if it were to have difficulty servicing the new debt, appear moderate. The company is not seasonal and does not appear dependent on potentially nervous supplier credit. Furthermore, a price war is not likely inasmuch as quality, innovation, and product consistency seem more important selling points than price. On the other hand, high customer switching costs could create some problems. The thought among existing customers of even a slight change in the color of those magenta tortilla chips resulting from a switch in suppliers has got to be a recurring nightmare. This suggests that existing Sensient customers would probably hang on to the bitter end. By the same token, however, potential new customers might be hesitant to sign a long-term supply contract with a financially weakened Sensient.

Flexibility

The tax benefits-distress costs perspective treats financing decisions as if they were one-time events. Should Sensient raise cash today by selling debt or equity? A broader perspective views such individual decisions

---

[2] Underinvestment problems can also arise in near-bankrupt companies when managers knowingly forgo attractive, safe investment opportunities because too much of the benefits accrue to creditors instead of shareholders.

within the context of a longer-run financing strategy that is shaped in large part by the firm's growth potential and its access to capital markets over time.

At one extreme, if a firm has the rare luxury of always being able to raise debt or equity capital on acceptable terms, its decision is straight-forward. The company can simply select a target capital structure premised on consideration of long-run tax benefits and distress costs and then base specific debt-equity choices on the proximity of its existing capital structure to the target. If the existing debt level is below target, debt financing is the obvious choice. If the current debt level is above target, time to issue equity.

In the more realistic case where continuous access to capital markets is not guaranteed, the decision becomes more complex. For now management must worry not only about long-run targets but also about how today's decision might affect future access to capital markets. This is the notion of financial flexibility: the concern that today's decision not jeopardize future financing options.

To illustrate the importance of financial flexibility to certain firms, consider the challenges faced by XYZ Enterprises, a rapidly growing business in continuing need of external financing. Even when an immediate debt issue appears attractive, XYZ management must understand that extensive reliance of debt financing will eventually "close off the top," meaning added debt financing would no longer be available without a proportional increase in equity. (Top as used here refers to the top portion of the liabilities side of an American balance sheet. British balance sheets show equity on top of liabilities, but then they drive on the wrong side too.) Having thus reached its debt capacity, XYZ would find itself dependent on the equity market for any additional external financing over the next few years. This is a precarious position because equity can be a fickle source of financing. Depending on market conditions and recent company performance, equity may not be available at a reasonable price—or indeed any price. And XYZ would then be forced to forgo attractive investment opportunities for lack of cash. This could prove very expensive, because the inability to make competitively mandated investments can result in a permanent loss of market position. On a more personal note, the CFO's admission that XYZ must pass up lucrative investment opportunities because he cannot raise the money to finance them will not be greeted warmly by his colleagues. Consequently, a concern for financing future growth suggests that XYZ avoid over-reliance on debt financing, thereby maintaining financial flexibility to meet future contingencies.

The situation is more extreme for most small companies and many larger ones that are unable or unwilling to sell new equity. For these firms the financing decision is not whether to issue debt or equity, but whether to issue debt or restrict growth. Of necessity, these companies need to place their financing decision in the larger context of managing growth. Recall from Chapter 4 that when a company is unable or unwilling to sell new equity, its sustainable growth rate is

$$g^* = PRA\hat{T}$$

where P, R, A, and $\hat{T}$ are profit margin, retention ratio, asset turnover ratio, and financial leverage, respectively. In this equation, P and A are determined on the operating side of the business. The financial challenge for these companies is to develop dividend, financing, and growth strategies that enable the firm to expand at an appropriate rate without using too much debt or resorting to common stock financing.

An executive student of mine once told me I would never do anything entrepreneurial because "you know too much about what could go wrong." In the case of debt financing, I am inclined to agree. Too many entrepreneurs, convinced of the eventual success of their endeavors, appear to view debt as an unmitigated blessing. In their eyes, debt's only attribute is that it enables them to expand the size of their empire beyond their own net worth; thus, their growth management strategy becomes to borrow as much money as creditors will lend. In other words, they maximize $\hat{T}$ in the preceding equation. Delegating the financing decision to creditors certainly simplifies life, but it also unwisely puts a critical management decision in the hands of self-interested outsiders. The smarter approach is to select a prudent capital structure and manage the firm's growth rate to lie within this constraint.

Reverse Engineering the Capital Structure Decision

Most companies select or stumble into a particular capital structure and then pray the rating agencies will treat them kindly when rating the debt. A growing number of businesses, however, are reverse engineering the process: first selecting the bond rating they want and then working backward to estimate the maximum amount of debt consistent with the chosen rating. Several consulting companies facilitate this effort by selling proprietary models—based on the observed pattern of past rating agency decisions—for predicting what bond rating a company will receive at differing debt levels.

The appeal of reverse engineering the capital structure decision is twofold. First, it reveals how much more debt a company can take on before suffering a rating downgrade. This is important information to businesses concerned about overuse of debt and to those interested in increasing the interest tax shields associated with debt financing. Second, it eliminates all speculation about how creditors will respond to a particular financing decision, enabling executives to focus instead on the more concrete question of what credit rating is appropriate for their company given its current prospects and strategy.

Market Signaling

Concern for future financial flexibility customarily favors equity financing today. A persuasive counterargument against equity financing, however, is the stock market's likely response. In Chapter 4, we mentioned that on balance, U.S. corporations do not make extensive use of new equity financing and suggested several possible explanations for this apparent bias. It is time now to discuss another.

Academic researchers have explored the stock market's reaction to various company announcements regarding future financing, and the results make fascinating reading. In one study, Paul Asquith and David Mullins, then of Harvard, were interested in what happens to a company's stock price when it announces a new equity sale.[3] To find out, they performed an event study, similar to the one described in Chapter 5, on 531 common stock offerings over the period 1963 to 1981. Defining the event date as the day of first public announcement, Asquith and Mullins found that more than 80 percent of the industrial firms sampled experienced a decline in stock price on the event date and that for the sample as a whole, the decline could not reasonably be attributed to random chance. Moreover, the observed decline did not appear to be recouped in subsequent trading; rather, it remained as a permanent wealth loss to existing owners.

The size of the announcement loss was startling, averaging *more than 30 percent* of the size of the new issue. To put this number into perspective, a 30 percent loss means a company announcing a $100 million equity issue could expect to suffer a permanent loss in the market value of existing equity of about $30 million the day it announced a $100 million equity issue (0.30 × $100 million = $30 million).

To complete the picture, similar studies of debt announcements have not observed the adverse price reactions found for equity financing. Further, it appears that equity announcements work both ways; that is, a company's announcement of its intention to repurchase some of its shares is greeted by a significant increase in stock price.

Why do these price reactions occur? Several explanations exist. One, suggested most often by executives and market practitioners, attributes the observed price reactions to dilution. According to this reasoning, a new equity issue slices the corporate pie into more pieces and reduces the portion of the pie owned by existing shareholders. It is therefore natural that the shares existing shareholders own will be worth less. Conversely, when a company repurchases its shares, each remaining

---

[3] Paul Asquith and David W. Mullins, Jr., "Equity Issues and Offering Dilution," *Journal of Financial Economics,* January–February 1986, pp. 61–89.

share represents ownership of a larger portion of the company and hence is worth more.

Other observers, including yours truly, remain unconvinced by this reasoning, pointing out that while an equity issue may be analogous to slicing a pie into more pieces, the pie also grows by virtue of the equity issue. When a company raises $100 million in an equity issue, it is clearly worth $100 million more than before the issue. And there is no reason to expect that a smaller slice of a larger pie is necessarily worth less; nor is there any reason to expect remaining shareholders to necessarily gain from a share repurchase. True, each post-repurchase share represents a larger percentage ownership claim, but the repurchase also reduces the size of the company.

A more intriguing explanation involves what is known as *market signaling*. Suppose, plausibly enough, that Sensient Technologies's top managers know much more about their company than do outside investors, and consider again Sensient's range of earnings chart in Figure 6.2. Begin by reflecting on which option you would recommend if, as Sensient's chief financial officer, you were highly optimistic about the company's performance in coming years. After a thorough analysis of the market for Sensient's products and its competitors, you are confident that EBIT can only grow over the next decade. If you have been awake the last few pages, you will know that the most attractive option in this circumstance is debt financing. The higher debt level produces a higher ROE today and puts the company on a steeper growth trajectory. Moreover, growing operating income will make it easier to support the higher financial burden of the debt.

Now reverse the exercise and consider which option you would recommend if you were concerned about Sensient's prospects, fearing that future EBIT might well decline. In this scenario, equity financing is the clear winner because of its superior coverage and higher ROE at low operating levels.

But if those who know the most about a company prefer debt when the future looks bright and equity when it looks grim, what does an equity announcement tell investors? Right: It signals the market that management is concerned about the future and has opted for the safe financing choice. Is it any wonder, then, that stock price falls on the announcement and that many companies are reluctant to even mention the "E" word, much less sell it?

The market signal conveyed by a share repurchase announcement is just the reverse. Top management is optimistic about the company's future prospects and perceives that current stock price is inexplicably low, so low that share repurchase constitutes an irresistible bargain. A repurchase announcement therefore signals good news to investors, and stock price rises.

A more Machiavellian view, which nonetheless comes to the same conclusion, sees management as exploiting new investors by opportunistically selling shares when they are overpriced and repurchasing them when they are underpriced. But regardless of whether management elects to sell new equity because it is concerned about the company's future or because it wants to gouge new investors, the signal is the same: New equity announcements are bad news and repurchase announcements are good news.

The need to sell equity at a discount is an example of what economists call the "lemons problem." Whenever the seller of an asset knows more about it than a buyer, the buyer, fearing she is being offered a lemon, will only purchase the asset at a bargain price. And the greater the information disparity between seller and buyer, the greater the discount will have to be. Your neighbor, who is trying to sell his month-old Mercedes, might be telling the truth when he says he only wants to sell it because his wife doesn't like the color. But then again, maybe he is not. Maybe the car has serious problems he is not revealing. Maybe it's a lemon. To guard against this possibility, a wise but uninformed buyer will only buy the car at a steep discount from the original price. Moreover, wise sellers, knowing they can only sell almost-new cars at a steep discount, will tell their wives to get used to the color, which, in turn, only increases the odds that the remaining almost-new cars for sale really are lemons.

Stewart Myers of MIT reasons that this lemons problem encourages companies to adopt what he calls a "pecking order" approach to financing.[4] At the top of the pecking order as the most preferred means of financing are internal sources, retained profits, depreciation, and excess cash accumulated from past profit retentions. Companies prefer internal financing sources because they avoid the lemons problem entirely. External sources are second in order of preference, with debt financing dominating equity because it is less likely to generate a negative signal. Or said differently, debt is preferred to equity because the information disparity between seller and buyer is less with debt, resulting in a smaller lemons problem. The financing decision, then, essentially amounts to working progressively down this pecking order in search of the first feasible source. Myers also notes that the observed debt-to-equity ratios of such pecking-order companies are less a product of a rational balancing of advantages and disadvantages of debt relative to equity and more the aggregate result over time of the company's profitability relative to its investment needs. Thus, high-profit-margin, modestly growing companies can get away with little or no debt, while

---

[4] Stewart C. Myers, "The Capital Structure Puzzle," *Journal of Finance,* July 1984, pp. 575–592.

lower-margin, more rapidly expanding businesses may be forced to live with higher leverage ratios.

Management Incentives

Incentive effects are not relevant in most financing decisions, but when relevant, their influence can be dominating.

Managers in many companies enjoy a degree of autonomy from owners. And human nature being what it is, they are inclined to use this autonomy to pursue their own interests rather than those of owners. This separation of ownership and control enables managers to indulge their personal preferences for such things as retaining profits in the business rather than returning them to owners, pursuing growth at the expense of profitability, and settling for satisfactory performance rather than excellence.

A virtue of aggressive debt financing in some instances is that it can reduce the gap between owners' interests and those of managers. The mechanics are simple. When a company's interest and principal repayment burden is high, even the most recalcitrant manager understands that he must generate healthy cash flows or risk losing the business and his job. With creditors breathing down their necks, managers quickly find there is no room for ill-advised investments or less than maximum effort. As discussed in more detail in Chapter 9, leveraged buyout firms have found that aggressive debt financing, especially when combined with significant management ownership, can create powerful incentives to improve performance. Ownership in such highly levered companies serves as a carrot to encourage superior performance, while the high debt level is a stick to punish inferior performance.

The Financing Decision and Growth

We have examined five ways in which a company's financing choices can affect its cash flows and hence its value. The art of the financing decision is to weigh the relative importance of these five forces for the specific firm. To illustrate the process, let's consider what these forces suggest about how debt levels should vary with firm growth.

Rapid Growth and the Virtues of Conservatism

Review of the likely effect of the five forces on rapidly growing businesses strongly suggests that high growth and high debt are a dangerous combination. First, the most powerful engine of value creation in a rapidly growing business is new investment, not interest tax shields or incentive effects that might accompany debt financing. Better, therefore, to make financing a passive servant to growth by striving to maintain unrestricted access to financial markets. This implies modest debt financing. Second, to the extent that high growth firms generate volatile income streams, chances of financial distress rise rapidly as interest coverage falls. Third, because much of a high-growth firm's value is represented by intangible growth opportunities, expected distress costs of such firms are large.

These considerations suggest the following financing polices for rapidly growing businesses:

- Maintain a conservative leverage ratio with ample unused borrowing capacity to ensure continuous access to financial markets.

- Adopt a modest dividend payout policy that enables the company to finance most of its growth internally.

- Use cash, marketable securities, and unused borrowing capacity as temporary liquidity buffers to provide financing in years when investment needs exceed internal sources.

- If external financing is necessary, use debt only to the point where the leverage ratio begins to affect financial flexibility.

- Sell equity rather than limit growth, thereby constraining growth only as a last resort after all other alternatives have been exhausted.

Low Growth and the Appeal of Aggressive Financing

Compared to their rapidly growing brethren, slow-growth companies have a much easier time with financing decisions. Because their chief financial problem is disposing of excess operating cash flow, concerns about financial flexibility and adverse market signaling are largely foreign to them. However, beyond merely eliminating a problem, this situation creates an opportunity that a number of companies have successfully exploited. The logic goes like this. Face the reality that the business has few attractive investment opportunities, and seek to create value for owners through aggressive use of debt financing. Use the company's healthy operating cash flow as the magnet for borrowing as much money as is feasible, and use the proceeds to repurchase shares.

Such a strategy promises at least three possible payoffs to owners. First, increased interest tax shields reduce income taxes, leaving more money for investors. Second, the share repurchase announcement should generate a positive market signal. Third, the high financial leverage may significantly improve management incentives. Thus, the burden high financial leverage imposes on management to make large, recurring interest and principal payments or face bankruptcy may be

---

Don't Talk to Deere & Company About Market Signaling

The experiences of Deere & Company, the world's largest farm equipment manufacturer, in the late 1970s and early 1980s provide a vivid object lesson for much of this chapter. Among the lessons illustrated are the value of financial flexibility, the use of finance as a competitive weapon, and the power of market signaling.

Beginning in 1976, rising oil prices, high and increasing inflation rates, and record-high interest rates sent the farm equipment industry into a severe tailspin. Much more conservative financially than its principal rivals, Massey Ferguson and International Harvester, Deere chose this moment to use its superior balance sheet strength as a competitive weapon. While competitors retrenched under the burden of high interest rates and heavy debt loads, Deere borrowed liberally to finance a major capital investment program and support financially distressed dealers. The strategy saw Deere's three-company market share rise from 38 percent in 1976 to 49 percent by 1980; such was the value of Deere's superior financial flexibility.

But by late 1980, with its borrowing capacity dwindling and the farm equipment market still depressed, Deere faced the difficult choice between curtailing its predatory expansion program and issuing new equity into the teeth of an industry depression. On January 5, 1981, the company announced a $172 million equity issue and watched the market value of its existing shares immediately fall by $241 million. So powerful was the announcement effect that Deere's existing shareholders lost more value than Deere stood to raise from the issue.

Despite the negative market response, Deere managers were so strongly convinced of the long-run virtues of their strategy that they gritted their teeth, issued the equity, and used the proceeds to reduce indebtedness. Deere thus regained the borrowing capacity and the financial flexibility it needed to continue expanding, while its rivals remained mired in financial distress.

---

just the elixir needed to encourage them to squeeze more cash flow out of the business.

In summary, an old saw among bank borrowers is that the only companies banks are willing to lend money to are those that don't need it. We see now that much the same dynamic may be at work on the borrowers' side. Slow-growth businesses that don't need external financing may find it attractive to finance aggressively, while rapidly growing businesses in need of external cash find it appealing to maintain conservative capital structures.

Empirical work supports the wisdom of this perspective. In their study of the ties between company value and the use of debt financing, John McConnell and Henri Servaes have found that for high-growth businesses increasing leverage reduces firm value, while precisely the reverse is true for slow-growth businesses.[5]

What does all this imply for Sensient Technologies's decision? Based on the information available, my advice, on balance, is to issue debt.

---

[5]John J. McConnell and Henri Servaes, "Equity Ownership and the Two Faces of Debt," *Journal of Financial Economics,* September 1995, pp. 131–57.

Colt Industries' Experience with Aggressive Financing

Colt Industries' late 1986 recapitalization illustrates the potential of aggressive financing in mature businesses. Facing increasing cash flows from its aerospace and automotive operations and a dearth of attractive investment opportunities, Colt decided to recapitalize its business by offering shareholders $85 in cash plus one share of stock in the newly recapitalized company in exchange for each old share held.

To finance the $85 cash payment, Colt borrowed $1.4 billion, raising total long-term debt to $1.6 billion and reducing the book value of shareholders' equity to *minus* $157 million. In other words, after the recapitalization, Colt's liabilities exceeded the book value of its assets by $157 million, yielding a negative book value of equity. We are talking serious leverage here. But book values are of secondary importance to lenders when the borrower has the cash flow to service its obligations, and this is where Colt's healthy operating cash flows were critical. Management's willingness to commit virtually all of its future cash flow to debt service enabled the company to secure the needed financing.

How did the shareholders make out? Quite well, thank you. Just prior to the announcement of the exchange offer, Colt's shares were trading at $67, and immediately after the exchange was completed, shares in the newly recapitalized company were trading for $10. So the offer came down to this: $85 cash plus one new share of stock worth $10 in exchange for each old share worth $67. This works out to a windfall gain to owners of $28 a share, or 42 percent ($28 = $85 + $10 − $67).

Debt's $11 million first year interest tax shield would be nice, while equity's $135 signaling cost would be quite painful ($135 = 30% × $450). The company does not anticipate raising capital from outside sources again in the near future, so flexibility is not an important concern. Moreover, the increased interest and principal requirements of the new debt might encourage management to work harder and smarter. As to risks, Sensient's historically very stable cash flows suggest that expected distress costs will remain modest, even at the lower interest coverage ratios created by the debt financing. Finally, debt financing will help solve Sensient's continuing problem of what to do with the excess cash being generated. In the future, they can use it to service the new debt. All in all, a nice package.

Selecting a Maturity Structure

When a company decides to raise debt, the next question is: What maturity should the debt have? Should the company take out a 1-year loan, sell 7-year notes, or market 30-year bonds? Looking at the firm's entire capital structure, the minimum-risk maturity structure occurs when the maturity of liabilities equals that of assets, for in this configuration, cash generated from operations over coming years should be sufficient to repay existing liabilities as they mature. In other words, the liabilities will be self-liquidating. If the maturity of liabilities is less than that of assets, the company incurs a refinancing risk because some maturing liabilities will have to be paid off from the proceeds of newly raised capital. Also, as noted in Chapter 5, the rollover of maturing debt is not an automatic feature of capital markets. When the maturity of liabilities is greater than that of assets, cash provided by operations should be more than sufficient to repay existing liabilities as they mature. This provides an extra margin of safety, but it also means the firm may have excess cash in some periods.

If maturity matching is minimum risk, why do anything else? Why allow the maturity of liabilities to be less than that of assets? Companies mismatch either because long-term debt is unavailable on acceptable terms or because management anticipates that mismatching will reduce total borrowing costs. For example, if the treasurer believes interest rates will decline in the future, an obvious strategy is to use short-term debt now and hope to roll it over into longer-term debt at lower rates in the future. Of course, efficient-markets advocates criticize this strategy on the grounds that the treasurer has no basis for believing she can forecast future interest rates.

Inflation and Financing Strategy

An old adage in finance is that it's good to be a debtor during inflation because the debtor repays the loan with depreciated dollars. It is important to understand, however, that this saying is correct only when the inflation is unexpected. When creditors expect inflation, the interest rate they charge rises to compensate for the expected decline in the purchasing power of the loan principal. This means it is not necessarily advantageous to borrow during inflation. In fact, if inflation unexpectedly declines during the life of a loan, it can work to the disadvantage of the borrower. The proper statement of the old adage, therefore, is that it's good to be a borrower during **unexpected** inflation.

APPENDIX

The Irrelevance Proposition

This appendix demonstrates the irrelevance of capital structure proposition mentioned in the chapter and illustrates in greater detail why the tax deductibility of interest favors debt financing. The irrelevance proposition says that holding expected cash flows constant, the way a company finances its operations has no effect on firm or shareholder value. As far as owners are concerned, a company might just as well use 90 percent debt financing as 10 percent.

The irrelevance proposition is significant not because it describes reality, but because it directs attention to what's important about financing decisions: understanding how financing choices affect firm cash flows. The proposition is also an interesting intellectual puzzle in its own right.

No Taxes

Legend has it that a waitress once asked Yogi Berra how many pieces he'd like his pizza cut into, and he replied, "You'd better make it six; I don't think I'm hungry enough to eat eight." Absent taxes, a company's financing decision can be likened to slicing Yogi's pizza: No matter how you slice up claims to the firm's cash flow, it is still the same firm with the same earning power and hence the same market value. The benefits of increased return to shareholders from higher leverage are precisely offset by the increased risks so that market value is unaffected by leverage.

Here is an example demonstrating this assertion. Your stockbroker has come up with two possible investments, Timid Inc. and Bold Company. The two firms happen to be identical in every respect except that Timid uses no debt financing while Bold relies on 80 percent debt at an annual interest cost of 10 percent. Each has $1,000 of assets and generates expected annual earnings before interest and tax of $400 in perpetuity. For simplicity, we will suppose that both companies distribute all their earnings every year as dividends.

The first two columns of Table 6A.1 show the bottom portion of pro forma income statements for the two companies in the absence of taxes. Note that Timid, Inc., shows higher earnings because it has no interest expense. Comparing Timid's $400 annual earnings to your prospective investment of $1,000 suggests a 40 percent annual return. Not bad! However, your broker recommends Bold Company, pointing out that because of the company's aggressive use of debt financing, you can purchase its entire equity for only $200. Comparing Bold Company's annual income of $320 to a $200 investment produces an expected annual return of 160% ($320/$200 = 160%). Wow!

But you have studied enough finance to know that the expected return to equity almost always rises with debt financing, so this result is not especially surprising. Moreover, a moment's reflection should convince you that it is incorrect to compare returns on two investments with

TABLE 6A.1   In the Absence of Taxes, Debt Financing Affects Neither Income nor Firm Value; In the Presence of Taxes, Prudent Debt Financing Increases Income and Firm Value

	No Taxes		Corporate Taxes at 40%	
	Timid Inc.	Bold Co.	Timid Inc.	Bold Co.
Corporate Income				
EBIT	$ 400	$400	$ 400	$400
Interest expense	0	80	0	80
Earnings before tax	400	320	400	320
Corporate tax	0	0	160	128
Earnings after tax	$ 400	$320	$ 240	$192
Investment	$1,000	$200	$1,000	$200
Rate of return	**40%**	**160%**	**24%**	**96%**
Personal Income				
Dividends received	400	320	240	192
Interest expense	80	0	80	0
Total income	$ 320	$320	$ 160	$192
Equity invested	$ 200	$200	$ 200	$200
Rate of return	**160%**	**160%**	**80%**	**96%**
Personal Taxes at 33%				
Income before tax			160	192
Personal taxes			53	63
Income after tax			$ 107	$129
Equity invested			$ 200	$200
Rate of return			**54%**	**64%**

different risk. If the return on investment A is greater than the return on investment B and they have the same risk, A is the better choice. But if A has a higher return and higher risk, as in the present case, all bets are off. Poker players and fighter pilots might prefer investment A despite its higher risk, while we more timid souls might reach the opposite conclusion.

More to the point, it is important to note that you are not dependent on Bold Company for financial leverage. You can borrow on your own account to help pay for your purchase of Timid's shares and in so doing precisely replicate Bold's numbers. The bottom portion of the left two columns in Table 6A.1, labeled Personal Income, show the results of your borrowing $800 at 10 percent interest to finance purchase of Timid's shares. Subtracting $80 interest and comparing your total income to your $200 equity investment, we find that your levered return on Timid stock is now also 160 percent. You can generate precisely the same return on either investment provided you are willing to substitute personal debt for corporate debt.

So what have we proven? We have shown that when investors can substitute homemade leverage for corporate leverage in the absence of taxes, the way a business is financed does not affect the total return to owners. And if total return is unaffected, neither is the value of the business. Firm value is independent of financing. If investors can replicate the leverage effects of corporate borrowing on their own account, there is no reason for them to pay more for a levered firm than an unlevered one. (If the logic here seems a bit counterintuitive, you will be heartened to learn that Franco Modigliani and Merton Miller won Nobel Prizes largely for explaining it.)

Taxes

Let us now repeat our saga in a more interesting world that includes taxes. The figures in the upper-right corner of Table 6A.1 show Timid and Bold's earnings after taxes in the presence of a 40 percent corporate tax rate. As before, absent any borrowing on your part, Bold continues to offer the more attractive return of 96 percent versus 24 percent for Timid. But contrary to the no-taxes case, the substitution of personal borrowing for corporate borrowing does not eliminate the differential. Even after borrowing $800 to help finance purchase of Timid, your return is only 80 percent versus 96 percent on Bold's stock. The levered business now offers a higher return and thus is more valuable than its unlevered cousin.

Why does debt financing increase the value of a business in the presence of taxes? Look at the tax bills of the two companies. Timid's taxes are $160, while Bold's are only $128, a saving of $32. Three parties share in the fruits of a company's success: creditors, owners, and the tax collector. Our example shows that debt financing, with its tax-deductible interest expense, reduces the tax collector's take in favor of the owners'. In other words, the financing decision increases expected cash flow to owners.

The bottom portion of Table 6A.1 is for suspicious readers who think these results might hinge on the omission of personal taxes. There you will note that imposition of a 33 percent personal tax on income reduces the annual after-tax advantage of debt financing from $32 to $22, but does not eliminate it. Note too that this conclusion holds at any personal tax rate, as long as it is the same for both firms. Because many investors, such as mutual funds and pension funds, do not pay taxes, the convention is to dodge the problem of defining an appropriate personal tax rate by concentrating on earnings after corporate taxes but before personal taxes. We will gratefully follow that convention here.

I should note that our finding of a tax law bias in favor of debt financing is largely an American result. In most other industrialized countries, corporate and personal taxes are at least partially integrated, meaning dividend recipients receive at least partial credit on their personal tax bills for corporate taxes paid on distributed profits. As in our no-tax example, there are no tax benefits to debt financing when corporate and personal taxes are fully integrated.

In the presence of American-style corporate taxes, then, the reshuffling of paper claims to include more debt does create value—at least from the shareholders' perspective, if not from that of the U.S. Treasury—because it increases the cash flow available to private investors. The amount of the increase in annual income to shareholders created by debt financing equals the corporate tax rate times the interest expense, or what we referred to earlier as the interest tax shield. In our example, annual company earnings after tax plus interest expense increases $32 a year ($192 + $80 − $240 = $32), which also equals the tax rate of 40 percent times the interest expense of $80.

Saying the same thing in symbols, if V_L is the value of the company when levered and V_U is its value unlevered, our example says that

$$V_L = V_U + \text{Value } (tI)$$

where t is the corporate tax rate, I is annual interest expense in dollars, and Value *(tI)* represents the value today of all future interest tax shields. In the next chapter, we will refer to this last term as the present value of future tax shields. In words, then, our equation says the value of a levered company equals the value of the same company unlevered plus the present value of the interest tax shields.

Taken at face value, this appendix suggests a disquieting conclusion: The value of a business is maximized when it is financed entirely with debt. But you know after reading the chapter that this is just the beginning of our story. For just as the tax deductibility of interest causes firm value to rise with leverage, the costs of financial distress cause it to fall. Add concerns about financial flexibility, market signaling, and incentive effects; season with a pinch of sustainable growth; and you have the recipe for the modern view on corporate financing decisions. Not a feast, perhaps, but certainly a hearty first course.

Stern, Joel M., and Donald H. Chew, Jr., ed., *The Revolution in Corporate Finance*, 4th ed. Malden, MA: Blackwell Publishing, 2003. 631 pages.

A collection of practitioner-oriented articles, many by leading academics, originally appearing in the *Journal of Applied Corporate Finance*. See especially "The Modigliani-Miller Proposition after 30 Years," by Merton Miller; "Raising Capital: Theory and Evidence," by Clifford W. Smith, Jr.; and "Still Searching for Optimal Capital Structure," by Stewart C. Myers. $60.

WEBSITES

www.abiworld.org
The American Bankruptcy Institute's website with news and statistics about many aspects of corporate and personal bankruptcy.

PROBLEMS

Answers to odd-numbered problems appear at the end of the book. For additional problems with answers, see **www.mhhe.com/higgins10e.**

1. Looking at Table 6.4, why do electric utilities have such a low times-interest-earned ratio? Why is the ratio for information technology companies so high?

2. What is operating leverage? How, if at all, is it similar to financial leverage? If a firm has high operating leverage, would you expect it to have high or low financial leverage? Explain your reasoning.

3. Explain why increasing financial leverage increases the risk borne by shareholders.

4. Explain how a company can incur costs of financial distress without ever going bankrupt. What is the nature of these costs?

5. One recommendation in the chapter is that companies with promising investment opportunities should strive to maintain a conservative capital structure. Yet many promising small businesses are heavily indebted.

   a. Why should most companies with promising investment opportunities strive to maintain conservative capital structures?

   b. Why do you suppose many promising small businesses fail to follow this recommendation?

6. Why might it make sense for a mature, slow-growth company to have a high debt ratio?

7. As the financial vice president of Progressive Media, you have the following information:

Next year's expected net income after tax but before new financing	$50 million
Sinking-fund payments due next year on existing debt	$17 million
Interest due next year on existing debt	$18 million
Company tax rate	35%
Common stock price, per share	$25
Common shares outstanding	20 million

   a. Calculate Progressive's times-interest-earned ratio for next year assuming the firm raises $50 million of new debt at an interest rate of 7 percent.

   b. Calculate Progressive's times-burden-covered ratio for next year assuming annual sinking-fund payments on the new debt will equal $8 million.

   c. Calculate next year's earnings per share assuming Progressive raises the $50 million of new debt.

   d. Calculate next year's times-interest-earned ratio, times-burden-covered ratio, and earnings per share if Progressive sells 2 million new shares at $20 a share instead of raising new debt.

8. A broker wants to sell a customer an investment costing $100 with an expected payoff in one year of $106. The customer indicates that a 6 percent return is not very attractive. The broker responds by suggesting the customer borrow $90 for one year at 4 percent interest to help pay for the investment.

   a. What is the customer's expected return if she borrows the money?

   b. Does borrowing the money make the investment more attractive?

   c. What does the Irrelevance Proposition say about whether borrowing the money makes the investment more attractive?

9. Explain how each of the following changes will affect a company's range of earnings chart such as that shown in Figure 6.2. Which changes would make increased financial leverage more attractive? Which would make it less attractive?

   a. An increase in the interest rate on the new debt to be raised.

   b. An increase in the company's stock price.

   c. Increased uncertainty about the issuing company's future earnings.

   d. Increased cash dividends paid on common stock.

   e. An increase in the amount of debt the company already has outstanding.

10. FARO Technologies, whose products include portable 3D measurement equipment, has 400 million shares outstanding trading at $5 a share. The company announces its intention to raise $200 million by selling new shares.

   a. What do market signaling studies suggest will happen to FARO's stock price on the announcement date? Why?

   b. How large a gain or loss in aggregate dollar terms do market signaling studies suggest existing FARO shareholders will experience on the announcement date?

   c. What percentage of the amount of money FARO intends to raise is this expected gain or loss?

   d. What percentage of the value of FARO's existing equity prior to the announcement is this expected gain or loss?

   e. At what price should FARO expect its existing shares to sell for immediately after the announcement?

11. This is a more difficult but informative problem. James Brodrick & Sons, Inc. is growing rapidly and, if at all possible, would like to finance its growth without selling new equity. Selected information from the company's five-year financial forecast follows.

Year	1	2	3	4	5
Earnings after tax (millions)	$100	$130	$170	$230	$300
Capital investment (millions)	$175	$300	$300	$350	$440
Target book value debt-to-equity ratio (%)	120	120	120	120	120
Dividend payout ratio (%)	?	?	?	?	?
Marketable securities (millions)	$200	$200	$200	$200	$200
(Year 0 marketable securities = $200 million.)					

   a. According to this forecast, what dividends will the company be able to distribute annually without raising new equity? What will the annual dividend payout ratio be? (Hint: remember sources of cash must equal uses at all times.)

   b. Assume the company wants a stable payout ratio over time and plans to use its marketable securities portfolio as a buffer to absorb year-to-year variations in earnings and investments. Set the annual payout ratio equal to the five-year sum of total dividends paid determined in part (a) divided by total earnings. Then solve for the size of the company's marketable securities portfolio each year.

   c. Suppose earnings fall below forecast every year. What options does the company have for continuing to fund its investments?

    d. What does the pecking-order theory say about how management will rank these options?

    e. Why might management be inclined to follow this pecking order?

12. An all-equity business has 100 million shares outstanding selling for $20 a share. Management believes that interest rates are unreasonably low and decides to execute a dividend recapitalization (a recap). It will raise $1 billion in debt and repurchase 50 million shares.

    a. What is the market value of the firm prior to the recap? What is the market value of equity?

    b. Assuming the Irrelevance Proposition holds, what is the market value of the firm after the recap? What is the market value of equity?

    c. Do equity shareholders appear to have gained or lost as a result of the recap? Please explain.

    d. Assume now that the recap increases total firm cash flows, which adds $100 million to the value of the firm. Now what is the market value of the firm? What is the market value of equity?

    e. Do equity shareholders appear to have gained or lost as a result of the recap in this revised scenario?

eXcel 13. This problem asks you to analyze the capital structure of HCA, Inc., the largest private operator of health care facilities in the world. In 2006, a syndicate of private equity firms bought the firm for $31.6 billion and took it private. In November 2010, as interest rates hit record lows, the company announced a dividend recapitalization in which it would distribute an extraordinary $2 billion dividend financed in large part by a $1.53 billion bond offering.

    An Excel spreadsheet with HCA's financial statements for 2005–2009 and specific questions is available at **www.mhhe.com/higgins10e.** (Select Student Edition > Choose a Chapter > Files.)

eXcel 14. This problem asks you to evaluate a major increase in financial leverage on the part of Avon Products, Inc. The company's financial statements for 2001–2003 and specific questions are available for download at **www.mhhe.com/higgins10e.** (Select Student Edition > Choose a Chapter > Files.) You may also find it useful to consult the company's past annual reports (10-Ks), available at **www.secinfo.com.**

eXcel 15. Problem 13, part (f) in Chapter 3 asks you to construct a five-year financial projection for Aquatic Supplies beginning in 2012. Based on your forecast or the suggested answer in the file C3_Problem_13_Answer.xlsx, answer the following questions. The file is available at

CHAPTER SEVEN

Discounted Cash Flow Techniques

A nearby penny is worth a distant dollar.

Anonymous

The chief determinant of what a company will become is the investments it makes today. The generation and evaluation of creative investment proposals is far too important a task to be left to finance specialists; instead, it is the ongoing responsibility of all managers throughout the organization. In well-managed companies, the process starts at a strategic level with senior management specifying the businesses in which the company will compete and determining the means of competition. Operating managers then translate these strategic goals into concrete action plans involving specific investment proposals. A key aspect of this process is the financial evaluation of investment proposals, or what is frequently called *capital budgeting*. The achievement of an objective requires the outlay of money today in expectation of increased future benefits. It is necessary to decide, first, whether the anticipated future benefits are large enough, given the risks, to justify the current expenditure, and second, whether the proposed investment is the most cost-effective way to achieve the objective. This and the following chapter address these questions.

Viewed broadly, the discounted cash flow techniques considered here and in the following chapters are relevant whenever a company contemplates an action entailing costs or benefits that extend beyond the current year. This covers a lot of ground, including such disparate topics as valuing stocks and bonds, analyzing equipment acquisitions or sales, choosing among competing production technologies, deciding whether to launch a new product, valuing divisions or whole companies for purchase or sale, assessing marketing campaigns and R&D programs, and even designing a corporate strategy. Indeed, it is not an exaggeration to say that discounted cash flow analysis is the backbone of modern finance and even modern business.

Figures of Merit

The financial evaluation of any investment opportunity involves three discrete steps:

1. Estimate the relevant cash flows.

2. Calculate a figure of merit for the investment.

3. Compare the figure of merit to an acceptance criterion.

A *figure of merit* is a number summarizing an investment's economic worth. A common figure of merit is the rate of return. Like the other figures of merit to be discussed, the rate of return translates the complicated cash inflows and outflows associated with an investment into a single number summarizing its economic worth. An *acceptance criterion*, on the other hand, is a standard of comparison that helps the analyst determine whether an investment's figure of merit is attractive enough to warrant acceptance. It's like a fisher who can keep only fish longer than 10 inches. To the fisher, the length of the fish is the relevant figure of merit, and 10 inches is the acceptance criterion.

Although determining figures of merit and acceptance criteria appears to be difficult on first exposure, the first step, estimating the relevant cash flows, is the most challenging in practice. Unlike the basically mechanical problems encountered in calculating figures of merit and acceptance criteria, estimating relevant cash flows is more of an art form, often requiring a thorough understanding of a company's markets, competitive position, and long-run intentions. Difficulties range from commonplace concerns with depreciation, financing costs, and working capital investments to more arcane questions of shared resources, excess capacity, and contingent opportunities. And pervading the whole topic is the fact that many important costs and benefits cannot be measured in monetary terms and so must be evaluated qualitatively.

In this chapter, we will initially set aside questions of relevant cash flows and acceptance criteria to concentrate on figures of merit. Later we will return to the estimation of relevant cash flows. Acceptance criteria will be addressed in the following chapter under the general heading "Risk Analysis in Investment Decisions."

To begin our discussion of figures of merit, let's consider a simple numerical example. Pacific Rim Resources, Inc., is contemplating construction of a container-loading pier in Seattle. The company's best estimate of the cash flows associated with constructing and operating the pier for a 10-year period appears in Table 7.1.

TABLE 7.1 Cash Flows for Container-Loading Pier ($ millions)

Year	0	1	2	3	4	5	6	7	8	9	10
Cash flow	($40)	7.5	7.5	7.5	7.5	7.5	7.5	7.5	7.5	7.5	17

FIGURE 7.1 Cash Flow Diagram for Container-Loading Pier

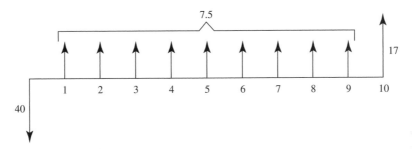

Figure 7.1 presents the same information in the form of a *cash flow diagram*, which is simply a graphical display of the pier's costs and benefits distributed along a time line. Despite its simplicity, I find that many common mistakes can be avoided by preparing such a diagram for even the most elementary investment opportunities. We see that the pier will cost $40 million to construct and is expected to generate cash inflows of $7.5 million annually for 10 years. In addition, the company expects to salvage the pier for $9.5 million at the end of its useful life, bringing the 10th-year cash flow to $17 million.

The Payback Period and the Accounting Rate of Return

Pacific's management wants to know whether the anticipated benefits from the pier justify the $40 million cost. As we will see shortly, a proper answer to this question must reflect the *time value of money*. But before addressing this topic, let's consider two commonly used, back-of-the-envelope-type figures of merit that, despite their popularity, suffer from some glaring weaknesses. One, known as the *payback period*, is defined as the time the company must wait before recouping its original investment. The pier's payback period is 5⅓ years, meaning the company will have to wait this long to recoup its original investment (5⅓ = 40/7.5).

The second widely used, but nonetheless deficient, figure of merit is the *accounting rate of return*, defined as

$$\text{Accounting rate of return} = \frac{\text{Annual average cash inflow}}{\text{Total cash outflow}}$$

The pier's accounting rate of return is 21.1 percent ([(7.5 × 9 + 17)/10]/40).

The problem with the accounting rate of return is its insensitivity to the timing of cash flows. For example, a postponement of all of the cash inflows from Pacific's container-loading pier to year 10 obviously reduces the value of the investment but does not affect the accounting rate of return. In addition to ignoring the timing of cash flows within the payback date, the payback period is insensitive to all cash flows occurring beyond this date. Thus, an increase in the salvage value of the pier from $9.5 million to $90.5 million clearly makes the investment more attractive. Yet it has no effect on the payback period, nor does any other change in cash flows in years 7 through 10.

In fairness to the payback period, I should add that although it is clearly an inadequate figure of investment merit, it has proven to be useful as a rough measure of investment risk. In most settings, the longer it takes to recoup an original investment, the greater the risk. This is especially true in high-technology environments where management can forecast only a few years into the future. Under these circumstances, an investment that does not promise to pay back within the forecasting horizon is equivalent to a night in Las Vegas without the floorshow.

The Time Value of Money

An accurate figure of merit must reflect the fact that a dollar today is worth more than a dollar in the future. This is the notion of the time value of money, and it exists for at least three reasons. One is that inflation reduces the purchasing power of future dollars relative to current ones; another is that in most instances, the uncertainty surrounding the receipt of a dollar increases as the date of receipt recedes into the future. Thus, the promise of $1 in 30 days is usually worth more than the promise of $1 in 30 months, simply because it is customarily more certain.

A third reason money has a time value involves the important notion of opportunity costs. By definition, the *opportunity cost* of any investment is the return one could earn on the next best alternative. A dollar today is worth more than a dollar in one year because the dollar today can be productively invested and will grow into more than a dollar in one year. Waiting to receive the dollar until next year carries an opportunity cost equal to the return on the forgone investment. Because there are always productive opportunities for investment dollars, all investments involve opportunity costs.

Compounding and Discounting

Because money has a time value, we cannot simply combine cash flows occurring at different dates as we do in calculating the payback period and the accounting rate of return. To adjust investment cash flows for their differing time value, we need to use the ideas of compounding and discounting. Anyone who has ever had a bank account knows intuitively what compounding is. Suppose you have a bank account paying 10 percent annual interest, and you deposit $1 at the start of the year. What will it be worth at the end of the year? Obviously, $1.10. Now suppose you leave the dollar in the account for two years. What will it be worth then? This is a little harder, but most of us realize that because you earn interest on your interest, the answer is $1.21. *Compounding* is the process of determining the future value of a present sum. The following simple cash flow diagrams summarize the exercise. And note the pattern: As the number of years increases, so too does the power by which we raise the interest rate term $(1 + .10)$. By extension, the future value of $1.00 in, say, 19 years at 10 percent interest is thus, $F_{19} = \$1(1 + .10)^{19} = \$6.12$.

Interest rate = 10%

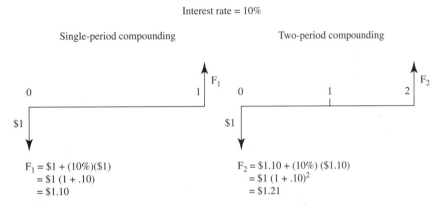

Single-period compounding

$F_1 = \$1 + (10\%)(\$1)$
$\quad = \$1\,(1 + .10)$
$\quad = \$1.10$

Two-period compounding

$F_2 = \$1.10 + (10\%)\,(\$1.10)$
$\quad = \$1\,(1 + .10)^2$
$\quad = \$1.21$

Discounting is simply compounding turned on its head: It is the process of finding the present value of a future sum. Yet despite the obvious similarities, many people find discounting somehow mysterious. And as luck would have it, the convention has become to use discounting rather than compounding to analyze investment opportunities.

Here is how discounting works. Suppose you can invest money to earn a 10 percent annual return and you are promised $1 in one year. What is the value of this promise today? Clearly, it is worth less than $1, but the exact figure is probably not something that pops immediately to mind. In fact, the answer is $0.909. This is the *present value* of $1 to be received in one year, because if you had $0.909 today, you could invest it at 10 percent interest, and it would grow into $1 in one year [$1.00 = 0.909(1 + 0.10)].

Now, if we complicate matters further and ask what is the value of one dollar to be received in two years, intuition fails most of us completely. We know the answer must be less than $0.909, but beyond that, things are a fog. In fact, the answer is $0.826. This sum, invested for two years at 10 percent interest, will grow, or compound, into $1 in two years. The following cash flow diagrams illustrate these discounting problems. Note the formal similarity to compounding. The only difference is that in compounding we know the present amount and seek the future sum, whereas in discounting we know the future sum and seek the present amount.

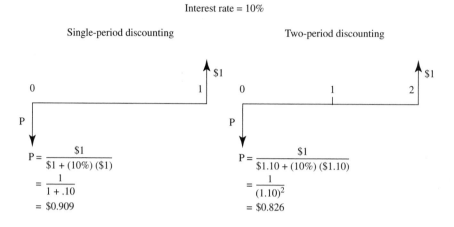

Interest rate = 10%

Single-period discounting

$$P = \frac{\$1}{\$1 + (10\%)\,(\$1)}$$

$$= \frac{1}{1 + .10}$$

$$= \$0.909$$

Two-period discounting

$$P = \frac{\$1}{\$1.10 + (10\%)\,(\$1.10)}$$

$$= \frac{1}{(1.10)^2}$$

$$= \$0.826$$

Present Value Calculations

How did I know the answers to these discounting problems? I could have done the arithmetic in any of three ways: use a computer to solve the formulas appearing below the cash flow diagrams; look up the answers in Appendix A at the back of the book; or punch the appropriate numbers into a financial calculator. In this instance, I opted for a calculator, but the choice is largely a matter of convenience.

Appendix A, appearing at the end of the book, is known as a *present value table*. It shows the present value of $1 to be received at the end of any number of periods from 1 to 50 and at interest rates ranging from 1 to 50 percent per period. The present values appearing in the table are generated from repeated application of the above formulas for differing time periods and interest rates. It might be useful to consult Appendix A for a moment to confirm the present values just mentioned.

As a matter of semantics, the interest rate in present value calculations is frequently called the *discount rate*. It can be interpreted two ways. If a company already has cash in hand, the discount rate is the rate of return available on alternative, similar-risk investments. In other words, it is the company's *opportunity cost of capital*. If a firm must raise the cash by selling securities, the discount rate is the rate of return expected by buyers of the securities. In other words, it is the investors' *opportunity cost of capital*. As we will see in Chapter 8, the discount rate is frequently used to adjust an investment's cash flows for risk and hence is also known as a *risk-adjusted discount rate*.

Appendix B at the end of the book is a close cousin to Appendix A. It shows the present value of $1 to be received at the end of *each period* for anywhere from 1 to 50 periods and at discount rates ranging from 1 to 50 percent. When cash flows are the same for a number of periods, as in this appendix, they are known as *annuities*. To illustrate both appendices, suppose the Cincinnati Reds sign a new, young catcher to a contract promising $2 million a year for four years. Let us calculate what the contract is worth today if the ballplayer has similar-risk investment opportunities yielding 15 percent a year.

The cash flow diagram for the contract is as follows:

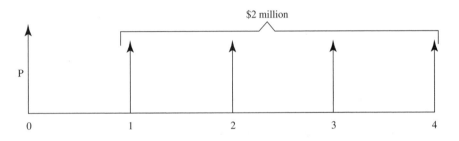

To find the present value, *P*, using Appendix A, we must find the present value at 15 percent of each individual payment. The arithmetic is

$$\begin{aligned}
\text{Present value of contract} &= 0.870 \times \$2 \text{ million} + 0.756 \times \$2 \text{ million} \\
&\quad + 0.658 \times \$2 \text{ million} + 0.572 \times \$2 \text{ million} \\
&= \$5,710,000
\end{aligned}$$

A much simpler approach is to recognize that since the dollar amount is an annuity, Appendix B can be used. Consulting Appendix B, we learn that the present value of $1 per period for four periods at a 15 percent discount rate is $2.855. Thus, the present value of $2 million per year is

$$\text{Present value of contract} = 2.855 \times \$2 \text{ million} = \$5,710,000$$

Although the baseball player expects to receive a total of $8 million over the next four years, the present value of these payments is barely over $5.7 million. Such is the power of compound interest.

A financial calculator is basically a family of automated present value tables where you provide the information and the calculator does the arithmetic. Five keys are of interest for discounted cash flow calculations: *n*, the number of periods; *i*, the interest rate; *PV*, a present cash flow; *PMT*, an annuity stream of cash flows; and *FV*, a future cash flow. The following diagram shows how these quantities relate to one another.

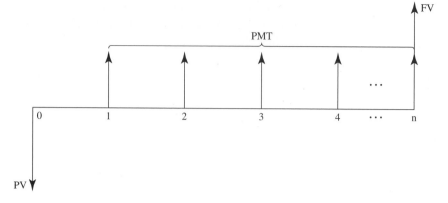

Here is a simple schematic illustrating the use of a financial calculator to find the present value of the catcher's contract. Begin by punching in the length of the contract, the interest rate, and the annual cash to be received, in any order. Then ask the calculator to find the present value, and it immediately returns the answer. The answer has a minus sign indicating this is the amount one should be willing to pay to receive the contract today.

Input: 4 15 ? 2 —

Output: −5.71

For convenience, I will use this schematic to describe subsequent discounted cash flow calculations, without suggesting this is the only way to perform them.

Equivalence

The important fact about the present value of future cash flows is that the present sum is *equivalent* in value to the future cash flows. It is equivalent because if you had the present value today, you could transform it into the future cash flows simply by investing it at the discount rate. To confirm this important fact, the following table shows the cash flows involved in transforming $5.71 million today into the baseball player's contract of $2 million a year for four years. We begin by investing the present value at 15 percent interest. At the end of the first year, the investment grows to over $6.5 million, but the first $2 million salary payment reduces the principal to just over $4.5 million. In the second year, the investment grows to over $5.2 million, but the second salary installment brings the principal down to just over $3.2 million. And so it goes until at the end of four years, the $2 million salary payment just exhausts the account. Hence, from the baseball player's perspective, $5.71 million today is equivalent in value to $2 million a year for four years because he can readily convert the former into the latter by investing it at 15 percent.

Year	Beginning-of-Period Principal	Interest at 15%	End-of-Period Principal	Withdrawal
1	$5,710,000	$856,500	$6,566,500	$2,000,000
2	4,566,500	684,975	5,251,475	2,000,000
3	3,251,475	487,721	3,739,196	2,000,000
4	1,739,196	260,879	2,000,075	2,000,000

Note: The $75 remaining in the account after the last withdrawal is due to round-off error.

The Net Present Value

Now that you have mastered compounding, discounting, and equivalence, let's use these concepts to analyze the container pier investment. More specifically, let us replace the future cash flows appearing in Figure 7.1 with a single cash flow of equivalent worth occurring today. Because all cash flows will then be in current dollars, we will have eliminated the time dimension from the decision and can proceed to a direct comparison of present value cash inflows against present value outflows.

Here is the arithmetic. Assuming other similar-risk investment opportunities are available yielding 10 percent annual interest, the present value of the cash inflows from the pier investment is $49.75 million.

Input:

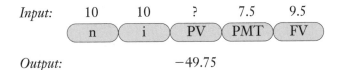

10	10	?	7.5	9.5
n	i	PV	PMT	FV

Output: −49.75

Note that the cash flow in year 10 here is composed of a $7.5 million annuity and a $9.5 million future amount, totaling $17 million.

The cash flow diagrams that follow provide a schematic representation of this calculation. The present value calculation transforms the messy original cash flows on the left into two cash flows of equivalent worth on the right, each occurring at time zero. And our decision becomes elementary. Should Pacific invest $40 million today for a stream of future cash flows with a value today of $49.75 million? Yes, obviously. Paying $40 million for something worth $49.75 million makes eminent sense.

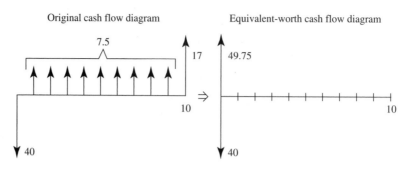

What we have just done is calculate the pier's *net present value*, or *NPV,* an important figure of investment merit:

$$\text{NPV} = \frac{\text{Present value of}}{\text{cash inflows}} - \frac{\text{Present value of}}{\text{cash outflows}}$$

The NPV for the container pier is $9.75 million.

NPV and Value Creation

The declaration that an investment's NPV is $9.75 million may not generate a lot of enthusiasm around the water cooler, so it is important to provide a more compelling definition of the concept. An investment's NPV is nothing less than a measure of how much richer you will become by undertaking the investment. Thus, Pacific's wealth rises $9.75 million when it builds the pier because it pays $40 million for an asset worth $49.75 million.

This is an important insight. For years, a common mantra among academics, management gurus, and an increasing number of senior executives has been that managers' purpose in life should be to create value for owners. A crowning achievement of finance has been to transform value creation from a catchy management slogan into a practical decision-making tool that not only indicates which activities create value but also estimates the amount of value created. Want to create value for owners? Here's how: Embrace positive-NPV activities—the higher the NPV, the better—and eschew negative-NPV activities. Treat zero-NPV activities as marginal because they neither create nor destroy wealth.

In symbols, when

NPV > 0, accept the investment.

NPV < 0, reject the investment.

NPV = 0, the investment is marginal.

The Benefit-Cost Ratio

The net present value is a perfectly respectable figure of investment merit, and if all you want is one way to analyze investment opportunities, feel free to skip ahead to the section "Determining Relevant Cash Flows." On the other hand, if you want to be able to communicate with people who use different but equally acceptable figures of merit, and if you want to reduce the work involved in analyzing certain types of investments, you will need to slog through a few more pages.

A second time-adjusted figure of investment merit popular in government circles is the *benefit-cost ratio (BCR)*, also known as the *profitability index*, defined as

$$BCR = \frac{\text{Present value of cash inflows}}{\text{Present value of cash outflows}}$$

The container pier's BCR is 1.24 ($49.75/$40). Obviously, an investment is attractive when its BCR exceeds 1.0 and is unattractive when its BCR is less than 1.0.

The Internal Rate of Return

Without doubt, the most popular figure of merit among executives is a close cousin to the NPV known as the investment's *internal rate of return*, or *IRR*. To illustrate the IRR and show its relation to the NPV, let's follow the fanciful exploits of the Seattle area manager of Pacific Rim Resources as he tries to win approval for the container pier investment. After determining that the pier's NPV is positive at a 10 percent discount rate, the manager forwards his analysis to the company treasurer with a request for approval. The treasurer responds that she is favorably impressed with the manager's methodology but believes that in today's interest rate environment, a discount rate of 12 percent is more appropriate. So the Seattle manager calculates a second NPV at a 12 percent discount rate and finds it to be $5.44 million—still positive but considerably lower than the original $9.75 million ($5.44 million = $45.44 million, as shown next, −$40 million).

Input:

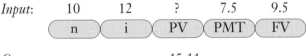

| 10 | 12 | ? | 7.5 | 9.5 |
| n | i | PV | PMT | FV |

Output: −45.44

Confronted with this evidence, the treasurer reluctantly agrees that the project is acceptable and forwards the proposal to the chief financial officer. (That the NPV falls as the discount rate rises here should come as no surprise, for all of the pier's cash inflows occur in the future, and a higher discount rate reduces the present value of future flows.)

The chief financial officer, who is even more conservative than the treasurer, also praises the methodology but argues that with all the risks involved and the difficulty in raising money, an 18 percent discount rate is called for. After doing his calculations a third time, the dejected Seattle manager now finds that at an 18 percent discount rate, the NPV is −$4.48 million (−$4.48 million = $35.52 million, as shown next, −$40 million).

Input: 10   18   ?   7.5   9.5

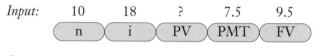

Output: −35.52

Because the NPV is now negative, the chief financial officer, betraying his former career as a bank loan officer, gleefully rejects the proposal. The manager's efforts prove unsuccessful, but in the process he has helped us to understand the IRR.

Table 7.2 summarizes the manager's calculations. From these figures, it is apparent that something critical happens to the investment merit of the container pier as the discount rate increases from 12 to 18 percent. Somewhere within this range, the NPV changes from positive to negative and the investment changes from acceptable to unacceptable. The critical discount rate at which this change occurs is the investment's IRR.

Formally, an investment's IRR is defined as

> IRR = Discount rate at which the investment's NPV equals zero

The IRR is yet another figure of merit. The corresponding acceptance criterion against which to compare the IRR is the opportunity cost of capital for the investment. If the investment's IRR exceeds the opportunity cost of capital, the investment is attractive, and vice versa. If the IRR equals the cost of capital, the investment is marginal.

In symbols, if K is the percentage cost of capital, then if

IRR > K, accept the investment.

IRR < K, reject the investment.

IRR = K, the investment is marginal.

TABLE 7.2 **NPV of Container Pier at Different Discount Rates**

Discount Rate	NPV	
10%	$9.75 million	
12	5.44	
		IRR = 15%
18	−4.48	

FIGURE 7.2 **NPV of Container Pier at Different Discount Rates**

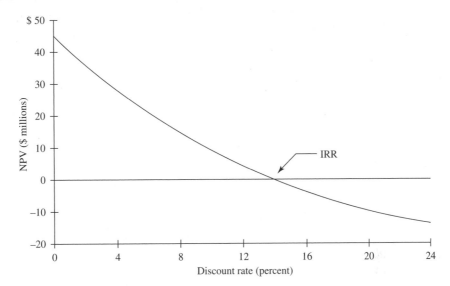

You will be relieved to learn that in most, but regrettably, not all, in-stances, the IRR and the NPV yield the same investment recommenda-tions. That is, in most instances, if an investment is attractive based on its IRR, it will also have a positive NPV, and vice versa. Figure 7.2 illustrates the relation between the container pier's NPV and its IRR by plotting the information in Table 7.2. Note that the pier's NPV = 0 at a discount rate of about 15 percent, so this by definition is the project's IRR. At capital costs below 15 percent, the NPV is positive and the IRR also exceeds the cost of capital, so the investment is acceptable on both counts. When the cost of capital exceeds 15 percent, the reverse is true, and the investment is unacceptable according to both criteria.

Figure 7.2 suggests several informative ways to interpret an invest-ment's IRR. One is that the IRR is a break-even return in the sense that at capital costs below the IRR the investment is attractive, but at capital costs greater than the IRR it is unattractive. A second, more important inter-pretation is that the IRR is the rate at which money remaining in an investment grows, or compounds. As such, an IRR is comparable in all respects to the interest rate on a bank loan or a savings deposit. This means you can compare the IRR of an investment directly to the annual percentage cost of the capital to be invested. We cannot say the same thing about other, simpler measures of return, such as the accounting rate of return, because they do not properly incorporate the time value of money.

The Container Pier Investment Is Economically Equivalent to a Bank Account Paying 15 Percent Annual Interest

To confirm that an investment's IRR is equivalent to the interest rate on a bank account, suppose that instead of building the pier, Pacific Rim Resources puts the $40 million cost of the pier in a bank account earning 15 percent annual interest. The table below demonstrates that Pacific can then use this bank account to replicate precisely the cash flows from the pier and that, just like the investment, the account will run dry in 10 years. In other words, ignoring any differences in risk, the fact that the pier's IRR is 15 percent means the investment is economically equivalent to a bank savings account yielding this rate.

	($ millions)			
Year	Beginning-of-Period Principal	Interest Earned at 15%	End-of-Period Principal	Withdrawals = Investment Cash Flows
1	$40.0	$6.0	$46.0	$ 7.5
2	38.5	5.8	44.3	7.5
3	36.8	5.5	42.3	7.5
4	34.8	5.2	40.0	7.5
5	32.5	4.9	37.4	7.5
6	29.9	4.5	34.4	7.5
7	26.9	4.0	30.9	7.5
8	23.4	3.5	26.9	7.5
9	19.4	2.9	22.3	7.5
10	14.8	2.2	17.0	17.0

Calculating an IRR typically involves a bit of trial-and-error searching for the right number. This can cause problems when using present value tables but presents no difficulties when using a computer or a calculator—although you may notice a pronounced pause with a calculator as it searches for the correct value. The following calculation confirms that the container pier's IRR is 15 percent.

Input: 10   ?   −40   7.5   9.5

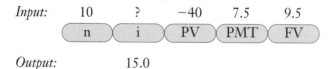

Output: 15.0

Table 7.3 illustrates the container pier calculations on an Excel spreadsheet. The three entries in the column labeled "Equation" would not normally appear on a spreadsheet. They are the equations I entered to coax the computer into calculating the figures of merit shown in the "Answer" column. Each equation takes advantage of the fact that spreadsheets contain a number of built-in functions for performing various financial calculations. In Excel, you can access these functions by selecting "Formulas,"

TABLE 7.3   Calculating Container Pier's Estimated NPV, IRR, and BCR with a Computer Spreadsheet

	A	B	C	D	E	F	...	K	L
1	**ESTIMATED ANNUAL CASH FLOWS ($ millions)**								
2	Year	*0*	*1*	*2*	*3*	*4*	...	*9*	*10*
3	Cash flow ($40)		7.5	7.5	7.5	7.5	...	7.5	17
4									
5	Discount rate:		10%						
6									
7					**Equation**			**Answer**	
8	Net present value (NPV)				= NPV (C5, C3:L3) + B3			$9.75	
9									
10	Benefit-Cost Ratio (BCR)				= NPV (C5, C3:L3)/ − B3			1.24	
11									
12	Internal Rate of Return (IRR)				= IRR (B3: L3, 0.12)			15%	

followed by "Financial." The NPV function calculates the net present value of the cash flows appearing in the range C3 through L3, at the interest rate specified in cell C5. From this present value, I have subtracted the initial $40 million expense in cell B3 to calculate the desired net present value. The IRR function calculates the internal rate of return of the numbers appearing in cells B3 through L3. To aid in the iterative search for the IRR, the function requests an initial guess of what the IRR might be. I have used 12 percent.

A common mistake to avoid: The NPV function calculates the net present value of an indicated range of numbers *as of one period before the first cash flow occurs.* This means that had I entered "npv(C5,B3:L3)," the computer would have calculated the NPV at time −1. To avoid this, I calculated the NPV of the cash flows in years 1 through 10, and then added the time 0 cash flow.

A Few Applications and Extensions

Discounted cash flow concepts are the foundation for much of finance. To demonstrate their versatility, to sharpen your mastery of the concepts, and to introduce some topics we will refer to later in the book, I want to consider several useful applications and extensions.

Bond Valuation

Investors regularly use discounted cash flow techniques to value bonds. For example, suppose ABC Corporation bonds have an 8 percent coupon rate paid annually, a par value of $1,000, and nine years to maturity. An investor wants to determine the most she can pay for the bonds if she wants to earn at least 7 percent on her investment. The relevant cash flow diagram is:

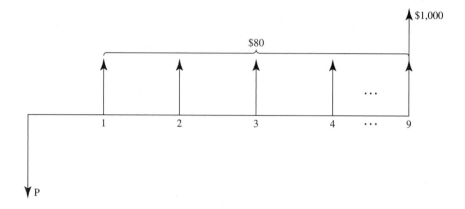

In essence, the investor wants to find P such that it is equivalent in value to the future cash receipts discounted at 7 percent. Calculating the present value, we find it equals $1,065.15, meaning her return over nine years will be precisely 7 percent when she pays this amount for the bond.

Input:

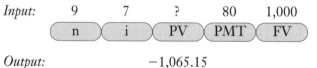

Output: $-1,065.15$

Moreover, we know her return will fall below 7 percent when she pays above this price, and rise above 7 percent when she pays less.

   More commonly, an investor knows the price of a bond and wants to know what return it implies. If ABC Corp. bonds are selling for $1,030, the investor wants to know the return she will earn if she buys the bonds and holds them to maturity. In the jargon of the trade, she wants to know the bond's *yield to maturity.* Performing the necessary calculation, we learn the bond's yield to maturity, or IRR, is 7.53 percent.

Input:

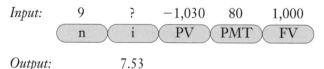

Output: 7.53

The IRR of a Perpetuity

Some financial instruments, including certain British and French government bonds, have no maturity date and simply promise to pay the stated interest every year forever. Annuities that last forever are called *perpetuities.*

Many preferred stocks are perpetuities. Later in Chapter 9 when valuing companies, we will occasionally find it convenient to think of company cash flows as perpetuities.

How can we calculate the present value of a perpetuity? It turns out to be embarrassingly easy. Begin by noting that the present value of an annuity paying $1 a year for 100 years discounted at, say, 12 percent is only $8.33!

Input: 100   12   ?   1   —

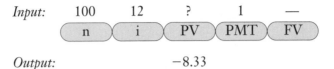

Output: −8.33

Think of it: Although the holder will receive a total of $100, the present value is less than $9. Why? Because if the investor put $8.33 in a bank account today yielding 12 percent a year, he could withdraw approximately $1 in interest every year *forever* without touching the principal (12% × $8.33 = $0.9996). Consequently, $8.33 today has approximately the same value as $1 a year forever.

This suggests the following simple formula for the present value of a perpetuity. Letting A equal the annual receipt, r the discount rate, and P the present value,

$$P = \frac{A}{r}$$

and

$$r = \frac{A}{P}$$

To illustrate, suppose a share of preferred stock sells for $480 and promises an annual dividend of $52 forever. Then its IRR is 10.8 percent (52/480). Because the equations are so simple, perpetuities are often used to value long-lived assets and in many textbook examples.

Equivalent Annual Cost

In most discounted cash flow calculations, we seek a present value or an internal rate of return, but this is not always the case. Suppose, for example, that Pacific Rim Resources is considering leasing its $40 million container pier to a large Korean shipping company for a period of 12 years. Pacific Rim believes the pier will have a $4 million continuing value at the end of the lease period. To consummate the deal, the company needs to know the annual fee it must charge to recover its investment, including the opportunity cost of the funds used. In essence, Pacific Rim needs a number that converts the initial expenditure and the salvage value into an equal value annual payment. At a 10 percent interest rate and ignoring taxes, the required annual lease payment is $5.68 million.

A Note on Differing Compounding Periods

For simplicity, I have assumed that the compounding period for all discounted cash flow calculations is one year. Of course, this is not always the case. In the United States and Britain, bond interest is calculated and paid semi-annually; many credit card issuers use monthly compounding; and some savings instruments advertise daily compounding.

The existence of different compounding intervals forces us to distinguish between two interest rates: a quoted interest rate, often called the *annual percentage rate* or APR, and a true rate, known as the *effective annual rate,* or EAR.

To appreciate the distinction, you know that $1 put to work at 10 percent interest, compounded annually, will be worth $1.10 in one year. But what will it be worth when the compounding period is semi-annual? To find out we need to divide the stated interest rate by 2 and double the number of compounding periods. Thus, at the end of six months, the investment will be worth $1.05, and at the end of the year it will be worth $1.1025 ($1.05 + .05 × $1.05). With semi-annual compounding, the interest earned in the first compounding period earns interest in the second, leading to a slightly higher ending value. So although the stated interest rate is 10 percent, semi-annual compounding boosts the effective return to 10.25 percent. The account's APR is 10 percent, but its EAR is 10.25 percent.

Letting *m* equal the number of compounding periods in a year, we can generalize this example to the following expression.

$$EAR = \left(1 + \frac{APR}{m}\right)^m - 1$$

Thus, the effective annual interest rate on a 6 percent savings account with daily compounding is $(1 + .06/365)^{365} - 1 = 6.18\%$, while the effective annual rate on a credit card loan charging 18 percent, compounded monthly, is $(1 + .18/12)^{12} - 1 = 19.56\%$.

There are two morals to this story. First, when an instrument's compounding period is less than one year, its true interest rate is its EAR, not its APR. And second, when comparing instruments with different compounding periods, you must look at their EARs, not their APRs. This might all be of only minor interest were it not for the fact that common practice, strongly supplemented by Federal Truth in Lending laws, emphasizes APRs to the virtual exclusion of EARs.

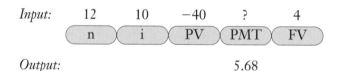

Input: 12   10   −40   ?   4

        (n)   (i)   (PV)   (PMT)   (FV)

Output: 5.68

This quantity, known as the investment's *equivalent annual cost*, is the effective, time-adjusted annual cost of the pier. The calculation tells us that if Pacific Rim sets the lease payment equal to the pier's equivalent annual cost, it will earn an IRR of precisely 10 percent on the investment. We will say more about equivalent annual costs in the chapter appendix.

Mutually Exclusive Alternatives and Capital Rationing

We now consider briefly two common occurrences that often complicate investment selection. The first is known as *mutually exclusive alternatives.* Frequently, there is more than one way to accomplish an objective, and the investment problem is to select the best alternative. In this case, the investments are said to be mutually exclusive. Examples of mutually exclusive alternatives abound, including the choice of whether to build a concrete or a wooden structure, whether to drive to work or take the bus, and whether to build a 40-story or a 30-story building. Even though each option gets the job done and may be attractive individually, it does not make economic sense to do more than one. If you decide to take the bus to work, driving to work as well could prove a difficult feat. When confronted with mutually exclusive alternatives, then, it is not enough to decide if each option is attractive individually; you must determine which is best. Mutually exclusive investments are in contrast to independent investments, where the capital budgeting problem is simply to accept or reject a single investment.

When investments are independent, all three figures of merit introduced earlier—the NPV, BCR, and IRR—will generate the same investment decision, but this is no longer true when the investments are mutually exclusive. In all of the preceding examples, we implicitly assumed independence.

A second complicating factor in many investment appraisals is known as *capital rationing*. So far, we have implicitly assumed that sufficient money is available to enable the company to undertake all attractive opportunities. In contrast, under capital rationing, the decision maker has a fixed investment budget that may not be exceeded. Such a limit on investment capital may be imposed externally by investors' unwillingness to supply more money, or it may be imposed internally by senior management as a way to control the amount of investment dollars each operating unit spends. In either case, the investment decision under capital rationing requires the analyst to *rank* the opportunities according to their investment merit and accept only the best.

Both mutually exclusive alternatives and capital rationing require a ranking of investments, but here the similarity ends. With mutually exclusive investments, money is available, but for technological reasons only certain investments can be accepted; under capital rationing, a lack of money is the complicating factor. Moreover, even the criteria used to rank the investments differ in the two cases, so the best investment among mutually exclusive alternatives may not be best under conditions of capital rationing. The appendix to this chapter discusses these technicalities and indicates which figures of merit are appropriate under which conditions.

The IRR in Perspective

Before turning to the determination of relevant cash flows in investment analysis, I want to offer a few concluding thoughts about the IRR. The stock a year ago at $100 a share and it is presently trading at $70. Even though you believe $70 is an excellent price for the stock given its current prospects, would you be prepared to admit your mistake and sell it now, or would you be tempted to hold it in the hope of recouping your original investment? The with-without principle says the $100 price is sunk and hence irrelevant, except for possible tax effects, so sell the stock. Natural human reluctance to admit a mistake and the daunting prospect of having to justify the mistake to a skeptical boss or spouse frequently muddy our thinking.

As another example, suppose the R&D department of a company has devoted 10 years and $10 million to perfecting a new, long-lasting light bulb. Its original estimate was a development time of two years at a cost of $1 million, and every year since R&D has progressively extended the development time and increased the cost. Now it is estimating only one more year and an added expenditure of only $1 million. Since the present value of the benefits from such a light bulb is only $4 million, there is strong feeling in the company that the project should be killed and whoever had been approving the budget increases throughout the years should be fired.

In retrospect, it is clear the company should never have begun work on the light bulb. Even if successful, the cost will be well in excess of the benefits. Yet at any point along the development process, including the current decision, it may have been perfectly rational to continue work. Past expenditures are sunk, so the only question at issue is whether the anticipated benefits exceed the *remaining* costs required to complete development. Past expenditures are relevant only to the extent that they influence one's assessment of whether the remaining costs are properly estimated. So if you believe the current estimates, the light bulb project should continue for yet another year.

Allocated Costs

The proper treatment of depreciation, working capital, and sunk costs in investment evaluation is comparatively straightforward. Now things get a bit murkier. According to Plasteel Communications's *Capital Budgeting Manual*,

> New investments that increase sales must bear their fair share of corporate overhead expenses. Therefore, all new-product proposals must include an annual overhead charge equal to 14 percent of sales, without exception.

Yet, as Table 7.4 reveals, division analysts ignored this directive in their analysis of the new phone. They did so on the grounds that the manual is simply wrong, that allocating overhead expenses to new products violates the with-without principle and stifles creativity. In their words, "If exciting projects like this one have to bear the deadweight costs of corporate overhead, we'll never be competitive in this business."

The point at issue here is whether expenses not directly associated with a new investment, such as the president's salary, legal department expenses, and accounting department expenses, are relevant to the decision. A straightforward reading of the with-without principle says that if the president's salary will not change as a result of the new investment, it is not relevant, nor are legal and accounting department expenses, if they will not change. This is clear enough. If they won't change, they aren't relevant.

But who is to say these expenses will not change with the new investment? Indeed, it appears to be an inexorable fact of life that over time, as companies grow, presidents' salaries become larger while legal and accounting departments expand. The issue therefore is not whether expenses are allocated but whether they vary with the size of the business. Although we may be unable to see a direct cause-effect tie between such expenses and increasing sales, a longer-run relation likely exists between the two. Consequently, it does make sense to require all sales-increasing investments to bear a portion of those allocated costs that grow with sales. Remember, allocated costs are not necessarily fixed costs.

A related problem arises with cost-reducing investments. To illustrate, as a part of their performance appraisal system, many companies allocate overhead costs to departments or divisions in proportion to the amount of direct labor expense the unit incurs. Suppose a department manager in such an environment has the opportunity to invest in a labor-saving asset. From the department's narrow perspective, such an asset offers two benefits: (1) a reduction in direct labor expense and (2) a reduction in the overhead costs allocated to the department. Yet from the total-company perspective and from the correct economic perspective, only the reduction in direct labor is a benefit because the total-company overhead costs are unaffected by the decision. They are simply reallocated from one cost center to another, and thus, are not relevant to the investment decision.

Cannibalization

During the meeting, a product manager in another division argued that the new phone proposal was "incomplete and overly optimistic." He stressed two points. First, the decision should be made from a corporate perspective, not from a narrow divisional one. Second, from this perspective the projected cash flows must reflect the reality that the new phone will cannibalize sales of existing offerings. That is, the new phone will attract a number of customers who would otherwise purchase one of the company's existing products. By his estimate, the new phone would attract about 10 percent of his division's customer base, resulting in lost cash flows of approximately $7 million a year. He argued that, at a minimum, this figure must appear as an annual cost in the new phone's projected cash flows.

Unequal Lives

The Petro Oil and Gas example conveniently assumed that both service station options had the same 10-year life. This, of course, is not always the case. When the alternatives have different lives, a simple comparison of NPVs is usually inappropriate. Consider the problem faced by a company trying to decide whether to build a wooden bridge or a steel one:

- The wooden bridge has an initial cost of $125,000, requires annual maintenance expenditures of $15,000, and will last 10 years.

- The steel bridge costs $200,000, requires $5,000 annual maintenance, and will last 40 years.

Which is the better buy? At a discount rate of, say, 15 percent, the present value cost of the wooden bridge over its expected life of 10 years is $200,282 ($125,000 initial cost + $75,282 present value of maintenance expenditures as shown next).

Input: 10   15   ?   15   —

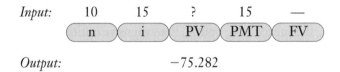

Output: −75.282

This compares with a figure for the steel bridge over its 40-year life of $233,209 ($200,000 initial cost + $33,209 present value of maintenance expenditures as shown next).

Input: 40   15   ?   5   —

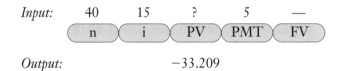

Output: −33.209

So if the object is to minimize the cost of the bridge, a simple comparison of present values would suggest that the wooden structure is a clear winner. However, this obviously overlooks the differing life expectancy of the two bridges, implicitly assuming that if the company builds the wooden bridge, it will not need a bridge after 10 years.

The message is clear: when comparing mutually exclusive alternatives having different service lives, it is necessary to reflect this difference in the analysis. One approach is to examine each alternative over the same common investment horizon. For example, suppose our company believes it will need a bridge for 20 years; due to inflation, the wooden bridge will cost $200,000 to reconstruct at the end of 10 years; and the salvage value of the steel bridge in 20 years will be $90,000. The cash flow diagrams for the two options are thus as follows:

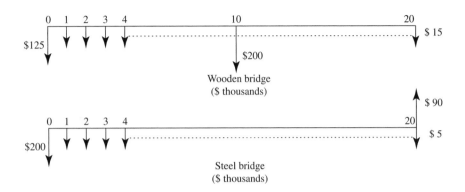

Wooden bridge
($ thousands)

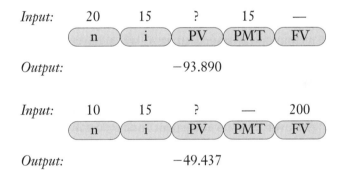

Steel bridge
($ thousands)

Now the present value cost of the wooden bridge is $268,327 ($125,000 initial cost + $93,890 present value of maintenance expenditures as shown below + $49,437 present value cost of a new bridge in 10 years as shown below).

Input: 20   15   ?   15   —

n   i   PV   PMT   FV

Output: −93.890

Input: 10   15   ?   —   200

n   i   PV   PMT   FV

Output: −49.437

And the cost of the steel bridge is $225,798 ($200,000 initial cost + $25,798 present value of maintenance expenditures net of salvage value).

Input: 20   15   ?   5   −90

n   i   PV   PMT   FV

Output: −25,798

Compared over a common 20-year investment horizon, the steel bridge has the lower present value cost and is thus superior.

A second way to choose among mutually exclusive alternatives with differing lives is to calculate the equivalent annual cost of each. Here's the arithmetic for the two bridges.

benefit per dollar invested when ranking investments. This is what the BCR does.

Two other details warrant mention. In the preceding example, the IRR provides the same ranking as the BCR, and although this is usually the case, it is not always so. It turns out that when the two rankings differ, the BCR ranking is the correct one. Why the rankings differ and why the BCR is superior are not worth explaining here. It is sufficient to remember that if you rank by IRR rather than BCR, you might occasionally be in error. A second detail is that when fractional investments are not possible— when it does not make sense for Sullivan Electronics to invest in $\frac{7}{12}$ of project B—rankings according to any figure of merit are unreliable, and one must resort to the tedious method of looking at each possible bundle of investments in search of the highest total NPV.

The Problem of Future Opportunities

Implicit in the preceding discussion is the assumption that as long as an investment has a positive NPV, it is better to make the investment than to let the money sit idle. However, under capital rationing, this may not be true. To illustrate, suppose the financial executive of Sullivan Electronics believes that within six months, company scientists will develop a new product costing $200,000 and having an NPV of $60,000. In this event, the company's best strategy is to forgo all of the investments presently under consideration and save its money for the new product.

This example illustrates that investment evaluation under capital rationing involves more than a simple appraisal of current opportunities; it also involves a comparison between current opportunities and future prospects. The difficulty with this comparison at a practical level is that it is unreasonable to expect a manager to have anything more than a vague impression of what investments are likely to arise in the future. Consequently, it is impossible to decide with any assurance whether it is better to invest in current projects or wait for brighter future opportunities. This means practical investment evaluation under capital rationing necessarily involves a high degree of subjective judgment.

A Decision Tree

Mutually exclusive investment alternatives and capital rationing complicate an already confusing topic. To provide a summary and an overview, Figure 7A.2 presents a capital budgeting decision tree. It indicates the figure or figures of merit that are appropriate under the various conditions discussed in the chapter. For example, following the lowest branch in the tree, we see that when evaluating investments under capital rationing that

FIGURE 7A.2 **Capital Budgeting Decision Tree**

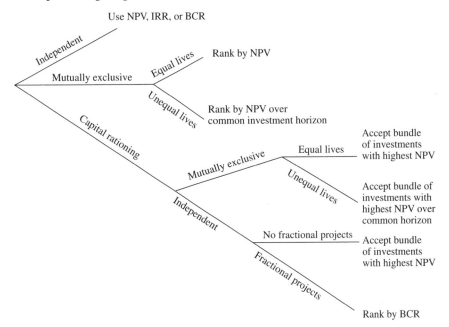

are independent and can be acquired fractionally, ranking by the BCR is the appropriate technique. To review your understanding of the material, see if you can explain why the recommended figures of merit are appropriate under the various conditions indicated, whereas the others are not.

SUMMARY

1. Evaluation of an investment opportunity involves three steps:
   - Estimate relevant cash flows.
   - Calculate a figure of merit.
   - Compare the figure of merit to an acceptance criterion.

2. Money has a time value because
   - Cash deferred imposes an opportunity cost.
   - Inflation reduces purchasing power over time.
   - Risk customarily increases with the futurity of a cash flow.

3. Equivalence
   - Says that a present sum and future cash flows have the same value when the present sum can be invested at the discount rate to replicate the future cash flows.

CHAPTER EIGHT

Risk Analysis in Investment Decisions

A man's gotta make at least one bet a day, else he could be walking around lucky and never know it.

Jimmy Jones, horse trainer

Most thoughtful individuals and some investment bankers know that all interesting financial decisions involve risk as well as return. By their nature, business investments require the expenditure of a known sum of money today in anticipation of uncertain future benefits. Consequently, if the discounted cash flow techniques discussed in the last chapter are to be useful in evaluating realistic investments, they must incorporate considerations of risk as well as return. Two such considerations are relevant. At an applied level, risk increases the difficulty of estimating relevant cash flows. More importantly at a conceptual level, risk itself enters as a fundamental determinant of investment value. Thus, if two investments promise the same expected return but have differing risks, most of us will prefer the low-risk alternative. In the jargon of economics, we are *risk averse*, and as a result, risk reduces investment value.

Risk aversion among individuals and corporations creates the common pattern of investment risk and return shown in Figure 8.1. The figure shows that for low-risk investments, such as government bonds, expected return is modest, but as risk increases, so too must the anticipated return. I say "must" because the risk-return pattern shown is more than wishful thinking. Unless higher-risk investments promise higher returns, you and I, as risk-averse investors, will not hold them.

This risk-return trade-off is fundamental to much of finance. Over the past four decades, researchers have demonstrated that under idealized conditions, and with risk defined in a specific way, the risk-return trade-off is a straight-line one as depicted in the figure. The line is known as the *market line* and represents the combinations of risk and expected return one can anticipate in a properly functioning economy.

FIGURE 8.1 The Risk-Return Trade-Off

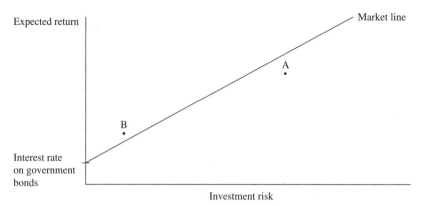

The details of the market line need not detain us here. What is important is the realization that knowledge of an investment's expected return is not enough to determine its worth. Instead, investment evaluation is a two-dimensional task involving a balancing of risk against return. The appropriate question when evaluating investment opportunities is not "What's the rate of return?" but "Is the return sufficient to justify the risk?" The investments represented by A and B in Figure 8.1 illustrate this point. Investment A has a higher expected return than B; nonetheless, B is the better investment. Despite its modest return, B lies above the market line, meaning it promises a higher expected return for its risk than available alternatives, whereas investment A lies below the market line, meaning alternative investments promising a higher expected return for the same risk are available.[1]

This chapter examines the incorporation of risk into investment evaluation. Central to our discussion of discounted cash flow techniques in the last chapter was a quantity variously referred to as the interest rate, the discount rate, and the opportunity cost of capital. While stressing that this quantity somehow reflected investment risk and the time value of money, I was purposely vague about its origins. It is time now to correct this omission by explaining how to incorporate investment risk into the discount rate. After defining investment risk in more detail, we will estimate the cost of capital to Sensient Technologies Corporation, the company profiled in earlier chapters, and will examine the strengths and weaknesses of the

---

[1] Saying the same thing more analytically, we know from our earlier study of financial leverage that owners of asset B need not settle for safe, low returns. Rather, they can use debt financing to lever B's expected return and risk to higher values. In fact, the market line tells us that with just the right amount of debt financing, owners of asset B can attain A's higher expected return, and more, with no greater risk. B is therefore the better investment.

Are You Risk Averse?

Here is a simple test to find out. Which of the following investment opportunities do you prefer?

1. You pay $10,000 today and flip a coin in one year to determine whether you will receive $50,000 or *pay* another $20,000.

2. You pay $10,000 today and receive $15,000 in one year.

If investment 2 sounds better than 1, join the crowd; you are risk averse. Even though both investments cost $10,000 and promise an expected one-year payoff of $15,000, or a 50 percent return, studies indicate that most people, when sober and not in a casino, prefer the certainty of option 2 to the uncertainty of option 1. The presence of risk reduces the value of 1 relative to 2.

For a simple, self-test of your risk tolerance from Rutgers University, see **njaes.rutgers .edu/money/riskquiz**.

cost of capital as a risk-adjusted discount rate. The chapter concludes with a look at several important pitfalls to avoid when evaluating investment opportunities and at economic value added, a hot topic in the world of performance appraisal. The appendix considers two logical extensions to the chapter material known as asset-betas and adjusted present value analysis, or APV.

You should know at the outset that the topics in this chapter are not simple, for the addition of a whole second dimension to investment analysis in the form of risk introduces a number of complexities and ambiguities. The chapter therefore will offer a general road map for how to proceed and an appreciation of available techniques rather than a detailed set of answers. But look on the bright side: If investment decisions were simple, there would be less demand for well-educated managers and aspiring financial writers.

Risk Defined

Speaking broadly, there are two aspects to investment risk: The *dispersion* of an investment's possible returns, and the *correlation* of these returns with those available on other assets. Looking first at dispersion, Figure 8.2 shows the possible rates of return that might be earned on two investments in the form of bell-shaped curves. According to the figure, the expected return on investment A is about 12 percent, while the corresponding figure for investment B is about 20 percent.

Dispersion risk captures the intuitively appealing notion that risk is tied to the range of possible outcomes, or alternatively to the uncertainty surrounding the outcome. Thus because investment A shows considerable bunching of possible returns about the expected return, its risk is low.

FIGURE 8.2 Illustration of Investment Risk: Investment A Has a Lower Expected Return and a Lower Risk than B

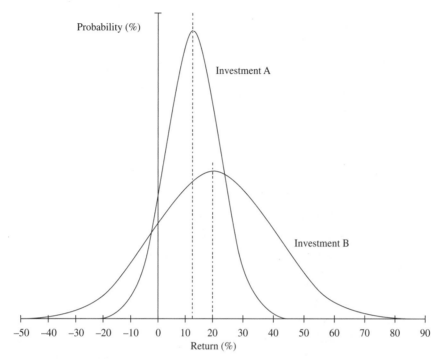

Investment B, on the other hand, evidences considerably less clustering, and is thus higher risk. Borrowing from statistics, one way to measure this clustering tendency is to calculate the standard deviation of return. The details of calculating an investment's expected return and standard deviation of return need not concern us here.[2] It is enough to know that

---

[2] An investment's expected return is the probability-weighted average of possible returns. If three returns are possible—8, 12, and 18 percent—and if the chance of each occurring is 40, 30, and 30 percent, respectively, the investment's expected return is

$$\text{Expected return} = 0.40 \times 8\% + 0.30 \times 12\% + 0.30 \times 18\% = 12.2\%$$

The standard deviation of return is the probability-weighted average of the deviations of possible returns from the expected return. To illustrate, the differences between the possible returns and the expected return in our example are $(8\% - 12.2\%)$, $(12\% - 12.2\%)$, and $(18\% - 12.2\%)$. Because some of these differences are positive and others are negative, they would tend to cancel one another out if we added them directly. So we square them to ensure the same sign, calculate the probability-weighted average of the squared deviations, and then find the square root.

$$\frac{\text{Standard}}{\text{deviation}} = [0.4(8\% - 12.2\%)^2 + 0.3(12\% - 12.2\%)^2 + 0.3(18\% - 12.2\%)^2]^{\frac{1}{2}} = 4.1\%$$

The probability-weighted average difference between the investment's possible returns and its expected return is 4.1 percentage points.

TABLE 8.1 **Diversification Reduces Risk**

Investment	Weather	Probability	Return on Investment		Weighted Outcome
Ice cream stand	Sun	0.50	60%		30%
	Rain	0.50	−20		−10
				Expected outcome =	20
Umbrella shop	Sun	0.50	−30		−15
	Rain	0.50	50		25
				Expected outcome =	10
Portfolio:					
1/2 Ice cream stand	Sun	0.50	15		7.5
and umbrella shop	Rain	0.50	15		7.5
				Expected outcome =	15%

risk relates to the dispersion, or uncertainty, in possible outcomes and that techniques exist to measure this dispersion.

Risk and Diversification

Dispersion risk, as just described, is often known as an investment's *total risk*, or more fancifully its Robinson Crusoe risk. It is the risk an owner would face if he were alone on a desert island unable to buy any other assets. The story changes dramatically, however, once the owner is off the desert island and again able to hold a diversified portfolio. For then the risk from holding a given asset is customarily less than the asset's total risk—frequently a lot less. In other words, there is more—or perhaps I should say less—to risk than simply dispersion in possible outcomes.

To see why, Table 8.1 presents information about two very simple risky investments: purchase of an ice cream stand and an umbrella shop.[3] For simplicity, let's suppose tomorrow's weather will be either rain or sun with equal probability. Purchase of the ice cream stand is clearly a risky undertaking, since the investor stands to make a 60 percent return on his investment if it is sunny tomorrow but lose 20 percent if it rains. The umbrella shop is also risky, since the investor will lose 30 percent if tomorrow is sunny but will make 50 percent if it rains.

Yet despite the fact that these two investments are risky when viewed in isolation, they are not risky when seen as members of a portfolio containing both investments. In a portfolio consisting of half ownership of the ice

[3] I used to think this was a fanciful example until I noticed how quickly street vendors in Washington D.C. switched between selling soft drinks and umbrellas depending on the weather.

cream stand and of the umbrella shop, the losses and gains from the two investments precisely counterbalance one another in each state, so that regardless of tomorrow's weather, the outcome is a certain 15 percent. (For example, if it is sunny tomorrow, the ice cream stand makes 60 percent on half of the portfolio and the umbrella shop loses 30 percent on the other half for a net of 15 percent [$15\% = 0.5 \times 60\% + 0.5 \times -30\%$].) The expected outcome from the portfolio is the average of the expected outcomes from each investment, but the risk of the portfolio is zero. Owning both assets eliminates the dispersion in possible returns. Despite what you may have heard, there really is a free lunch in finance. It is called diversification.

This is an extreme example, but it does illustrate an important fact about risk: When it is possible to own a diversified portfolio, the relevant risk is not the investment's risk in isolation—its Robinson Crusoe risk—but its risk as part of the portfolio. And, as the example demonstrates, the difference between these two perspectives can be substantial.

An asset's risk in isolation is greater than its risk as part of a portfolio whenever the asset's returns and the portfolio's returns are less than perfectly correlated. In this commonplace situation, some of the asset's return variability is offset by variability in the portfolio's returns, and the effective risk borne by the investor declines. Look again at Table 8.1. The return on the ice cream stand is highly variable, but because it hits a trough precisely when the umbrella shop return hits a peak, return variability for the two investments combined disappears. The portfolio will earn 15 percent rain or shine. In other words, when assets are combined in a portfolio an "averaging out" process occurs that reduces risk.

Because most business investments depend to some extent on the same underlying economic forces, it is unusual to find investment opportunities with perfectly inversely correlated returns as in the ice cream stand–umbrella shop example. However, the described diversification effect still exists. Whenever investment returns, or cash flows, are less than perfectly positively correlated—whenever individual investments are unique in some respects—an investment's risk as part of a portfolio is less than the dispersion of its possible returns.

Saying the same thing more formally, it is possible to partition an investment's total risk into two parts as follows:

$$\text{Total risk} = \text{Systematic risk} + \text{Unsystematic risk}$$

Systematic risk reflects exposure to economywide, or marketwide events, such as interest rate changes and business cycles, and cannot be reduced by diversification. Unsystematic risk, on the other hand, reflects investment-specific events, such as fires and lawsuits, which can be eliminated through

FIGURE 8.3   **The Power of Diversification in Common Stock Portfolios**

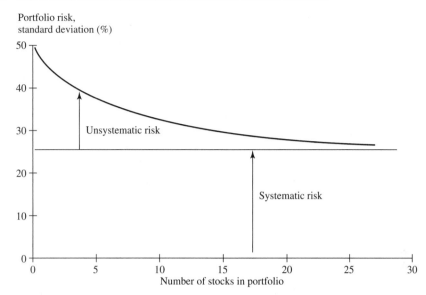

diversification. Because savvy shareholders own diversified investment portfolios, only systematic risk is relevant for evaluating investment opportunities. The rest can be diversified away.

Figure 8.3 demonstrates the power of diversification in common stock portfolios. It shows the relationship between the variability of portfolio returns, as measured by the standard deviation of return, and the number of randomly chosen stocks in the portfolio. Note that variability is high when the number of stocks is low but declines rapidly as the number increases. As the number of stocks in the portfolio grows, the "averaging out" effect takes place, and unsystematic risk declines. Studies suggest that unsystematic risk all but vanishes when portfolio size exceeds about 30 randomly chosen stocks, and that diversification eliminates approximately one-half of total risk.[4]

Estimating Investment Risk

Having defined risk and risk aversion in at least a general way, let us next consider how we might estimate the amount of risk present in a particular investment opportunity. In some business situations, an investment's risk can be calculated objectively from scientific or historical evidence. This is

[4] Meir Statman, "How Many Stocks Make a Diversified Portfolio?" *Journal of Financial and Quantitative Analysis* 22 (September 1987), pp. 353–63.

Systematic Risk and Conglomerate Diversification

Some executives seize on the idea that diversification reduces risk as a justification for conglomerate diversification. Even when a merger promises no increase in profitability, it is said to be beneficial because the resulting diversification reduces the risk of company cash flows. Because shareholders are risk averse, this reduction in risk is said to increase the value of the firm.

Such reasoning is at best incomplete. If shareholders wanted the risk reduction benefits of such a conglomerate merger, they could achieve them much more simply by just owning shares of the two independent companies in their own portfolios. Shareholders do not depend on company management for such benefits. Executives intent on acquiring other firms must look elsewhere to find a rationale for their actions.

true, for instance, of oil and gas development wells. Once an exploration company has found a field and mapped out its general configuration, the probability that a development well drilled within the boundaries of the field will be commercially successful can be determined with reasonable accuracy.

Sometimes history can be a guide. A company that has opened 1,000 fast-food restaurants around the world should have a good idea about the expected return and risk of opening the 1,001st. Similarly, if you are thinking about buying IBM stock, the historical record of the past variability of annual returns to IBM shareholders is an important starting point when estimating the risk of IBM shares. I will say more about measuring the systematic risk of traded assets, such as IBM shares, in a few pages.

These are the easy situations. More often, business ventures are one-of-a-kind investments for which the estimation of risk must be largely subjective. When a company is contemplating a new-product investment, for example, there is frequently little technical or historical experience on which to base an estimate of investment risk. In this situation, risk appraisal depends on the perceptions of the managers participating in the decision, their knowledge of the economics of the industry, and their understanding of the investment's ramifications.

Three Techniques for Estimating Investment Risk

Three previously mentioned techniques—sensitivity analysis, scenario analysis, and simulation—are useful for making subjective estimates of investment risk. Although none of the techniques provides an objective measure of investment risk, they all help the executive to think systematically about the sources of risk and their effect on project return. Reviewing briefly, an investment's IRR or NPV depends on a number of uncertain economic factors, such as selling price, quantity sold, useful life, and so on.

Sensitivity analysis involves an estimation of how the investment's figure of merit varies with changes in one of these uncertain factors. One commonly used approach is to calculate three returns corresponding to an optimistic, a pessimistic, and a most likely forecast of the uncertain variables. This provides some indication of the range of possible outcomes. Scenario analysis is a modest extension that changes several of the uncertain variables in a mutually consistent way to describe a particular event.

We looked at simulation in some detail in Chapter 3 as a tool for financial planning. Recall that simulation is an extension of sensitivity and scenario analysis in which the analyst assigns a probability distribution to each uncertain factor, specifies any interdependence among the factors, and asks a computer repeatedly to select values for the factors according to their probability of occurring. For each set of values chosen, the computer calculates a particular outcome. The result is a graph, similar to Figure 3.1, plotting project return against frequency of occurrence. The chief benefits of sensitivity analysis, scenario analysis, and simulation are that they force the analyst to think systematically about the individual economic determinants of investment risk, indicate the sensitivity of the investment's return to each of these determinants, and provide information about the range of possible returns.

Including Risk in Investment Evaluation

Once you have an idea of the degree of risk inherent in an investment, the second step is to incorporate this information into your evaluation of the opportunity.

Risk-Adjusted Discount Rates

The most common way to do this is to add an increment to the discount rate; that is, discount the expected value of the risky cash flows at a discount rate that includes a premium for risk. Alternatively, you can compare an investment's IRR, based on expected cash flows, to a required rate of return that again includes a risk premium. The size of the premium naturally increases with the perceived risk of the investment.

To illustrate the use of such risk-adjusted discount rates, consider a $10 million investment promising risky cash flows with an expected value of $2 million annually for 10 years. What is the investment's NPV when the risk-free interest rate is 5 percent and management has decided to use a 7 percent risk premium to compensate for the uncertainty of the cash flows?

A little figure work reveals that at a 12 percent, risk-adjusted discount rate the investment's NPV is $1.3 million ($11.3 million present value of future cash flows, less $10 million initial cost). The positive NPV indicates that the investment is attractive even after adjusting for risk. An equivalent approach is to calculate the investment's IRR of 15.1 percent and note that it exceeds the 12 percent risk-adjusted rate, again signaling the investment's merit.

Note how the risk-adjusted discount rate reduces the investment's appeal. If the investment were riskless, its NPV at a 5 percent discount rate would be $5.4 million, but because a higher risk-adjusted rate is deemed appropriate, NPV falls by over $4 million. In essence, management requires an inducement of at least this amount before it is willing to make the investment.

A virtue of risk-adjusted discount rates is that most executives have at least a rough idea of how an investment's required rate of return should vary with risk. Stated differently, they have a basic idea of the position of the market line in Figure 8.1. For instance, they know from the historical data in Table 5.1 of Chapter 5 that over many years, common stocks have yielded an average annual return about 6.2 percentage points higher than the return on government bonds. If the present return on government bonds is 4 percent, it is plausible to expect an investment that is about as risky as common stocks to yield a return of about 10.2 percent. Similarly, executives know that an investment promising a return of 40 percent is attractive unless its risk is extraordinarily high. Granted, such reasoning is imprecise; nonetheless, it does lend some objectivity to risk assessment.

The Cost of Capital

Now that we introduced risk-adjusted discount rates and illustrated their use, the remaining challenge is to identify the appropriate rate for a specific investment. Do we just add 7 percentage points to the risk-free rate, or is there a more objective process?

There is a more objective process, and it rests on the notion of the *cost of capital*. When creditors and owners invest in a business, they incur opportunity costs equal to the returns they could have earned on alternative, similar-risk investments. Together these opportunity costs define the minimum rate of return the company must earn on existing assets to meet the expectations of its capital providers. This is the firm's cost of capital. If we can estimate this minimum required rate of return, we have an objectively determined risk-adjusted discount rate suitable for evaluating typical, or average risk, investments undertaken by a firm. Rather than relying on managers' "gut feelings" about investment risk, the cost of capital methodology enables us to look to financial markets for valuable information about the appropriate risk-adjusted discount rate.

Moreover, once we know how to estimate one company's cost of capital, we can use the technique to estimate the risk-adjusted discount rate applicable to a wide variety of project risks. The trick is to reason by analogy as follows. If Project A appears to be about as risky as investments undertaken by Company 1, use Company 1's cost of capital as the required return for Project A, or better yet, use an average of the cost of capital to Company 1 and all its industry peers. Thus, if a traditional pharmaceutical company is contemplating an investment in the biotech industry, a suitable required rate of return for the decision is the average cost of capital to existing biotech firms. In the following paragraphs, we define the cost of capital more precisely, estimate Sensient Technologies's cost of capital, and discuss its use as a risk-adjustment vehicle.

The Cost of Capital Defined

Suppose we want to estimate the cost of capital to XYZ Corporation and we have the following information:

	XYZ Liabilities and Owners' Equity	Opportunity Cost of Capital
Debt	$100	10%
Equity	200	20

We will discuss the origins of the opportunity costs of capital in a few pages. For now just assume we know that given alternative investment opportunities, creditors expect to earn at least 10 percent on their loans and shareholders expect to earn at least 20 percent on their ownership of XYZ shares. With this information, we need answer only two simple questions to calculate XYZ's cost of capital:

1. *How much money must XYZ earn annually on existing assets to meet the expectations of creditors and owners?*

   The creditors expect a 10 percent return on their $100 loan, or $10. However, because interest payments are tax deductible, the effective after-tax cost to a profitable company in, say, the 50 percent tax bracket is only $5. The owners expect 20 percent on their $200 investment, or $40. So in total, XYZ must earn $45 [$45 = (1 − 0.5)(10%)$100 + (20%)$200].

2. *What rate of return must the company earn on existing assets to meet the expectations of creditors and owners?*

   A total of $300 is invested in XYZ on which the company must earn $45, so the required rate of return is 15 percent ($45/$300). This is XYZ's cost of capital.

Let's repeat the preceding reasoning using symbols. The money XYZ must earn annually on existing capital is

$$(1 - t)K_D D + K_E E$$

where t is the tax rate, K_D is the expected return on debt or the cost of debt, D is the amount of interest-bearing debt in XYZ's capital structure, K_E is the expected return on equity or the cost of equity, and E is the amount of equity in XYZ's capital structure. Similarly, the annual return XYZ must earn on existing capital is

$$K_W = \frac{(1 - t)K_D D + K_E E}{D + E} \tag{8.1}$$

where K_W is the cost of capital.

From the preceding example,

$$15\% = \frac{(1 - 50\%)10\% \times \$100 + \$20\% \times \$200}{\$100 + \$200}$$

In words, a company's cost of capital is the cost of the individual sources of capital, weighted by their importance in the firm's capital structure. The subscript W appears in the expression to denote that the cost of capital is a weighted-average cost. This is also why the cost of capital is often denoted by the acronym WACC for weighted-average cost of capital. To demonstrate that K_W is a weighted-average cost, note that one-third of XYZ's capital is debt and two-thirds is equity, so its WACC is one-third the cost of debt plus two-thirds the cost of equity:

$$15\% = (1/3 \times 5\%) + (2/3 \times 20\%)$$

The Cost of Capital and Stock Price

An important tie exists between a company's cost of capital and its stock price. To see the linkage, ask yourself what happens when XYZ Corporation earns a return on existing assets greater than its cost of capital. Because the return to creditors is fixed by contract, the excess return accrues entirely to shareholders. And because the company can earn more than shareholders' opportunity cost of capital, XYZ's stock price will rise as new investors are attracted by the excess return. Conversely, if XYZ earns a return below its cost of capital on existing assets, shareholders will not receive their expected return, and its stock price will fall. The price will continue falling until the prospective return to new buyers again equals equity investors' opportunity cost of capital. Another definition of the cost of capital, therefore, is *the return a firm must earn on existing assets to keep its stock price constant*. Finally, from a shareholder value perspective, we can say that management creates value when it earns returns above the firm's cost of capital and destroys value when it earns returns below this target.

Cost of Capital for Sensient Technologies Corporation

To use the cost of capital as a risk-adjusted discount rate, we must be able to measure it. This involves assigning values to all of the quantities on the right side of equation 8.1. To illustrate the process, let's estimate Sensient Technologies's cost of capital at year-end 2010.

The Weights

We begin by measuring the weights, D and E. There are two common ways to do this, only one of which is correct: Use the book values of debt and equity appearing on the company's balance sheet, or use the market values. By *market value*, I mean the price of the company's bonds and common shares in securities markets multiplied by the number of each security type outstanding. As Table 8.2 shows, the book values of Sensient's debt and equity at the end of 2010 were $349.9 million and $983.8 million, respectively. The figure for debt includes only interest-bearing debt because other liabilities are either the result of tax accruals that are subsumed in the estimation of after-tax cash flow or spontaneous sources of cash that are part of working capital in the investment's cash flows. The table also indicates that the market value of Sensient's debt and equity on the same date were $349.9 million and $1,821.8 million, respectively.

Consistent with common practice, I have assumed here that the market value of Sensient's debt equals its book value. This assumption is almost certainly incorrect, but just as certainly the difference between the book and market values of debt is quite small compared to that for equity. The market value of Sensient's equity is its price per share at year-end of $36.73 times 49.6 million common shares outstanding. The market value of equity exceeds the book value by a ratio of almost 2 to 1 because investors are upbeat about the company's future prospects.

TABLE 8.2 **Book and Market Values of Debt and Equity for Sensient Technologies Corporation (December 31, 2010)**

Source	Book Value Amount ($ millions)	Book Value Percentage of Total	Market Value Amount ($ millions)	Market Value Percentage of Total
Debt	$ 349.9	26.2%	$ 349.9	16.1%
Equity	983.8	73.8%	1,821.8	83.9%
Total	$1,333.7	100.0%	$ 2,171.7	100.0%

To decide whether book weights or market weights are appropriate for measuring the cost of capital, consider the following. Suppose that 10 years ago you invested $20,000 in a portfolio of common stocks that, through no doing of your own, is now worth $50,000. After talking to stockbrokers and investment consultants, you believe a reasonable return on the portfolio, given present market conditions, is 10 percent a year. Would you be satisfied with a 10 percent return on the original $20,000 cost of the portfolio, or would you expect to earn 10 percent on the current $50,000 market value? Obviously, the current market value is relevant for decision making; the original cost is sunk and therefore irrelevant. Similarly, Sensient Technologies's owners and creditors have investments worth $1,821.8 million and $349.9 million, respectively, on which they expect to earn competitive returns. Thus, the market values of debt and equity are appropriate for measuring the cost of capital.

The Cost of Debt

This is an easy one. Bonds with risk and maturity similar to Sensient's were yielding a return of approximately 6.1 percent in December 2010, and the company's marginal tax rate is about 35 percent. Consequently, the after-tax cost of debt to Sensient was 4.0 percent $[(1 - 35\%) \times 6.1\%]$. Some financial neophytes are tempted to use the coupon rate on the debt rather than the prevailing market rate in this calculation. But the coupon rate is, of course, a sunk cost. Moreover, because we want to use the cost of capital to evaluate new investments, we want the cost of new debt.

The Cost of Equity

Estimating the cost of equity is as hard as estimating debt was easy. With debt, or preferred stock, the company promises the holder a specified stream of future payments. Knowing these promised payments and the current price of the security, it is a simple matter to calculate the expected return. This is what we did in the last chapter when we calculated the yield to maturity on a bond. With common stock, the situation is more complex. Because the company makes no promises about future payments to shareholders, there is no simple way to calculate the return expected.

Assume a Perpetuity

One way out of this dilemma recalls the story of the physicist, the chemist, and the economist trapped at the bottom of a 40-foot pit. After failing with a number of schemes based on their knowledge of physics and chemistry to extract themselves from the pit, the two finally turn to the economist in desperation and ask if there isn't anything in his professional training that might help them devise a means of escape. "Why, yes," he replies. "The problem is really quite elementary. Simply assume a ladder." Here our "ladder" is an assumption about the future payments shareholders expect. From this heroic beginning, the problem really does become quite elementary. To illustrate, suppose equity investors expect to receive an annual dividend of $d per share forever. Because we know the current price, P, and have assumed a future payment stream, all that remains is to find the discount rate that makes the present value of the payment stream equal the current price. From the last chapter, we know that the present value of such a perpetuity at a discount rate of K_E is

$$P = \frac{d}{K_E}$$

and, solving for the discount rate,

$$K_E = \frac{d}{p}$$

In words, if you are willing to assume investors expect a company's stock to behave like a perpetuity, the cost of equity capital is simply the dividend yield.

Perpetual Growth

A somewhat more plausible assumption is that shareholders expect a per share dividend next year of $d and expect this dividend to grow at the rate of g percent per annum *forever*. Fortunately, it turns out that this cash flow stream also has an unusually simple solution. Without boring you with the arithmetic details, the present value of the assumed payment stream at a discount rate of K_E is

$$P = \frac{d}{K_E - g}$$

and, solving for the discount rate,

$$K_E = \frac{d}{P} + g$$

This equation says that if the perpetual growth assumption is correct, the cost of equity capital equals the company's dividend yield (d/P), plus the growth rate in dividends. This is known as the *perpetual growth equation* for K_E.

The problem with the perpetual growth estimate of K_E is that it is only as good as the assumption on which it is based. For mature companies such as railroads, electric utilities, and steel mills, it may be reasonable to assume that observed growth rates will continue indefinitely. And in these cases, the perpetual growth equation yields a plausible estimate of the cost of equity capital. In all other instances, when it is implausible to think the company can maintain its current rate of growth indefinitely, the equation over-estimates the cost of equity.

Let History Be Your Guide

A second and generally more fruitful approach to estimating the cost of equity capital looks at the determinants of expected returns on risky investments. In general, the expected return on any risky asset is composed of three factors:

$$\begin{matrix} \text{Expected return} \\ \text{on risky asset} \end{matrix} = \begin{matrix} \text{Risk-free} \\ \text{interest rate} \end{matrix} + \begin{matrix} \text{Inflation} \\ \text{premium} \end{matrix} + \begin{matrix} \text{Risk} \\ \text{premium} \end{matrix}$$

The equation says that the owner of a risky asset should expect to earn a return from three sources. The first is compensation for the opportunity cost incurred in holding the asset. This is the risk-free interest rate. The second is compensation for the declining purchasing power of the currency over time. This is the inflation premium. The third is compensation for bearing the asset's systematic risk. This is the risk premium. Fortunately, we do not need to treat the first two terms as separate factors because together they equal the expected return on a default-free bond such as a government bond. Since we can readily determine the government bond interest rate, the only challenge is to estimate the risk premium.

When the risky asset is a common stock, it is useful to let history be our guide and recall from Table 5.1 that on average over the last century, the annual return on U.S. common stocks has exceeded that on government bonds by 6.2 percentage points. As a reward for bearing the added systematic risk, common stockholders earned a 6.2 percentage point higher annual return than government bondholders. Treating this as a risk premium and adding it to a 2010 long-term government bond rate of 4.2 percent yields an estimate of 10.4 percent as the cost of equity capital for a typical company.

What is the logic of treating the 6.2 percentage point historical excess return as a risk premium? Essentially, it is that over a long enough time, the return investors receive and what they expect to receive should approximate each other. For example, suppose investors expect a 20-percentage-point excess return on common stocks but the actual return keeps turning out to be 3 percentage points. Then two things should happen: Investors should lower their expectations, and selling by disappointed investors should increase subsequent realized returns. Eventually expectations and reality should come into rough parity.

We now have an estimate of the cost of capital to an "average-risk" company, but of course few companies are precisely average-risk. How, then, can we customize our average cost expression to reflect the risk of a specific firm? The answer is to insert a "customization factor," known as the company's *equity beta*, into the expression so that it becomes

$$\frac{\text{Cost of equity}}{\text{capital}} = \frac{\text{Interest rate on}}{\text{government bond}} + \beta_e \left(\frac{\text{Historical excess return}}{\text{on common stocks}} \right)$$

or in symbols,

$$K_E = i_g + \beta_e \times Rp \qquad (8.2)$$

where i_g is a government bond rate, β_e is the equity beta of the target company, and Rp is the excess return on common stocks. You can think of β_e as a scale factor reflecting the systematic risk of a specific company's shares relative to that of an average share. When the stock's systematic risk equals that of an average share, β_e equals 1.0, and the historical risk premium applies directly. But for above-average risk shares, β_e exceeds 1.0, and the risk premium grows accordingly. Conversely, for below-average risk shares, β_e is below 1.0, and only a fraction of the historical risk premium applies.

Estimating Beta

But, you might well ask, how do we estimate a company's beta? Actually, it's pretty simple. Figure 8.4 provides everything required to estimate Sensient Technologies's beta. It shows the monthly realized returns on Sensient's

FIGURE 8.4 **Sensient Technologies's Beta is the Slope of the Best-Fit Line Below**
Monthly Returns of Sensient Technologies Corporation v. S&P 500, 60 Months through December 2010

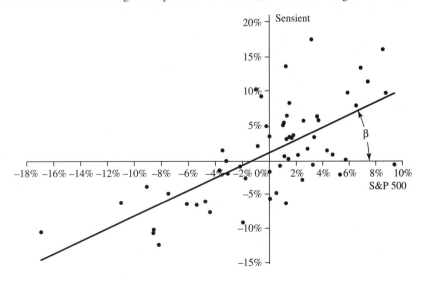

A Virtue of Statistics

Many of the concepts in this chapter can be described quite simply with the aid of a little statistics. As already noted, an investment's *total risk* refers to its dispersion in possible returns, commonly represented by the standard deviation of returns, while its *systematic risk* depends on the extent to which the investment's returns correlate with those on a broadly diversified portfolio. We can thus represent the systematic risk of investment j as

$$\text{Systematic risk} = \rho_{jm}\sigma_j$$

where ρ_{jm} is the correlation coefficient between investment j and well-diversified portfolio m, and σ_j is the standard deviation of returns on investment j. The correlation coefficient is, of course, a dimensionless number ranging between $+1$ and -1, with $+1$ characterizing perfectly positively correlated returns and -1 perfectly inversely correlated returns. For most business investments, ρ_{jm} is in the range of 0.5 to 0.8, meaning that 20 to 50 percent of the investment's total risk can be diversified away.

A common stock's *equity beta* equals its systematic risk relative to that of a well-diversified portfolio, or in symbols, stock j's equity beta is

$$\beta_j = \frac{\rho_{jm}\sigma_j}{\rho_{mm}\sigma_m}$$

But because any variable must be perfectly positively correlated with itself, this expression reduces to

$$\beta_j = \frac{\rho_{jm}\sigma_j}{\sigma_m}$$

In addition to representing stock j's equity beta, this expression also equals the slope coefficient of the regression of r_j on r_m, where r_j and r_m are realized returns on stock j and the diversified portfolio, respectively.

---

common stock relative to returns on the Standard & Poor's 500 Stock Index over the past 60 months. For example, in October 2008, the S&P index fell 17 percent, while Sensient's stock fell 10 percent. This return pair constitutes one point on the graph. The S&P 500 index is a broadly diversified portfolio containing many common shares; so its systematic risk is a reasonable surrogate for the systematic risk of an average share, and of the market as a whole. Also appearing in the figure is a best-fit, straight line indicating the average relationship among the paired returns. (If you are familiar with regression analysis, this is a simple regression line.)

The slope of this line is the beta estimate we seek. It measures the sensitivity of Sensient's equity returns to movements in the S&P index. The indicated slope of 0.92 means that on average, the return on Sensient's equity rises or falls 0.92 percent for every one percent change in the index, indicating that Sensient's equity is lower risk than average. Clearly if this line were less steeply sloped, Sensient's stock would be less sensitive to market movements, or alternatively to economy-wide events, and thus less risky. A more steeply sloped line would imply just the reverse.

The fact that all of the return pairs plotted in the figure do not lie precisely on the straight line reflects the importance of unsystematic risk in determining Sensient's monthly returns. Remember that because unsystematic risk can be eliminated through diversification, it should play no role in determining required returns or prices.

Fortunately, you do not need to worry about calculating betas yourself. Beta risk is so important a factor in security analysis that many stockbrokerage companies and investment advisors regularly publish the betas of virtually all publicly traded common stocks. Table 8.3 presents recent betas for a representative sample of firms. Observe that beta ranges from a low of 0.31 for Consolidated Edison, an electric utility, to a high of 3.75 for American International Group, the infamous insurer rescued by the government in the recent crisis. Note, too, that the numbers are intuitively plausible, with high-risk businesses such as technology and Internet companies having high betas, while low-risk companies such as food processors, and grocery stores have lower betas.

Inserting Sensient's estimated equity beta of 0.92 into equation 8.2 yields the following cost of equity capital:

$$K_E = 4.2\% + 0.92 \times 6.2\% = 9.9\%$$

TABLE 8.3 **Representative Company Betas**

Source: Standard & Poor's Compustat.

Company	Beta	Company	Beta
Advanced Micro Devices	2.19	Costco Wholesale	0.74
Amazon.com	1.17	Cummins	1.96
American Electric Power	0.59	Dean Foods	0.70
American International Group	3.75	Dell	1.38
Apple	1.38	Duke Energy	0.43
AT&T INC	0.67	Exxon Mobil	0.49
Avon Products	1.50	Goldman Sachs	1.40
Bank of New York	0.73	H & R Block	0.52
Baxter International	0.51	IBM	0.73
Berkshire Hathaway	0.46	Intel	1.10
Boeing	1.25	JDS Uniphase	2.30
Carmax	1.32	Microsoft	1.08
Caterpillar	1.74	Safeway	0.71
CBS	2.05	Southern Company	0.36
Chevron	0.75	Southwest Airlines	1.10
Coca-Cola	0.60	Wellpoint	0.97
Consolidated Edison	0.31	Wells Fargo Bank	1.38

TABLE 8.4 Calculation of Sensient Technologies Corporation's Weighted-Average Cost of Capital*

Source	Amount ($ millions)	Percentage of Total	Cost after Tax	Weighted Cost
Debt	$ 349.9	16.1%	3.9%	0.6%
Equity	1,821.8	83.9%	9.9%	8.3%
			Weighted-Average Cost of Capital =	8.9%

*Totals may not add due to rounding.

Sensient Technologies's Weighted-Average Cost of Capital

All that remains now is the figure work. Table 8.4 presents my estimate of Sensient's cost of capital in tabular form. Sensient's weighted-average cost of capital is 8.9 percent. This means that at year-end 2010, Sensient needed to earn at least this percentage return on the market value of existing assets to meet the expectations of creditors and shareholders and, by inference, to maintain its stock price. In equation form,

$$K_W = \frac{(1 - 0.35)(6.1\%)(\$349.9 \text{ million}) + (9.9\%)(\$1,821.8 \text{ million})}{\$349.9 \text{ million} + \$1,821.8 \text{ million}}$$

$$= 8.9\%$$

Before leaving our discussion of beta, I should note that while the motivation offered for equation 8.2 has been largely intuitive, the equation actually rests on a solid conceptual foundation known as the Capital Asset Pricing Model, or the CAPM. According to the CAPM, equation 8.2 is nothing less than the equation of the market line shown earlier in Figure 8.1. As such, it describes the equilibrium relationship between the expected return on any risky asset and its systematic risk. Said differently, Equation 8.2 defines the minimum acceptable rate of return an investor should demand on any risky asset.

The Cost of Capital in Investment Appraisal

The fact that the cost of capital is the return a company must earn on *existing assets* to meet creditor and shareholder expectations is an interesting detail, but we are after bigger game here: We want to use the cost of capital as an acceptance criterion for *new investments*.

Are there any problems in applying a concept derived for existing assets to new investments? Not if one critical assumption holds: The new investment must have the same risk existing assets do. If it does, the new investment is essentially a "carbon copy" of existing assets, and the cost of capital is the appropriate risk-adjusted discount rate. If it does not, we must proceed more carefully.

FIGURE 8.5 **An Investment's Risk-Adjusted Discount Rate Increases with Risk**

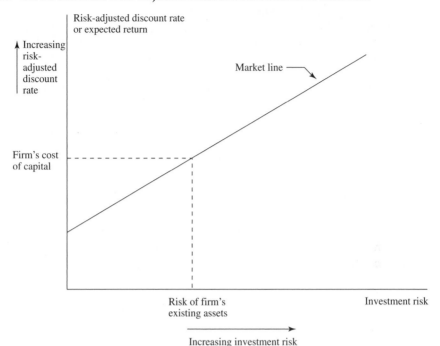

The market line in Figure 8.5 clearly illustrates the importance of the equal-risk assumption. It emphasizes that the rate of return risk-averse individuals anticipate rises with risk. This means, for example, that management should demand a higher expected return when introducing a new product than when replacing aged equipment, because the new product is presumably riskier and therefore warrants a higher return. The figure also shows that a company's cost of capital is but one of many possible risk-adjusted discount rates, the one corresponding to the risk of the firm's existing assets. We conclude that the cost of capital is an appropriate acceptance criterion only when the risk of the new investment equals that of existing assets. For all other investments, the cost of capital is inappropriate. But do not despair, for even when inappropriate itself, the cost of capital concept is central to identifying a correct risk-adjusted rate.

Multiple Hurdle Rates

Companies adjust their hurdle rates for differing investment risks in at least three possible ways. The first two are straightforward extensions of the cost of capital. For large projects, the approach is to identify an industry in which the contemplated investment would be considered average risk, estimate

---

The Cost of Capital to a Private Company

Two hurdles exist to estimating a private company's cost of capital. The first is conceptual. Some owners of private companies argue that because their company's securities do not trade on public markets, any cost of capital based on these markets is not relevant to them. This reasoning is incorrect. Financial markets define the opportunity costs incurred by all individuals when they make investment decisions regardless of whether those investments are publicly traded or privately held. A private business owner would obviously be foolish to make a business investment promising a 5 percent return when comparable-risk investments promising 15 percent are available in public markets.

The second hurdle is one of measurement. Without market values for the company's debt and equity and without equity returns on which to base a beta estimate, what do we do? I recommend the strategy described above for estimating project and divisional capital costs. Identify one or more public competitors, estimate their capital costs, and use the resulting average to represent the private firm's cost of capital. In instances where the private business has a much different capital structure from the public competitors, it may be necessary to do some further adjusting of the kind described in the appendix. When the private firm is much smaller than the public competitors, it may also be appropriate to make an upward adjustment in the cost of capital, amounting to perhaps two percentage points, to reflect the added risks faced by small firms.

---

the weighted-average cost of capital for several companies in the industry, and use an average of these estimates as the project's required rate of return. For example, when a pharmaceutical company contemplates a biotechnology investment, a reasonable hurdle rate for the decision is an average of the capital costs to existing biotechnology companies.

A challenge when applying this approach is deciding which companies to include in the sample. The cost of capital to a diversified firm is the weighted-average of the capital costs prevailing in each of its businesses. This means that even when a diversified company is a major competitor in the target business, its cost of capital may not accurately reflect the risk of that business. As a result, the best sample candidates are "pure-plays," undiversified firms that compete only in the target business. However, pure-plays are not always available, and in their absence considerable judgment and a certain amount of art must be applied when selecting sample companies and deciding how best to weight their numbers.

A second risk adjustment technique used by multidivision companies is to calculate a separate cost of capital for each division. As just noted, the cost of capital to a multidivision company will be an average of the costs of capital appropriate to each business line. When such companies use a single, corporatewide cost of capital across all divisions, they risk committing two types of errors. In low-risk divisions they are inclined to reject some worthwhile, low-risk investments for lack of expected return, while in their high-risk divisions, they are inclined to do just the opposite: accept uneconomic, high-risk investments because of their prospective returns. Over time, such companies find their lower-risk divisions withering for lack of capital, while their higher-risk divisions are force-fed too much capital.

To avoid this dilemma, many multidivision companies use the methods just described to estimate a different hurdle rate for each division. They begin by identifying several primary division competitors—hopefully including a few pure-plays. They then estimate the weighted-average cost of capital of these competitors, and use an average of these numbers as the division's cost of capital.

The third approach is more *ad hoc*. Many companies adjust for differing project risks by defining several risk buckets and assigning a different hurdle rate to each bucket. For example, Sensient might use the following four buckets.

Type of Investment	Discount Rate (%)
Replacement or repair	6.5
Cost reduction	7.0
Expansion	8.9
New product	14.0

Investments to expand capacity in existing products are essentially carbon-copy investments, so their hurdle rates equal Sensient's cost of capital. Other types of investments have a higher or lower hurdle rate, depending on their risk relative to expansion investments. Replacement or repair investments are the safest because virtually all of the cash flows are well known from past experience. Cost reduction investments are somewhat riskier, because the magnitude of potential savings is uncertain. New-product investments are the riskiest type of all, because both revenues and costs are uncertain.

Multiple hurdle rates are consistent with risk aversion and with the market line, but the amount by which the hurdle rate should be adjusted for each level of risk is largely arbitrary. Whether the hurdle rate for new product investments should be 3 or 6 percentage points above Sensient's cost of capital cannot be determined objectively.

Four Pitfalls in the Use of Discounted Cash Flow Techniques

You now know the basics of investment appraisal: Estimate the opportunity's annual, expected after-tax cash flows and discount them to the present at a risk-adjusted discount rate appropriate to the risk of the cash flows. When the opportunity is a "carbon-copy" investment, the firm's weighted-average cost of capital is the appropriate discount rate. In other

---

The Fallacy of the Marginal Cost of Capital

Some readers, especially engineers, look at equation 8.1 and naively conclude that it is possible to reduce a company's weighted-average cost of capital by using more of the cheap source of financing, debt, and less of the expensive source, equity. In other words, they conclude that increasing leverage will reduce the cost of capital. This reasoning, however, evidences an incomplete understanding of leverage. As we observed in Chapter 6, increasing leverage increases the risk borne by shareholders. Because they are risk averse, shareholders react by demanding a higher return on their investment. Thus, K_E and, to a lesser extent, K_D rise as leverage increases. This means that increasing leverage affects a company's cost of capital in two opposing ways: Increasing use of cheap debt reduces K_W, but the rise in K_E and K_D that accompanies added leverage increases it.

To review this reasoning, ask yourself how you would respond to a subordinate who made the following argument in favor of an investment: "I know the company's cost of capital is 12 percent and the IRR of this carbon-copy investment is only 10 percent. But at the last directors' meeting, we decided to finance this year's investments with new debt. Since new debt has a cost of only about 4 percent after tax, it is clearly in our shareholders' interest to invest 4 percent money to earn a 10 percent return."

The subordinate's reasoning is incorrect. Financing with debt means increasing leverage and increasing K_E. Adding the change in K_E to the 4 percent interest cost means the true *marginal* cost of the debt is well above the interest cost. In fact, it is probably quite close to K_W.

---

instances, an upward or downward adjustment to the firm's cost of capital is necessary.

In the interest of full disclosure, I will now gingerly mention four pitfalls in the practical application of discounted cash flow techniques. The first two are easily avoided once you are aware of them; the last two highlight important limitations of discounted cash flow techniques as conventionally applied. Collectively these pitfalls mean you need to master several more topics before attempting to pass as an expert.

The Enterprise Perspective versus the Equity Perspective

Any corporate investment partially financed with debt can be analyzed from either of two perspectives: that of the company, commonly known as the *enterprise* perspective, or that of its owners, often referred to as the *equity* perspective. As the following example demonstrates, these two perspectives are functionally equivalent in the sense that when properly applied they yield the same investment decision—but woe be to him who confuses the two.

Suppose ABC Industries has a capital structure composed of 40 percent debt, costing 5 percent after tax, and 60 percent equity, costing 20 percent. Its WACC is therefore

$$K_W = 5\% \times 0.40 + 20\% \times 0.60 = 14\%$$

The company is considering an average-risk investment costing $100 million and promising an after-tax cash flow of $14 million a year in perpetuity. If undertaken, ABC plans to finance the investment with $40 million in new borrowings and $60 million in equity. Should ABC make the investment?

The Enterprise Perspective

The left side of the following diagram shows the investment's cash flows from the enterprise perspective. Applying our now standard approach, the investment is a perpetuity with a 14 percent internal rate of return. Comparing this return to ABC's weighted-average cost of capital, also 14 percent, we conclude that the investment is marginal. Undertaking it will neither create nor destroy shareholder value.

The Equity Perspective

The right side of the diagram shows the same investment from the owners' viewpoint, or the equity perspective. Because $40 million of the initial cost will be financed by debt, the equity outlay is only $60 million. Similarly, because $2 million after-tax must be paid to creditors each year as interest, the residual cash flow to equity will be only $12 million. The investment's internal rate of return from the equity perspective is therefore 20 percent.

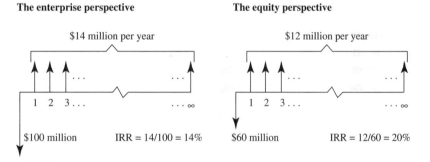

Does the fact that the return is now 20 percent mean the investment is suddenly an attractive one? Clearly, no. Because the equity cash flows are levered, they are riskier than the original cash flows and hence require a higher risk-adjusted discount rate. Indeed, the appropriate acceptance criterion for these equity cash flows is ABC's cost of equity capital, or 20 percent. (Remember, the discount rate should reflect the risk of the cash flows to be discounted.) Comparing the project's 20 percent IRR to equity with ABC's cost of equity, we again conclude that the investment is only marginal.

It is not an accident that the enterprise and equity perspectives yield the same result. Because the weighted-average cost of capital is defined to ensure that each supplier of capital receives a return equal to her opportunity cost, we know that an investment by ABC earning 14 percent, from the enterprise perspective, will earn just enough to service the debt and generate a 20 percent IRR on invested equity. Problems arise only when you mix the two perspectives, using K_E to discount enterprise cash flows or, more commonly, using K_W to discount equity cash flows.

Which perspective is better? Some of my best friends use the equity perspective, but I believe the enterprise perspective is easier to apply in practice. The problem with the equity perspective is that both the IRR to equity and the appropriate risk-adjusted discount rate vary with the amount of leverage used. The IRR to equity on ABC Industries' investment is 20 percent with $40 million of debt financing but jumps to 95 percent with $90 million of debt and rises to infinity with all-debt financing.

The interdependency between the means of financing and the risk-adjusted discount rate is easily handled in a classroom, but when real money is on the line, we often become so enthralled by the return-enhancing aspect of debt that we forget the required rate of return rises as well. Moreover, even when we remember that leverage increases risk as well as return, it is devilishly hard to estimate exactly how much the cost of equity should change with leverage.

Life is short. I recommend that you avoid unnecessary complications by using the enterprise perspective whenever possible. Assess the economic merit of the investment without regard to how it will be financed or how you will divvy up the spoils. If the investment meets this fundamental test, you can then turn to the nuances of how best to finance it.

Inflation

The second pitfall involves the improper handling of inflation. Too often managers ignore inflation when estimating an investment's cash flows but inadvertently include it in their discount rate. The effect of this mismatch is to make companies overly conservative in their investment appraisal, especially with regard to long-lived assets. Table 8.5 illustrates the point. A company with a 15 percent cost of capital is considering a $10 million, carbon-copy investment. The investment has a four-year life and is expected to increase production capacity by 10,000 units annually. Because the product sells for $900, the company estimates that annual revenues will rise $9 million ($900 $\times$ 10,000 units), which, after subtracting production costs, yields an increase in annual after-tax cash flows of $3.3 million. The IRR of the investment is calculated to be 12 percent, which is below the firm's cost of capital.

Did you spot the error? By assuming a constant selling price and constant production costs over four years, management has implicitly estimated real, or constant-dollar, cash flows, whereas the cost of capital as

TABLE 8.5   When Evaluating Investments under Inflation, Always Compare Nominal Cash Flows to a Nominal Discount Rate or Real Cash Flows to a Real Discount Rate ($ millions)

(a) Incorrect Investment Evaluation Comparing Real Cash Flows to a Nominal Discount Rate					
	2009	**2010**	**2011**	**2012**	**2013**
After-tax cash flow	$(10.0)	$3.3	$3.3	$3.3	$3.3
		IRR = 12%			
		K_W = 15%			
		Decision: **Reject**			
(b) Correct Investment Evaluation Comparing Nominal Cash Flows to a Nominal Discount Rate					
	2009	**2010**	**2011**	**2012**	**2013**
After-tax cash flow	$(10.0)	$3.5	$3.8	$4.0	$4.3
		IRR = 20%			
		K_W = 15%			
		Decision: **Accept**			

calculated earlier in the chapter is a nominal one. It is nominal because both the cost of debt and the cost of equity include a premium for expected inflation.

The key to capital budgeting under inflation is to always compare like to like. When cash flows are in nominal dollars, use a nominal discount rate. When cash flows are in real, or constant, dollars, use a real discount rate. The bottom portion of Table 8.5 illustrates a proper evaluation of the investment. After including a 5 percent annual increase in selling price and in variable production costs, the expected nominal cash flows from the investment are as shown. As one would expect, the nominal cash flows exceed the constant-dollar cash flows by a growing amount in each year. The IRR of these flows is 20 percent, which now exceeds the firm's cost of capital.[5]

Real Options

The third pitfall involves possible omission of valuable managerial options inherent in many corporate investments. Conventional discounted cash flow analysis fails to capture these options because it implicitly ignores managerial flexibility—the ability to alter an investment in response to changing circumstances. This omission might be appropriate when dealing with passive stock and bond investments, but

---

[5] An alternative approach would have been to calculate the firm's real cost of capital and compare it to a real IRR. But because this approach is more work and is fraught with potential errors, I recommend working with nominal cash flows and a nominal discount rate instead.

can be quite inappropriate when managers are able to make various mid-course corrections. Examples of what are often called *real options* in recognition of their formal equivalence to traded financial options, include

- the option to abandon an investment if cash flows do not meet expectations,
- the option to make follow-on investments if the initial undertaking is successful, and
- the option to reduce uncertainty by deferring investments to a later date.

In each instance, the option gives managers the ability to cherry pick: to act when the odds are in their favor but to walk away when they are not. (The appendix to Chapter 5 provides a brief overview of financial options, and the recommended readings at the end of the chapter offer more rigorous treatments of real options and their valuation.)

Formal real options analysis has been slow to catch on in many businesses, due primarily to its complexity.[6] At a more informal level, however, the realization that many corporate investments contain potentially valuable embedded options has altered the way executives think about these opportunities. An increasingly common item on an analyst's checklist is to identify any real options embedded in a project and to estimate, at least qualitatively, their significance to the business. The next few pages offer an intuitive look at three common real options faced by businesses and illustrate how an understanding of real options can sharpen thinking about corporate investment decisions.

Decision Trees

General Design Corporation is considering investing $100 million to launch a new line of high-speed semiconductors based on an emerging diamond film technology. This is a risky investment. Management thinks the odds of success are only about 50 percent and have decided to apply a high-risk discount rate of 25 percent in their analysis. As shown in Panel (a) of Table 8.6, they estimate that if successful, the present value of expected free cash inflows over the life of the project will total $134 million, while if it is unsuccessful, the same figure will be negative $27 million. Should General Design make the investment?

Panel (a) contains a conventional discounted cash flow analysis of the investment in the form of what is known as a "decision tree," a simple graphical technique to portray an uncertain decision. Decision trees are

---

[6] Edward Teach, "Will Real Options Take Root? Why Companies Have Been Slow to Adopt the Valuation Technique," *CFO Magazine*, July, 2003, pp. 1–4.

especially useful when the decision involves several interrelated decisions and chance events. Square nodes in the tree represent decisions, while circular nodes denote chance events. Here, there is only one decision: to invest or not, and one chance event: success or failure. Decision trees are drawn from the left, beginning with the most immediate decision and

TABLE 8.6   General Design's Diamond Film Project ($ millions)*

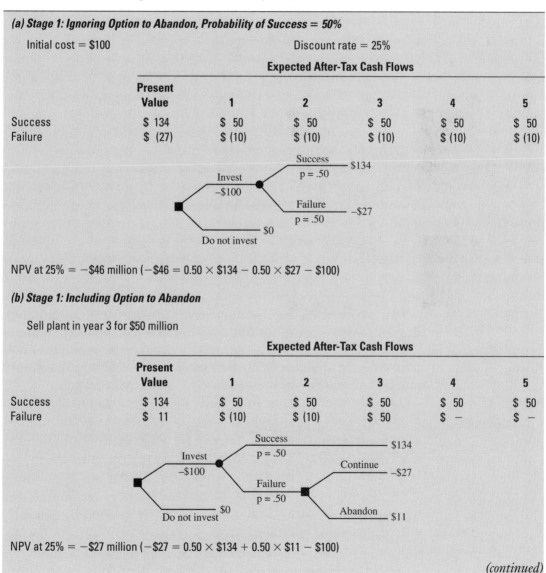

(a) Stage 1: Ignoring Option to Abandon, Probability of Success = 50%

Initial cost = $100   Discount rate = 25%

Expected After-Tax Cash Flows

	Present Value	1	2	3	4	5
Success	$ 134	$ 50	$ 50	$ 50	$ 50	$ 50
Failure	$ (27)	$ (10)	$ (10)	$ (10)	$ (10)	$ (10)

NPV at 25% = −$46 million (−$46 = 0.50 × $134 − 0.50 × $27 − $100)

(b) Stage 1: Including Option to Abandon

Sell plant in year 3 for $50 million

Expected After-Tax Cash Flows

	Present Value	1	2	3	4	5
Success	$ 134	$ 50	$ 50	$ 50	$ 50	$ 50
Failure	$ 11	$ (10)	$ (10)	$ 50	$ —	$ —

NPV at 25% = −$27 million (−$27 = 0.50 × $134 + 0.50 × $11 − $100)

(continued)

TABLE 8.6 General Design's Diamond Film Project ($ millions)*(*continued*)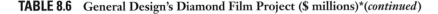

(c) Stage 2: Option to Expand, Probability of Success (Assuming Stage 1 Successful) = 90%

Invest $500 million in year 2 if Stage 1 is successful (present value at 25% = $320)

| | Present Value | Expected After-Tax Cash Flows | | | | | | |
		1	2	3	4	5	6	7
Success	$ 430	$ —	$ —	$ 250	$ 250	$ 250	$ 250	$ 250
Failure	$ 36	$ —	$ —	$ (50)	$ (50)	$ 250	$ —	$ —

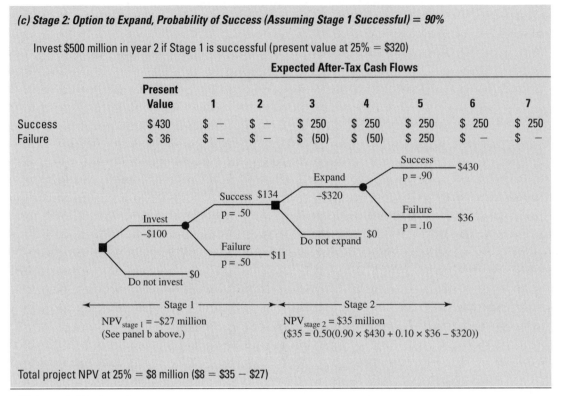

Stage 1 ⟶ ⟵ Stage 2

NPV$_{stage\ 1}$ = –$27 million
(See panel b above.)

NPV$_{stage\ 2}$ = $35 million
($35 = 0.50(0.90 × $430 + 0.10 × $36 – $320))

Total project NPV at 25% = $8 million ($8 = $35 – $27)

*Totals may not add due to rounding.

moving to the right along various branches to subsequent chance events, decisions, and outcomes. Analysis of a decision tree, however, moves in the opposite direction—from right to left. Begin at the most distant outcomes, decide what they imply for the most distant decisions, and work progressively back along the branches to the current decision.

The two rightmost outcomes in Panel (a) promise cash flows of $134 million and –$27 million with equal probability, so working to the left along the "success" and "failure" branches, it is easy to calculate that the chance node has an expected value of $54 million ($54 = .50 × $134 – .50 × $27). Combining this expected inflow with the $100 million outlay appearing under the "Invest" branch yields a net present value of –$46 million.

The Option to Abandon

The diamond film project is clearly unacceptable according to conventional analysis. But after reviewing the decision tree for a moment, one General Design executive observes that "this decision tree commits us to manufacturing the new semiconductors, even after we learn the product's a bust. Wouldn't we be smarter in that scenario to just close down the line and sell the plant?" In essence, the executive is suggesting that the conventional analysis in Panel (a) ignores a potentially valuable abandonment option: the right to terminate the project whenever the plant's resale value exceeds present value of operating cash flows generated by the plant.

Assuming General Design would abandon the project after two years of losses and sell the plant for $50 million, the decision tree in Panel (b) of Table 8.6 adds this abandonment option to the previous tree. Beginning at the right, General Design will clearly want to continue making semiconductors when sales are high, but should abandon the project when sales are low. According to the figures, including the abandonment option increases the project's net present value by $19 million to a still negative −$27 million (Revised NPV = .50 × $134 + .50 × $11 − $100 = −$27). Recognizing that the company has the option to abandon the project when conditions warrant adds $19 million to its value. This is the value of the abandonment option and also the amount by which conventional investment analysis understates the project's worth.

Before considering the second type of real option companies frequently encounter, it is appropriate to say a few more words about the strengths and weaknesses of decision trees for analyzing real options. Decision trees are a handy tool for illustrating the compound, contingent nature of many investment decisions, and they help to demonstrate how management flexibility can add value to investment opportunities. However, they also suffer from several conspicuous weaknesses. One is that decision trees quickly morph from well-behaved trees into unruly bushes as decisions become more complex and as chance events sprout more possible outcomes. Decision trees are also unable to handle decisions with continuous as opposed to discrete outcomes and when uncertainty resolves gradually over time as opposed to all at once on a specific date. But the most serious weakness is that the solution technique of calculating probability-weighted expected values of distant outcomes and rolling the results back to the present is only approximately correct when valuing real options.[7] Taken together, these observations are a reminder that our discussion here is only an introductory overview, and that rigorous real option analysis requires modeling and valuation techniques that are beyond the scope of this book.

---

[7] The problem lies with the risk-adjusted discount rate, which varies in complex ways throughout the tree depending on which options are exercised.

The Option to Grow

A chief attraction of many new-technology investments is that success today creates the option to make highly profitable follow-on investments tomorrow. To illustrate, assume General Design believes initial success in diamond film semiconductors will open the door to a stage 2, follow-on investment in two years that will be five times as large as today's stage 1 investment and cost $500 million—which at a 25 percent discount rate is equivalent to a present value cost of $320 million.

The probability management assigns to a stage 2 success is critical here. If the stage 2 investment were made today, it would be no more likely to succeed than would stage 1; after all, it is the same technology only five times larger. But, of course, the company does not need to make the stage 2 decision today. It has the option to wait until the initial results from stage 1 are in, and it is able to make a more informed choice. The stage 1 investment effectively buys the company an option to grow if future conditions prove attractive.

Panel (c) in Table 8.6 expands the decision tree further to include the stage 2 growth option. It assumes that stage 2 will only be undertaken if stage 1 is successful and that management believes the chance stage 2 will succeed, given that stage 1 has succeeded, is 90 percent. Starting again on the far right, the present value of the expected cash inflows at the stage 2 event node equals $391 million and, after subtracting $320 million present value cost of the stage 2 investment, the NPV of stage 2 is $71 million ($71 = .90 × $430 + .10 × $36 − $320). Recognizing that there is only a 50 percent chance the stage 2 investment will ever be made, its expected NPV is $35 million ($35 = .50 × $71). Finally, adding this figure to the −$27 million NPV from stage 1 generates a combined NPV for both stages of $8 million. Explicit consideration of the option to expand adds $35 million to the investment's value and transforms it into an acceptable project.

The Timing Option

The third common corporate real option is known as a timing option. In addition to passive managers, conventional discounted cash flow analysis also assumes investment decisions are "now or never." Do we make the investment immediately or not at all? Many corporate decisions, however, are of a subtler "now or later" variety. Do we invest today or wait to some more propitious future date? Here is an example of a timing option.

Wind Resources, Inc. (WRI) designs, builds, and sells wind farms to financial investors interested in stable cash flows and lucrative tax shields. Key to the price WRI can charge for a completed wind farm is the long-term contract it is able to negotiate with an electric utility to purchase the wind farm's power. The terms of this contract depend, in turn, on the prevailing price of natural gas, the utility's most common alternative energy source. WRI is considering developing an attractive wind farm site it owns in Southern California. A consultant estimates that at the current natural gas price of 6¢/kWh (cents per kilowatt hour), immediate development will yield a profit of $10 million.

Several company executives endorse the consultant's analysis and recommend immediate development. However, one of the younger managers disagrees, arguing that despite the $10 million profit from immediate development, he favors waiting for a time. He reasons that natural gas prices might rise in the future, enabling WRI to get a better selling price if it waits. Others sharply disagree, arguing that "gas prices could just as easily go down as up in the future, and anyway, WRI isn't in the business of speculating on natural gas prices." The dissenter responds that there is more involved than just getting lucky on gas prices, and offers the following illustration.

Consider the choice between developing the site today or in one year. Natural gas prices are quite volatile, so suppose the price in one year is either 8¢/kWh or 4¢/kWh with equal probability. A chart in the consultant's report indicates that WRI's profit will jump to $30 million at a price of 8¢/kWh and fall to a loss of $10 million at 4¢/kWh. Because the company won't receive these profits for one year, suppose we discount them to the present at a high, risk-adjusted rate of 25 percent. This yields present value profits of $24 million or −$8 million.

What should WRI do? A naïve expected value analysis suggests that develop now at a profit of $10 million is better than develop in one year at an expected profit of only $8 million ($8 = .50 × $24 − .50 × $8). But of course, as a moment's reflection will confirm, WRI would never develop the property only to sell it for a loss. Instead, if natural gas prices fall, the company will just postpone development until they improve, and if they do not improve, WRI will not develop.

The decision tree in Figure 8.6 shows the timing decision in more detail. If gas prices rise, WRI will develop the wind farm in one year at a present value profit of $24 million, but if they fall, it will defer development to a future date at no cost. The expected profit for the "Wait" alternative is thus, $12 million, $2 million higher than the "Develop now" path. The value of WRI's timing option in this scenario is thus, $2 million, even at a 25 percent discount rate. Note, too, that the option's value rises with uncertainty, so that the wider the dispersion in future natural gas prices, the higher the value of WRI's option to wait. As mentioned in the appendix to Chapter 5, this is an important characteristic of all options, where value increases with the volatility of the underlying asset.

FIGURE 8.6 Timing Option for Wind Resources Investment ($ millions)

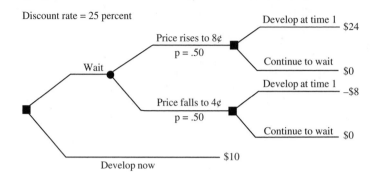

Discount rate = 25 percent

$\text{NPV}_{\text{wait}} = \$12 \text{ million } (\$12 = 0.50 \times \$24 - 0.50 \times \$0)$

The observation that the ability to postpone an investment is valuable raises an obvious question. If WRI should not invest now, when should it invest? When should management quit stalling and build the wind farm? Ironically, the answer to this question in many instances is that the company should wait as long as possible. Because a timing option can only be exercised once and because doing so destroys its value, development should only occur when the resulting gains exceed the value of the option sacrificed. With some opportunities, management may want to invest immediately to take advantage of short-lived profit opportunities, to capture first-mover advantages, or to avoid rising construction costs. But, unless these costs of waiting exceed the value of the option destroyed, it makes sense to wait. In WRI's case, the only significant costs of waiting appear to be the threat of declining government subsidies and of rising construction costs.

In sum, this brief look at real options has demonstrated several important facts:

- Standard DCF analysis of investments containing embedded options systematically understates their value.
- The NPV of such investments equals their NPV ignoring the options, plus the NPV of the options.
- When opportunities contain timing options, it may make sense to defer investment even when the NPV of immediate investment is positive.
- Because option values rise with uncertainty, the incentive to acquire growth options via research and development or other means rises with uncertainty, as does the incentive to delay investing in opportunities containing timing options.
- The logic and vocabulary of real options are increasingly pervading corporate thinking and discussion, even in the absence of rigorous quantitative analysis.

- Smart managers think systematically about the presence of embedded options and assess their value in at least qualitative terms.
- Smart companies realize that embedded options are valuable and work systematically to maintain and acquire them.

The moral should be clear: Failure to appreciate the value of real options embedded in some corporate investment opportunities leads to inaccurate decision making and unnecessary timidity in the face of certain high-risk, high-payoff opportunities.

Excessive Risk Adjustment

Our last pitfall is a subtle one concerning the proper use of risk-adjusted discount rates. Adding an increment to the discount rate to adjust for an investment's risk makes intuitive sense. You need to be aware, however, that as you apply this discount rate to more distant cash flows, the arithmetic of the discounting process compounds the risk adjustment. Table 8.7 illustrates the effect. It shows the present value of $1 in 1 year and in 10 years, first at a risk-free discount rate of 5 percent and then at a risk-adjusted rate of 10 percent. Comparing these present values, note that addition of the risk premium knocks a modest 4 cents off the value of a dollar in 1 year but a sizable 23 cents off in 10 years. Clearly, use of a constant risk-adjusted discount rate is appropriate only when the risk of a cash flow grows as the cash flow recedes farther into the future.

For many, if not most, business investments, the assumption that risk increases with the remoteness of a cash flow is quite appropriate, but as we will see by looking again at General Design's diamond film project, this is not always the case.

Recall that General Design is contemplating a possible two-stage investment. The first stage, costing $100 million, is attractive chiefly because it gives management the option to make a much more lucrative

TABLE 8.7 **Use of a Constant Risk-Adjusted Discount Rate Implies that Risk Increases with the Remoteness of a Cash Flow (risk-free rate = 5%; risk-adjusted rate = 10%)**

	Present Value of $1	
	Received in 1 Year	**Received in 10 Years**
Discounted at risk-free rate	$0.95	$0.61
Discounted at risk-adjusted rate	0.91	0.39
Reduction in present value due to risk	$0.04	$0.23

follow-on investment. Because both stages depend on a new, untested diamond film technology, the discount rate used throughout the analysis was General Design's high-risk hurdle rate of 25 percent.

Given the speculative nature of this investment, many executives would argue that it is entirely appropriate to use a high risk-adjusted discount rate throughout. But is it really? The investment clearly involves high risk, but because most of the risk will be resolved in the first two years, use of a constant risk-adjusted discount rate is overly conservative.

To see the logic, suppose you are at time 2, stage 1 has been successful, and the company is about to launch stage 2. Because the stage 2 cash flows are now relatively certain, their value *at time 2* is their expected value as shown in Table 8.6 Panel (c), discounted at General Design's discount rate for average-risk investments of, say, 15 percent. This amounts to $263 million.[8]

As seen from the present, therefore, General Design's decision to invest in stage 1 gives it a 50 percent chance at a follow-on investment worth $263 million in two years. And because the next two years are high risk, it makes sense to value stage 2 today by discounting this sum to the present at a 25 percent discount rate and then applying a 50 percent probability. This produces a revised stage 2 NPV of $84 million.

Adding this figure to the original stage 1 NPV of −$27 million produces a revised total NPV for both stages equal to $57 million, $49 million higher than the earlier figure.

To recap, whenever you encounter an investment with two or more distinct risk phases, be careful about using a constant risk-adjusted discount rate, for although such investments may be comparatively rare, they are also frequently the type of opportunities companies can ill afford to waste.

Economic Value Added

In late 1993, *Fortune* magazine ran a cover story entitled "The Real Key to Creating Wealth," which trumpeted, "Rewarded by knockout results, managers and investors are peering into the heart of what makes businesses valuable by using a tool called Economic Value Added."[9] With publicity like this and a steady stream of laudatory articles since, it is little wonder that many otherwise placid executives and investors are interested in what *Fortune* called "today's hottest financial idea and getting hotter."

[8] The present value of "success" cash flows at time 2 discounted at 15 percent is $836 million. The corresponding figure for "failure" cash flows is $83 million. At a 90 percent chance of success, the expected present value of cash inflows is $763 million ($763 = .90 × $836 + .10 × $83). Subtracting the initial cost of $500 million yields $263 million.
[9] Shawn Tully, "The Real Key to Creating Wealth," *Fortune,* September 20, 1993, p. 38.

Having mastered the intricacies of the cost of capital, you will find economic value added, or EVA, to be little more than a restatement of what you already know. The central message of this and the preceding chapter has been that an investment creates value for its owners only when its expected return exceeds its cost of capital. In essence, EVA simply extends the cost of capital imperative to performance appraisal. It says that a company or a business unit creates value for owners only when its operating income exceeds the cost of capital employed. In symbols,

$$EVA = EBIT(1 - Tax\ rate) - K_W C$$

where $EBIT(1 - Tax\ rate)$ is the unit's after-tax operating income, K_W is its WACC, and C is the capital employed by the unit. $K_W C$, then, represents an annual capital charge. The capital-employed variable, C, equals the money invested in the unit over time by creditors and owners. As a first approximation, C is the sum of interest-bearing debt plus the book value of equity or, more generally, all sources of capital to the business on which it must earn a return.[10]

Plugging Sensient Technologies's 2010 numbers into this expression, we find that

$$EVA_{10} = \$173.2(1 - 30.5\%) - 8.9\%(\$349.9 + \$983.8)$$
$$= \$1.6\ million.$$

Although estimating economic values from accounting data is always problematic, these numbers suggest that Sensient earned just enough in 2010 to cover the cost of capital employed and created $1.6 million in new value for its owners—a marginal performance.

EVA and Investment Analysis

An important attribute of economic value added is that the present value of an investment's annual EVA stream equals the investment's NPV. This makes it possible to talk about investment appraisal in terms of EVA rather than NPV—provided, of course, there is something to be gained by doing so. The numerical example in Table 8.8 demonstrates this equality. Part *a* of the table is a conventional net present value analysis of a very simple investment. The investment requires an initial outlay of $100, which will be depreciated on a straight-line basis to zero over four years. Adding depreciation to prospective income after tax and discounting the resulting after-tax cash flow at 10 percent yields an NPV of $58.50.

Part *b* of the table presents a discounted EVA treatment of the same investment. To calculate EVA, we need a dollar figure for the annual

---

[10] For details, see G. Bennett Stewart III, *The Quest for Value* (New York: HarperBusiness, 1991).

TABLE 8.8 **Discounting an Investment's Annual EVA Stream Is Equivalent to Calculating the Investment's NPV**

(a) Standard NPV Analysis

		Year			
	0	**1**	**2**	**3**	**4**
Initial investment	−$100.00				
Revenue		$ 80.00	$80.00	$80.00	$80.00
Cash expenses		13.33	13.33	13.33	13.33
Depreciation		25.00	25.00	25.00	25.00
Income before tax		41.67	41.67	41.67	41.67
Tax at 40%		16.67	16.67	16.67	16.67
Income after tax		25.00	25.00	25.00	25.00
Depreciation		25.00	25.00	25.00	25.00
After-tax cash flow	−$100.00	$ 50.00	$50.00	$50.00	$50.00
NPV at 10%	$ 58.50				

(b) Discounted EVA Analysis

		Year			
	0	**1**	**2**	**3**	**4**
Capital employed		$100.00	$75.00	$50.00	$25.00
K_W		0.10	0.10	0.10	0.10
$K_W \times$ Capital		10.00	7.50	5.00	2.50
EBIT$(1 - t)$		25.00	25.00	25.00	25.00
$- K_W \times$ Capital		10.00	7.50	5.00	2.50
EVA		$ 15.00	$17.50	$20.00	$22.50
EVA discounted at 10%	$ 58.50				

opportunity cost of capital employed. This equals the percentage cost of capital times the book value of the investment at the beginning of each year. Subtracting this quantity from EBIT after-tax yields annual project EVA, which, discounted at 10 percent, yields a discounted EVA of $58.50— precisely the NPV calculated in part *a*. Thus, another way to evaluate investment opportunities, which is equivalent to NPV analysis, is to calculate the present value of the investment's annual EVA. Still to be answered is why one might want to calculate discounted EVA instead of NPV.[11]

[11] Why the equality? The difference between the two approaches lies in the treatment of the initial investment. NPV records the full cost of the investment at time zero. EVA ignores the initial cost but records an annual depreciation charge plus a carrying cost equal to the WACC times the undepreciated asset value. It turns out that the present value of these two annual charges always equals the initial cost of the investment, regardless of the method of depreciation employed. Therefore, the two methods must yield the same result.

EVA's Appeal

If EVA looks vaguely familiar, it should. The fact that capital provided by creditors and owners is costly and this cost is relevant for measuring economic performance has been recognized for many years. Indeed, we made the point in Chapter 1 when we noted that accounting income overstates true, economic income because it ignores the cost of equity. So novelty cannot explain EVA's sudden appeal, nor can EVA's superiority to return on investment, ROI, as a measure of business performance. For the problems with ROI, defined as operating income over operating assets, have also been widely known for a long while.[12] So why the sudden appeal of EVA after all these years?

The answer, I think, is that EVA, in its present incarnation, addresses a pervasive business problem, one that has greatly undermined many managers' acceptance of modern finance. EVA's appeal is that it integrates three crucial management functions: capital budgeting, performance appraisal, and incentive compensation. Together these functions are intended to positively influence management behavior, but too often, they work at cross-purposes, giving managers confusing and apparently conflicting signals about what to do. Thus, in the absence of EVA, managers are told to use NPV, IRR, or BCR to analyze investment opportunities but to look at ROE, ROI, or earnings per share growth when assessing business unit performance. And all the while, the company's incentive compensation plan relies on still other metrics, requires an advanced degree to fully comprehend, and changes more often than the Italian government. Is it any wonder, then, that many operating managers faced with this apparent confusion take none of it very seriously and rely instead on common sense to muddle through?

Contrast this with EVA-based management. The business goal is to create EVA. Capital budgeting decisions are based on discounted EVA at an appropriate cost of capital. Unit EVA, or change in EVA, measures business unit performance, and incentive compensation depends on unit EVA relative to an appropriate target—clean, simple, and straightforward. Consultants Stern Stewart & Company have even developed a clever method of distributing a manager's bonus over several periods, known as the bonus

---

[12] Here is one problem with ROI. Imagine a division with an ROI of only 2 percent and ask what type of investments the division manager is apt to favor. Charged with the task of raising division ROI, the manager will naturally look favorably on any investment promising an ROI above 2 percent regardless of the investment's NPV. Conversely, managers in divisions with high ROIs will be quite conservative in their investment decisions for fear of lowering ROI. A company in which unsuccessful divisions invest aggressively while successful ones invest conservatively is probably not what shareholders want to see.

bank, that puts middle managers at risk much as though they were owners and also helps to discourage myopic, single-period decision making.[13]

EVA certainly has its own problems, and some of its virtues are more cosmetic than real. But it does address an important barrier to the acceptance of the financial way of thinking in many companies, and for this reason alone deserves our attention. Or, as *Fortune's* purple prose might put it, "EVA promises to complete the transformation of value creation from a mere slogan into a powerful management tool, one that may at last move modern finance out of the classroom and into the boardroom—perhaps even onto the shop floor!"

A Cautionary Note

An always present danger when using analytic or numerical techniques in business decision making is that the "hard facts" will assume exaggerated importance compared to more qualitative issues and that the manipulation of these facts will become a substitute for creative effort. It is important to bear in mind that numbers and theories don't get things done; people do. And the best investments will fail unless capable workers are committed to their success. As Barbara Tuchman put it in another context, "In military as in other human affairs will is what makes things happen. There are circumstances that can modify or nullify it, but for offense or defense its presence is essential and its absence fatal."[14]

APPENDIX

Asset Beta and Adjusted Present Value

Most companies have two betas: An observable equity beta, discussed at some length in the chapter, and an unobservable asset beta. Equity beta measures the systematic risk of a company's shares, while asset beta measures the systematic risk of its assets. In rare instances when a company is all-equity financed, the risk of its common stock equals that of its assets, and equity beta equals asset beta. For this reason, asset beta is also commonly referred to as the firm's *unlevered* beta. It is the equity beta a firm would report if it were all-equity financed.

---

[13] See Stewart, *The Quest for Value*, Chapter 6.
[14] Barbara W. Tuchman, *Stilwell and the American Experience in China 1911–1945* (New York: Bantam Books, 1971), pp. 561–62.

One important use of asset betas is to improve the accuracy by which equity betas are measured. To illustrate, when I estimated Sensient Technologies's equity beta by regressing the company's monthly, realized returns against those of the Standard & Poor's 500 Stock Index, I calculated an equity beta of 0.92, as reported in the chapter. But I also found a standard error of estimate equal to 0.13. Standard error is a statistical indicator of the precision of the beta estimate. As a benchmark, when the deviations of the individual observations from the regression line are distributed in a normal, bell-shaped pattern, we know there is a two-thirds chance that the true slope of the regression line is within plus or minus one standard error of the observed slope. This means we can state with some confidence that Sensient's equity beta is somewhere in the range of 0.79 to 1.05—not an especially comforting conclusion.

A second important use of asset beta is in conjunction with a net present value technique called *Adjusted Present Value*, or *APV*. Together asset beta and APV offer a flexible alternative to the standard WACC-based approach to investment appraisal described in the chapter. This alternative is especially attractive when evaluating complex investment opportunities.

Beta and Financial Leverage

Our starting point in the consideration of asset beta and adjusted present value is the effect of financial leverage on equity beta. Recalling our discussion of company financing decisions in Chapter 6, you know that shareholders face two distinct risks: the basic business risk inherent in the markets in which the firm competes, plus the added financial risk created by the use of debt financing. Asset beta measures the business risk, while equity beta reflects the combined effect of business and financial risks. To appreciate the tie between equity beta and financial leverage, recall from Chapter 6 that debt financing increases the dispersion in possible returns to shareholders, which in turn increases the firm's equity beta.

Because most businesses are levered, it is generally impossible to observe asset beta directly. However, with the aid of the following formula, we can easily calculate asset beta given equity beta, and vice versa.[1]

---

[1] We can express the market value of a levered firm in two ways: as the market value of its debt plus equity, and as the value of the same firm unlevered plus the present value of the tax shields from debt financing. Equating these two expressions,

$$D + E = V_u + tD$$

where D is interest-bearing debt, E is the market value of equity, V_u is the value of the firm without any debt, and t is the marginal tax rate.

$$\beta_A = \frac{E}{V}\beta_E$$

where β_A is asset beta, β_E is equity beta, and $\frac{E}{V}$ is the equity-to-firm value ratio, measured at market. This equation says that $\beta_A = \beta_E$ when debt is zero and that β_E rises above β_A by a growing amount as leverage increases. Plugging Sensient's numbers into the equation, we learn that if the company's equity beta is 0.92, its asset beta must be 0.77 [0.77 = ($1,821.8 / $2,171.7) × 0.92]. Calculating asset beta from equity beta in this manner is known in the trade as *unlevering* beta, while applying the equation in reverse to calculate equity beta from asset beta is referred to as *relevering* beta.

Using Asset Beta to Estimate Equity Beta

The ability to unlever and relever betas is the key to improving equity beta estimates. Three steps are required:

- Identify industry competitors of the target company, and calculate each competitor's asset beta by unlevering its observed equity beta.
- Average these asset betas, or use their median value, to estimate an industry asset beta.
- Relever this industry asset beta to the target company's capital structure.

The logic of this approach is that firms in the same industry should face the same or similar business risks and should therefore have similar asset betas. Unlevering the observed equity betas removes the differential effects of financial leverage for each company, allowing us to estimate an industry asset beta based on observations from several firms. Then relevering this asset beta to the target's capital structure produces an equity beta consistent with the target's unique structure. The payoff from this approach is that an equity beta estimate based on data from a number of firms should reduce the unavoidable noise inherent in the conventional, single-firm approach.

---

[1](continued) An important property of beta is that the beta of a portfolio is the weighted-average of the betas of the individual assets comprising the portfolio. Applying this insight to both sides of the equation above,

$$\frac{D}{D + E}\beta_D + \frac{E}{D + E}\beta_E = \frac{V_u}{V_u + tD}\beta_A + \frac{tD}{V_u + tD}\beta_{ITS}$$

where β_D is the beta of debt, β_E is the beta of equity, β_A is the beta of the unlevered firm, or equivalently, the firm's asset beta, and β_{ITS} is the beta of the firm's interest tax shields.

Assuming for simplicity (1) the firm's debt is risk-free, so $\beta_D = 0$, and (2) the risk of interest tax shields equals the risk of the firm's unlevered asset cash flows, so $\beta_{ITS} = \beta_A$, the above equation simplifies to the equation in the text.

A possible alternative assumption is $\beta_{ITS} = \beta_D = 0$, which yields a more complex expression. For details, see Richard S. Ruback, "Capital Cash Flows: A Simple Approach to Valuing Risky Cash Flows," *Financial Management*, Summer 2002, pp. 85–103.

TABLE 8A.1   **Estimate of Industry Asset Beta for Sensient Technologies Corporation**

Company	Equity Beta	Equity/Firm Value	Asset Beta	Market Value Equity	% of Total Market Value	Weighted-Asset Beta
Albemarle Corporation	1.49	86%	1.27	$5,109	24%	0.30
Cabot Corporation	1.67	79%	1.32	$2,461	11%	0.15
Corn Products Int'l	1.20	66%	0.80	$3,497	16%	0.13
Intl Flavors & Fragrances	0.92	83%	0.76	$4,459	21%	0.16
McCormick & Company	0.41	88%	0.36	$6,193	29%	0.10
					Industry asset beta	**0.83**

Table 8A.1 illustrates the mechanics. It presents an estimate of Sensient's industry asset beta based on numbers for five competitors of Sensient identified in Chapter 2. To avoid giving undue weight to smaller firms, I weighted the firm asset betas by relative market value of equity in calculating the industry figure. The resulting industry asset beta is 0.83. Relevering this industry beta to reflect Sensient's unique capital structure yields an estimated equity beta of 0.99, about 8 percent above the number reported in the chapter, [0.99 = ($2,171.7/$1,821.8) × 0.83].

Asset Beta and Adjusted Present Value

In the standard WACC-based approach to investment appraisal described in the chapter, we ask the weighted average cost of capital to do double duty: to adjust for the risk of the cash flows being discounted, and to capture the tax-shield advantages of the debt financing used by the firm. We reflect these tax shield advantages by using the after-tax cost of debt in the weighted-average calculation. In most instances, this creates no problem; however, difficulties can arise when the firm's capital structure is changing over time, or when the project's debt capacity differs from that implicit in the WACC.

In these situations it becomes advantageous to use an Adjusted Present Value approach, or what is sometimes called "valuation by parts." First, abstract entirely from anything to do with debt financing by estimating the project's NPV assuming all-equity financing. Then capture the tax shield effects of debt financing, and any other "side effects," in separate add-on terms. If the sum of these separate present value terms is positive, the opportunity is financially attractive, and vice versa. In symbols,

$$APV = NPV_{\text{all-equity financing}} + PV_{\text{interest tax shields}} + PV_{\text{any other side effects}}$$

At its root, APV is nothing more than a formalization of the idea that when evaluating investment opportunities, the whole should equal the sum of the parts.

Asset beta and APV are ideal partners because asset beta enables us to estimate the appropriate discount rate for valuing investments that are all-equity financed. A moment's review of the WACC equation in the chapter will convince you that in the absence of debt financing, WACC collapses to the cost of equity. The discount rate for evaluating all-equity financed investments is therefore represented by equation 8.2 in the chapter, with β_A replacing β_E.

$$K_A = i_g + \beta_A \times Rp$$

where i_g is a government bond rate, β_A is the investment's asset beta, and Rp is the risk premium, usually approximated by the excess return on common stocks over government bonds.

To illustrate the combined use of APV and asset beta, consider the investment opportunity under review by Delaney Pumps. Delaney Pumps manufactures and distributes an extensive line of agricultural irrigation systems. In recent years, computerized control systems used to automate irrigation and to conserve water have become increasingly important in selling high-end systems. And Delaney management is actively considering investing $160 million to develop a state-of-the-art, computerized controller that promises to leapfrog competition. Development work would be contracted to a software development company on a cost-plus basis. Revenue would come from a new product line featuring the controller and from license fees from selected competitors who elected to include the controller in their products. Projected cash flows for the investment appear in Table 8A.2. The projections extend for only four years because management anticipates that other, more advanced controllers will be available by this time.

Two challenges confronted Delaney management as they began their deliberations. Because the digital controller appeared much riskier than the

TABLE 8A.2   Adjusted Present Value Analysis of Automated Irrigation Controller ($ in millions)

		Year			
	0	**1**	**2**	**3**	**4**
Earnings before interest and taxes		$50.0	$150.0	$80.0	$30.0
Expected free cash flow	(160.0)	30.0	120.0	60.0	70.0
Interest expense		5.0	15.0	8.0	3.0
Interest tax-shield @ 40% tax rate		2.0	6.0	3.2	1.2
Asset beta	2.41				
NPV all-equity	20.1				
PV tax-shields	8.4				
APV	**$ 28.5**				

company's usual capital expenditures, managers were uncomfortable using the company's 10 percent weighted-average cost of capital as the hurdle rate. In addition, Delaney had traditionally financed its business with the goal of maintaining a target times-interest-earned ratio of about 3 to 1. But because this project consisted almost entirely of intangible computer code and because its cash flows were quite uncertain, Delaney's treasurer thought it prudent to target a higher interest coverage of 10 to 1 on this project.

To address these challenges, the treasurer decided to do an APV analysis. Reasoning that the digital controller would probably be an average-risk investment for software companies, she identified five smaller, publicly traded firms specializing in business automation software. She then unlevered the equity betas of these firms and calculated an industry average asset beta equal to 2.41, confirming her intuition that business automation software is indeed a risky business. Combining this asset beta with a 4.2 percent riskless borrowing rate and a 6.2 percent historical risk premium in the earlier equation, she calculated a hurdle rate for unlevered, business automation software investments equal to 19.1 percent (19.1 = 4.2% + 2.41 × 6.2%). Using this rate to discount the expected free cash flows in Table 8A.2, she found the project's NPV assuming all-equity financing to be $20.1 million.

The investment's principal side effect was the interest-tax shields it would generate over time. At a target times-interest-earned ratio of 10 to 1 and a 40 percent tax rate, the annual interest expense appearing in the table equals one-tenth of projected EBIT, while the corresponding tax shield is 40 percent of this amount. The discount rate used to calculate the present value of these tax shields should, of course, reflect the risk of the cash flows being discounted. Some executives argue that because interest tax shields are debtlike in terms of risk, they should be discounted at a corporate debt rate. Others maintain that while individual debt contracts may generate predictable cash flows, the total debt a business carries varies with its size and cash flows, in which case a discount rate more like K_A is appropriate. Here, because the tax shields are tied mechanically to operating income, K_A is the proper rate. Discounting at this rate, the tax shields are worth $8.4 million, so the investment's APV is an attractive $28.5 million.

$$APV = NPV_{\text{all-equity financing}} + PV_{\text{interest tax shields}}$$
$$\$28.5 \text{ million} = \$20.1 \text{ million} + \$8.4 \text{ million}$$

Note carefully in this analysis that the treasurer's tax shield calculations had nothing to do with the way Delaney intended to finance the investment and everything to do with how much debt the treasurer believed the project could prudently support. For tactical reasons, companies routinely finance some investments entirely with debt and others entirely with retained profits, but this information is irrelevant to judging an investment's debt capacity and its consequent claim to interest tax shields. To think otherwise would be to commit a variation of the "marginal cost of capital fallacy."

This example deals with a straightforward investment possessing one simple side effect, but I hope it hints at the power of the technique. APV's divide-and-conquer perspective makes it possible to break even very complex problems into a series of tractable, smaller problems, and to solve the complex problem by stringing together solutions to the smaller ones. We can thus analyze a cross-border investment involving several currencies and subsidized financing as the sum of separate NPV calculations for cash flows in each currency translated into the home currency at prevailing exchange rates, plus a separate term capturing the value of the subsidized finance. And we can even apply a separate, customized hurdle rate to each cash flow stream. In a complicated world, APV and its cousin, asset beta, are indeed welcome additions to our tool kit.

SUMMARY

1. An investment's total risk
   - Refers to the range of possible returns.
   - Can be estimated for traded assets as the standard deviation of returns.
   - Can be avoided to some extent by diversifying.

2. Systematic risk
   - Is the part of total risk that cannot be avoided by diversifying.
   - Equals about half of total risk, on average, for stocks.
   - Is the only part of total risk that should affect asset prices and returns.
   - Is positively related to the return demanded by risk-averse investors.
   - Can be estimated as the product of total risk and the correlation coefficient between an asset's returns and those on a well-diversified portfolio.

3. The cost of capital
   - Is a risk-adjusted discount rate.
   - Equals the value-weighted average of the opportunity costs incurred by owners and creditors.
   - Is the return a firm must earn on existing assets to at least maintain stock price.

- Is relevant for private firms and not-for-profits as well as public firms.
- Is the appropriate hurdle rate for evaluating carbon copy investments.
- Can be an appropriate hurdle rate for evaluating non–carbon copy investments when it is the cost of capital of other firms for which the investment *is* carbon copy.

4. The cost of equity capital
   - Is the opportunity cost incurred by owners.
   - Is the most challenging variable to estimate when measuring a firm's cost of capital.
   - Is best approximated as the sum of an interest rate on a government bond plus a risk premium.
   - Increases with financial leverage.

5. Beta
   - Measures an asset's relative systematic risk.
   - Can be estimated by regressing an asset's periodic realized returns on those of a well-diversified portfolio.
   - When multiplied by the realized excess return on stocks relative to bonds, yields a suitable risk premium for estimating the cost of equity.
   - Increases with financial leverage.

6. Four pitfalls to avoid in discounted cash flow analysis are
   - Confounding an enterprise perspective with an equity perspective.
   - Using a nominal discount rate to value real cash flows, or vice versa.
   - Ignoring possibly valuable real options embedded in firm investments.
   - Forgetting that a constant discount rate implies risk grows with the futurity of the cash flow.

7. Economic Value Added
   - Is a popular measure of firm or division performance.
   - Equals a unit's operating income after tax less an annual charge for capital employed.
   - Helps unify three apparently disparate topics:
     – Investment evaluation.
     – Performance appraisal.
     – Incentive compensation.

ADDITIONAL RESOURCES

Bernstein, Peter L. *Against the Gods: The Remarkable Story of Risk*. New York: John Wiley and Sons, 1998. 383 pages.

A stimulating history of man's attempt to cope with risk in human affairs from the 13th century to the present. Bernstein

other, estimating the value of debt amounts to nothing more than grabbing a few numbers off the company's balance sheet.[1] If the fair market value of a business is $4 million and the firm has $1.5 million in debt outstanding, its equity is worth $2.5 million. It's that simple.[2] (We ignore non-interest-bearing debt such as accounts payable and deferred taxes here because they are treated as part of free cash flow, to be described momentarily.)

Free Cash Flow

As in all capital expenditure decisions, the biggest practical challenge in business valuation is estimating the relevant cash flows to be discounted. In Chapter 7, we said the relevant cash flows are the project's annual free cash flows (FCF), defined as EBIT after tax plus depreciation, less investment. When valuing a company, this translates into the following:

$$\frac{\text{Free}}{\text{cash flow}} = \text{EBIT}(1 - \text{Tax rate}) + \text{Depreciation} - \frac{\text{Capital}}{\text{expenditures}} - \frac{\text{Working capital}}{\text{investments}}$$

where EBIT is earnings before interest and taxes.

The rationale for using free cash flow goes like this. EBIT is the income the company earns without regard to how the business is financed; so EBIT$(1 - \text{Tax rate})$ is income after tax excluding the effects of debt financing. Adding depreciation and any other noncash items yields after-tax cash flow. If management were prepared to run the company into the ground, it could distribute this cash flow to owners and creditors, and that would be the end of it. But in most companies, management retains some or all of this cash flow in the business to pay for new capital expenditures and additions to short-term assets. The annual cash flow available for distribution to owners and creditors is thus operating cash flow after tax less capital expenditures and working capital investments.

The working capital term in this expression can be tricky. Working capital investment equals the increase in current assets necessary to support operations, less any accompanying increases in non-interest-bearing current liabilities, or what I referred to in Chapter 7 as "spontaneous

---

[1] There are two instances in which the market value and the book value of debt will differ significantly: Default risk has changed significantly since issue, and the debt is fixed rate and interest rates have changed significantly since issue. In these instances, it pays to estimate the market value of the debt independently.

[2] An alternative approach to equity valuation is to estimate the present value of expected cash flows to equity discounted at the target's cost of equity capital. Executed correctly, this equity approach yields the same answer as the enterprise approach described above; however, I find it more difficult to apply in practice. See the section "The Enterprise Perspective versus the Equity Perspective" in Chapter 8 for details.

sources." This difference equals the net investment in current assets that must be financed by creditors and owners. A second challenge is how to treat any excess cash a company accumulates over and above the amount necessary to support operations. My advice is to omit excess cash from the discounted cash flow valuation and treat it as a separate add-on term.

The Terminal Value

We now come to a serious practical problem. Our equation says that the FMV of a business equals the present value of all future free cash flows. Yet because companies typically have an indefinitely long life expectancy, the literal application of this equation would have us estimating free cash flows for perhaps hundreds of years into the far distant future—a clearly unreasonable task.

The standard way around this impasse is to think of the target company's future as composed of two discrete periods. During the first period, of some 5 to 15 years, we presume the company has a unique cash flow pattern and growth trajectory that we seek to capture by estimating individual, annual free cash flows just as the equation suggests. However, by the end of this forecast period, we assume the company has lost its individuality—has grown up, if you will—and become a stable, slow-growth business. From this date forward, we cease worrying about annual cash flows and instead estimate a single *terminal value* representing the worth of all subsequent free cash flows. If the initial forecast period is, say, 10 years, our valuation equation becomes

$$\text{FMV of firm} = \text{PV(FCF years } 1-10 + \text{Terminal value at year 10)}$$

Introduction of a terminal value, of course, only trades one problem for another, for now we need to know how to estimate a company's terminal value. I wish I could assure you that financial economists have solved this problem and present a simple, accurate expression for a company's terminal value, but I can't. Instead, the best I can offer are several plausible alternative estimates and some general advice on how to proceed.

Following are five alternative ways to estimate a company's terminal value with accompanying explanatory comments and observations. To use these estimates effectively, note first that no single estimate is always best; rather, each is more or less appropriate depending on circumstances. Thus, liquidation value may be highly relevant when valuing a mining operation with 10 years of reserves but quite irrelevant when valuing a rapidly growing software company. Second, resist the natural temptation to pick what appears to be the best technique for the situation at hand, ignoring all others. Avoid too the simple averaging of several estimates. Instead, calculate a number of terminal value estimates and begin by asking why they differ. In some instances, the differences will be readily explainable; in others, you may find it necessary to revise your assumptions to reconcile the differing values. Then, once you understand why remaining differences exist and feel comfortable with the magnitude of the differences, select a terminal value based on your assessment of the relative merits of each estimate for the target company.

Five Terminal Value Estimates

Liquidation Value   Highly relevant when liquidation at the end of the forecast period is under consideration, liquidation value usually grossly understates a healthy business's terminal value.

Book Value   Popular perhaps among accountants, book value usually yields a quite conservative terminal value estimate.

Warranted Price-to-Earnings Multiple   To implement this approach, multiply the target firm's estimated earnings to common stock at the end of the forecast horizon by a "warranted" price-to-earnings ratio; then add projected interest-bearing liabilities to estimate the firm's terminal value. As a warranted price-to-earnings ratio, consider the multiples of publicly traded firms that you believe represent what the target will become by the end of the forecast period.[3] If, for example, the target company is a startup but you believe it will be representative of other, mature companies in its industry by the end of the forecast period, the industry's current price-to-earnings multiple may be a suitable ratio. Another strategy is to bracket the value by trying multiples of, say, 10 and 20 times. The approach generalizes easily to other "warranted" ratios, such as market value to book value, price to cash flow, or price to sales.

No-Growth Perpetuity   We saw in Chapter 7 that the present value of a no-growth perpetuity is the annual cash flow divided by the discount rate. This suggests the following terminal value estimate:

$$\text{Terminal value of no-growth firm} = \frac{\text{FCF}_{T+1}}{K_W}$$

where FCF_{T+1} is free cash flow in the first year beyond the forecast horizon and K_W is the target's weighted-average cost of capital. As further refinement, we might note that when a company is not growing, its capital expenditures should about equal its annual depreciation charges and its net working capital should neither increase nor decrease over time, both of which imply that free cash flow should simplify to EBIT(1 − Tax rate).

[3] For industry price-to-earnings ratios, see **pages.stern.nyu.edu/~adamodar/**. Select "Updated Data" and under "Data Sets" go to "multiples."

Because most businesses expand over time, if due only to inflation, many analysts believe this equation understates the terminal value of a typical business. I am more skeptical. For, as noted repeatedly in earlier chapters, growth creates value only when it generates returns above capital costs; and in competitive product markets over the long run, such performance is more the exception than the rule. Hence, even if many companies are capable of expanding, they may be worth no more than their no-growth brethren. The implication is that the no-growth equation is applicable to more firms than might first be supposed. I am also mindful of economist Kenneth Boulding's observation that, "Anyone who believes that exponential growth can go on forever in a finite world is either a madman or an economist."

Perpetual Growth In Chapter 8, we saw that the present value of a perpetually growing stream of cash equals next year's cash flow divided by the difference between the discount rate and the growth rate. Thus, another terminal value estimate is

$$\text{Terminal value of perpetually growing firm} = \frac{\text{FCF}_{T+1}}{K_W - g}$$

where g is the perpetual-growth rate of free cash flow.

A few words of caution are in order about this popular expression. It is a simple arithmetic fact that any business growing faster than the economy *forever* must eventually become the economy. (When I made this point one time at a Microsoft seminar, the immediate response was "Yeah! Yeah! We can do it!") The intended conclusion for mere mortal firms is that the absolute upper limit on g must be the long-run growth rate of the economy, or about 2 to 3 percent a year, plus expected inflation. Moreover, because even inflationary growth invariably requires higher capital expenditures and increases in working capital, free cash flow falls as g rises. This implies that unless this inverse relation is kept in mind, the preceding expression may well overstate a company's terminal value—even when the perpetual growth rate is kept to a low figure.[4]

---

[4] Here is a modestly more complex version of the perpetual-growth expression, to which I am partial:

$$\text{Terminal value} = \frac{\text{EBIT}_{T+1}(1 - \text{Tax rate})(1 - g/r)}{K_W - g}$$

where r is the rate of return on new investment. One virtue of this expression is that growth does not add value unless returns exceed capital cost. To confirm this, set $r = K_W$ and note that the expression collapses to the no-growth equation. A second virtue is that growth is not free, for as growth rises, so must capital expenditures and net working capital. In the equation, higher g reduces the numerator, which is equivalent to reducing free cash flow. See page 39 in the Koller, Goedhart, and Wessels book referenced at the end of this chapter for a demonstration that this expression is mathematically equivalent to the earlier perpetual-growth equation.

The Forecast Horizon

Terminal values of growing businesses can easily exceed 60 percent of firm value, so it goes without saying that proper selection of the forecast horizon and terminal value are critical to the successful application of discounted cash flow approaches to business valuation. Because most tractable terminal value estimates implicitly assume the firm is a mature, slow-growth, or no-growth perpetuity from that date forward, it is important to extend the forecast horizon far enough into the future that this assumption plausibly applies. When valuing a rapidly growing business, this perspective suggests estimating how long the company can be expected to sustain its supernormal growth before reaching maturity and setting the forecast horizon at or beyond this date.

A Numerical Example

Table 9.1 offers a quick look at a discounted cash flow valuation of our friend from earlier chapters, Sensient Technologies Corporation. It goes

TABLE 9.1 Discounted Cash Flow Valuation of Sensient Technologies Corporation on December 31, 2010 ($ millions except per share)

	Year					
	2011	**2012**	**2013**	**2014**	**2015**	**2016**
Sales	$1,421	$1,520	$1,627	$1,741	$1,863	
EBIT	185	198	211	226	242	
Tax at 31%	57	61	66	70	75	
Earnings after tax	127	136	146	156	167	
+ Depreciation	48	52	55	59	63	
− Capital expenditures	57	61	65	70	75	
− Increase in working capital	20	21	23	24	26	
Free cash flow	$ 99	$ 106	$ 113	$ 121	$ 130	$135
$PV_{@8.9\%}$ of FCFs11−15	$ 439					

Terminal value estimates:	Terminal value in 2015
Perpetual growth at 4% [$FCF_{16}/(K_W − g)$]	$2,755
Warranted MV firm/EBIT(1 − Tax rate) in 2015 = 17.0 times	2,839
Projected book value of debt and equity in 2015	1,871
Best guess terminal value	**2,800**

PV of terminal value	**$ 1,828**
Estimated value of firm	**$ 2,267**
Value of debt	350
Value of equity	**$ 1,917**
Shares outstanding	49.6 million
Estimated value per share	**$38.66**

without saying that if I were being paid by the hour to value Sensient and you were being similarly compensated to read about it, we would both proceed much more thoroughly and deliberately. In particular, we would want to know a great deal more about the company's products, markets, and competitors, for a discounted cash flow valuation is only as good as the projections on which it is based. Nonetheless, the table should give you a basic understanding of how to execute a discounted cash flow valuation.

The valuation date is December 31, 2010. The free cash flows appearing in the table are percent-of-sales projections assuming 7 percent annual sales growth for the next five years. The percentages used in the forecast are based on careful review of the common-size historical financial statements appearing in Chapter 2, Table 2.3, while the growth rate reflects security analysts' expectations.[5] The present value of these free cash flows discounted at Sensient's 8.9 percent weighted-average cost of capital, estimated in the last chapter, amounts to $439 million.

The valuation considers three terminal value estimates. The first relies on the perpetual-growth equation and assumes that beginning in 2016 Sensient's free cash flows will commence growing at 4 percent a year into the indefinite future. Free cash flow in 2016 will, thus, be $135 million [$135 = $130 × (1 + .04)]. Plugging these values into the perpetual growth equation, one estimate of Sensient's terminal value at the end of 2015 is

$$\text{Terminal value} = \frac{FCF \text{ in } 2016}{K_W - g} = \frac{\$135 \text{ million}}{0.089 - 0.04} = \$2{,}755 \text{ million}$$

The second terminal value estimate assumes that at the end of the forecast horizon, Sensient Technologies will command a price-to-earnings multiple of 17.0 times EBIT after tax, a figure reflecting current valuations of comparable firms. I will say more about this multiple in a few pages. Applying this warranted price-to-earnings ratio to Sensient's EBIT after tax in 2015 yields a second terminal value estimate:

$$\text{Terminal value} = 17.0 \times \$167 \text{ million} = \$2{,}839 \text{ million}$$

(I will let you decide whether these terminal value estimates are so close because I am really good at this or really lucky. I know where my vote lies.)

Finally, I estimate that Sensient's projected book value of interest-bearing debt and equity in 2015 will be $1,871. This constitutes a third estimate of the company's terminal value, although certainly a low one.

---

[5] See **www.reuters.com/finance/stocks** and **Yahoo.finance.com.**

how much investors are paying per dollar of current income, sales, or invested capital for each firm. Thus, the first indicator says that $1.00 of Albemarle Corporation's (ALB) current income costs $15.80, while Corn Products International's (CPO) goes for $20.70. Similarly, the third indicator says that $1.00 of IFF's sales cost $1.70, and the last indicator says $1.00 of MKC's assets, measured at book, cost $2.00. The first, third, and fifth indicators focus on equity value, while the other three concentrate on enterprise value.

Reflecting on how Sensient stacks up against its peers in terms of growth and risk, the valuation challenge is to decide what indicators of value are appropriate for Sensient. The third group of numbers on the lower left contains my necessarily subjective estimates. In coming to these estimates, I considered several factors. First, I believe the first two indicators of value are generally more reliable than the others because they tie market value to income as opposed to sales or assets. With rare exceptions, investors are interested in a company's income potential when they buy its shares, not its sales or the assets it owns. Asset-based indicators of value are more relevant when liquidation is contemplated. Sales-based ratios tend to be of interest when current earnings are unrepresentative of long-run potential or when investors lose faith in the accuracy of reported earnings. This is not to say that sales are immune to manipulation but only that they are somewhat less manipulable than earnings.

Second, when choosing between indicators focusing on equity value or enterprise value, I prefer the enterprise value ratios because they are less affected by the way a business is financed. The problem with the equity approach is that leverage affects a company's price-to-earnings ratio in complex ways, so that, for example, inferring a highly levered firm's price-to-earnings ratio from those of more modestly levered peers can lead to errors.

Third, it makes sense to assign more importance to those indicators of value that are more stable across peer companies. If the calculated value of one indicator was 10.0 for every comparable company, I would deem it a more reliable indicator of value than if it varied from 1.0 to 30.0 from firm to firm. Here, the first two ratios, those based on earnings, are noticeably more stable than the others.

Fourth, Sensient's smaller size, marginally lower expected growth rate, and slightly more precarious capital structure all suggest the company should be in the lower half of the indicated valuation ranges. On the other hand, the earlier-noted remarkable stability of the firm's cash flows, right through the recent sharp recession, speaks in its favor. I have selected multiples for the first two ratios that are a few percent below the figures for IFF and MKC, and also modestly below the peer group medians. Because Sensient has lower operating margins than its peers, I expect investors to pay less per dollar of sales for Sensient than the other firms, resulting in below-average values for the next two sales-based multiples. Finally, I have chosen similarly conservative figures for the remaining two book-value multiples.

The last set of numbers on the lower right of Table 9.2 presents the price of Sensient's stock implied by each chosen indicator of value. To the right of each stock price is an equation demonstrating how I translated the chosen indicator of value into an implied stock price. To illustrate the second equation, I estimated that Sensient's total enterprise value should be 17.0 times its EBIT after tax. Sensient's EBIT after tax in 2010 was $120.4 million, so its implied enterprise value is $2,046.4 million. Subtracting interest-bearing debt of $349.9 million and dividing by 49.6 million shares yields an estimated stock price of $34.20. The other implied share prices are calculated similarly. Reflecting on the observations made earlier, my best guess of a fair price for Sensient Technologies's shares on the valuation date is $36.00 a share, or about 2 percent below the actual price of $36.73. (I don't usually come this close . . . I wonder if it is too late to change careers.)

Lack of Marketability

An important difference between owning stock in a publicly traded company and owning stock in a private one is that the publicly traded shares are more liquid; they can be sold quickly for cash without significant loss of value. Because liquidity is a valued attribute of any asset, it is necessary to reduce the FMV of a private company estimated by reference to publicly traded comparable firms. Without boring you with details, a representative lack of marketability discount is on the order of 25 percent.[6] Of course, if the purpose of the valuation is to price an initial public offering of common stock, the shares will soon be liquid, and no discount is required.

A second possible adjustment when using the comparable-trades approach to valuation is a premium for control. Quoted prices for public companies are invariably for a minority interest in the firm, while many valuations involve transactions in which operating control passes from seller to buyer. Because control is valuable, it is necessary in these instances to add a premium to the estimated value of the target firm to reflect the value of control. Estimating the size of this control premium is our next task. But first, I want to call your attention to a close cousin of comparable trades valuation known as comparable *transactions* valuation. The two techniques are identical except that the latter substitutes prices struck in recent

---

[6] Shannon P. Pratt, Robert F. Reilly, and Robert P. Schweihs. *Valuing a Business: The Analysis and Appraisal of Closely Held Companies*, 4th ed. (New York: Irwin/McGraw-Hill, 2000).

corporate acquisitions for publicly quoted stock prices. Transactions prices are obviously much less common than quoted stock prices and are often proprietary. However, in most instances, they are probably a better reflection of the value inherent in an acquisition candidate, and they already contain a premium for control.

The Market for Control

We have noted on several occasions that buying a minority interest in a company differs fundamentally from buying control. With a minority interest, the investor is a passive observer; with control, she has complete freedom to change the way the company does business and perhaps increase its value significantly. Indeed, the two situations are so disparate that it is appropriate to speak of stock as selling in two separate markets: the market in which you and I trade minority claims on future cash flows and the market in which Kraft Foods and other acquirers trade the right to control the firm. The latter, the *market for control*, involves a two-in-one sale. In addition to claims on future cash flows, the buyer in this market also gains the privilege of structuring the company as he or she wishes. Because shares trading in the two markets are really different assets, they naturally sell at different prices.

The Premium for Control

Figure 9.2 illustrates this two-tier market. From the perspective of minority investors, the fair market value of a company's equity, represented in the figure by m, is the present value of cash flows to equity given current management and strategy. To a corporation or an individual seeking control, however, the FMV is c, which may be well above m. The difference, $(c - m)$, is the value of control. It is the maximum premium over the minority fair market value an acquirer should pay to gain control. It is also the expected increase in shareholder value created by acquisition. When an acquirer pays FMVc for a target, all of the increased value will be realized by the seller's shareholders, while at any lower price, part of the increased value will accrue to the acquirer's shareholders as well. FMVc is therefore the maximum acquisition price a buyer can justify paying. Said differently, it is the price at which the net present value of the acquisition to the buyer is zero.

What Price Control?

There are two ways to determine how large a control premium an acquirer can afford to pay. The brute force approach values the business first assuming the merger takes place and then assuming it does not. The difference

FIGURE 9.2   **FMV of a Corporation to Investors Seeking Control May Exceed FMV to Minority Investors**

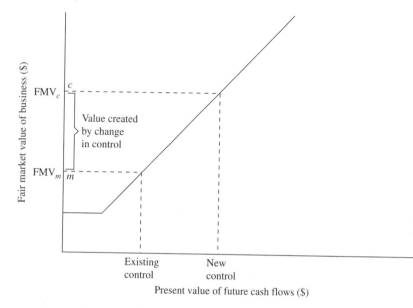

between these values is the maximum premium an acquirer can justify paying. The second, often more practical approach focuses on the anticipated gains from the merger. In equation form,

$$FMV_c = FMV_m + Enhancements$$

where c and m again denote controlling and minority interest, respectively. This expression says the value of controlling interest in a business equals the business's FMV under the present stewardship, or what is often called the business's *stand-alone value*, plus whatever enhancements to value the new buyer envisions. If the buyer intends to make no changes in the business now or in the future, the enhancements are zero, and no premium over stand-alone value can be justified. On the other hand, if the buyer believes the merging of two businesses will create vast new profit opportunities, enhancements can be quite large.

Putting a price tag on the value of enhancements resulting from an acquisition is a straightforward undertaking conceptually: Make a detailed list of all the ways the acquisition will increase free cash flows, estimate the magnitude and timing of the cash flows involved, calculate their present values, and sum:

Enhancements = PV {All value-increasing changes due to acquisition}

Kissing Toads

The Oracle of Omaha, Warren Buffett, attributes corporate executives' willingness to pay large control premiums to three very human factors: an abundance of animal spirits, an unwarranted emphasis on company size as opposed to profitability, and overexposure during youth to "the story in which the imprisoned handsome prince is released from a toad's body by a kiss from a beautiful princess. [From this tale, executives] are certain their managerial kiss will do wonders for the profitability of Company T(arget)." Why else, Buffett asks, would an acquiring company pay a premium to control another business when it could avoid the premium altogether by simply purchasing a minority interest?

"In other words, investors can always buy toads at the going price for toads. If investors instead bankroll princesses who wish to pay double for the right to kiss the toad, those kisses had better pack some real dynamite. We've observed many kisses but very few miracles. Nonetheless, many managerial princesses remain serenely confident about the future potency of their kisses—even after their corporate backyards are knee-deep in unresponsive toads."

Source: Warren Buffett, Berkshire Hathaway, Inc. 1981 annual report.

Global Investing Partners believes 2M's management may be interested in a leveraged buyout (LBO) and has approached it with a proposal to form a new corporation, invariably called NEWCO, to purchase all of 2M's equity in the open market. Because 2M's cash flows are very stable, Global figures it can finance most of the purchase price by borrowing $190 million on a 10-year loan at 10 percent interest. The loan will be interest-only for the first five years. In the longer run, Global believes 2M can easily support annual interest expenses of $10 million. The value of the anticipated interest tax shields to NEWCO, discounted at a 12 percent rate, is as follows:

Year	Interest Expense	Tax Shield at 40% Tax Rate
1	$19.00	$7.60
2	19.00	7.60
3	19.00	7.60
4	19.00	7.60
5	19.00	7.60
6	19.00	7.60
7	15.89	6.36
8	12.46	4.98
9	10.00	4.00
10	10.00	4.00

Present value of tax shields years 1–10 at 12%	= $38.87
Present value of tax shields years 10 and beyond at 12%	= 10.73
Total	$49.60 million

Ignoring the increased costs of financial distress that customarily accompany higher financial leverage, these figures suggest that NEWCO can bid up to $249.60 million to purchase Mature Manufacturing, a 25 percent premium over the current market price ($249.60 million = $200 million stand-alone value + $49.60 million of enhancements). Moreover, Global's required equity investment at this price would be only $59.60 million ($249.60 million acquisition price − $190 million in new debt), implying a post acquisition debt-to-assets ratio of 76 percent. This, believe it or not, is representative financing by LBO standards. LBOs are indeed aptly named.

A final judgment on the value of interest tax shields in leveraged restructurings, of course, rests on a qualitative weighting of the indicated tax savings against the costs of financial distress as discussed in Chapter 6. A reduced tax bill isn't especially attractive when the added debt frightens customers, drives away creditors, and emboldens competitors.

Note that if increased interest tax shields are the objective, an LBO is not the only way to obtain them. 2M can generate much the same effect by simply issuing debt and distributing the proceeds to owners as a large dividend or by a share repurchase. This was Colt Industries' strategy (described in Chapter 6) when it floated a huge debt issue to finance distribution of a special dividend and ended up with $1.6 billion in long-term debt and a negative net worth of $1 billion. But what's to fear from a mountain of debt as long as you have the cash flow to service it? And if you don't, your creditors have so much at stake in your company that they are more likely to behave like partners than police.

Nor must a leveraged buyout necessarily involve a takeover. Many LBOs are initiated by incumbent management who team up with outside investors to purchase all of the company's stock and take it private. Management risks its own money in return for a sizable equity position in the restructured company.

Incentive Effects

Tax shield enhancements are clearly just a game: To the extent that shareholders win, "we, the people" (in the form of the U.S. Treasury) lose. If this were the only financial gain to takeovers and restructurings, the phenomena would not command serious public attention. Best that we eliminate the tax benefits and get back to producing goods and services instead of stocks and bonds.

The other two potential enhancements are not so easily dismissed. Both involve free cash flow, and both are premised on the belief that restructuring powerfully affects the performance incentives confronting senior management. To examine the incentive effects of restructuring in more detail, let's return to Mature Manufacturing, Inc.

Avoiding Dilution in Earnings per Share

An all-too-popular alternative approach to determining how much one company can afford to bid for another looks at the impact of the acquisition on the acquirer's earnings per share (EPS). Popularity is about all this approach has to recommend it, for it grossly oversimplifies the financial effects of an acquisition, and it rests on an inappropriate decision criterion.

Suppose the following data apply to an acquiring firm, A, and its target, T, in an exchange-of-shares merger; that is, A will give T's shareholders newly printed shares of A in exchange for their shares of T.

	Company A	Company T	Merged Company
Earnings ($ millions)	$ 100	$ 20	$130
Number of shares (millions)	20	40	26
Earnings per share	$ 5	$0.50	$ 5 (minimum)
Stock price	$ 70	$ 5	
Market value of equity (millions)	$1,400	$ 200	

The suggested decision criterion is that A should avoid dilution in EPS. If earnings of the merged firm are forecasted to be $130 million, the figures above indicate that A can issue as many as 6 million shares without suffering dilution [6 million shares = ($130 million/$5) − 20 million]. At $70 a share, this implies a maximum price of $420 million for T ($70 × 6 million), or a 110 percent premium [(420 − 200)/200]. It also suggests a maximum exchange ratio of 0.15 shares of A for each share of T (6 million/40 million).

The obvious shortcomings of this simplistic approach are, first, that earnings are not the cash flows that determine value and, second, that it is grossly inappropriate to base an acquisition decision on only one year's results. Doing so is comparable to making investments because they promise to increase next year's profits. If T's growth prospects are sufficiently bright, it may be perfectly reasonable to sacrifice near-term EPS in anticipation of long-run gains.

Academics have been stamping on this weed for decades, but it never seems to die. Witness the following from *The Wall Street Journal* announcing the Daimler-Chrysler merger in 1998. "[T]he cross-border union is actually typical of the stock-for-stock deals that have made the 1990s merger boom so fertile: a combination using favorable accounting in which the buyer has a high price-to-earnings ratio that can make a deal 'accretive' because the seller has a low P/E. Chrysler's price-to-earnings ratio has long been around eight times earnings, analysts say, and has only recently crept up to nine times. Daimler's P/E, meanwhile, is more like 20 times profits, giving the buyer the financial firepower to pay 11 to 12 times earnings and still have the transaction 'accretive,' or beneficial to the earnings of the new DaimlerChrysler."* Business valuation is tough in practice, but there is no reason to use flawed techniques just because they are tractable.

*Steven Lipin and Brandon Mitchener, "Daimler-Chrysler Merger to Produce $3 Billion in Savings, Revenue Gains Within 3 to 5 Years," *The Wall Street Journal,* May 8, 1998.

Before restructuring, the life of a senior manager at Mature Manufacturing, Inc., may well have been an enviable one. With very stable cash flows, a mature business, and no debt, managers had no pressing reason to improve performance. They could pay themselves and their employees generously, make sizable corporate contributions to charity, and, if the president was so inclined, sponsor an Indy race car or an unlimited hydroplane. Alternatively, if they wanted 2M to grow, the company could acquire other firms. This might involve some uneconomical investments, but hey—as long as cash flows are strong, almost anything is possible.

Samuel Johnson once observed, "The certainty of hanging in a fortnight focuses the mind wonderfully." Restructuring can have a similar effect, for it fundamentally changes the world of 2M senior executives. Because they probably have invested much of their own resources in the equity of the newly restructured company, their own material well-being is closely tied to that of the business. Moreover, the huge debt service burden restructuring frequently creates forces management to generate healthy cash flows or face bankruptcy—no more "corpocracy" at 2M. The carrot of ownership and the stick of possible financial ruin create significant incentives for management to maximize free cash flow and spend it for the benefit of owners.

Controlling Free Cash Flow

In addition to interest tax shields and incentive effects of high leverage, a third possible enhancement in restructurings rests on the perception that public companies are not always run solely for the benefit of owners. In this view, value can be created by gaining control of such firms and refocusing the business on the single goal of creating shareholder value. Adherents of this view see shareholder-manager relations as an ongoing tug-of-war for control of the firm's free cash flow. When shareholders have the upper hand, companies are run to maximize shareholder value; but when management is in the driver's seat, increasing value is only one of a number of competing corporate goals. After more than 50 years on the losing end of this tug-of-war, the emergence of the hostile raider in the mid-1980s enabled shareholders to gain the ascendancy and force companies to restructure. According to this view, the hostile acquisitions and restructurings during the latter half of the 1980s were a boon not only to shareholders but to the entire economy; for to the extent that shareholders can force management to increase firm value, the economy's resources are allocated more efficiently.

Consistent with this adversarial view of corporate governance, many takeovers and restructurings occur in mature or declining industries. Because investment opportunities in these industries are low, affected businesses often have large free cash flows. At the same time, industry decline creates real concern in the minds of executives about the continued survival of their organization. And although the proper strategy from a purely financial perspective may be to shrink or terminate the business, management often takes another tack. Out of a deep commitment to the business and concern for employees, the community, and their own welfare, some managers continue to fight the good fight by reinvesting in the business despite its poor returns, or by entering new businesses despite any convincing reasons to expect success. The purpose of restructuring in these instances is brutally basic: Wrest control of free cash flow away from management and put it in the hands of owners.

How, you might ask, does incumbent management ever gain control of a business in the first place? In theory, managers should be incapable of acting in opposition to owners for at least two reasons. First, if a company operates in highly competitive markets, management has very little discretion; it must maximize value or the firm will be driven from the industry. Second, all corporations have boards of directors with the power to hire and fire management and the responsibility to represent owners' interests.

Theory, however, often differs from reality. Many corporations operate in less than perfectly competitive markets, and corporate boards have not always been an effective, independent shareholder voice. One reason is that most senior executives, usually supported by the courts, believe that a board's primary responsibility is to help incumbent management run the business, not to represent shareholder interests. As a result, boards are often more closely affiliated with management than with owners. Many directors are company insiders; other directors have important ties to the enterprise other than ownership and are more beholden to the chief executive than to shareholders for their seat on the board. Consequently, while such boards may help keep the shelves stocked, they are not about to recommend selling the store.

A second reason directors do not always represent shareholder interests traces to the process by which they are chosen. In the great majority of instances, the proxy materials sent annually to shareholders propose a single, unopposed slate of board candidates nominated by management. And even then, shareholders may not vote against a candidate, but may only withhold approval. The only way disaffected shareholders can contest a board seat is to propose their own candidate and use their own money to campaign against management's choice in a proxy contest. Meanwhile, management is free to use corporate funds to defeat its rivals. Little wonder then that management effectively controls most company boards.

The SEC recently sought to reduce management control of board elections by forcing companies to accept limited shareholder nominations under certain specified conditions. However, a federal appeals court struck down the controversial regulation before it could be implemented, and it is unclear at this date how the SEC will respond.

The new proxy regulations are the product of a long simmering shareholder rights movement initiated by activist investors. Having tasted the fruits of control in the form of unusually high returns during the hostile takeover era, these investors have found new ways to challenge incumbent managers for free cash flow. Unlike hostile acquirers of the 1980s, the goal of activist investors is not to gain control of a target company, but to browbeat management into actions investors believe will increase shareholder value. These actions usually involve repurchasing shares with excess cash, selling underperforming assets, or putting the company itself up for sale. Many believe activist investing got its start when shareholders grew tired of watching buyout firms make large fortunes executing strategies that incumbent managers could just as easily implement themselves. The goal of activist investors is to provide the requisite motivation. Or in the words of meta-activist Carl Icahn "We do the job the LBO guys do, but for all the shareholders."

Does activist investing work? Accumulating evidence indicates it does. Writing in 2009, April Klein and Emanuel Zur look at the campaigns of 151 hedge fund activists and 154 other types of activists. Hedge funds are lightly regulated, private equity partnerships that have grown rapidly in the past several decades, to the point where there are now thought to be upward of 8,000 in existence. The authors found that the activist's targets experienced abnormal returns of 5.1 to 10.2 percent, depending on the sample, in the period immediately surrounding public announcement of the activists' intentions and generated additional abnormal returns of 11.4 to 17.8 percent over the following year. They also found that activists were successful 60 to 65 percent of the time in getting incumbent management to acquiesce to their demands. Other studies have found that activist investors also earn higher risk-adjusted returns than their more passive brethren.[7]

As debate topics go, the question of whether management should have broader social responsibilities than simply creating shareholder value is among the more intriguing. Like many important societal questions, however, the issue tends to be resolved more on the basis of power than of logic. Throughout most of the twentieth century, incumbent management retained the power to interpret its responsibilities broadly and to treat shareholders as only one of several constituencies possessing a claim on the corporation. The balance of power shifted abruptly in shareholders' favor during the era of the

[7] April Klein and Emanuel Zur, "Entrepreneurial Shareholder Activism: Hedge Funds and Other Private Investors," *Journal of Finance*, February 2009, pp. 187–229. See also, Nicole M. Boyson and Robert M. Mooradian, "Hedge Funds as Shareholder Activists from 1994–2005," Working paper, July 2007. Available at **ssrn.com/abstract=992739**.

too little for Cadbury, I can assure you that having paid an estimated $440 million in combined fees, Kraft and Cadbury had numerous valuation studies of the type described here supporting the acquisition pricing. Whether the assumptions and forecasts underlying those studies were accurate remains to be seen.

To most observers, Kraft's justification for buying Cadbury read like the syllabus of a business strategy course, replete with appropriate buzzwords. The company spoke of "a compelling financial rationale" based on "increased scope and scale, complementary brands, a strengthened geographic footprint, and complementary routes to market producing meaningful cost savings and synergies." Setting aside the rhetoric, Cadbury's most compelling attraction appeared to be its distribution network in emerging markets, especially India and Mexico. Kraft seemed convinced that emerging market consumers were anxious to eat a lot more Kraft cheeses and Oreo cookies if just given a proper chance. In more concrete terms, Kraft's chief executive claimed to have identified annual cost savings of $675 million achievable within three years. (At a 35 percent tax rate, a 10 percent discount rate, and three percent perpetual growth, the present value of these savings totals roughly $6 billion or about 80 percent of the acquisition premium paid [$6 billion = $(1 - .35) \times$ $675 million/ $(.10 - .03)$]).

Despite statements to the contrary, Cadbury appeared to have been grooming itself for a takeover since early 2007 when activist investor Nelson Peltz first took an interest in the company. Mr. Peltz's investment vehicle, Trian Fund Management, frequently buys into poorly performing companies, often in the food business, and exerts increasing public pressure on management to take actions Trian perceives will improve performance. When Trian first bought into Cadbury, the company was known as Cadbury Schweppes and consisted of an attractive confectionary business married to a dead-end soft drinks operation. Some even spoke of the drinks business as Cadbury's personalized "poison pill," reasoning that no suitor would be interested in the company as long as it held on to soft drinks. Almost immediately after Trian purchased shares in Cadbury, the company announced its intention to dispose of soft drinks, and in mid-May 2008, it did so by spinning the operation off into a new company, Snapple Group, Inc. This set Cadbury up as an attractive, pure-play acquisition target for the likes of Hershey, Nestle, or Kraft.

Kraft ran into two unanticipated problems in its pursuit of Cadbury. Just as the company was finalizing its offer preparatory to a shareholder vote, Warren Buffett of Berkshire Hathaway, Kraft's largest shareholder, strongly condemned the deal and announced he would vote against it. He noted that Kraft's shares were currently undervalued by his reckoning and, thus, made an expensive currency to pay in an acquisition. Although critical of Kraft, Mr. Buffett's comments drove Kraft's stock up and Cadbury's down as investors perceived that Kraft would now have to exercise more restraint in bidding up the acquisition price—perhaps Mr. Buffett's intent all along. Kraft responded by quickly selling its DiGiorno Pizza operations to Nestle and using the proceeds to increase the cash portion of its offer. This assuaged Mr. Buffett's concern directly by reducing the number of shares Kraft needed to issue, and, quite fortuitously, I am sure, eliminated the need for a shareholder vote at all by cutting the issue size below 20 percent of shares outstanding. Mr. Buffett was now free to have his own opinion about the deal but was powerless to prevent it.

Kraft's second problem was more embarrassing. As the much beloved Cadburys of their youth—the makers of Crème Eggs no less—many British were upset to think of yet another British institution being gobbled up by a crass American giant, this time by the maker of what one critic called "plastic cheese." To polish its image a bit during negotiations, Kraft magnanimously announced that if successful, it was prepared to save 400 local jobs by keeping open an elderly Cadbury facility, known as the Somerdale plant, located in Southwest England. Cadbury management had recently announced their intention to close the plant and move all the work to Poland. Unfortunately, applause soon turned to jeers when just seven days after closing the deal Kraft announced they had changed their minds and would be closing the plant and moving the work to Poland after all. It seems that Kraft had been lax in its due diligence and had not realized Cadbury was so close to completing the move. On closer inspection, keeping the Somerdale plant open now looked too expensive.

Sometimes timing is more important than skill. In this instance, Kraft committed its blunder right in the middle of heated British national elections. Politicians of all stripes instantly seized on the event to excoriate unscrupulous foreign raiders, short-term speculators, greedy business executives, outrageous salaries, lax takeover regulations, and all the other usual suspects. *The Economist* aptly caught the fervid atmosphere in its headline "Small Island for Sale." In retrospect, Kraft's faux pas did not affect the terms of the acquisition, but it did decimate the company's reputation in Britain and set back the cause of an open market for corporate control in Britain. At this writing, work by the government panel reviewing British takeover regulations is still underway, but with the election safely in the past, calmer heads appear to be prevailing. Only Kraft can say how badly the Somerdale fiasco has hurt efforts to integrate the two companies.

The Venture Capital Method of Valuation

Venture capitalists are the carrier pilots of corporate finance. They make high-risk, high-return investments in new or early stage companies thought capable of growing rapidly into sizeable enterprises. Their investment horizon is typically five or six years, at which time they expect to cash out as the target company goes public or sells out to a competitor. To manage risk, venture capitalists typically make staged investments in which the company must meet a stated business milestone before qualifying for the next financing round. Venture capitalists often specialize in a particular financing round, such as startup, early stage, or mezzanine. The mezzanine round is the company's last private financing round prior to going public, or merging. In most instances, the risk to new investors and, hence, the return demanded, diminishes from one financing round to the next.

The standard discounted cash flow valuation technique discussed in the chapter is ill-suited to venture investing for several reasons. First, the cash infusions from venture investors are intended to cover near-term, negative free cash flows, so projecting and discounting annual free cash flows is not relevant. Second and more fundamentally, the standard approach to business valuation does not gracefully accommodate multiple financing rounds at different required rates of return.

Rather than use the standard approach, venture capitalists employ a specialized discounted cash flow technique that is better suited to their needs. Our purpose here is to illustrate the venture capital method of valuation, to indicate the level of target returns used in the industry, and to offer several explanations of why these targets appear so outlandishly high. We begin with a simple example of a company in need of only one financing round. We then build on this example to consider a more realistic situation involving multiple financing rounds.

The Venture Capital Method—One Financing Round

Jerry Cross and Greg Robinson, two veteran computer programmers, have what they believe is a pathbreaking idea for a new product. Soon after incorporating as ZMW Enterprises and arbitrarily awarding themselves 2,000,000 shares of common stock, Cross and Robinson prepared a detailed business plan and began talking to venture capitalists about funding their company. The business plan envisions an immediate $6 million venture capital investment, profits of $5 million in year 5, and rapid growth thereafter. The plan indicates that $6 million will be sufficient to commence operations and to cover all anticipated cash needs until the company begins generating positive cash flows in year 5.

After hearing the entrepreneurs' pitch, a senior partner at Touchstone Ventures, a local venture capital company, expressed interest in financing ZMW but demanded 3.393 million shares in return for his firm's $6 million investment. He also mentioned in passing that his offer implied a pre-money valuation for ZMW of $3.537 million and a post-money value of $9.537 million. Determined not to be intimidated, Greg Robinson challenged the venture capitalist to justify his numbers, hoping in the process to learn what he meant by pre- and post-money.

Panel A of Table 9A.1 presents a valuation of ZMW using the venture capital method. Three steps are involved.

1. Estimate ZMW's value at some future date, often based on a conventional comparable trades or comparable transactions analysis.

TABLE 9.A1   The Venture Capital Method of Valuation

Panel A: One Financing Round						
Facts and Assumptions (000 omitted)						
Net income year 5	$ 5,000					
Price-to-earnings ratio in year 5	20					
Investment required at time 0	$ 6,000					
Touchstone Ventures'						
target rate of return	60%					
Time 0 shares outstanding	2,000					
Cash Flow and Valuation						
Year	**0**	**1**	**2**	**3**	**4**	**5**
Investment	$ 6,000					
ZMW value in year 5						$100,000
PV at time 0 of year 5 value						
discounted at 60%	$ 9,537					
Time 5 Touchstone ownership						
to earn target return	**62.9%**					
Shares purchased						
by Touchstone[1]	3,393					
Price per share	$ 1.77					
Pre-money value of ZMW	$ 3,537					
Post-money value of ZMW	$ 9,537					

(continued)

TABLE 9.A1   The Venture Capital Method of Valuation (*continued*)

Panel B: Two Financing Rounds						

Facts and Assumptions (000 omitted)

Net income year 5	$ 5,000
Price-to-earnings ratio in year 5	20
Investment required at time 0	$ 6,000
Investment required at time 2	$ 4,000
Touchstone Ventures' target rate of return	60%
Second-round investor's target rate of return	40%
Time 0 shares outstanding	2,000

Cash Flow and Valuation

Year	0	1	2	3	4	5
Investment	$ 6,000		$ 4,000			
Terminal value yr. 5						$100,000

Second-Round Investor

PV at time 2 of year 5 value discounted at 40%			$36,443			
Time 5 ownership to earn target return			11.0%			

Touchstone Ventures

PV at time 0 of year 5 value discounted at 60%	$ 9,537
Time 5 Touchstone ownership to earn target return	62.9%
Retention ratio[2]	89.0%
Time 0 Touchstone ownership to earn target return	70.7%
Shares purchased by Touchstone[1]	4,819
Price per share	$ 1.24
Pre-money value of ZMW	$ 2,490
Post-money value of ZMW	$ 8,490

Second-Round Investor

Shares purchased by second round investor[1]			841			
Price per share			$ 4.76			
Pre-money value of ZMW			$32,443			
Post-money value of ZMW			$36,443			

[1] If x equals the number of shares purchased by new investors, y is the number of shares currently outstanding, and p is the percentage of the firm purchased by new investors, then $x/(y + x) = p$, and $x = py/(1 - p)$.

[2] Retention ratio = (1– second round investor's percentage ownership) = $(1 - 22.9\%)$. In general, the retention ratio = $(1 - d_1)(1 - d_2)...(1 - d_n)$, where d_n is the % ownership given to the nth subsequent round of investors.

2. Discount this future value to the present at the venture capitalist's target internal rate of return.

3. Divide the venture capitalist's investment by ZMW's present value to calculate the venture capitalist's required percentage ownership.

As shown in Panel A, Touchstone accepted the entrepreneurs' projection that ZMW would earn $5 million in year 5. They then multiplied this amount by a "warranted" price-to-earnings ratio of 20 to calculate a firm value of $100 million. The price-to-earnings ratio used here typically reflects the multiples implied by other recent venture financings or the multiples presently commanded by public companies in the same or related industries.

Discounting the year 5 value to the present at Touchstone's 60 percent target rate of return yields a present value for ZMW of $9.537 million [$9.537 million = $100 million/$(1 + 0.60)^5$]. This, in turn, implies a percentage ownership for Touchstone of 62.9 percent. The logic here is that if the company is worth $9.537 million after the investment, and if Touchstone contributes $6 million to this total, its fractional ownership should be $6 million/$9.537 million, or 62.9 percent. To confirm this logic, note that if ZMW is worth $100 million in five years, Touchstone's 62.9 percent ownership will be worth $62.9 million, which translates into an internal rate of return of precisely 60 percent.

The rest is just algebra. If Touchstone is to own 62.9 percent of ZMW and the company presently has 2 million shares outstanding, Touchstone needs to receive 3.393 million new shares [62.9% = 3.393/(2 + 3.393)], which, in turn, implies a per share price of $1.77 ($6 million/3.393 million shares). ZMW's estimated value before Touchstone's investment, or its pre-money value, is, thus, $3.537 million ($1.77 per share × 2 million shares), and its value after the investment, or its post-money value, is $9.537 million (1.77 per share × 5.393 million shares).

Cross and Robinson are likely to be of two minds about this valuation: flabbergasted that Touchstone would demand a 60 percent return when all they do is put up money, but pleased to learn that Touchstone apparently puts a $3.537 million price tag on their idea.

The Venture Capital Method—Multiple Financing Rounds

The venture capital method is easy to apply when there is only one financing round prior to the valuation date. Things get more complicated, and more realistic, when there are multiple rounds. To illustrate, let's change the ZMW example by supposing that Cross and Robinson's business plan calls for two financing rounds: the original $6 million at time 0, plus a second investment of $4 million at time 2. Because ZMW will be a functioning company at time 2, it is reasonable to suppose that second-round investors will demand a lower rate of return. Based on Touchstone's experience, let us assume that second-round investors will demand "only" 40 percent. Reworking the earlier figures, as shown in Panel B of Table 9A.1, Touchstone will now demand 4.819 million shares, or 70.7 percent ownership, in return for their $6 million investment.

To arrive at these figures, note that each subsequent financing round will dilute Touchstone's investment. Therefore, owning 62.9 percent of ZMW today, as in our first example, will no longer be adequate. To capture the effect of dilution imposed by subsequent financing rounds, it is necessary to apply the logic described earlier recursively to each financing round, beginning with the most distant. Panel B shows that at a discount rate of 40 percent, the time 2 value of ZMW to a new investor will be $36.443 million, so round 2 investors will demand 11.0 percent of the company for their $4 million investment (11.0% = $4 million/ $36.443 million).

Once we know this number, we are ready to calculate Touchstone's initial ownership. We know that Touchstone wants 62.9 percent of ZMW in year 5 and that round 2 dilution makes it necessary to gross this number up by some amount. To determine how much, we divide 62.9 percent by what is known as a *retention ratio*. Here, the retention ratio turns out to be 0.89, so Touchstone's current ownership must be 70.7 percent (70.7% = 62.9%/0.89). The logic of the retention ratio goes like this. If y represents Touchstone's initial ownership, then $y - 0.11y = 0.629$, so $y = 0.629/(1 - 0.11) = 70.7\%$. The quantity in parentheses is the retention ratio.

Extending this reasoning to an arbitrary number of financing rounds, the retention ratio for the ith financing round is

$$R_i = (1 - d_{i+1})(1 - d_{i+2}) \ldots (1 - d_n),$$

where d_{i+1} is the percentage ownership given to the ith + 1 round investors, and n is the total number of subsequent financing rounds. With only one subsequent financing round, Touchstone's retention ratio is $(1 - 0.11) = 0.89$. The need to work recursively from the most distant financing round to the present should now be clear. Because the retention ratio for each round depends on dilution created by all subsequent rounds, it is impossible to calculate the initial percentage ownership of early-round investors without knowing that of all later rounds.

Once we know the percentage ownership at each financing round, it is easy to calculate stock prices as well as pre- and post-money values. As noted in Panel B, ZMW's pre-money value at time 0 is $2.49 million,

TABLE 9.A2   **Prospective Returns to Investors in ZMW**

	Year					
	0	**1**	**2**	**3**	**4**	**5**
Touchstone Ventures						
Free cash flows	$(6,000)	0	0	0	0	$ 62,915
Internal rate of return	**60%**					
Second round investor						
Free cash flows			$(4,000)	0	0	$ 10,976
Internal rate of return			**40%**			
Entrepreneurs' cash flows						
Value of idea	$(2,490)	0	0	0	0	$ 26,109
IRR	**60%**					
Total						**$100,000**

while the same quantity at time 2 is $32.443 million. The corresponding share prices are $1.24 and $4.76, respectively.

Table 9A.2 confirms the validity of the venture capital method. It shows the resulting cash flows to Touchstone Ventures, the second-round investor, and the founding entrepreneurs—assuming that ZMW can achieve its business plan. Observe that these cash flows yield precisely the target rates of return demanded by the venture capitalists. Note too that although the entrepreneurs lose majority control of their company, the prospect of owning shares worth $26.109 million in five years should provide some consolation.

Why Do Venture Capitalists Demand Such High Returns?

To begin, it is important to understand that the sky-high target returns demanded by venture capitalists do not come close to approximating the realized returns they actually earn. Although estimating realized returns in venture capital is difficult for a number of reasons, the best current estimates suggest that after adjusting for differences in investment risk and liquidity, realized returns in venture capital do not differ systematically from comparable stock market returns.[1] They might be consistently better for some leading venture firms and for the industry as a whole in some years, but the figures do not suggest that venture capitalists are systematically gouging the entrepreneurs with whom they partner.

[1] Steven Kaplan and Josh Lerner, "It Ain't Broke: The Past, Present, and Future of Venture Capital," *Journal of Applied Corporate Finance*, Spring 2010, pp. 36–47.

Why then are target returns so high? There are at least four possible explanations. First, venture investing is a very risky business, and high risk invariably commands high return. When venture investors must screen as many as 100 proposals for each investment made, and when they earn real money on only 1 or 2 investments in 10, target rates must be high to compensate for the many disappointments. Second, high target rates have history on their side. They have been consistent over the years with adequate-deal flow and, as just noted, the realized returns earned using these high targets have been sufficient to attract new investment capital. Third, venture capitalists argue that they provide much more than money when they invest and that they deserve compensation for these ancillary services. Rather than bill directly for their counsel, connections, and occasional outright direction, venture capitalists bundle their fees into the required target return.

Finally, high target returns may be a natural outgrowth of the dynamic between venture capitalist and entrepreneur. Venture capitalists consistently maintain that the business plans crossing their desks are overly optimistic. It is not so much that the numbers in the plan are unobtainable, but rather that the plan ignores the myriad ways in which a startup business can fail. So instead of representing the expected outcome, the plan is essentially a best-case scenario. When presented with such projections, the venture capitalist has two choices: Try to argue the entrepreneur down to more reasonable numbers, or accept the entrepreneur's numbers at face value and discount them at an inflated target rate.

Two forces favor the "inflated target" strategy. For psychological reasons, the venture capitalist would prefer that the entrepreneur strive to meet his optimistic plan rather than settle for a lower, albeit more realistic, objective. Moreover, for practical reasons, the venture capitalist will find it difficult to convince the entrepreneur—who typically knows more about the business than the venture capitalist—that his plan is overly optimistic. Better to concede gracefully on the business plan, and recoup by demanding a high target return. This might suggest a war of escalating projections in which entrepreneurs progressively ratchet up their forecasts to counteract venture capitalists' artificially high rates, while venture investors progressively raise their target rates to offset entrepreneurs' increasingly implausible projections. However, this is unlikely to occur. Venture capitalists are expert at ferreting out overblown forecasts, so unless the entrepreneur truly believes her numbers, she has little chance of convincing venture capitalists of their plausibility.

SUMMARY

1. Valuing a business
   - Is the art of pricing all or part of a business.
   - Is the central discipline underlying all corporate restructurings, including:
     – Leveraged buyouts, acquisitions, large stock repurchases, sale or purchase of a division, recapitalizations, spin-offs, and carveouts.
   - Begins by answering three questions:
     – Value a firm's assets or its equity?
     – Value the business dead or alive?
     – Value a minority interest or control?

2. Discounted cash flow valuation
   - Views a business as if it were a large capital expenditure opportunity.
   - Estimates the present value of a target's free cash flows discounted at its weighted-average cost of capital.
   - Presents two major challenges:
     – Estimating a forecast horizon when the target can be treated as mature.
     – Estimating a terminal value applicable at the forecast horizon, possibly based on liquidation value, book value, a warranted price-to-earnings multiple, a no-growth perpetuity, or a perpetually growing cash flow.

3. Comparable trades valuation
   - Infers value from the prices at which comparable public firms trade.
   - Requires identifying suitable indicators of value such as
     – Price to earnings.
     – Price to sales.
     – Price to book value.
   - May require a discount for lack of marketability, or a premium for control.
   - Is a close cousin to comparable transactions valuation.

4. The premium for control
   - Is the excess above a firm's stand-alone value **paid** by an acquirer.
   - Should not exceed the present value of all enhancements anticipated by the buyer.
   - May include the value of three possible financial enhancements:
     – Increased tax shields.
     – Improved incentives from new ownership.
     – Shareholders wresting control of free cash flow from managers.

Present Value of \$1 in Year *n*, Discounted at Discount Rate *k* (*concluded*)

Period (*n*)	13%	14%	15%	16%	17%	18%	19%	20%	25%	30%	35%	40%	50%
1	0.885	0.877	0.870	0.862	0.855	0.847	0.840	0.833	0.800	0.769	0.741	0.714	0.667
2	0.783	0.769	0.756	0.743	0.731	0.718	0.706	0.694	0.640	0.592	0.549	0.510	0.444
3	0.693	0.675	0.658	0.641	0.624	0.609	0.593	0.579	0.512	0.455	0.406	0.364	0.296
4	0.613	0.592	0.572	0.552	0.534	0.515	0.499	0.482	0.410	0.350	0.301	0.260	0.198
5	0.543	0.519	0.497	0.476	0.456	0.437	0.419	0.402	0.320	0.269	0.223	0.186	0.132
6	0.480	0.456	0.432	0.410	0.390	0.370	0.352	0.335	0.262	0.207	0.165	0.133	0.088
7	0.425	0.400	0.376	0.354	0.333	0.314	0.296	0.279	0.210	0.159	0.122	0.095	0.059
8	0.376	0.351	0.327	0.305	0.285	0.266	0.249	0.233	0.168	0.123	0.091	0.068	0.039
9	0.333	0.308	0.284	0.263	0.243	0.225	0.209	0.194	0.134	0.094	0.067	0.048	0.026
10	0.295	0.270	0.247	0.227	0.208	0.191	0.176	0.162	0.107	0.073	0.050	0.035	0.017
11	0.261	0.237	0.215	0.195	0.178	0.162	0.148	0.135	0.086	0.056	0.037	0.025	0.012
12	0.231	0.208	0.187	0.168	0.152	0.137	0.124	0.112	0.069	0.043	0.027	0.018	0.008
13	0.204	0.182	0.163	0.145	0.130	0.116	0.104	0.093	0.055	0.033	0.020	0.013	0.005
14	0.181	0.160	0.141	0.125	0.111	0.099	0.088	0.078	0.044	0.025	0.015	0.009	0.003
15	0.160	0.140	0.123	0.108	0.095	0.084	0.074	0.065	0.035	0.020	0.011	0.006	0.002
16	0.141	0.123	0.107	0.093	0.081	0.071	0.062	0.054	0.028	0.015	0.008	0.005	0.002
17	0.125	0.108	0.093	0.080	0.069	0.060	0.052	0.045	0.023	0.012	0.006	0.003	0.001
18	0.111	0.095	0.081	0.069	0.059	0.051	0.044	0.038	0.018	0.009	0.005	0.002	0.001
19	0.098	0.083	0.070	0.060	0.051	0.043	0.037	0.031	0.014	0.007	0.003	0.002	0.000
20	0.087	0.073	0.061	0.051	0.043	0.037	0.031	0.026	0.012	0.005	0.002	0.001	0.000
25	0.047	0.038	0.030	0.024	0.020	0.016	0.013	0.010	0.004	0.001	0.001	0.000	0.000
30	0.026	0.020	0.015	0.012	0.009	0.007	0.005	0.004	0.001	0.000	0.000	0.000	0.000
40	0.008	0.005	0.004	0.003	0.002	0.001	0.001	0.001	0.000	0.000	0.000	0.000	0.000
50	0.002	0.001	0.001	0.001	0.000	0.000	0.000	0.000	0.000	0.000	0.000	0.000	0.000

Present Value of an Annuity of $1 for *n* Years, Discounted at Rate *k*

Period (*n*)	1%	2%	3%	4%	5%	6%	7%	8%	9%	10%	11%	12%
1	0.990	0.980	0.971	0.962	0.952	0.943	0.935	0.926	0.917	0.909	0.901	0.893
2	1.970	1.942	1.913	1.886	1.859	1.833	1.808	1.783	1.759	1.736	1.713	1.690
3	2.941	2.884	2.829	2.775	2.723	2.673	2.624	2.577	2.531	2.487	2.444	2.402
4	3.902	3.808	3.717	3.630	3.546	3.465	3.387	3.312	3.240	3.170	3.102	3.037
5	4.853	4.710	4.580	4.452	4.329	4.212	4.100	3.993	3.890	3.791	3.696	3.605
6	5.795	5.601	5.417	5.242	5.076	4.917	4.767	4.623	4.486	4.355	4.231	4.111
7	6.728	6.472	6.230	6.002	5.786	5.582	5.389	5.206	5.033	4.868	4.712	4.564
8	7.652	7.325	7.020	6.733	6.463	6.210	5.971	5.747	5.535	5.335	5.146	4.968
9	8.566	8.162	7.786	7.435	7.108	6.802	6.515	6.247	5.995	5.759	5.537	5.328
10	9.471	8.983	8.530	8.111	7.722	7.360	7.024	6.710	6.418	6.145	5.889	5.650
11	10.368	9.787	9.253	8.760	8.306	7.887	7.499	7.139	6.805	6.495	6.207	5.938
12	11.255	10.575	9.954	9.385	8.863	8.384	7.943	7.536	7.161	6.814	6.492	6.194
13	12.134	11.348	10.635	9.986	9.394	8.853	8.358	7.904	7.487	7.103	6.750	6.424
14	13.004	12.106	11.296	10.563	9.899	9.295	8.745	8.244	7.786	7.367	6.982	6.628
15	13.865	12.849	11.939	11.118	10.380	9.712	9.108	8.559	8.061	7.606	7.191	6.811
16	14.718	13.578	12.561	11.652	10.838	10.106	9.447	8.851	8.313	7.824	7.379	6.974
17	15.562	14.292	13.166	12.166	11.274	10.477	9.763	9.122	8.544	8.022	7.549	7.102
18	16.398	14.992	13.754	12.659	11.690	10.828	10.059	9.372	8.756	8.201	7.702	7.250
19	17.226	15.678	14.324	13.134	12.085	11.158	10.336	9.604	8.950	8.365	7.839	7.366
20	18.046	16.351	14.877	13.590	12.462	11.470	10.594	9.818	9.129	8.514	7.963	7.469
25	22.023	19.523	17.413	15.622	14.094	12.783	11.654	10.675	9.823	9.077	8.422	7.843
30	25.808	22.396	19.600	17.292	15.372	13.765	12.409	11.258	10.274	9.427	8.694	8.055
40	32.835	27.355	23.115	19.793	17.159	15.046	13.332	11.925	10.757	9.779	8.951	8.244
50	39.196	31.424	25.730	21.482	18.256	15.762	13.801	12.233	10.962	9.915	9.042	8.304

(continued)

Present Value of an Annuity of $1 for *n* Years, Discounted at Rate *k* (*concluded*)

Period (*n*)	13%	14%	15%	16%	17%	18%	19%	20%	25%	30%	35%	40%	50%
1	0.885	0.877	0.870	0.862	0.855	0.847	0.840	0.833	0.800	0.769	0.741	0.714	0.667
2	1.668	1.647	1.626	1.605	1.585	1.566	1.547	1.528	1.440	1.361	1.289	1.224	1.111
3	2.361	2.322	2.283	2.246	2.210	2.174	2.140	2.106	1.952	1.816	1.696	1.589	1.407
4	2.974	2.914	2.855	2.798	2.743	2.690	2.639	2.589	2.362	2.166	1.997	1.849	1.605
5	3.517	3.433	3.352	3.274	3.199	3.127	3.058	2.991	2.689	2.436	2.220	2.035	1.737
6	3.998	3.889	3.784	3.685	3.589	3.498	3.410	3.326	2.951	2.643	2.385	2.168	1.824
7	4.423	4.288	4.160	4.039	3.922	3.812	3.706	3.605	3.161	2.802	2.508	2.263	1.883
8	4.799	4.639	4.487	4.344	4.207	4.078	3.954	3.837	3.329	2.925	2.598	2.331	1.922
9	5.132	4.946	4.772	4.607	4.451	4.303	4.163	4.031	3.463	3.019	2.665	2.370	1.948
10	5.426	5.216	5.019	4.833	4.659	4.494	4.339	4.192	3.571	3.092	2.715	2.414	1.965
11	5.687	5.453	5.234	5.029	4.836	4.656	4.486	4.327	3.656	3.147	2.752	2.438	1.977
12	5.918	5.660	5.421	5.197	4.988	4.793	4.611	4.439	3.725	3.190	2.779	2.456	1.985
13	6.122	5.842	5.583	5.342	5.118	4.910	4.715	4.533	3.780	3.223	2.799	2.469	1.990
14	6.302	6.002	5.724	5.468	5.229	5.008	4.802	4.611	3.824	3.249	2.814	2.478	1.993
15	6.462	6.142	5.847	5.575	5.324	5.092	4.876	4.675	3.859	3.268	2.825	2.484	1.995
16	6.604	6.265	5.954	5.668	5.405	5.162	4.938	4.730	3.887	3.283	2.834	2.489	1.997
17	6.729	6.373	6.047	5.749	5.475	5.222	4.988	4.775	3.910	3.295	2.840	2.492	1.998
18	6.840	6.467	6.128	5.818	5.534	5.273	5.033	4.812	3.928	3.304	2.844	2.494	1.999
19	6.938	6.550	6.198	5.877	5.584	5.316	5.070	4.843	3.942	3.311	2.848	2.496	1.999
20	7.025	6.623	6.259	5.929	5.628	5.353	5.101	4.870	3.954	3.316	2.850	2.497	1.999
25	7.330	6.873	6.464	6.097	5.766	5.467	5.195	4.948	3.985	3.329	2.856	2.499	2.000
30	7.496	7.003	6.566	6.177	5.829	5.517	5.235	4.979	3.995	3.332	2.857	2.500	2.000
40	7.634	7.105	6.642	6.233	5.871	5.548	5.258	4.997	3.999	3.333	2.857	2.500	2.000
50	7.675	7.133	6.661	6.246	5.880	5.554	5.262	4.999	4.000	3.333	2.857	2.500	2.000

Glossary

A

accelerated depreciation Any *depreciation*[1] that produces larger deductions for depreciation in the early years of a project's life.

acceptance criterion Any minimum standard of performance in investment analysis (cf. *hurdle rate*).

accounting income An economic agent's *realized income* as shown on financial statements (cf. *economic income*).

accounting rate of return A figure of investment merit, defined as average annual cash inflow divided by total cash outflow (cf. *internal rate of return*).

accounts payable (payables, trade payables) Money owed to suppliers. Obligations due to trade suppliers within one year.

accounts receivable (receivables, trade credit) Money owed by customers.

accrual accounting A method of accounting in which *revenue* is recognized when earned and expenses are recognized when incurred without regard to the timing of cash receipts and expenditures (cf. *cash accounting*).

accrued liabilities *Other liabilities*. A catchall accounting term referring to a collection of unpaid expenses that are individually too small to warrant a separate line on the balance sheet.

acid test (quick ratio) A measure of *liquidity*, defined as *current assets* less inventories divided by *current liabilities*.

activist investor A professional investor, not a company insider, who seeks to initiate significant corporate actions to improve her investment returns.

adjusted present value (APV) *Net present value* of an asset if financed entirely by equity plus the present value of any side effects, such as interest tax shields.

[1]Words in italics are defined elsewhere in the glossary.

after-tax cash flow Total cash generated by an investment annually, defined as profit after tax plus depreciation or, equivalently, operating income after tax plus the tax rate times depreciation.

allocated costs Costs systematically assigned or distributed among products, departments, or other elements.

amortization The provision for the gradual elimination of an asset or a liability by regular payments or charges. Often synonymous with depreciation.

annuity A level stream of cash flows for a limited number of years (cf. *perpetuity*).

asset Anything with value in exchange.

asset turnover ratio A broad measure of asset efficiency, defined as net sales divided by total assets.

B

bankruptcy A legal condition in which an entity receives court protection from its creditors. Bankruptcy can result in *liquidation* or reorganization.

bearer securities Any securities that are not registered on the books of the issuing corporation. Payments are made to whoever presents the appropriate coupon. Bearer securities facilitate tax avoidance.

benefit-cost ratio *Profitability index.*

β-risk (systematic risk, nondiversifiable risk) Risk that cannot be diversified away.

bond Long-term publicly issued debt.

bond rating An appraisal by a recognized financial organization of the soundness of a *bond* as an investment.

book value The value at which an item is reported in financial statements (cf. *market value*).

401

nondiversifiable risk   β-*risk*, *systematic risk*.

notes payable   The total amount of interest-bearing short-term obligations.

O

operating leverage   Fixed operating costs that tend to increase the variation in profits (cf. *financial leverage*).

opportunity cost   Income forgone by an investor when he or she chooses one action over another. Expected income on next best alternative.

opportunity cost of capital   *Cost of capital*.

option   See *call option, put option*.

option premium   The amount paid per unit by an option buyer to the option seller for an option contract.

other assets   A catchall accounting term referring to a collection of assets that are individually too small to warrant a separate line on the balance sheet.

other expenses   A catchall accounting term referring to a collection of expenses that are individually too small to warrant a separate line on the income statement.

over-the-counter (OTC) market   Informal market in which securities not listed on organized exchanges trade.

owners' equity   *Equity*.

P

paid-in capital   That portion of *shareholders' equity* that has been paid in directly, as opposed to earned profits retained in the business.

par value   An arbitrary value set as the face amount of a security. Bondholders receive par value for their bonds on maturity.

payables period   A measure of a company's use of trade credit financing, defined as accounts payable divided by purchases per day.

payback period   A crude figure of investment merit and a better measure of investment risk, defined as the time an investor must wait to recoup his or her initial investment.

perpetual-growth equation   An equation representing the *present value* of a *perpetuity* growing at the rate of *g* percent per annum. Defined as next year's receipts divided by the difference between the *discount rate* and *g*.

perpetuity   An *annuity* that lasts forever.

plug   Jargon for the unknown quantity in a pro forma forecast.

portfolio   Holdings of a diverse group of assets by an individual or a company.

position diagram   A graph relating the value of an investment position on the vertical axis to the price of an underlying asset on the horizontal axis.

post-money value   A company's equity value implied by the price per share an investor pays, after investing (cf. *pre-money value*).

preferred stock   A class of stock, usually fixed-income, that carries some form of preference to income or assets over *common stock* (cf. *cumulative preferred stock*).

premium for control   The premium over and above the existing *market value* of a company's *equity* that an acquirer is willing to pay to gain control of the company.

pre-money value   A company's equity value implied by the price per share an investor agrees to pay prior to investing (cf. *post-money value*).

prepaid income taxes   A prepayment of taxes treated as an asset until taxes become due.

present value   The present worth of a future sum of money.

price-to-earnings ratio (P/E ratio)   Amount investors are willing to pay for $1 of a firm's current earnings. Price per share divided by earnings per share over the most recent 12 months.

principal   The original, or face, amount of a loan. Interest is earned on the principal.

private placement   The raising of capital for a business through the sale of securities to a limited number of well-informed investors rather than through a public offering.

profitability index (benefit-cost ratio)   A figure of investment merit, defined as the *present value* of cash inflows divided by the present value of cash outflows.

profit center   An organizational unit within a company that produces revenue and for which a profit can be calculated.

profit margin   The proportion of each sales dollar that filters down to *income*, defined as income divided by *net sales*.

profits   *Earnings.*

pro forma statement   A financial statement prepared on the basis of some assumed future events.

property, plant, and equipment   The cost of tangible fixed property used in the production of revenue.

protective covenant   *Covenant.*

provision for income taxes   Taxes due for the year based on reported income. Often differs from taxes paid, which are based on separate tax accounting rules.

public issue (public offering)   Newly issued securities sold directly to the public (cf. *private placement*).

purchasing power parity   A theory stating that foreign exchange rates should adjust so that in equilibrium, commodities in different countries cost the same amount when prices are expressed in the same currency.

put option   Option to sell an asset at a specified exercise price on or before a specified maturity date (cf. *call option*).

Q

quick ratio   *Acid test.*

R

range of earnings chart   Graph relating *return on equity (ROE)* or *earnings per share (EPS)* to earnings before interest and taxes (*EBIT*) under alternative financing options.

rate of return   Yield obtainable on an asset.

ratio analysis   Analysis of financial statements by means of ratios.

real amount   Any quantity that has been adjusted for changes in the purchasing power of the currency due to inflation (cf. *nominal amount*).

realized income   The earning of income related to a transaction as distinguished from a paper gain.

residual income security   A security that has last claim on company income. Usually the beneficiary of company growth.

residual profits   An alternative to *return on investment* as a measure of *profit center* performance, defined as *income* less the annual cost of the capital employed by the profit center.

retained earnings (earned surplus)   The amount of earnings retained and reinvested in a business and not distributed to stockholders as dividends.

return on assets (ROA)   A measure of the productivity of assets, defined as *income* divided by total assets. A superior but less common definition includes interest expense and preferred dividends in the numerator.

return on equity (ROE)   A measure of the productivity or efficiency with which shareholders' equity is employed, defined as *income* divided by *equity*.

return on invested capital (ROIC)   A fundamental measure of the earning power of a company that is unaffected by the way the company is financed. It is equal to earnings before interest and tax times 1 minus the tax rate, all divided by *debt* plus *equity*.

return on investment (ROI)   The productivity of an investment or a profit center, defined as *income* divided by *book value* of investment or *profit center* (cf. *return on assets*).

revenues   *Sales.*

rights of absolute priority   Specification in bankruptcy law stating that each class of claimants with a prior claim on assets in liquidation will be paid off in full before any junior claimants receive anything.

risk-adjusted discount rate (cost of capital, hurdle rate)   A *discount rate* that includes a premium for risk.

risk aversion   An unwillingness to bear risk without compensation of some form.

risk-free interest rate   The interest rate prevailing on a default-free bond in the absence of inflation.

risk premium   The increased return on a security required to compensate investors for the risk borne.

S

sales (revenue)   The inflow of resources to a business for a period from sale of goods or provision of services (cf. *net sales*).

secured creditor   A creditor whose obligation is backed by the pledge of some asset. In liquidation, the secured creditor receives the cash from the sale of the pledged asset to the extent of his or her loan.

Securities and Exchange Commission (SEC)   Federal government agency that regulates securities markets.

selling, general, and administrative expenses   All expenses of operation not directly related to product production incurred in the generation of operating income.

semistrong-form efficient market   A market in which prices instantaneously reflect all publicly available information.

senior creditor   Any creditor with a claim on income or assets prior to that of *general creditors*.

sensitivity analysis   Analysis of the effect on a plan or forecast of a change in one of the input variables.

shareholders' equity   *Equity, net worth.*

shelf registration   SEC program under which a company can file a general-purpose prospectus describing its possible financing plans for up to two years. This eliminates time lags for new public security issues.

simulation (Monte Carlo simulation)   Computer-based extension of *sensitivity analysis* that calculates the probability distribution of a forecast outcome.

sinking fund   A fund of cash set aside for the payment of a future obligation. A bond sinking fund is a payment of cash to creditors.

solvency   The state of being able to pay debts as they come due.

sources and uses statement   A document showing where a company got its cash and where it spent the cash over a specific period of time. It is constructed by segregating all changes in balance sheet accounts into those that provided cash and those that consumed cash.

spontaneous sources of cash   Those liabilities, such as accounts payable and accrued wages, that arise automatically, without negotiation, in the course of doing business.

spot market   A market in which prices are determined for immediate trade.

spread   Investment banker jargon for the difference between the issue price of a new security and the net to the company.

standard deviation of return   A measure of variability. The square root of the mean squared deviation from the *expected return*.

statement of changes in financial position   A financial statement showing the sources and uses of working capital for the period.

stock   *Common stock.*

stock option   A contractual privilege sometimes provided to company officers giving the holder the right to purchase a specified number of shares at a specified price within a stated period of time.

strike price (exercise price)   The fixed price for which a stock can be purchased in a call contract or sold in a put contract (cf. *call option, put option*).

strong-form efficient market   A market in which prices instantaneously reflect all information, public or private.

subordinated creditor   A creditor who holds a debenture having a lower chance of payment than other liabilities of the firm.

sunk cost   A previous outlay that cannot be changed by any current or future action.

sustainable growth rate   The rate of increase in sales a company can attain without changing its profit margin, assets-to-sales ratio, debt-to equity ratio, or dividend payout ratio. The rate of growth a company can finance without excessive borrowing or issuing new stock.

T

tax shield   The reduction in a company's tax bill caused by an increase in a tax-deductible expense, usually depreciation or interest. The magnitude of the tax shield equals the tax rate times the increase in the expense.

times burden covered   A *coverage ratio* measure of *financial leverage*, defined as earnings before interest and taxes divided by interest expense plus principal payments grossed up to their before-tax equivalents.

times interest earned   A *coverage ratio* measure of *financial leverage*, defined as earnings before interest and taxes divided by interest expense.

total capital   All long-term sources of financing to a business.

total enterprise value (TEV)   *Market value of the firm.* The market value of equity plus the market value of debt.

trade payables   *Accounts payable.*

transfer price   An internal price at which units of the same company trade goods or services among themselves.

treasury stock   The value of a company's common stock that has been repurchased. Treasury shares neither receive dividends nor vote.

U

underwriting syndicate   A group of *investment banks* that band together for a brief time to guarantee a specified price to a company for newly issued securities.

unrealized income   Earned income for which there is no confirming transaction. A paper gain.

V

variable cost   Any expense that varies with sales over the observation period.

volatility   The standard deviation of the return on an asset. A measure of asset risk.

W

warrant   A security issued by a company granting the right to purchase shares of another security of the company at a specified price and for a stated time.

weak-form efficient market   A market in which prices instantaneously reflect information about past prices.

weighted-average cost of capital   *Cost of capital.*

with-without principle   Principle defining those cash flows that are relevant to an investment decision. It states that if there are two worlds, one with the investment and one without it, all cash flows that differ in these two worlds are relevant and all cash flows that are the same are irrelevant.

working capital (net working capital)   The excess of current assets over current liabilities.

working capital cycle   The periodic transformation of cash through current assets and current liabilities and back to cash (cf. *cash flowcycle*).

Y

yield to maturity   The *internal rate of return* on a bond when held to maturity.

Suggested Answers to Odd-Numbered Problems

Chapter 1

1. a. It means that the company's operating activities consumed cash. A combination of two things can cause this: operating losses, and increases in accounts receivable and inventories. Operating losses can obviously be dangerous. Rising receivables and inventories need not be dangerous provided they are growing in step with sales, and provided the company is able to finance the cash shortfalls. Rising receivables and inventories relative to sales suggests slackening management control of important operating assets, a potential danger.

    b. This means that the company's investing activities consumed cash, that the company purchased more property, plant, equipment, or marketable securities than it disposed of during the year. For most growing, stable companies, cash flows from investing activities are negative as firms build production capacity and replace used equipment. Positive cash flows from investing activities can signal problems, suggesting the firm has no attractive investment opportunities or that it might be liquidating productive assets due to financial difficulties.

    c. Negative cash flows from financing activities means that the firm is paying out more money to investors (in the form of debt principal repayment, interest payments, dividends, and share repurchases) than it is raising from investors. Usually, negative cash flows from financing activities are associated with mature companies generating more than enough cash from operations to fund future activities. It is not necessarily bad news. Conversely, early-stage firms, rapidly growing firms, and those in financial distress typically have positive cash flows from financing activities.

3. a. False. Shareholders' equity is on the liabilities side of the balance sheet. It represents owners' claims on company assets. Or said differently, the money contributed by owners and supplemented by retained profits has already been spent to acquire company assets.

    b. False. The book value of equity is simply the "plug" number that makes the book value of assets equal the sum of the book value of liabilities and the book value of equity. If the book value of liabilities is greater than the book value of assets, then (by definition)

413

book value of equity must be negative. This does not automatically spell bankruptcy. Bankruptcy occurs when a firm cannot pay its bills in a timely manner and creditors force it to seek, or it voluntarily seeks, court protection.

c. True. With two balance sheets, it is possible to construct a sources and uses statement.

d. False. Goodwill arises when one firm acquires another at a price above its book value. For example, if one firm acquires another for $10 million in cash but the target has a book value of only $8 million, the accountants record a $10 million reduction in the acquirer's cash, an $8 million increase in assets, and a $2 million increase in goodwill to balance the accounts.

e. False. It's just the reverse. As an asset account decreases, cash is made available for other uses. Thus, decreases in assets are sources of cash. In order to decrease a liability account, the firm must use cash to lower the liability. Thus, decreases in liability accounts are uses of cash.

5. Because the accountant's primary goal is to measure earnings, not cash generated. She sees earnings as a fundamental indicator of viability, not cash generation. A more balanced perspective is that, over the long run, successful companies must be both profitable and solvent, that is, they must be profitable and have cash in the bank to pay their bills when due. This means that you should pay attention to both earnings and cash flows.

7. The General Secretary has confused accounting profits with economic profits. Earning $300 million on a $7.5 billion equity investment is a return of only four percent. This is poor performance and is too low for the company to continue attracting new investment necessary for growth. The company is certainly not covering its cost of equity.

9. Mead, Inc. generated $330,000 of cash during the year. The $400,000 net income ignores the fact that accounts receivable rose $250,000, a use of cash. It also treats $180,000 depreciation as an expense, whereas it is a non-cash charge. The $20,000 increase in market value of assets adds to the market value of the business, but is not a cash flow. Here are the figures.

Accounting Income	$400,000
Depreciation (a non-cash charge)	+ $180,000
Increase in Accounts Receivable	− $250,000
Cash Generated	$330,000

11. a. In 2011, company sales were $782 million, but accounts receivable rose $30 million, meaning the company received only $752 million in cash. (This ignores possible changes in bad debt reserves.) Letting bop stand for beginning of period, and eop for end of period, the relevant equation is

$$\text{Accounts receivable}_{eop} = \text{Accounts receivable}_{bop} + \text{Credit sales} - \text{Collections}$$

$$\text{Collections} = \text{Credit sales} - \text{Change in accounts receivable}$$

$$\$752 \text{ million} = \$782 \text{ million} - \$30 \text{ million}$$

b. During 2011, the company sold $502 million of merchandise at cost, but finished goods inventory fell $10 million, indicating that the company produced only $492 million of merchandise. The equation is

$$\text{Inventory}_{eop} = \text{Inventory}_{bop} + \text{Production} - \text{Cost of sales}$$

$$\text{Production} = \text{Cost of sales} + \text{Change in inventory}$$

$$\$492 \text{ million} = \$502 \text{ million} - \$10 \text{ million}$$

c. Net fixed assets rose $78 million, depreciation reduced net fixed assets $61 million, so capital expenditures must have been $139 million (ignoring asset sales or write-offs).

$$\text{Net fixed assets}_{eop} = \text{Net fixed assets}_{bop} + \text{Capital expenditures} - \text{Depreciation}$$

$$\text{Capital expenditures} = \text{Change in net fixed assets} + \text{Depreciation}$$

$$\$139 \text{ million} = \$78 \text{ million} + \$61 \text{ million}$$

d. There are two ways to derive cash flow from operations. If there were no financing cash flows for the year, then changes in the year-end cash balance must be due to cash flows from operations and investing activities. The capital expenditures of $139 million represent the investing cash flows of the firm. Thus, we can use the change in the cash balance from 2010 to 2011 ($49 million) and the cash flows from investing to obtain cash flow from operations.

$$\text{Change in cash balance} = \text{CF from ops} + \text{CF from investing} + \text{CF from financing}$$

$$\$49 \text{ million} = \text{CF from ops} + (-\$139 \text{ million}) + 0$$

$$\text{CF from operations} = \$49 + \$139 = \$188 \text{ million}$$

Alternatively, you can calculate the cash flow from operations from the items in the table. Begin with net income, remove any non-cash items (such as depreciation) and add any cash transactions that are not captured by the income statement (such as changes to working capital accounts). We can see that accounts receivable increased by $30 million, finished goods inventory decreased by $10 million, and accounts payable increased by $5 million. Depreciation was $61 million.

CF from operations = Net income − Increase in acct. receivable
+ Decrease in inventory + Increase in
acct. payable + Depreciation

CF from operations = 142 − 30 + 10 + 5 + 61 = $188 million

13. a. Stock price per share = $15 million/700,000 shares = $21.43 per share. Book value per share = $9 million/700,000 = $12.86 per share.

b. Epic Trucking will pay $21.43 per share for the 175,000 shares it repurchases. This reduces the book value of equity by $3,750,250. Assuming all else remains the same, the new book value will be $5,249,750.

c. Since nothing else has changed, investors do not change their perceptions of the firm, and there are no taxes or transaction costs, the market value should fall by exactly the amount of the cash paid in the transaction. The new market value should be $11,249,750. Another way to think about the question is to note that repurchase of the shares will reduce cash by $3,750,250 or increase liabilities by the same amount if they finance the repurchase with debt. Either way, the firm is worth $3,750,250 less to owners after the repurchase, or $11,249,750. With 525,000 shares outstanding after repurchase, the price per share remains $21.43 ($11,249,750/525,000 shares). (In practice, share repurchases often have a positive price effect at the time of announcement. There are several explanations for this effect, some of which we will cover in later chapters.)

d. Shares outstanding increase 20 percent, or 140,000 shares. At $21.43 per share, Epic Trucking would raise $3,000,200. Assuming all else remains the same, the new book value of equity will be $12,000,200 ($9 million + $3,000,200).

e. Due to the same reasoning as in part c, the market value should rise by $3,000,200. In essence, the sale raises company cash by $3,000,200, increasing the value of the firm by just this amount. The new market value should be $18,000,200. The price per share should remain $21.43 ($18,000,200/840,000 shares = $21.43).

In practice, such equity sales often cause investors to be less optimistic about the firm's future performance and thus generate negative price effects at the time of announcement. We will discuss this topic more in Chapter 6.

Chapter 2

1. The CEO is correct that ROE is the product of profit margin, asset turnover, and financial leverage, but an increase in prices will not necessarily increase ROE because increased prices will likely reduce sales. If operating costs are fixed, the profit margin could actually fall when prices rise. Even if operating costs are variable, a decrease in sales will reduce the asset turnover, and thus reduce ROE. It is uncertain whether the effect of the increase in profit margin on ROE will outweigh the effect of the decrease in asset turnover. When thinking about the levers of performance, it is important to remember that changes in company strategy can affect several levers, often in different directions.

3. a. True. Let L = liabilities, E = equity, and A = assets. Does A/E = 1 + L/E? Does A/E = (E + L)/E? Yes.

   b. True. The numerators of the two ratios are identical. ROA can exceed ROE only if assets are less than equity, which implies that liabilities would have to be negative.

   c. False. A payables period longer than the collection period would be nice because trade credit would finance accounts receivable. However, payables periods and collections periods are typically determined by industry practice and the relative bargaining power of the firms involved; depending on a company's circumstances, it may have to gracefully put up with a collection period longer than its payables period.

   d. True. The two ratios are the same except that inventory, a positive quantity, is subtracted from the numerator to calculate the acid test.

   e. True. Decomposing ROE shows that a higher asset turnover ratio increases ROE. Thus, a firm wants to maximize asset turnover (all else being equal, of course).

   f. False. Earnings yields and price-to-earnings ratios are the inverse of one another. If two firms have identical earnings yields, they will have identical price-to-earnings ratios.

   g. False. Ignoring taxes and transactions costs, unrealized gains can always be realized by the act of selling, so they must be worth as much as a comparable amount of realized gains.

5. a.

	Year 1	Year 2
Current Ratio	9.70	2.80
Quick Ratio	9.61	2.31

Industrial's short-run liquidity has deteriorated considerably, but from a high initial base.

b.

	Year 1	Year 2
Collection period (days)	28.3	28.1
Inventory turnover (times)	38.5	4.7
Payables period (days)	42.3	24.3
Days' sales in cash (including marketable securities)	919.3	243.7
Gross margin	8%	25%
Profit margin	−57%	−88%

c. The company lost money in both years, more in the second year than the first. Cash flow from operations is negative in both years but has improved. Liquidity has fallen and the inventory turnover is down sharply. The more than 10-fold increase in inventory suggests that Industrial was either wildly optimistic about potential sales or completely lost control of its inventory. A third possibility is that the company is building inventory in anticipation of a major sales increase next year. In any case, the inventory investment warrants close scrutiny. In general, these numbers look like those of an unstable startup operation.

7. a.

	Locktite Inc.	Stork Systems
ROE	30%	57%
ROA	23%	11%
ROIC	25%	17%

b. Stork's higher ROE is a natural reflection of its higher financial leverage. It does not mean that Stork is the better company.

c. This is also due to Stork's higher leverage. ROA penalizes levered companies by comparing the net income available to equity to the capital provided by owners *and* creditors. It does not mean that Stork is a worse company than Locktite.

d. ROIC abstracts from differences in leverage to provide a direct comparison of the earning power of the two companies' assets.

On this metric, Locktite is the superior performer, although both percentages are quite attractive. Before drawing any firm conclusions, however, it is important to ask how the business risks faced by the companies compare and whether the observed ratios reflect long-run capabilities or transitory events.

9.   Collection period = Accounts receivable / Credit sales per day
Credit Sales = 0.75 × $420 million = $315 million

Accounts receivable = Collection period × Credit sales per day
= 55 × $315 million / 365 = $47.5 million

Inventory turnover = COGS / Ending inventory
COGS = Sales * (1 − Gross Margin) = $420 million
× (1 − 0.40) = $252 million

Inventory = COGS / Inventory turnover
= $252 million/8 = $31.5 million

Payables Period = Accounts payable / Purchases per day
(Since information is not available on Purchases, use COGS.)

Accounts payable = Payables period × COGS per day
= 40 × $252 million/365
= $27.6 million

11. Sales = (Cash / Days sales in cash) × 365 = (1,100,000/34) × 365
= $11,808,824

Accounts receivable = Collection period × credit sales per day
= Collection period × (Sales/365)
= 71 × 11,808,824/365 = $2,297,059

Cost of goods sold = Inventory turnover × Ending inventory
= 5 × 1,900,000 = $9,500,000

Accounts payable = Payables period × (Cost of goods sold/365)
= 36 × 9,500,000 / 365 = $936,986

Total liabilities = Assets × Liabilities to assets
= 8,000,000 × 0.75 = $6,000,000

Shareholders' equity = Total assets − Total liabilities
= 8,000,000 − 6,000,000 = $2,000,000

Current liabilities = Current assets/Current ratio
= 5,297,059 / 2.6 = $2,037,330

Assets	
Current:	
Cash	$1,100,000
Accounts receivable	$2,297,059
Inventory	$1,900,000
Total current assets	$5,297,059
Net fixed assets	$2,702,941
Total assets	$8,000,000
Liabilities and shareholders' equity	
Current liabilities:	
Accounts payable	$ 936,986
Short-term debt	$1,100,344
Total current liabilities	$2,037,330
Long-term debt	$3,962,670
Shareholders' equity	$2,000,000
Total liabilities and equity	$8,000,000

13. You will find suggested answers to this problem on the Web at **www.mhhe.com/higgins10e.** Select Student Edition > Choose Chapter > Files. Select the spreadsheet for problem 13.

Chapter 3

1. A negative value implies that the company has excess cash above its desired minimum. You can confirm this on the balance sheet by setting the external financing requirement to zero and adding the figure for external financing required to cash. You will find that assets equal liabilities plus owners' equity in this circumstance; in other words, the balance sheet balances.

3. This would tell me I had erred in constructing one or both of the forecasts. Using the same assumptions and avoiding accounting and arithmetic errors, estimated external financing required should equal estimated cash surplus or deficit for the same date.

5. The company needs a certain level of cash in order to operate efficiently. Operating cash flows can be volatile and difficult to predict from day to day. Companies rely on a cash cushion to cover periodic cash flow imbalances. The amount of cushion depends on many things, including the volatility of the cash flows and the availability of other sources of liquidity, such as unused bank credit lines. While one might argue that the company could get by with less than 18 days' sales in cash as implied in the forecast, this figure is a good bit less than the recent median for nonfinancial firms in the S&P 500 of about 43 days.

7. Pro Forma Forecast for R&E Supplies 2013

Income Statement	
Net sales	$33,496
Cost of goods sold	28,807
Gross profit	4,689
General, selling, and administrative expense	3,685
Interest expense	327
Earnings before tax	678
Tax	305
Earnings after tax	373
Dividends paid	187
Additions to retained earnings	$ 187
Balance Sheet Forecast	
Current assets	$ 9,714
Net fixed assets	270
Total assets	$ 9,984
Current liabilities	$ 4,823
Long-term debt	560
Equity	1,995
Total liabilities and shareholders' equity	$ 7,378
External Financing Required	**$ 2,606**

a. Projected external financing required in 2013 is $2.606 million, over $1 million more than in 2012. R&E Supplies needs to get off this treadmill as soon as possible.
b. External financing required falls to $2.416 million, down 7.3 percent.
c. External financing required rises to $2.977 million, up 14.2 percent in this recession scenario.

9.

Pepperton Income Statement	
January 1, 2012–March 31, 2012 ($ thousands)	
Net sales	$1,080
Cost of sales	540
Gross profit	540
Selling and administrative expense	540
Interest	90
Depreciation	30
Net profit before tax	(120)
Tax at 33%	(40)
Net profit after tax	($80)
Dividends	300
Additions to retained earnings	(380)

Balance Sheet—March 31, 2012 ($ thousands)

Assets	
Cash	$ 150
Accounts receivable	192
Inventory	1,800
Total current assets	2,142
Gross fixed assets	900
−Accumulated depreciation	180
Net fixed assets	720
Total assets	$2,862
Liabilities	
Bank loan	**$1,362**
Accounts payable	240
Miscellaneous accruals	60
Current portion long-term debt	0
Taxes payable	80
Total current liabilities	1,742
Long-term debt	990
Shareholders' equity	130
Total liabilities and equity	$2,862

Comments:
Inventory is estimated as follows:

Beginning inventory Jan. 1	$1,800
+ 1st quarter purchases	540
− 1st quarter cost of goods sold	540
Ending inventory March 31	$1,800

Taxes payable are estimated as follows:

Taxes payable Dec. 31, 2008	$ 300
− Payments	180
+ 1st quarter taxes accrued	−40
Taxes payable March 31	$ 80

a. Estimated external financing need on March 31: $1,362,000.

b. Yes, they are the same. If they weren't, it would indicate I had made a mistake or used different assumptions for the two forecasts.

c. Yes, the pro-forma forecasts can be analyzed in the usual manner to assess the firm's financial health.

d. They say little about financing needs at any time other than the forecast date.

11. a. Negative numbers for taxes mean the company's tax liability will fall by this amount. If the company does not have an accrued tax liability but has paid taxes in the recent past, it can file for a rebate of past taxes paid.

b. Cash balances exceed the minimum required level because the company has excess cash in these quarters. Cash balances are determined in these periods by first noting that external financing required is negative when cash is set at the minimum level. External financing required is then set to zero and cash becomes the balancing item equating assets to liabilities and owners' equity.

c. When greater than zero, external financing required becomes the balancing item equating assets to liabilities and owners' equity.

d. The company should easily be able to borrow the money. The amounts required are less than one-quarter of accounts receivable in each quarter.

13. See the Suggested Answers worksheet in C3_Problem_13.xlsx available at **www.mhhe.com/higgins10e.** (Select Student Edition > Choose Chapter > Files.)

15. See the Suggested Answers worksheet in C3_Problem_15.xlsx available at **www.mhhe.com/higgins10e.** (Select Student Edition > Choose Chapter > Files.)

Chapter 4

1. This statement is incorrect and evidences a basic misunderstanding of the chapter. A correct statement would be "An important top-management job is to anticipate differences between their company's actual and sustainable growth rates and to have a plan in place to prudently manage these differences." Constraining a rapidly growing company's actual growth rate to approximate its sustainable rate risks needlessly sacrificing valuable growth, while boosting the growth rate of a slow-growth business risks promoting value-destroying growth.

3. a. False. In addition to issuing new equity, companies can grow at rates above their current sustainable rate by increasing any of the four ratios comprising the sustainable growth rate: their profit margin, asset turnover, financial leverage, or retention ratio. The problem is that there are limits to a company's ability to increase these ratios.

b. False. Glamorous companies such as Clearwire with an exciting story to tell can raise equity despite operating losses. More traditional companies have much more difficulty.

c. True. Repurchases reduce the number of shares outstanding, which contributes to increasing earnings per share. At the same time, the money used to repurchase the shares has a cost, which reduces earnings and tends to reduce earnings per share. In most instances, the former offsets the latter and earnings per share rise when shares are repurchased.

d. True. Survey evidence suggests that most managers, most of the time, believe their shares are under-valued. Repurchasing under-valued stock is a productive use of company resources benefiting remaining shareholders.

e. False. A major theme of this chapter has been that slow-growth companies have subtle and often more serious growth management problems than their rapidly growing neighbors.

f. False. Good growth yielding returns above cost increases stock price. Bad growth at returns below cost destroys value and will reduce the stock price sooner or later.

5. In most years since 1985, net equity issuance has been negative, meaning U.S. corporations have retired more shares measured in terms of value than they have issued. In aggregate then, new equity has been a use of capital to U.S. corporations, not a source. (At the same time, Figure 4.6 illustrates that new equity has been an important source to a certain subset of companies characterized primarily by high growth.)

7. a. Biosite's sustainable growth rates are

	2000	2001	2002	2003	2004
Sustainable growth rate (%)	NA	9.3	14.7	23.0	26.9

For example, in 2001 $g^* = 10.3\% \times 100\% \times 0.64 \times \$102.7/\$72.9 = 9.3\%$.

b. Biosite's actual growth rate in every year exceeded its sustainable growth rate by a wide margin. The company was growing at a rate well above its sustainable growth rate. Its challenge was how to manage this growth without growing broke.

c. Biosite increased every ratio except its retention ratio (which was already at 100%). Had Biosite not improved its operating performance, as reflected in profit margin and asset turnover, the financial leverage required to generate the company's sustainable growth rate would have been almost twice as high as observed.

9. a.

	2000	2001	2002	2003	2004
Sustainable growth rate	X	28.6	30.6	31.5	26.0
Actual growth rate	17.8	16.4	21.4	14.0	8.5

b. Harley-Davidson does have a sustainable growth problem. Its actual growth rate is much lower than its sustainable growth rate.

c. The decreases in asset turnover, retention ratio, and financial leverage are helping to decrease the sustainable growth rate. But, the spread between the two rates is still substantial in 2004.

11. See the worksheet entitled Suggested Answers in the file C4_Problem_9 .xlsx available at **www.mhhe.com/higgins10e.** (Select Student Edition > Choose Chapter > Files.)

Chapter 5

1. Common stocks are more risky than U.S. government bonds. Risk-averse investors demand higher returns on common stocks than government bonds as compensation for the added risk. If returns on government bonds were, on average, as high as those on common stocks, prices of government bonds would rise and prices of common stocks would fall as investors fled to the safer but equally promising bonds. This would result in lower expected returns on bonds for new investors and higher expected returns on stocks until the tradeoff of risk for return reappeared.

3. The percentage of the company owned is most important to the investor. This determines the size of her claims on company cash flows and, hence, the value of her investment. A company's share price, and the number of shares outstanding, can be arbitrarily changed by splitting the shares. Share price and number of shares owned are of interest only to the extent that they help the investor calculate more meaningful dollar or percentage ownership numbers.

5. a. The holding period return is -4.76 percent [($60 − $110)/$1,050].

   b. The bond's price might have fallen because investor perceptions of its risk rose or because interest rates rose. The price of a bond is the present value of future cash receipts. As interest rates rise, the present value of future cash flows falls, as does the price of the bond. See Chapter 7 for details.

7. a.

Stock price	$75.00
− 8% underpricing	6.00
Issue price	69.00
− 7% spread	4.83
Net to company	$64.17

Number of shares = $500 million/$64.17 = 7.79 million

    b. Investment bankers' revenue = $4.83 × 7.79 million = $37.63 million

    c. Underpricing is not a cash flow. It is, however, an opportunity cost to current owners because it means that more shares must be sold to raise $500 million and each existing share will represent a smaller ownership interest in the company. P.S. Opportunity costs are just as real as cash flow costs.

9. While intriguing, this is not evidence of market inefficiency. Think of flipping a coin and trying to get "heads." If skill is involved, you would expect to get heads more than 50% of the time. But if coin flipping is just luck, you would only get heads, on average, half of the time. Thus, if mutual fund returns were random, you would expect to see about half of all mutual funds outperform the market each year. Of these "winning" mutual funds, about half would again outperform the market in the subsequent year (in coin-flipping terms, when you flip heads, the next flip will result in heads approximately half of the time). After five years, you would expect that roughly 1/32 of the original sample of mutual funds would have outperformed the market each year $((1/2)^5 = 1/32)$. When you start with 5,600 mutual funds, one would expect that, if no skill is involved, about 175 would have outperformed the market each year for five years $(5,600/32 = 175)$. Given that only 104 have done so, it seems that luck (and not skill) is the likely cause of their success.

11. a. Suppose Liquid Force shares sell for $40 and it has announced a $6 per share dividend. Buy Liquid Force stock immediately prior to the announced dividend date for $40, receive the $6 dividend, and immediately sell the stock for $37. You invest $40 and immediately after the sale have $43 in cash. Easy money.

    b. Liquid Force's stock price would rise prior to the dividend and fall more when the dividend is paid. As more and more investors pursue this strategy, the price drop will fall until the decline equals the dividend, ignoring any taxes or transaction costs.

    c. Suppose Liquid Force stock sells for $40 before the dividend and the dividend is $6. You want to sell Liquid Force's stock short: Borrow Liquid Force stock from a shareholder and sell it immediately prior to the dividend for $40, pay the $6 dividend to the person from whom you borrowed the stock, and buy the stock for $28. Cover the short sale by returning the stock to the lender. You invest $34 ($28 + $6) and, immediately after the transaction, you have $40 cash. Again, easy money.

    d. Liquid Force's stock price would fall prior to the dividend and fall less when the dividend is paid. As more and more investors pursue this strategy, the price drop will equal the dividend (in the absence of transaction costs and taxes).

e. Such trading guarantees that the stock price will drop by an amount equal to the dividend payment.

f. Ignoring taxes and transactions costs, a $1 increase in dividends results in a $1 decline in stock price, and thus, a $1 reduction in capital appreciation. Rational investors are indifferent to whether they receive their return as dividends or price appreciation, so increasing the dividend cannot benefit investors.

13. The analogy is an appropriate one. Think of equity as a call option on the company's assets with a strike price equal to the value of debt outstanding. When the value of company assets is very low, equity holders' call option is out of the money. If they wish, they can walk away, leaving their option unexercised and firm assets in the hands of creditors. When the value of company assets exceeds the value of debt, the owners' call option is in the money. They can exercise their option by paying the value of the debt to creditors and owning the assets free and clear. The value of equity relative to the value of the firm looks like the payoff diagram for a call option.

Chapter 6

1. Electric utilities have very stable cash flows. Few of us turn off our lights or take cold showers during recessions. Stable cash flows are just what are needed to support large interest obligations. In addition, electric utilities have large investments in land and fixed assets, excellent sources of loan collateral.

   Information technology companies, on the other hand, have highly uncertain cash flows, the kind ill-suited to servicing interest obligations. They also aspire to rapid growth, meaning that maintaining the flexibility necessary to assure access to financial markets is important. They are thus wary of "closing off the top" by borrowing aggressively.

3. Because all firms face business risk, company EBIT varies over time. Debt is a fixed income security, meaning interest expense does not vary with EBIT. As a result, all of the variability in EBIT is borne by equity investors, who hold a residual income security. As leverage increases, the same variability in EBIT is borne by a smaller equity investment, causing variability per dollar invested to rise. This results in increased volatility in shareholder returns—or increased risk. Also, as evident from the range of earnings chart,

leverage increases the slope of line relating EBIT to EPS or ROE, and the steeper the slope, the greater the variability in EPS, and ROE, for any given variability in EBIT.

5. a. There are several reasons. First, companies with promising investment opportunities typically have valuable intangible assets whose value would decline sharply if the company got into financial difficulty; that is, the resale value of their assets is low. Second, it is important for such companies to maintain the financial flexibility that comes with a conservative capital structure to assure funding for future investment opportunities. They are making money on the asset side of the business and are, thus, ill-advised to do anything on the liability side to jeopardize future investments.

   b. Most would follow this recommendation if they could, but lack of sufficient operating cash flow and the inability to raise additional equity force many small businesses to an extensive reliance on debt financing. For these companies, it is either growth with debt or do not grow. Also, many entrepreneurs view debt as a way to stretch their limited equity to gain control over more assets. In essence, they like playing with someone else's chips.

7. a. EBIT = Income before tax + Interest expense = $50/(1 - 0.35) + 18 = \$94.9$.
   Interest $= \$18 + 0.07(50) = \$21.5$. Times interest earned $= 94.9/21.5 = 4.41$ times.

   b. Burden of interest and sinking fund before tax $= 21.5 + (17 + 8)/(1 - 0.35) = \$59.96$.

   Times burden covered $= 94.9/59.96 = 1.58$ times

   c. EPS $= (94.9 - 21.5)(1 - 0.35)/20 = \$2.39$.

   d. Times interest earned $= 94.9/18 = 5.27$ times. Times burden covered $= 94.9/[18 + 17/(1 - 0.35)] = 2.15$ times. EPS $= (94.9 - 18)(1 - 0.35)/(20 + 2) = \$2.27$.

9. a. An increase in the interest rate would lower the debt financing line in the range-of-earnings chart. This would reduce the ROE or EPS advantage of the increased leverage, or increase the disadvantage if EBIT is below the crossover point. It would also increase the crossover EBIT. Both changes would reduce the attractiveness of increased financial leverage.

   b. An increased stock price would reduce the number of shares the company would need to sell to raise targeted funds. This would increase ROE at all EBIT levels under the equity-financing alternative, making increased leverage less attractive. Said differently, a higher stock price would raise the equity financing line at all EBIT values, making debt financing less attractive relative to equity financing.

c. The range-of-earnings chart will be unchanged, but increased uncertainty will increase the probability that EBIT will fall below the crossover point. Such increased business risk will make debt financing riskier and, hence, less attractive.

d. Increased common dividends will not affect the range-of-earnings chart. The increased dividends will reduce the times-common-covered ratio for both options. But because there are more shares outstanding with the equity issue, the higher dividend will make a debt issue relatively more attractive.

e. An increase in the amount of debt already outstanding will increase interest expense and lower ROE under both options. This will lower both lines in the range-of-earnings chart by the same amount, but will not affect the attractiveness of the one option relative to the other; at least as far as the range-of-earnings chart is concerned. Interest coverage obviously falls as existing debt rises, which makes additional debt financing riskier and thus less attractive.

11. a. Each year sources of cash must equal uses. Sources are earnings plus new borrowing. Uses are investment and dividends. So each year the following equation applies: $E + 1.2(E - D) = I + D$, where E is earnings, 1.2 is the target debt-to-equity ratio, D is dividends, and I is investment. [The target debt-to-equity ratio is Debt = $1.2 \times$ Equity. Annual additions to equity = retained profits = $E - D$. Annual new borrowing, thus, equals $1.2(E - D)$.] Solving for D, $D = E - I/2.2$. The following table presents the resulting annual dividend and payout ratio.

b. Summing dividends and dividing by total earnings, the stable payout ratio is $219/$930 = 24$ percent. Substituting this into the sources and uses equation, $E + 1.2(E - .24E) = I + .24E + CM$, where CM is the change in the marketable securities portfolio. Solving for CM, $CM = 1.67E - I$. The resulting values for CM and the year-end marketable securities portfolio appear in the following table. (Had I carried out the calculations with more accuracy, the ending marketable securities would have equaled the beginning value, $200.)

Year	($ millions)				
	1	**2**	**3**	**4**	**5**
Dividends ($)	20	−6	34	71	100
Payout ratio (%)	20	−5	20	31	33
Stable payout ratio (%)	24	24	24	24	24
Stable dividend ($)	24	31	41	55	72
Change in marketable securities ($)	−8	−83	−16	34	61
Marketable securities ($)	192	109	93	127	188

c. The company can do any or some combination of the following: reduce marketable securities, increase leverage, sell new equity, cut dividends.

d. The pecking-order theory predicts a company will favor internal financing sources over external and, among external sources, it will favor lower risk assets, such as bonds, over equity. The options are ranked according to the pecking order as they appear in the answer to question c. Although cutting dividends is technically an internal source of financing, the adverse signaling associated with cutting dividends when the firm has a history of stable dividends is so strong I expect firms would list it behind selling new equity in their pecking order. Feel free to ignore cutting dividends in grading your answer to this question.

e. The pecking-order theory follows from the desire to avoid negative signaling (or lemon) effects of new equity issues, supplemented by the desire to maintain access to financial markets. If these goals are important to managers, they will naturally follow the pecking order.

13. See the file C6_Problem_13_Answer.xlsx, available at **www.mhhe .com/higgins10e.** (Select Student Edition > Choose Chapter > Files.)

15. See the file C6_Problem_15_Answer.xlsx, available at **www.mhhe .com/higgins10e.** (Select Student Edition > Choose Chapter > Files.)

Chapter 7

1. a.

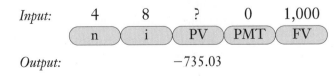

Input:	4	8	?	0	1,000
	n	i	PV	PMT	FV

Output: −735.03

b. PV = 540.27. Present value is less because the present sum has more time to grow into $1,000.

Input: 8   8   ?   0   1,000

n   i   PV   PMT   FV

Output: −540.27

c. PV = $20,565.89.

Input: 7   8   −12,000   0   ?

n   i   PV   PMT   FV

Output: 20,565.89

d. PV = 4,629.63 + 3,429.36 + 3,705.55 = $11,764.54.

Input: 1   8   ?   0   5,000

n   i   PV   PMT   FV

Output: −4,629.63

Input: 2   8   ?   0   4,000

n   i   PV   PMT   FV

Output: −3,429.36

Input: 10   8   ?   0   8,000

n   i   PV   PMT   FV

Output: −3,705.55

e.

Input: ?   8   −2,000   0   4,000

n   i   PV   PMT   FV

Output: 9.01

f.

Input: 20   8   0   −500   ?

n   i   PV   PMT   FV

Output: 22,880.98

g.

Input: 18   8   0   ?   250,000

n   i   PV   PMT   FV

Output: −6,675.52

h. If the stream lasted forever, PV = 600/.08 = $7,500.00. Hence, the stream must be a perpetuity. If the stream lasted only five years, the salvage value would have to be $7,500. This is the amount required to be invested at 8 percent to generate $600 per year in perpetuity from year 5 on.

Rate of Return Problems

i.

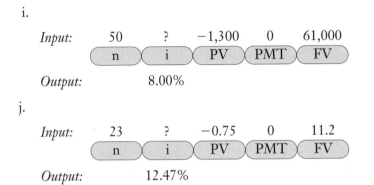

Input:	50	?	−1,300	0	61,000
	n	i	PV	PMT	FV

Output: 8.00%

j.

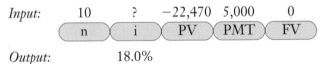

Input:	23	?	−0.75	0	11.2
	n	i	PV	PMT	FV

Output: 12.47%

k. IRR = 18%. Paying less than $22,470 implies an IRR greater than 18, and vice versa.

Input:	10	?	−22,470	5,000	0
	n	i	PV	PMT	FV

Output: 18.0%

l. Assume you invest $1.00 today and receive $2.00 in five years.

Input:	5	?	−1.00	0	2.0
	n	i	PV	PMT	FV

Output: 14.87%

m. Enter the investment cash flows in row 1, columns A through F on an Excel spreadsheet. IRR = (IRR,A1:F1) = 10.4 percent.

n. The internal rate of return is 13.69 percent. Once again, we see the power of compound interest. This does not suggest that investing in fine art is especially attractive. It ignores the costs of maintaining, insuring, and protecting a valuable painting; and the return on a Van Gogh can be expected to be much higher than the return on a typical fine art investment, even if it is one of his lesser works.

Input:	98	?	−125	0	36,000,000
	n	i	PV	PMT	FV

Output: 13.69

Bank Loan, Bond and Stock Problems

o. PV = $932.90.

Input: 10   8   ?   70   1,000

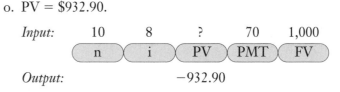

Output: −932.90

p. PV = 5/.08 = $62.50.

q. The annual payment necessary to amass $150 million in eight years is $14.10 million.

Input: 8   8   0   ?   150

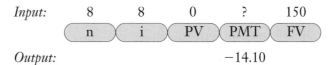

Output: −14.10

If the money is deposited at the beginning of each year, bring the $14.10 million deposit forward one year. The answer is $13.06 million.

Input: 1   8   ?   —   14.10

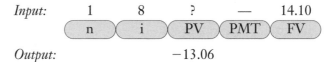

Output: −13.06

r. Annual payments must be $25,960.

Input: 6   8   120   ?   0

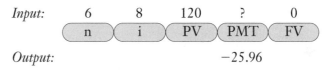

Output: −25.96

3. The effective interest rate on the time purchase plan is the discount rate that makes the seller indifferent to a cash sale for $48,959 and a time payment sale for $10,000 now and $10,000 for each of the next five years plus $2,000 fees.

> 48,959 = 2,000 + 10,000 + X, where X = the present value of a $10,000 annual payment for five years

Solving for X, X = $36,959. The interest rate at which the present value of a $10,000 annual payment for five years equals $36,969 is 11 percent.

Input: 5   ?   −36,959   10,000   0

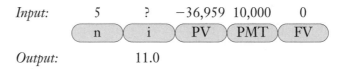

Output: 11.0

The interest rate = the internal rate of return = 11%.

5. The value of a constant stream of cash flows one year before the first cash flow can be determined using the perpetuity formula. The present value of the scholarship fund at time 2 is

$$PV = \$45,000/0.05 = \$900,000$$

In order to have $900,000 in the scholarship fund in two years, it would be necessary to contribute $816,330 today.

Input: 2   5   ?   0   900

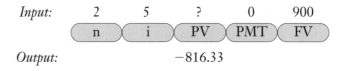

Output: −816.33

7. This is a straightforward replacement problem.

	Old Roasters	New Roasters
Gross profit	$600,000	$1,200,000
− Depreciation	300,000	450,000
Profit before tax	300,000	750,000
Tax at 45%	135,000	338,000
Profit after tax	165,000	412,000
+ Depreciation	300,000	450,000
After-tax cash flow	$465,000	$862,000

If the company keeps the old roasters, NPV = $2.857 million.

Input: 10   10   ?   465   —

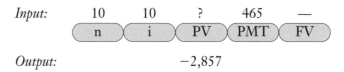

Output: −2,857

The present value of the after-tax cash flows from the new roasters is $5,297 million. If they sell the old roasters and buy the new ones, NPV = −4.500 + 1.500 + 5.297 = $2.297 million. Therefore, keep the old roasters.

Input: 10   10   ?   862   —

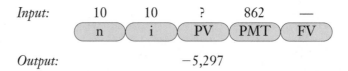

Output: −5,297

Alternatively, one can look at the difference in cash flows between the two alternatives. This amounts to analyzing the *incremental* cash flows.

Subtracting the old roasters' cash flows from the new roasters' cash flows,

Input: 10   10   ?   397   —

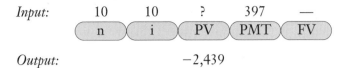

Output: −2,439

and NPV = −3.000 + 2.439 = −0.561 million, indicating that spending an incremental $3 million to buy the new roasters is not attractive. It should not surprise you to learn that this NPV equals the difference in the NPVs of the two options. That is, −0.561 million = $2.297 million − $2.857 million.

The IRR of the incremental cash flows is 5.4 percent, which because it is below 10 percent again indicates the incremental investment is unwarranted.

9. The after-tax cash flows from the investment are:

Year	0	1	2	3	4	5
Initial cost	$ 15,000					
Revenue		$20,000	$20,000	$20,000	$20,000	$20,000
Operating expense		13,000	13,000	13,000	13,000	13,000
Depreciation		3,000	3,000	3,000	3,000	3,000
Income before tax		4,000	4,000	4,000	4,000	4,000
Tax @ 40%		1,600	1,600	1,600	1,600	1,600
Income after tax		2,400	2,400	2,400	2,400	2,400
+ Depreciation		3,000	3,000	3,000	3,000	3,000
After-tax cash flow	$(15,000)	$ 5,400	$ 5,400	$ 5,400	$ 5,400	$ 5,400

The investment is quite attractive. Its internal rate of return is 23.4 percent, well above the minimum target of 10 percent.

Input: 5   ?   −15,000   5,400   —

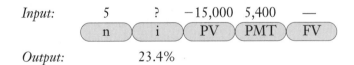

Output: 23.4%

11. **What's Wrong with This Picture?**
    a. Add back depreciation to calculate after-tax cash flow. We are interested in the cash generated by the project, not the accounting profits. Using a salvage value less than initial cost captures the reality of depreciation. To also subtract an annual amount would be double counting.

b. Do not subtract interest expense. The opportunity cost of money invested is captured in the discount rate. To also subtract financing costs would again be double counting. More broadly, you should separate the investment and the financing decision whenever possible. If you must mix the two, it is possible to analyze the project from a purely equity perspective, but then you must also subtract principal payments to determine cash flows to equity. As we will see in Chapter 8, this equity perspective can be tricky to apply in practice.

c. A 15 percent annual growth in earnings is not an appropriate corporate goal because it is not necessarily consistent with increasing shareholder value, or anyone else's value for that matter. Accounting numbers can easily be manipulated to create apparent growth even when none exists. Blind pursuit of growth biases management in favor of retaining income to invest in even very low return projects because they generate growth while dividends do not. The appropriate corporate objective is to create shareholder value, to undertake projects promising a positive NPV.

d. Thirty percent is the accounting rate of return, not the correct internal rate of return.

e. Increases in accounts receivable and "stuff like that" are relevant. True, much of the investment in working capital is recovered at the end of the project's life, but because money has a time value, the present value of the recovered working capital investment is less than the original outlay, and thus constitutes a relevant cash flow.

f. Extra selling and administrative costs are relevant if they are incremental to the project. Remember the with-without principle. If surplus employees would be laid off in the absence of this project, retaining them to work on this project generates incremental costs. If surplus employees would be retained and remain idle in the absence of this project, the costs would exist even without this project and would, thus, be irrelevant. The former situation appears more likely. I agree with Loretta: dump Denny as rapidly as possible.

13. See C7_Problem_13_Answer.xlsx, available at **www.mhhe.com/ higgins10e.** (Select Student Edition > Choose Chapter > Files.)

15. See C7_Problem_15_Answer.xlsx, available at **www.mhhe.com/ higgins10e.** (Select Student Edition > Choose Chapter >Files.)

CHAPTER 8

1. a. False. Future cash flows are discounted more than near cash flows for risk because the discount rate in the denominator is raised to a higher power. A constant discount rate assumes risk increases at a constant geometric rate as the cash flow recedes in time.

   b. True. The WACC is the appropriate discount rate to use for projects that have the same risk as existing assets of the firm. If a project is either safer (riskier) than average, it should be evaluated at a discount rate below (above) the firm's WACC.

   c. False. This is yet another example of the marginal cost of capital fallacy. A company may be able to borrow the entire cost of a project. However, this does not imply that the cost of capital for the investment equals the borrowing rate. Increasing leverage increases the risks borne by shareholders, which increases the cost of equity capital. Alternatively, the discount rate for an investment is an opportunity cost reflecting the return available on same-risk investments elsewhere in the economy. It is not the cost of any particular funding source.

   d. False. Interest expense reflects the coupon rate on debt outstanding when payments were made. There are several reasons interest expense/end-of-period debt outstanding may be a poor estimate of a firm's cost of debt. First, the amount of debt outstanding may vary over time, so the end-of-period debt does not equal the debt outstanding when payments were made. Second, we want the cost of new debt, and interest expense/end-of-period debt outstanding is an historical number. If market interest rates, or the company's creditworthiness, have changed since existing debt was issued, the historical cost will differ from the cost of new debt. Third, debt coupon rates may not equal the full return expected by the lender. An extreme example is zero-coupon debt where all of the return is in the form of price appreciation. The cost of debt is best approximated by the yield to maturity on existing debt; this is the rate of return investors demand today on new debt.

   e. False. A firm's equity beta depends on two factors: the business risk of the firm and the financial risk imposed by the firm's capital structure. While firms in the same industry should have similar business risks, there is no guarantee that the firms will have the similar financial risk.

3. The lowest rate of return the entrepreneur should be willing to accept has nothing to do with the presence of an interest-free loan. The lowest acceptable rate is the rate the entrepreneur could expect to earn on

the next best alternative investment at the same risk. The cost of capital is an opportunity cost determined by the attractiveness of alternative investment opportunities.

5. When an investment lies below the market line, it is possible to make equal-risk investments promising higher expected returns. Conversely, investments above the market line, promise expected returns above those available on equal-risk, ready alternatives.

7. Increasing financial leverage increases the risk borne by equity investors and hence increases the cost of equity capital. The company's equity beta will rise as well. Indeed, the rising equity beta causes the cost of equity to rise. Figure 6.1 shows the relationship graphically.

9. a. IRR of perpetuity = Annual receipt/Initial investment. We want $IRR_e = 20\% = (\$3 \text{ million} - (1 - .50)8\%X)/(\$25 \text{ million} - X)$, where X = Required loan. X = \$12.5 million. So the investor can pay \$25 million for the property financed with a \$12.5 million loan and earn an expected 20 percent return on her investment.

   b. $90\% = (\$3 \text{ million} - (1 - .50)8\%X)/(\$25 \text{ million} - X)$. X = \$22.67 million. All she needs to do is borrow \$22.67 million of the required \$25 million investment.

   c. Make certain you understand this answer. It's important. An investor would settle for a lower return because it takes less debt financing to achieve it. Leverage increases expected return to equity but also the risk to equity. Indeed, if the investor can borrow at 8 percent on her own, the broker is not making this investment any more attractive by borrowing more to increase the return to equity. See Chapter 6.

11. a. The annual debt service payment = \$83.09 million. (\$83.09 = PMT[6%, 5 yrs, \$350]).

   b. The equity investor invests \$50 million at time 0 and receives \$16.91 million annually for five years (\$100 − \$83.09 = \$16.91). The internal rate of return on this cash flow is 20.5 percent.

   c. This is a poor investment. Discounting the company's free cash flows at its cost of capital, its enterprise value is only \$379.08 million. Buying the company for \$400 million implies a negative NPV of −\$20.92 million. (If the problem had not instructed us to ignore taxes, an additional source of value would be the present value of interest tax shields. But that term is not relevant here.) A 20.5 percent return to equity looks attractive, but this is just leverage talking. The return to equity is not sufficient to justify the risk borne. The investment is below the market line.

13. a. It is a call option. It gives General Design the option to "purchase" the expansion.

   b. The strike price is the price at which General Design can purchase the expansion, or $500 million.

15. a. Voice Division EVA = $220 × (1 − 40%) − 10% × $1,000 = **$32 million**. Data Division EVA = $130 × (1 − 40%) −15% × $600 = **−$12 million**.

   b. The fact that the Data Division's EVA is negative should be a source of concern but not justification for immediately eliminating the division. Here are some reasons EVA numbers should be treated cautiously in strategic decision making:

   - EVA numbers are backward-looking. Strategic decisions are based on expectations.

   - The EVAs calculated are for only one year. Entry and exit decisions have implications over many years.

   - The Data Division is young and growing rapidly. It might make perfect sense to suffer negative EVAs or even losses for a period to establish a position in what could be lucrative businesses in the future.

   - The EVA calculations may be inaccurate. In particular, practitioners argue that it is necessary to make a number of complex adjustments to balance sheet assets before the number can be used to represent capital employed in an EVA calculation.

   In my opinion, divisional EVAs can yield useful information but should never be used mechanically. Rather than eliminating the Data Division in this instance, I might be inclined to show the Data Division manager the EVA numbers and put the heat on him to name a date by which division EVA will be positive, and then hold him to this projection.

17. See C8_Problem_17_Answer.xlsx, available at **www.mhhe.com/ higgins10e.** (Select Student Edition > Choose Chapter > Files.)

CHAPTER 9

1. a. False. Quoting from one study, "Investigators found that the combined market value of buyers' and sellers' shares rose an average of 7.4 percent on the [acquisition] announcement. However, they also found that virtually all of the increased stock market value flowed to selling shareholders, who saw their stock rise just over 30 percent on average. Buyers' shares, on the other hand, rose only about

1 percent …. In the last four years of the study, the price of acquiring firms' shares fell some 3 percent on the announcement."

b. False. A discounted cash flow valuation of a target company discounts the target's estimated free cash flows at the TARGET'S cost of capital. The basic principle is: The discount rate should reflect the risk of the cash flows discounted. Here the risk of the cash flows discounted is that of the target.

c. False. Acquirers make money by buying poorly run companies and improving their performance. When a company is well run, the likelihood of materially improving performance is small, and the control premium should be correspondingly modest.

d. False. The liquidation decision is in the hands of controlling shareholders—or if ownership is widely disbursed, incumbent management. These parties are under no obligation to liquidate, even when the firm is worth more dead than alive. If controlling parties are optimistic about the firm's prospects or if they are receiving large nonpecuniary firm rewards, they may elect to continue operations even when others believe the firm is worth more in liquidation.

e. True. Say a company's stock price is $30, while management believes it is worth $80. Buying an $80 asset for $30—usually with the financial help of a buyout firm—has got to be an attractive investment. It can also create a major conflict of interest as management realizes they can get an even better price if they run down the company before buying it.

3. The value of control is the difference between the bid price and the price immediately prior to the bid, times the number of shares outstanding, or $2.21 billion ([$60 − $33] × 82 million shares).

5. Free cash flow $=$ EBIT(1 − Tax rate) + Depreciation − Fixed investment − Working capital investment.

$$\text{EBIT} = \text{Income before tax} + \text{Interest} = 1{,}800 + 570 = \$2{,}370.$$

$$\text{Tax rate} = 612/1{,}800 = .34$$

$$\text{Free cash flow} = 2{,}370(1 - .34) + 800 - 510 - 340 = \$1{,}514.20.$$

7. a. Any time one company acquires another, its sales and assets increase. Further, if the acquired company's earnings exceed the interest cost of any debt issued in the acquisition, earnings will increase as well. This is no surprise.

b. Value per share before proposal $= \$12/0.15 = \$80$.

c. Value per share after proposal $= \$6/(1 + .15) + (\$12.75/.15) / (1 + .15) = \$79.13$.

d. Clearly, owners of Flatbush should oppose the president's plan. It may result in a larger company, but it will destroy shareholder value; that is, stock price will fall under the plan. The problem with the president's plan is that it takes money with an opportunity cost of 15 percent to owners and invests it in a venture yielding only 12.5 percent ($0.75 per year added dividend in perpetuity for a $6 investment yields 12.5 percent return).

7. a.

	P	V1	P + V1	V2	P + V2
Earnings after tax ($ millions)	2	1	3	1	3
Price-to-earnings ratio (X)	30	8		35	
Market value of equity ($ millions)	60	8		35	
Number of equity shares ($ millions)	1	1	1.5	1	1.5
Earnings per share ($ millions)	2	$1	2	$ 1	2
Price per share ($ millions)	60	8		35	
Maximum new shares issued ($ millions)		.5		.5	
Value of new shares issued ($ millions)		30		30	
Maximum acquisition premium (%)		**275%**		**−14%**	

b. This problem illustrates why concern with earnings-per-share dilution or accretion is short-sided. Here, Procureps is tempted to pay a huge premium to buy V1 but is disinclined to even look at V2. Yet V2 is the exciting firm with future potential.

11. a. FMV = PV{FCF, '12 – '15} + PV{Terminal value}. PV{FCF, '12 – '15} = $155.9 million. Terminal value = EBIT(1 − Tax rate)/0.11 = $120/0.11 = $1,090.9 million. PV{Terminal value} = $1,090.9 million/$(1 + 0.11)^4$ = $718.6 million. Summing, FMV = $874.5 million.

b. FMV of equity = ($874.5 − $250)/40 = $15.61 per share.

c. Terminal value = FCF in 2016/(0.11 − 0.05). FCF in 2016 = $200(1.05)(1 − .4) − 30 − 15 = $81. So terminal value = $81/(.11 − .05) = $1,350. Present value of terminal value = $889.3. FMV of company = $155.9 + $889.3 = $1,045.2 million. FMV of equity per share = ($1,045.2 − $250)/40 = $19.88.

d. Terminal value = Value of equity + Value of interest-bearing liabilities. Value of equity = 12 × Net income in 2015 = 12 × (200 − 0.10 × 250)(1 − .40) = $1,260 million. Terminal value = $1,260 million + $250 million = $1,510. Present value of terminal value = $994.7. Therefore, FMV of company on valuation date = $155.8 + $994.7 = $1,150.6 million. Value per share = ($1,150.6 million − $250 million)/40 = $22.51.

13.

Employee ownership at time 5		20.0%
Round 2 VC's ownership at time 5		11.0%
Round 2 VC's retention ratio	= (1 − .20)	0.80
Round 2 VC's ownership at time 2	= 0.11/0.80	13.8%
Touchstone ownership at time 5		62.9%
Touchstone retention ratio	= (1 − .20)(1 − .138)	0.69
Touchstone ownership at time 0	= 0.629/0.69	91.2%

Confirmation of Answer

Let X equal total shares outstanding at time 5 and recall that the founders own 2 million shares. Then $.20X + .11X + .629X + 2$ million $= X$.

Total shares at time 5		32.79 million
Touchstone ownership at time 5	= .629 × 32.79	20.62 million
Price per share at time 5	= $100 million/32.79	$3.05
Value of Touchstone shares at time 5	= 20.62 million × $3.05	$62.9 million
IRR to Touchstone	See Table 9.A2	60%
Round 2 VC's ownership at 5	= .11 × 32.79	3.61 million
Value of R'nd 2 VC's shares at time 5	= 3.61 million × $3.05	$11.0 million
IRR to Round 2 VC	See Table 9.A2	40%
Value of options	= 20% × $100 million	$20 million
Value of founders' ownership	= 2 million × $3.05	$6.1 million

Note that the founders effectively pay for the employee options. Touchstone and the second-round VC still get their target returns of 60 percent and 40 percent, respectively, while the value of the founders' time 5 ownership falls from $26.1 million (see Table 9.A2) to $6.1 million, with the missing $20 million going to employee options.

15. See C9_Problem_15_Answer.xlsx, available at **www.mhhe.com/ higgins10e.** (Select Student Edition > Choose Chapter > Files.)

Index

Page numbers followed by n refer to footnotes.